G000082385

NEW YORK
2008

NEW YORK

2008

Amanda Statham

foulsham

LONDON • NEW YORK • TORONTO • SYDNEY

foulsham

The Publishing House, Bennetts Close, Cippenham, Slough, Berkshire, SL1 5AP, England

Foulsham books can be found in all good bookshops and direct from www.foulsham.com

ISBN: 978-0-572-03371-2

Copyright © 2008 W. Foulsham & Co. Ltd

Cover photographs © Getty Images

Maps by PC Graphics (UK) Limited

A CIP record for this book is available from the British Library

The moral right of the author has been asserted

While every effort has been made to ensure the accuracy of all the information contained within this book, neither the author nor the publisher can be liable for any errors. In particular, since prices, times and any hotel, holiday or venue details change from time to time, it is vital that each individual checks relevant information for themselves.

Look out for the latest editions in this series:
Brit's Guide to Disneyland Resort Paris, Simon and Susan Veness
Brit's Guide to Choosing a Cruise, Simon Veness
Brit's Guide to Las Vegas, Karen Marchbank with Richard Evans
Brit's Guide to Orlando and Walt Disney World, Simon and Susan Veness

Printed in Dubai

Contents

Acknowledgements

With thanks to travel writer Nicki Grihault for sharing the research.

With grateful thanks for all their help to Ryan Levitt and Anna Catchpole at Hillsbalfour Synergy PR, which represents NYC & Co in the UK. All at NYC Visit.com, Niagara Falls Convention and Visitors Bureau and the New York State Department of Economic Development.

Thanks also to the Lower East Side Tenement Museum, the Metropolitan Museum of Art, Ellis Island Immigration Museum, the Museum of Modern Art, the Museum of Jewish Heritage, the Whitney Museum of American Art, Intrepid Sea-Air-Space Museum, the Frick Collection, the Skyscraper Museum, the National Museum of the American Indian, the Children's Museum of Manhattan, the Empire State Building, the American Museum of Natural History, the New York Stock Exchange, the Brooklyn Museum of Art, NY Waterways, the Sex And The City Tour, Harlem Spirituals, the Big Apple Greeters, David Watkins and Ponycabs, the Queens Jazz Trail, Gangland Tours, Big Onion Walking Tours, Rabbi Beryl Epstein and the Hassidic Discovery Center, former NYPD cop Gary Gorman, Gray Line, Food Tours of Greenwich, The Ritz-Carlton at Battery Park, The Warwick, The Mark, Waldorf Astoria, Le Parker Meridien, The Marriott Marquis, The Wellington, The Doral, Le Cirque, The Bull & Bear, The View at the Marriot Marquis, American Park at the Battery, Serafina Fabulous Grill, The Boathouse, Picholine, Sylvia's Restaurant, The River Café, The Water Club, World Yacht Dining Cruise, Europa Grill, The 21 Club, Tavern on the Green, Zoe's Restaurant and ONE c.p.s.

Photograph Acknowledgements

Steve Brickles: 111, 118, 119, 121, 125, 130, 134, 137, 151, 155, 158, 161 bottom, 162, 169, 172, 174, 192, 214, 219, 220, 284.

Christopher Martin Hobson: 2, 6, 7, 9, 10, 12, 18, 19, 20, 21, 23, 24, 25, 31, 39, 41, 43, 46, 60, 61, 63, 68, 69, 70, 71, 75, 76, 77, 78, 80, 81, 83, 84, 85, 87, 94, 103, 104, 106, 113, 122, 129, 141, 144, 147, 152, 159, 163 top, 167, 175, 190, 195, 205 top, 209, 211, 218, 222, 233, 237, 239 bottom, 244, 250, 252 bottom, 258, 259, 262, 263, 281, 283.

Leonardo.com: 161 top, 213, 221, 223, 225, 226, 228, 231, 232, 234, 235, 236, 238, 239 top, 240, 241, 242, 246.

NYC & Company Inc.: 54, 59, 93, 95, 100, 108, 109 bottom, 160, 173, 196, 208, 248, 253, 254, 256, 257, 265, 269, 272, 273, 277, 279, 282; **NYC/Jordan Gary:** 143, 145, 150, 160, 200, 217, 251 top, 268; **NYC/Jeff Greenberg:** 11, 14, 16, 22, 28, 34, 39, 66, 73, 79, 89, 109 top, 116, 123, 135, 138, 142, 170, 185, 203, 205 bottom, 206, 207 bottom, 249 top, 251 bottom, 252 top, 260, 261, 264, 267; **NYC/Darren McGee:** 98; **NYC/Macy's East Inc.:** 255; **NYC/Mesa Grill:** 177; **NYC/Linda Turley:** 191.

Other contributors: 60 Thompson/Full Picture 230; Peter Aaron/Esto for the Jewish Museum 96; Anthony Anderson 107; atpm.com 45; Barbetta 168; Battery Gardens 148; Big Apple Ticket 210; bigapplejazz.com 199; Daniel Boulud 163 bottom (G. Vitieri). 178 (P. Medilek); Brooklyn Environmental Health 270 bottom; Chelsea Savoy 212; Curtains 208; Jake Dobkin (www.bluejake.com) 13, 179 top, 247; End Point Corporation 157; Four Seasons 164, 243; C. S. Helsinki 215; HK Hotels 229; J. Horey 27; Ithaka 179 bottom; jewishtours.com; Korova Milk Bar 186; Le Cirque 166; Lower East Side Tenement Museum 97; Manhattan Oriental Hotel Group 194; Joan Marcus 207 top; John Mariani 154; Mick Hales/Metropolitan Museum of Art 92; MoMA 101; New York City Ballet 249 bottom; NoCa 202; Prospect Park 270 top; Ritz-Carlton Hotel 224; Ruby Foo's 181; Savory Sojourns 81; Streetblog.org 105; Mark Thomas 49; Therapy 215; Time's Up 37; Union Square Hospitality Group 167; Woodbury Common 146; Zoe 171.

Introduction

Welcome to the 2008 edition of the *Brit's Guide to New York*, the guidebook that aims to be your very own personal tour guide to this amazing city.

We hope the guide will inspire you to want to visit the Big Apple again and again, for this is a city that really does capture the heart. Very few people visit once and don't return, simply because they're always left with the feeling that there's so much more to see and do. Once you've ticked the major sights off your list – such as the Empire State Building, Statue of Liberty and Central Park – you can start investigating the cosmopolitan neighbourhoods of the likes of SoHo, Greenwich Village and Chelsea and, in each new place you venture into, you'll discover a veritable treasure of shops, cafés, hotels and bars and witness the 'zoo' of residents going about their daily business.

A record 44 million visitors from around the world visited the city last year, a major step towards New York city's Mayor Bloomberg's goal of attracting 50 million tourists by 2015. The UK is the Big Apple's biggest market, with more than 1.2 million of us making the journey over the pond last year. So what is it that makes us love this city so much?

One of the reasons for its magnetism is that it is a relatively new city that is in a constant process of renewal, regeneration and regrowth. Quite simply, there's always something new to see and do. This year there is set to be a dizzying array of new hotel rooms, global cuisine, blockbuster Broadway shows, exceptional exhibitions and incomparable shopping. The record number of visitors flocking to the city proves that the insatiable demand for all things New York continues to climb and that the dark day of 11 September 2001, when terrorists destroyed the twin towers of the World Trade Center and killed nearly 3,000 people, is well and truly behind it.

Manhattan and Central Park

THE NEW YORK STATE OF MIND

While New York is undoubtedly a melting pot of cultures and religions (Italians, Chinese, Jews, Africans, Irish and French to name but a few) there is one thing that unites everyone living in this cosmopolitan city: attitude. Resident New Yorkers are a breed unto themselves, unlike other American states where you're constantly instructed to 'have a nice day', they're not prone to saccharine sweetness. Here's how to spot a genuine New Yorker: on face value, they tend to have a sort of totally cheesed-off-with-the-world, don't-mess-with-me look. They also speak incredibly quickly as if they were eating their own words, so it can be hard to understand them.

Scratch the surface, though, and you just have your ordinary, everyday kind of person with the same kind of worries, fears and doubts as the rest of us. We've discovered two things that work a treat: firstly, smiling like mad and being genuinely polite; secondly, the British accent. You can see them looking at you askance when you smile (smile? Who on earth does that in New York?), but then deciding that you must be one of those British eccentrics they've heard about. It does the trick, though, because more often than not they'll respond in a helpful way.

And don't go thinking that all New Yorkers will tell you to f*** off if you ask for directions. Many are happy to help and we've even had people stop to help us work out where we're going when they've spotted us studying a map. This heady mix of rudeness and helpfulness is no better demonstrated than in the following anecdote from New York author Douglas Kennedy:

'On a crosstown bus I noticed two visitors from Japan having difficulty with the exact change for the fare,' he recounts. 'The driver, an overweight guy with a scowl, started giving them a hard time. "Like can't you read English or what?" he said loudly. "It says a buck-fifty. Surely they teach you how to count in Japan."

The Japanese looked as if they wanted to commit hara-kiri on the spot until an elegantly dressed woman in her late sixties seated opposite the door came to their defence. Out of nowhere she turned to the driver and said: "Hey asshole, be polite".

It's typical of the spirit of this vibrant, beautiful city that it has come back stronger than ever before; foreign visitors from all over the world continue to pour into the Big Apple, trade is booming and it's brimming with life and excitement whichever neighbourhood you venture into. Every New Yorker has a story about that day, but all are concentrating on the future and how to make the city bigger and better than ever.

BRITTIP

If you do want to pay your respects at Ground Zero, remember that this is also an ideal place from which to visit Wall Street and the Statue of Liberty, so give yourself time to explore Lower Manhattan.

There has been much discussion over the last five years as to what would fill the space that has been left by the fall of the Twin Towers. At the moment you can head to Lower Manhattan to pay your respects at the Tribute WTC Visitor Center, which opened in 2006, and which will act as a point of focus while the planned memorial and museum are being completed. The memorial, Reflecting Absence, by architect Michael Arad was chosen in 2004 from more than 5,200 entrants from 63 nations, and will consist of two massive voids in the one-acre space left by the towers, with waterfalls cascading down their sides into two reflecting pools with the names of the 2,979 people from 92 countries who died inscribed in the walls. It's scheduled to open in 2009.

PLANNING YOUR HOLIDAY

One of New York's greatest charms is its cosmopolitan nature, its hugely diverse ethnic mix. In this city you will find any type of cuisine, often available at any time of the day or night. Where music is concerned, everything from jazz and R&B to techno and rap is out there on any night of the week and the many nightclubs are among the hottest and most stylish of any in the world.

The drawback is that it may seem a bit overwhelming and it doesn't help that everyone gives the impression of being in the biggest hurry ever and far too busy to help. But beneath the ice-cool veneer of

The Winter Garden

most New Yorkers you'll find people willing to answer any question or plea for help.

In this book, we hope not only to provide all the information you need about the sights, sounds and attractions, but also to give an insight into what makes the city tick and how to get the most out of it. The book is filled with tips and insider information, but we are always open to hearing other people's views and are happy to receive suggestions by email at amanda@mrhoppy.freeserve.co.uk.

◀▶ BRITTIP

If you really want to get an insight into how a New Yorker thinks, log on to *The New York Times* website www.nytimes.com, and read the Metropolitan Diaries, stories of city life supplied by the locals.

Once you have decided to go to New York, the next step is to work out what you want to do there, otherwise you could end up wasting a lot of valuable time. The city is so big and diverse and everyone's tastes are so different that each visit to New York is a unique experience. Are you a museum buff? Do you like to get off the beaten track? Want to see a great Broadway show and some of the outstanding sights of the city? Your priorities will reflect not only your

tastes, but also whether it is your first or second visit to the Big Apple, or whether you are becoming an old friend, as well as the time you have available. Whatever the case, the key to making the most of your time is in the planning.

The thing we emphasise most is the importance of location. When you fly into New York, seeing all the skyscrapers from your lofty perch makes Manhattan look pretty small, but do not be fooled by this. It is a narrow island, but it's longer than it looks from high in the sky – 21km (13 miles) in fact – so don't be duped into believing it is easy to walk from Downtown to the Upper East Side. Nothing could be further from the truth.

Central Park from a helicopter

Queensborough Bridge

It's also the case that the city's subway is nowhere near as fast as our much-maligned tube system in London, nor is it that good for getting from east to west or vice versa. That means using buses is often the better option and they, like taxis, can get stuck in heavy traffic. So, when planning your activities for the day, it is a good idea to stick to one particular area so that walking everywhere – the best way to see the city – won't be so tiring.

Most New York trips are for between two and seven days. For the former, it's like

> ◀▮▶ **BRITTIP**
> Make the most of your time by planning each day carefully – but don't try to do too much, and give yourself enough breaks each day to recharge your batteries.

dipping your toes in the water; for the latter it's a big commitment to getting to know the city. Regardless of how many days you have, though, you won't be able to see everything, so you'll need to be selective.

HOW TO USE YOUR GUIDEBOOK

We've tried to help you with your choices in as many ways as possible. The top sights and museums are listed in alphabetical order so you can go straight to the ones you will most likely want to see, and in each case the area they are in has been specified – again to help you plan your day. Be sure to look out for our 'Top Fives', which are scattered throughout the chapters. They are designed to give you instant snippets of information – for example, the best restaurants with an outside garden area, or the five best shops for accessories – and provide a certain degree of insider knowledge. The same is true for our Brit Tips, which give you extra titbits of facts and advice that you probably won't find elsewhere.

As a Broadway show is one of the most popular things for tourists to do in New York, we've created a new chapter called Theatre and Film, which will help you plan your trip more easily. The restaurant chapter gives an alphabetical area-by-area guide that makes light work of planning lunch and dinner. We've also provided a complete outline of all the different transport systems in New York and how to use them, plus a description of the different neighbourhoods so that you will be able to get the most out of what each one offers.

The accommodation chapter has been placed towards the back of the book because choosing a hotel should be one of your final decisions. If the sights, sounds, shops and museums you want to see are all in a particular area, then you should try to find a hotel or accommodation as close to it as possible. That way you can reduce the time and money you spend on getting around. Unless, of course, the hotel is the reason you're travelling to the city; for some people the experience of staying in exclusive accommodation such as The Waldorf is worth a visit to NYC before they've even thought about sightseeing.

We've tried to include everything we believe the average Brit will be interested in visiting in New York, but if you come across a sight, museum, shop, gallery, coffee shop, club, hotel or restaurant not in this book, which you think is worth including, email us at amanda@mrhoppy.freeserve.co.uk.

Finally, we'd just like to wish you a wonderful trip to one of the greatest cities in the world.

CHAPTER 1

Knowing New York

So what is New York all about? Due to the vast number of movies set in different periods of the city, many of the key people in its history, sights and areas are familiar to us Brits, though you may be a little hazy as to their whereabouts or true influence.

A BRIEF HISTORY OF NEW YORK

Understanding a little of the city's history is a good way of understanding its modern-day psyche, and familiarising yourself with the different areas of New York and the buildings named after its great movers and shakers. Many of them were men and women of great vision and courage, and their contributions to New York's rich and diverse culture, business and entertainment are all part of what makes the city so remarkable today.

The great story of New York started in 1524 when Florentine Giovanni da Verrazano arrived on the island now known as Manhattan. It was a mixture of marshes, woodland, rivers and meadows, and was home to the Algonquin and Iroquois tribes of Native Americans.

No one settled on the island, though, until British explorer Henry Hudson arrived in 1609. Working for the Dutch West India Company, he discovered Indians who were happy to trade in furs, skins, birds and fruit. In 1613, a trading post was set up at Fort Nassau, and by 1624 the Dutch West India Company was given the right to govern the area by the Dutch government.

Dutch settlers soon began to arrive; Manhattan was named New Amsterdam and governor Peter Minuit bought the island for $24-worth of trinkets and blankets. The Dutch, of course, thought they had a bargain. The irony is that they were trading with a tribe of Indians who were simply passing through the area! Peaceful relations between the Europeans and Native Americans were disturbed, however, by the settlers' insistence on taking over the land, and a costly and bloody war ensued, lasting two and a half years. Finally, Peter Stuyvesant was hired by the Dutch West India Company to restore peace.

Stuyvesant was an experienced colonialist and went about establishing a strong community with a proper infrastructure. One of the first things he did was to order the building of a defensive wall and ditch along what we know today as Wall Street. The new settlement prospered and even doubled in size, but Governor Stuyvesant was not well liked. He introduced new taxes, persecuted Jews and Quakers, and even limited the amount of alcohol people could drink. Trouble followed, and the locals became less and less inclined to obey him. By the time four British warships sailed into the harbour in late 1664, he had no alternative but to surrender to Colonel Richard Nichols without a shot being fired. The colony was immediately renamed New York in honour of the Duke of York, brother to the English king, and thereafter remained mostly in the hands of the British until the end of the American Revolution.

UN and Chrysler Buildings

Columbus Circle

A NEW VOICE

By 1700, the population had reached 20,000, made up of immigrants from England, Holland, Germany, Ireland and Sweden. It was already the rich melting-pot of cultures and religions that it remains today. Over the next 74 years, the colony gradually began to establish itself and there was a growing belief among well-educated and powerful Americans – including Thomas Jefferson and Benjamin Franklin – that the government should be fair and democratic.

In 1764, following the Seven Years War between the British and French, the Brits passed a number of laws, including the Stamp Act, allowing them to raise taxes in the colony. In response, Americans from all over the country banded together and rescinded Britain's right to collect taxes from them. The Stamp Act was repealed but it seemed that the Brits hadn't learned their lesson. They introduced the Townshend Act, which imposed taxes on various imports and led to a bloody confrontation in 1770. In 1774, the Americans set up the Continental Congress, made up of representatives from each of the colonies. Later that year, those representatives urged all Americans to stop paying their taxes, and just two years later the Declaration of Independence was drawn up, largely by Jefferson.

During the War of Independence that inevitably followed, New York was considered strategically vital, as it stood between the New England colonies and those in the south. In 1776, British commander Lord Howe sailed 500 ships into the harbour and occupied the city. George Washington's army was defeated and forced to leave. The peace process began in 1779 and led to a treaty in 1783. The Brits, who had remained in New York since the end of the war, left just before George Washington returned to claim victory.

New York then became the country's first capital and George Washington its first president, taking his oath of office in 1789. The city was capital for just one year, but business boomed. The New York Stock Exchange, established under a tree on Wall

WHAT'S IN A NAME?

The Big Apple has become synonymous with New York City, but came into being during the 1920s when horse-racing writer John Fitzgerald popularised the term. On assignment in New Orleans for *The Morning Telegraph*, he overheard stablehands refer to New York City racing tracks as The Big Apple and decided to call his column on New York's racing scene 'Around the Big Apple'.

A decade later, jazz musicians adopted the term to refer to New York City. The favourite story of Big Onion tour guides is related to Small's Big Apple jazz club in Harlem. The story goes that when the musicians from the club went on tour around America they'd say to each other: 'I'll see you in the Big Apple'. But the term was still relatively unknown until it was adopted by the New York Convention and Visitors' Bureau in 1971, when they launched The Big Apple campaign.

So there you have it – the name Big Apple is a marketing device invented by the city to lure in visitors and it certainly seems to work as around 44 million business people and tourists arrive each year, 1.2 million of them Brits.

Many New Yorkers also like to call the city Gotham – taken from the Batman stories that are based in Gotham City and believed by many to be a thinly veiled reference to New York. The name Manhattan is derived from Mannahatta, or 'land of many hills', the name given to the island by its first inhabitants, the Algonquin Indians.

TOP FIVE BOOKS ON NEW YORK HISTORY

Herbert Asbury: *The Gangs of New York; An Informal History of the Underworld*, Arrow Books (2003)
Sanna Feirstein: *Naming New York*, New York University Press (2000)
Kenneth T Jackson: *The Encyclopedia of New York City*, Yale University Press (1995)
Mike Wallace and Edwin G Burrows: Gotham: *A History of New York City to 1898*, Oxford University Press Inc. USA (1999)
Shaun O'Connell: *Remarkable, Unspeakable New York*, Beacon Press (1997)

Street by Alexander Hamilton in 1792, positively buzzed with activity as new companies were set up, bought and sold.

As the city grew, it became clear that a proper infrastructure and sanitation system was needed, so the governors introduced a grid system throughout the entire island. North of 14th Street, it abandoned all the existing roads except for Broadway, which followed an old Indian trail, and set up wide avenues that ran south to north and streets that ran between the rivers. Everything, it seemed, was pushing the city north, from illness to prosperity: while the grid system was being put on paper, a series of epidemics drove residents from the old Downtown into what is now known as Greenwich Village.

THE RICH GET RICHER...

By 1818, reliable shipping services between New York and other American cities and Europe were well established and trade was booming. It was boosted further by the opening of the Erie Canal in 1825, which, together with the new railroads, opened trade routes to the Midwest. With so much spare cash to play with, businessmen started to build large summer estates and mansions along 5th Avenue up to Madison Square. At the same time, many charities and philanthropic institutions were set up and great libraries were built, as education was seen as being very important.

But the divide between rich and poor was getting wider. While water supplies, indoor plumbing and central heating were being installed in the 5th Avenue mansions, thousands of immigrant families – particularly from Ireland – had no choice but to live in the appalling tenement buildings that were being erected on the Lower East Side of Manhattan.

These people were forced to eke out a wretched existence in the old sweatshops by day and contend with the punitive living conditions of the tenements by night. Entire families were crammed into one or two rooms that had no windows, no hot water, no heat and, of course, no bathroom. Toilet facilities had to be shared with neighbours.

The impending Civil War over the question of slavery became a major issue for the poor of New York, who couldn't afford to buy their way out of conscription. Uppermost in their minds was the concern that freed slaves would be going after their jobs. The fear reached fever pitch and led to America's worst-ever riot, a four-day-long affair in which over 100 people died and thousands, mostly blacks, were injured. By 1865, however, the abolitionists won the war, finally freeing four million black people from the plight of slavery.

BOOM TIME FOR IMMIGRATION

At the same time, New York and Boston were being hit by great tidal waves of immigrants. In the 1840s and 1850s it was the Irish fleeing famine; in the 1860s it was the Germans fleeing persecution; and in the 1870s it was the Chinese, brought into America specifically to build the railroads. In the 1880s it was the turn of the Russians, along with 1.5 million Eastern European Jews. Over eight million immigrants went through Castle Clinton in Battery Park between 1855 and 1890. Then the Ellis Island centre was built in 1892 and handled double that number. Between 1880 and

Rockefeller Center

KNOWING NEW YORK

USEFUL WEBSITES

www.cityguideny.com The online site of the weekly *City Guide* that is provided to hotels, with all the latest events, activities, etc.

www.citysearchnyc.com Packed with information on New York, events and what's happening.

www.clubplanet.com Complete list of what's cool, where and why; the final word on nightlife.

www.manhattanusersguide.com The insider's guide to what's going on where.

www.downtownny.com Directory of places to visit in Downtown.

www.nyctourist.com An official tourism site for the city.

www.nycvisit.com The New York Convention and Visitors' Bureau's comprehensive listing includes suggested itineraries for where to stay and shop and what to do.

www.nytab.com The New York Travel Advisory Bureau's site is helpful for trip planning and gives information on major savings.

www.newyorkology.com Everything from arrivology to technology!

www.nytimes.com The online site for *The New York Times*.

www.villagevoice.com The online site of *The Village Voice*.

1910, 17 million immigrants passed through the city and, by 1900, the population had reached 3.4 million.

Most of the new arrivals who chose to stay in New York ended up in the crowded tenements of the Lower East Side. Finally in 1879, after the terrible conditions were brought to light, the city passed new housing laws requiring landlords to increase water supplies and toilets, install fire escapes and build air shafts between buildings to let in air and light. The introduction of streetcars and elevated railways also helped to alleviate the transport problem.

THE GILDED AGE

Meanwhile, the wealthy were enjoying the Gilded Age, as Mark Twain dubbed it. Central Park opened in 1858 and more and more mansions were built on 5th Avenue for the likes of the Whitneys, Vanderbilts and Astors. Row houses were also being built on the Upper West Side for wealthy European immigrants. Henry Frick, who made his

Met Life Tower and the Flatiron Building

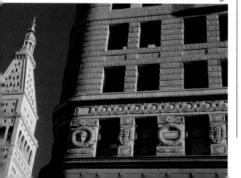

fortune in steel and the railroads, built a mansion (now a museum) on the east side of the park at 70th Street, just 10 blocks from the new Metropolitan Museum of Art. Luxury hotels such as the original Waldorf Astoria and the Plaza opened, as did the original Metropolitan Opera House. The Statue of Liberty, St Patrick's Cathedral, the Brooklyn Bridge and Carnegie Hall were all built at this time.

Those were the days of the people whose names we associate with New York but don't necessarily know: like Cornelius Vanderbilt, a shipping and railroad magnate; Andrew Carnegie, a steel and railroad baron; and John D Rockefeller, who made his millions in oil. The names of many of these millionaires live on in the gifts they gave back to the city: they provided concert halls, libraries and art museums, and donated entire collections to put in them. Carnegie built and donated Carnegie Hall to the city, Rockefeller was one of three major backers behind the opening of the Museum of Modern Art, and the Whitneys created a museum containing their own collection of modern American works of art.

At the same time, the structure of the city itself was undergoing a transformation. In 1904, the IRT subway opened 135km (84 miles) of track, which meant that people could move away from the polluted downtown areas, and by 1918 the New York City Transit System was complete.

The turn of the century also saw the birth of another phenomenon – the skyscraper. First to be built was the Flatiron Building in

1902, which was constructed using the new technology for the mass production of cast iron. Frank Woolworth's Gothic structure followed in 1913. The beautiful Chrysler Building went up in 1929 and the Empire State Building was completed in 1931.

PROHIBITION ARRIVES

In the meantime, the Volstead Act of 1919 banned the sale of alcohol at the start of the Roaring Twenties. Fuelled by lively speakeasies, illegal booze, gangsters, the Charleston and jazz, this was the real heyday of famous venues like Harlem's Cotton Club and the Apollo Theater. After several glittering years, the fun and frolics came to an abrupt end with the collapse of the Wall Street stock market on 29 October 1929. It destroyed most small investors and led to huge unemployment and poverty across the whole of America. Things started to turn for the better only after President Franklin D Roosevelt introduced the New Deal, employing people to build new roads, houses and parks.

In New York, Fiorello LaGuardia (pronounced La-gwar-dia), was elected mayor and set up his austerity programme to enable the city to claw its way back to financial security. During his 12 years in office, LaGuardia worked hard at fighting corruption and organised crime, and introduced a massive public housing project.

◄📖 BRITTIP

One of the most famous speakeasies during Prohibition was Jack & Charlies 21. You can visit it today as the rather more respectable 21 Club at 21 West 52nd Street (Tel 212-582 7200, www.21club.com).

These were also the days of a great literary and artistic scene in the city. Giants of the spoken and written word, including Dorothy Parker and George Kaufman, would meet at the famous Round Table of the Algonquin Hotel, where they were joined by stage and screen legends Tallulah Bankhead, Douglas Fairbanks and the Marx Brothers.

The Second World War was another watershed for New York, as people fled war-ravaged Europe and headed for the metropolis. Both during and after the war, huge new waves of immigrants arrived, fleeing first the Nazis and then the

BEAT IT

The 1950s Beat Movement was a partly social, partly literary phenomenon with three centres – Greenwich Village in New York, the North Beach district of San Francisco and Venice West in Los Angeles. Socially, the movement was all about rejecting middle-class values and commercialism and embracing poverty, individualism and release through jazz, sexual experience and drugs. The term 'beat' conveys not only the American connotations of being worn-out and exhausted, but also suggests 'beatitude' or 'blessedness'. The chief spokesmen were Allen Ginsberg, Jack Kerouac, whose most famous novel is *On The Road*, Gregory Corso, William S Burroughs, Lawrence Ferlinghetti and Gary Snyder.

Communists. New York was as affected by McCarthy's hunt for 'reds' among the cultural and intellectual elite as was the rest of the country, but it bounced back when a new building boom followed the election of President Harry S Truman, whose policies were aimed specifically at helping the poor.

The Port Authority Bus Terminal was finished in 1950, the mammoth United Nations Headquarters was completed in 1953, and in 1959 work started on the huge Lincoln Center complex – built on the slums of the San Juan district that were the setting for *West Side Story*.

FROM BOOM TO BUST

By the 1950s, a new period of affluence had started for the middle classes of New York. The descendants of the earlier Irish, Italian and Jewish immigrants moved out to the new towns that were springing up outside Manhattan, leaving space for a whole new wave of immigrants from Puerto Rico and the southern states of America. It was also the decade of the Beat generation, epitomised by Jack Kerouac and Allen Ginsberg, which evolved into the hippy culture of the 1960s. This was when Greenwich Village became the centre of a new wave of artists extolling the virtues of equality for all.

By the 1970s, however, this laissez-faire attitude, coupled with New York's position as a major gateway for illegal drug importation and the general demoralisation of the working classes and ethnic groups, led to an escalation in crime. Muggings and murder

The Woolworth Building

tax incentives to rejuvenate New York's business community. A boom followed, reflected in the erection of a series of mammoth new skyscrapers, including the World Trade Center and Trump Tower.

The transformation was completed in the 1990s with Mayor Giuliani's clean-up operation. This was unpopular with the more liberal New Yorkers, but many believe it was his policies that turned New York into a city fit for the new millennium.

From the time of the earliest immigrants, New York has represented a gateway to a new life, a place of hope: the American dream offered a future filled with happiness and success. And nowadays New York still draws in people in their thousands. After all, as the Sinatra song goes, 'If you can make it there, you'll make it anywhere.'

were rampant, and the city was brought to the brink of bankruptcy.

Chaos was averted only by the introduction of austerity measures, which unfortunately primarily affected the poor. But good news was just around the corner, as new mayor Ed Koch implemented major

THE BEST TIMES TO GO

January to March, and July and August are best for accommodation and good for flights. Just bear in mind that July and August are the hottest months, though it is not as bad as you might expect because all the shops and cabs have air-conditioning

AT-A-GLANCE HISTORY

1524	Giovanni da Verrazano arrives on Manhattan
1613	Trading post is set up at Fort Nassau
1624	Dutch West India Company establishes rule and settlers name Manhattan New Amsterdam
1626	Peter Minuit buys Manhattan for trinkets worth $24
1664	Dutch surrender to the British and New Amsterdam is renamed New York after the Duke of York
1776	War of Independence and battle for New York begins
1785	New York becomes the nation's capital
1792	New York Stock Exchange is founded
1811	Grid plan for Manhattan is introduced
1827	Slavery is officially abolished in New York
1858	Work on Central Park begins
1883	Brooklyn Bridge opens
1886	Statue of Liberty is built
1892	Ellis Island opens
1902	The Fuller (Flatiron) Building becomes the world's first skyscraper
1904	New York's first subway line opens
1919	Prohibition Act sees alcohol sales banned in New York
1923	Yankee Stadium opens
1929	New York stock market crashes
1931	Empire State Building opens
1950	United Nations building completed
1970	First New York City Marathon
1993	A terrorist bomb in the World Trade Center kills six and injures 1,000
1994	Rudy Giuliani appointed mayor and brings crime to an all-time low
2001	World Trade Centre Twin Towers hit by terrorists, killing 3,000

SEASONAL WEATHER

Month	Temp	Rainfall
Jan	-3-3°C (27-38°F)	8cm (3in)
Feb	-3-5°C (27-40°F)	8cm (3in)
Mar	1-9°C (34-49°F)	11cm (4¼in)
Apr	7-16°C (44-61°F)	10cm (4in)
May	12-22°C (53-72°F)	10cm (4in)
June	17-27°C (63-80°F)	8cm (3in)
July	20-29°C (68-85°F)	10cm (4in)
Aug	19-29°C (67-85°F)	10cm (4in)
Sep	16-25°C (60-77°F)	9cm (3½in)
Oct	10-19°C (50-66°F)	9cm (3½in)
Nov	5-12°C (41-54°F)	11cm (4¼in)
Dec	-1-6°C (31-42°F)	10cm (4in)

and you get blasts of lovely cool air from the shops as you pass.

In the run-up to Christmas it is very difficult to find accommodation in Manhattan, due to the number of conventions in September and October. Surprisingly, the times around Thanksgiving and between Christmas and New Year are good times to go because people tend to be at home with their families. April to June should be pleasantly cool (though it can also be surprisingly warm) and is a popular time to visit.

Check Chapter 12 Festivals and Parades (page 247) to find out when the major events are happening in the city, as it tends to be more crowded at these times.

WHAT TO WEAR

Layers are the key to comfortable clothes in New York, no matter what time of year you go.

In summer the air-con in buildings can get pretty cold, while outside it is stiflingly hot. If you take a lightweight, rainproof jacket, you'll be covered for all eventualities, including the odd shower.

In winter it is the other way round – warm buildings and cold streets – so it's best to have an overcoat of some sort, but nothing too heavy unless you're planning to

BRITTIP

Don't worry if you spill wine all over your favourite outfit; most hotels have a valet service that can clean it for you overnight or there are plenty of dry cleaners throughout the city. Ask at the hotel reception desk.

be out of doors a lot. Also make sure you have a hat, scarf and gloves in your bag for times of emergency. At any time of the year, the skyscrapers of the city act as a kind of wind tunnel and unless you're in the sun it can get nippy pretty quickly – another reason to make sure you have a cardigan or lightweight jacket in the summer.

NEW YORK FOR FAMILIES

New York is like a giant playground to a child, so it is a great place to go with the family. Towering skyscrapers, mammoth bridges, vast parks, circuses and shows, bright lights and rows of shops packed with enticing kid-friendly products are enough on their own to keep children entertained for a week. But there are plenty of other

BRITTIP

Pick up the NY Convention Bureau's *Kids Guide to New York City* from www.nycvisit.com or, hot off the press, *Miffy Loves New York City* ($9.99 from the Visitors' Information Center Bookshops), in which the popular bunny takes parents and kids around 30 family-friendly sites.

attractions to hunt out that can make a stay in NYC for the under 16s even more exciting. Central Park, for example, has a wealth of entertainment year-round, while some of

BRITTIP

To inspire kids aged 8 to 12 about their trip, get a copy of *Melanie in Manhattan* by Carol Weston (www.melaniemartin.com), a novel about a girl and her family travelling in the Big Apple.

the museums offer some real hands-on, fun activities. A word of warning: visiting any of the incredible children's stores with a real-life child in tow is likely to lead to plastic card meltdown!

TOP FIVE ATTRACTIONS FOR KIDS
Circle Line Sightseeing Cruise (page 77)
Statue of Liberty (page 60)
Empire State Building (page 61)
Times Square (page 185)
Central Park (pages 257–260)

DISABLED TRAVELLERS

According to the disabled people we've spoken to, New York is one of the easier destinations to tackle – and certainly puts Britain to shame. Most of the road corners, for instance, have kerbs that dip to the ground, making it a lot easier to wheel yourself about the city. Again, for the wheelchair-bound, bus platforms can be lowered to the same level as the pavement to allow easy access and, where possible, some of the subway stations have had elevators installed. To find out which 59 stations are accessible to wheelchair passengers, check the MTA site www.mta.info. For up-to-date information on the accessibility status of lifts and escalators, call 718-596 8585/8273 (TTY) daily 6am–10pm. Access-A-Ride (AAR) is a 24-hour door-to-door shared ride service offered by them to people who are unable to use the subway or bus (tel 877-337 2017 toll free or 718-393 4999/4259 (TTY) 7am–5pm for information and to reserve a trip). Proof of disability needed. Able-Ride is a shared ride kerb-to-kerb bus services in New York State that disabled visitors can apply for (tel 516-228 4000). Full details on both can be found at the MTA site.

If you'd like to travel in style, Vega Transportation (tel 718-507 0500, www.vegatransportation.com) offers the luxury of a chauffeur-driven car for those in a wheelchair. You can rent a wheelchair on arrival (7-day, 24-hour service) from ScootAround (tel 888-441 7575, www.scootaround.com).

Washington Memorial Arch

One of our favourite New York tales comes from Colin Macrae, a disabled person who regularly travels all over the world with his wife Joan. They were in New York one cold Christmas and Colin was sitting in his wheelchair all by himself, huddled up against the biting wind, while his wife went off to sort out tickets for the Circle Line cruise. As he waited, Colin was approached by a tramp, who pressed a quarter into his hand saying: 'I don't have much, but you can have what I've got.' Then he rushed off before Colin could reply or give him his money back. Just goes to show, the most unexpected and heart-warming things can happen in this amazing city.

Anyway, to make your life as easy as possible, here are the main organisations that deal with different aspects of travel for the disabled.

RESOURCES FOR THE DISABLED

Note: TDD or TTY = Telecommunications devices for the deaf.

Hospital Audiences Inc (HAI): 3rd Floor, 548 Broadway. Tel 212-575 7676, www.hospaud.org. Publishes a book, *Access for All* ($5), which gives comprehensive information on venue access, toilet facilities and water fountains at a whole range of cultural centres from theatres to museums and major sights.

In addition, it has audio description services for people who are blind or visually impaired. Called Describe, this contains Program Notes, which describe all aspects of a show and staging in an audio cassette you can listen to before the performance. It also transmits a live Audio Description, during a pause in the dialogue, to audience members who have a small receiver. Reservations for both the tickets, which have to be bought either through HAI or the theatre, and receivers, which are provided free of charge, must be made through HAI. For more information, call Describe on 212-575 7663.

New York Society for the Deaf: 817 Broadway at 12th Street. Tel 212-777 3900. Provides advice and information on facilities for the deaf.

Hands On: Suite 7F, 159-00 Riverside Drive West. Tel 212-740 3087/TTY use relay 711, http://handson.org. Provides accessibility to arts and cultural events for the hard of hearing through sign interpreted performances and a monthly cultural calendar of accessible events.

Big Apple Greeter Access Coordinator:
1 Center Street, Room 2035, New York, NY
10007. Tel 212-669 3602 (voice) or 212-669
8273 (TDD), www.bigapplegreeter.org. Will
provide a free tour guide for anyone with a
disability. Reserve though, three to four
weeks ahead.

BRITTIP
The booklet *On the Go*,
available from Hospital
Audiences Inc (HAI) (tel 212-575
7676, www.hospaud.org) gives
discounts on admission costs around
the city for seniors, all in one place,
as well as food outlets nearby and
other useful information.

SIGN LANGUAGE INTERPRETED PERFORMANCES
The Theater Access Program: TAP is
specifically for Broadway shows and is run
by the Theater Development Fund. Apply
online at www.tdf.org or email
access@tdf.org. Reservations for free
infrared headsets or neckloops for Broadway
shows can be made by calling Sound
Associates. 424 West 45th Street. Tel 212-
757 5679, www.soundassociates.com.

Lighthouse International: 111 East 59th
Street. Tel 212-821 9200 (voice) or 212-821
9713 (TTY), www.lighthouse.org. Provides
help and advice for blind people living in or
visiting the city.

COMMUNICATIONS
The American ringing tone is long and the
engaged tone is very short and high-pitched,
almost like a beep. Public phone booths can
be found all over the city. These booths are
coin or card operated, with prepaid cards
bought from drugstores, news-stands and
'candy stores' for international calls, ranging
from $5 to $100. To save you the bother,
many phones take credit cards. Toll-free calls
for booking lines or attractions when in New
York save on costs and are mentioned when
available. These start with the codes 800,
888, 866 and 877.

BRITTIP
Visit www.nycvisit.com to check
something while in town at
public phone booths with internet
access. Print off the locations from
the site before you go.

PHONES
To call New York from abroad: Dial 001
and the prefix – for instance, the main prefix
for Manhattan is 212 – then dial the 7-digit
number. The code for Brooklyn, Queens, The
Bronx and Staten Island are 718 and 347.
Mobile phones usually use the 917 prefix.

To call abroad from New York: Dial 011 +
country code + area code (dropping the first
0) + local number. The code for Britain is 44.
To call any number in New York from New
York: Always dial 1 + the area code + the
number.

Useful numbers:

Operator: 0

Directory enquiries: 411 (free from
payphones)

Long distance directory enquiries: 1 +
area code + 555 1212

Free numbers directory: 1 + 800 + 555
1212 (no charge)

MOBILE PHONES
You can, if you wish, get a mobile phone for
use in New York. Cellhire USA supplies
competitively priced mobiles (or cell phones
in American-speak) to international business
travellers to the city. Tel toll free 866-235
5447 or 877 244-7242, www.cellhire.com.

BRITTIP
If you make any calls at all
from your hotel you will pay a
tremendous premium. To avoid this,
you can either get a whole bucket of
quarters to use in a public payphone
or buy an international phone card
before you leave home. Local calls
cost a minimum of 50c.

POST
To send a postcard costs 70c, to send a letter
costs 80c for the first 25g (1oz). You can buy
stamps in shops – the Duane Reade chain of
chemists has machines – but there is a
mark-up. If you don't want to pay over the

Manhattan Bridge

odds for the convenience of these stamps, then go to one of the many post offices dotted around the city (call 800-275 877 or visit www.usps.com).

The main post office on 34th Street at 8th Avenue is a beautiful Beaux Arts building and incredibly large. If the queues are long, you can buy stamps from the vending machines.

Post boxes are square, dark blue metal boxes about 1.2m (4ft) tall with a rounded top that has a pull-down handle. They have a sign saying *US Mail* and a striking big American eagle logo on the side and can be found on street corners.

THE INTERNET

easyEverything: 234 West 42nd Street between 7th and 8th Avenues. Tel 212-398 0724, www.easyinternetcafe.com. Subway A, C, E, 1, 2, 3, 7, 9, N, R, S, B, D, F, Q to Port Authority/42nd Street/Times Square. Area: Theater District. Open 24 hours, the world's largest internet cafe, in the *Guinness Book of Records*, has 648 computers, plus scanners. Prices start at just $1 and it is open 7 days a week, 7am–1am.

Cybercafé: 250 West 49th Street between Broadway and 8th Avenue. Tel 212-333 4109, www.cyber-cafe.com. Subway N, R, 1, 9, to 49th Street, A, C, E to 50th Street. Open 8.30am–11pm Mon–Fri and 11am–11pm Sat–Sun and costs $6.40 for half an hour on the internet.

AMERICAN-SPEAK

It has often been said that the Brits and Americans are two races divided by a common language, and when you make an unexpected faux pas you'll certainly learn how true this is. For instance, never ask for a packet of fags as this is the American slang word for gays! There are plenty of other differences, too, which may not necessarily cause offence, but that will cause confusion. So to help you on your way, here is a guide to American-speak.

Ticket booths for Circle Line cruises

General:

English	American
Air hostess	Flight attendant
Anti-clockwise	Counterclockwise
At weekends	On weekends
Autumn	Fall
Behind	In back of
Camp bed	Cot
Cinema	Movie theater
City/town centre	Downtown (not Lower Manhattan)
Coach	Bus
Cot	Crib
Diary (appointments)	Calendar
Diary (records)	Journal
Football	Soccer
From... to...	Through
Lift	Elevator
Long-distance call	Trunk call
Nappy	Diaper
Ordinary	Regular, normal
Paddling pool	Wading pool
Plaster	Band Aid
Post, postbox	Mail, mailbox
Pram, pushchair	Stroller
Receptionist	Desk clerk
Tap	Faucet
Toilet	Restroom (public) or bathroom (private)

Money:

English	American
Banknote	Bill
Bill	Check or tab
Cashpoint/cash machine	ATM
Cheque	Check
1 dollar	Single
25 cents	Quarter
10 cents	Dime
5 cents	Nickel
1 cent	Penny

BRITTIP

There are no ground floors in America; what we call the ground floor, they call the first floor. It may seem a silly point, but it can cause confusion!

Food and drink:
One of the biggest disappointments we had on our first trip to America was to order our breakfast eggs 'sunny-side up', only to end up with what seemed like a half-cooked egg! The Americans don't flick fat over the top of the egg when frying it, but turn it over to

Break dancers at Columbus Circle

cook on both sides. So for eggs cooked on both sides but soft, order eggs 'over easy' and if you like yours well done, then ask for eggs 'over hard'.

There are plenty of other anomalies. Many standard American dishes come with a biscuit – which is a corn scone to us. Breakfast may also include grits, a porridge-like dish of ground, boiled corn, and hash browns – grated, fried potatoes. You'll find foods and food terms that are specific to New York on page 176.

English	American
Aubergine	Eggplant
Biscuit (savoury)	Cracker
Biscuit (sweet)	Cookie
Chick pea	Garbanzo bean
Chips	(French) fries
Choux bun	Cream puff
Clingfilm	Plastic wrap
Cornflour	Cornstarch
Courgette	Zucchini
Crayfish	Crawfish
Crisps	Chips
Crystallised	Candied
Cutlery	Silverware or place-setting
Demerara sugar	Light-brown sugar
Desiccated coconut	Shredded coconut
Digestive biscuit	Graham cracker
Double cream	Heavy cream
Essence (eg vanilla)	Extract or flavouring
Filled baguette	Sub or hero
Fillet (of meat/fish)	Filet
Fizzy drink	Soda
Golden syrup	Corn syrup

Grated, fried potatoes	Hash browns
Grilled	Broiled
Icing sugar	Powdered/confectioners' sugar
Jam	Jelly/conserve
Jelly	Jello
Ketchup	Catsup
King prawn	Shrimp
Main course	Entrée
Measure	Shot
Mince	Ground meat
Off-licence	Liquor store
Pastry case	Pie shell
Pips	Seeds (in fruit)
Plain/dark chocolate	Semi-sweet or unsweetened chocolate
Pumpkin	Squash
Scone	Biscuit
Shortcrust pastry	Pie dough
Single cream	Light cream
Soda water	Seltzer
Sorbet	Sherbet
Soya	Soy
Spirits	Liquor
Sponge finger biscuits	Lady fingers
Spring onion	Scallion
Starter	Appetiser
Stoned (cherries etc)	Pitted
Sultanas	Golden raisins
Sweet shop	Candy store
Takeaway	To go
Tomato purée	Tomato paste
Water biscuit	Cracker

BRITTIP

New Yorkers may consider themselves broad-minded but, like any American, will be genuinely shocked if you ask where the toilet is. Ask for the restroom in a public place and the bathroom if you're in someone's house.

Shopping:

English	American
Braces	Suspenders
Bumbag	Fanny pack
Chemist	Drug store
Flip-flops	Thongs
Ground floor	First floor
Handbag	Purse
High street	Main street
Jumper	Sweater
Knickers	Panties

Muslin	Cheesecloth
Queue	Line, line up
Suspenders	Garters
Tights	Pantyhose
Till	Check-out
Trainers	Sneakers
Trousers	Pants
Underpants	Shorts, underwear
Vest	Undershirt
Waistcoat	Vest
Zip	Zipper

Travelling around:

English	American
Aerial	Antenna
Articulated truck	Semi
Bonnet	Hood
Boot	Trunk
Caravan	House trailer
Car park	Parking lot
Carriage (on a train)	Car
Car silencer	Muffler
Crossroads/junction	Intersection
Demister	Defogger
Dipswitch	Dimmer
Dual carriageway	Four-lane (or divided) highway
Flyover	Overpass
Give way	Yield
Jump lead	Jumper cables
Layby	Pull-off
Lorry	Truck
Manual transmission	Stickshift
Motorway	Highway, freeway, expressway
Pavement	Sidewalk
Petrol	Gas
Request stop	Flag stop
Ring road	Beltway
Roundabout	Traffic circle
Slip road	Ramp
Subway	Pedestrian underpass
Turning	Turnoff
Underground	Subway
Walk	Hike
Wheel clamp	Denver boot
Windscreen	Windshield
Wing	Fender
Zebra crossing	Cross walk

BRITTIP

While you're at the NYC visitor centre in New York, pick up a copy of the *NYC Guide*. It has up-to-date listings of Broadway shows, plus various money-off coupons.

NYC&Co. Visitor Information Kiosk

TOURIST INFORMATION

NYC & COMPANY CONVENTION & VISITORS BUREAU
www.nycvisit.com

London: Tel 020 7922 1100 (line open Mon–Fri 9.30am–5.30pm).
New York City's official tourism agency – call to discuss any queries you have with the information officers or ask them to send you a Visitors' Guide.

New York: 810 7th Avenue at 53rd Street. Tel 212-484 1222. Mon–Fri 8.30am–6pm; Sat and Sun 8.30am–5pm. Subway N, R, S, Q to 57th Street, B, D, E to 7th Avenue/53rd Street or 1, 9 to 50th Street/Rockefeller Center.

BRITTIP

NYC & Company New York Open/Book campaign tells you the best value time of the year for a visit to New York City – usually around major US holiday times.

A state-of-the-art visitors' information centre in Midtown with touch-screen kiosks that provide up-to-date information on the city's attractions and events accompanied by a detailed map. There is also a cashpoint and a souvenir shop, plus an incredible range of brochures covering hotels, shops, museums, sights, tours and Broadway shows. There are also visitors' centres in Downtown, Chinatown, Harlem and the Financial District.

TIPS ON TIPPING

You won't get a lunch, drink, ride or even a taxi door being opened for you without a tip being involved in America and it can add quite a lot to your overall expenses when you're on holiday. It's something that doesn't come naturally to us Brits, but you need to get used to it quickly.

Bartender: $1 a round.

Hotel doormen: $1 for hailing a cab.

Maid service: Around $1–$10 per day when you leave your accommodation.

Porters: $1 per bag.

Taxi drivers: 15 per cent, and if you travel by private car or limousine they'll automatically add 20 per cent to the bill.

Waiters: General rule of thumb is 15–20 per cent. The best way to work it out is to double the sales tax, which will come to 17 per cent, and add a little more if you are very impressed. Just remember, at a posh restaurant the tip alone can come to more than the price of a decent meal!

NEW YORK TRAVEL ADVISORY BUREAU

www.nytab.com

An independently run tourism agency, which is most famous for its own pocket guide to New York, the NYPages, and the NYCard, which gives discounts to hotels, museums and attractions – check the website for the latest update on all their available discounts. It also has downloadable walking maps and up-to-the-minute top picks.

LOST YOUR PASSPORT?

If you lose your passport or have any big problems, call the emergency number at the New York British Consulate on 212-745 0202 option 2, www.britainusa.com.

CURRENCY

Exchange rate for the US dollar at the time of writing is around $2/£1. UK banks' and travel agencies' rates vary, so shop around to find the best. Also check the commission – some will charge for both selling and buying back, but many will only charge once, so you can return unused dollars you bought from them free of charge. Travel agencies tend to compete with each other on rates and don't charge commission. The Post Office and Marks & Spencer do not charge commission.

A lot of people use travellers' cheques, but it is often a real palaver to cash them, especially at banks in New York. Many banks simply won't take them, and if they do they'll need photo ID so you'll have to carry your passport around with you. Chase Bank, Manhattan has more than 400 branches and doesn't charge a fee for exchanging currencies. Visit www.chase.com to find a branch with full contact details including phone numbers.

BRITTIP

You must have plenty of change and singles ($1 notes) as you'll be tipping everyone for everything, and you'll also need change for the buses.

BRITTIP

For a quick currency converter go to www.xe.com/ucc/, which also offers free exchange rates.

Inside the Empire State Building

KNOWING NEW YORK

The alternative is to exchange a reasonable amount of cash in one hit to use for tips, buses and in cafés, then use your credit card as much as possible (the exchange rate is generally reasonable). If you need extra cash, make sure you know your PIN number for your credit card and you'll be able to use any of the many cashpoints (ATMs) around the city, for which there is usually a fee.

DISCOUNT DIVAS

NYC & Co (see page 22) runs various money-off campaigns in association with the American Express Card that cover restaurants, hotels, theatres and sightseeing tours. The main one is Paint the Town Red, which runs from early January until the end of March and includes the Winter Restaurant Week as well as the January sales. Log onto www.nycvisit.com/paintthe town for a list of offers or call 1-800-NYC GUIDE for a free discount brochure.

BRITTIP

Smoking is not allowed in taxis, buses or subways and banned in most indoor places, including restaurants and bars. If you're gasping, there's a list of smoker-friendly restaurants, clubs and bars on http://newyork.citysearch.com.

Each year the popular Summer Restaurant Week takes place for two weeks from mid-July when you can get three-course meals at more than 150 of the city's top restaurants for around $25 (excluding tip, tax and drinks). Many restaurants also continue serving their prix-fixe lunches to the end of August. Establishments include Nobu, Union Square Café, Spice Market, 66, Blue Water Grill and Vento. For further information visit www.nycvisit.com/restaurantweek or phone either 1-800 NYC VISIT (toll-free within America) or 212-484 1222.

NEW YORK TALK

Of course, in addition to the differences between American and Brit-speak, the locals have a dialect and phraseology all their own, influenced mainly by the Brooklyn accent, Mafia-speak and the fact that people often talk so quickly that words run into each other. Here are just a few examples that you may well come across:

All right already: Stop it, that's enough!
Big one: A $1,000 bill
Bloomies: Bloomingdale's
Capeesh: Pronunciation of capisce, Italian for 'understand'
Cattle call: A theatre casting call
Dead soldier: Empty beer can or bottle
Do me a solid: Do me a favour
Don't jerk my chain: Don't fool with me
DPh: Damned fool, based on transposing PhD
Eighth Wonder of the World: Brooklyn Bridge
Finger: Pickpocket (also mechanic, dip, cannon, goniff or moll buzzer)
Fuggedaboduid: No way
Guppies: Gay yuppies
In line: Stand in a queue
JAPs: Jewish American princesses
Jocks: Sporty types, after their straps
Mazuma: Slang for money
Meet me between the lions: A favourite meeting place: the lion statues at the New York Public Library
Met: The Metropolitan Opera House or the Metropolitan Museum
No problem: You're welcome
Nudnik or nudge: A persistently dull and boring person
On account: Because
Out in left field: Weird, unorthodox
Ozone: Very fresh, pure air
Shoot the works: Gamble or risk everything
Straphanger: Subway commuter
Suit: Businessman
Yard: Back garden

View from the Empire State Building

CHAPTER 2

New York
Neighbourhoods

It's worth getting to know the neighbourhoods of Manhattan as each one has a distinct flavour and is filled with its own unique sights and sounds. From the historic Downtown area of the Financial District to the charming cobbled streets of Greenwich Village and the vibrancy of Times Square, every one is well worth visiting in its own right.

Here's an outline of what you'll find in each neighbourhood, what makes them so special and how to make the most of your time there. They are placed in alphabetical order for ease of reference.

34TH STREET

At a glance: Empire State Building * Herald Square * Penn Station * shopping at Macy's

You'll have two major reasons for coming to this part of New York (Map 3) – the divine **Empire State Building** (page 61) and the shopping. **Macy's** is here (page 113), as well as a range of chains and most importantly a lot of retail outlets for the nearby Garment District. This was once a pretty seedy area, but thanks to the efforts of the 34th Street Business Improvement District Partnership (BID), it has been transformed.

Now the streets are constantly maintained, clean and lined with pretty flower tubs and green benches. The BID has even installed some smart green telephones with a semi-enclosure to block out some of the street noise. The kiosk at Herald Square is in matching green, as is the city's one and only automatic pay toilet next door. It's pretty swanky and, most importantly, it's clean! The size of the average New York bedroom, you've enough room to swing a cat if you feel like it and 25c gives you 20 minutes inside.

If you plan to do the Empire State Building, make it your first port of call before the crowds and queues build up. Take the B, D, F, N, Q, R, V, W to 34th Street and walk one block east to 5th Avenue where you'll find the beautiful Art Deco entrance.

Once you've come back down to earth,

take a cheap coffee break at the little-known **Graduate Center** (www.gc.cuny.edu/) at 365 5th Avenue on the corner of 34th Street, diagonally opposite the Empire State Building. Here you can buy filtered coffee or a luscious latte with a croissant and sit in relative peace at any time of the day before 4pm, which is when the graduates start pouring in. The building used to be a department store, which is why there are ribbons and ties sculpted into the exterior columns. Now it is used as a research centre for students and holds free concerts. Anyone can sign up to use a computer here for up to two hours for free.

HERALD SQUARE

Herald Square, which is named after the now defunct newspaper, is home to the famous **Macy's** (www.macys.com), the world's largest retail outlet (the best subways for East 34th Street are the B, D, F, N, Q, R, V, W to 34th Street/Herald Square). Prior to Macy's opening in 1901, the area was down-at-heel, with lots of bordellos and seedy clubs. The opening of the department store was a fashion moment and improved the entire district.

The Empire State Building from the Circle Line Ferry

The store's top-sellers among the Brits are the extremely well-priced Levi's and beauty products, while the seventh floor is dedicated to children's goods and it even has a McDonald's – the only department store in town to make such a proud boast.

For the grown-ups there is the wonderful **Cucina & Co.** (page 143) in the basement. A combination of buffet foods to eat in and take away, a grill restaurant and a coffee shop, it also has a sandwich station, pasta station and take-aways at incredible prices. Bearing in mind the average New Yorker spends $10 for a sandwich-style lunch and drink, Cucina's lunches are amazing value, as are their meal specials.

But don't expect it to look cheap; this is a wonderful space filled with fabulously fresh food in an indoor-market setting. Adjacent to it is **Macy's Cellar**, where a complete dinner for two costs $24.95.

SHOPPERS' PARADISE

Between 5th and 8th Avenues on 34th Street is a shopper's paradise and one of the highlights is the **Sephora** beauty emporium, which has branches all over the city (page 130). With its sparkling floor-to-ceiling windows and stylish displays, this is a pristine shrine to beauty products and fragrances.

Other great shops in the area include **Old Navy**, the high-value end of the **Banana Republic** chain, **Kids R Us**, **Daffy's** and its amazingly cheap designer selection, plus **HMV**, **H&M** and **Kmart**.

PENN STATION

One block south on 33rd Street and 7th Avenue is the entrance to **Penn Station**, short for Pennsylvania Station (subways 1, 2, 3, 9 to 34th Street–Penn Station). Before you enter you'll see a **Lindy's** pastry shop. The original Lindy's in the theatre area was famous for its cheesecake, and this and the other branch (in Times Square), trade off the

---

BRITTIP

If you're on the west side of Penn Station, you're just a stone's throw from the block-long B&H Photo & Video store (www.bhphotovideo.com) on 9th Avenue from 33rd to 34th Street (page 141). It has 625 staff over its four floors selling thousands of items to both amateurs and professionals.

---

name but they're pricey and not unique.

As you enter Penn Station, you'll see a handy Duane Reade (think Boots the Chemist) on the left. Walk down to the round area that sits under the **Madison Square Garden** building and on your left you'll see the information booth for the **34th Street BID Partnership**. All around are coffee shops, bakeries and a sit-down restaurant called **Kabooz**. None of them is a patch on Cucina & Co. or the Graduate Center, though. The restrooms are terrible; they have running water, but it just happens to be all over the floor! A good alternative is to head for the **Hotel Pennsylvania** on 7th Avenue opposite Penn Station, where you'll find clean WCs situated on the ground floor.

BRITTIP

There's a free tour of Penn Station on the fourth Monday of each month starting from the 34th Street Partnership Information Kiosk at 12.30pm. Tel 212-484 1222.

The main taxi ranks for Penn Station are on 7th Avenue opposite the Pennsylvania Hotel and on 8th Avenue opposite the majestic Beaux Arts General Post Office building. If you want a taxi from here, it's best to walk a block north as the queues can get quite long, or use the A, C, E, 1, 2, 3, 9 subways at 34th Street–Penn Station.

CHELSEA

At a glance: art galleries * Chelsea Hotel * Joyce Theater

This neighbourhood is only likely to be on your list of places to see if you like art galleries, want to go clubbing or if you're gay. However, it's actually worth a visit if you want to see an up-and-coming area in the process of gentrification. Originally farmland in 1750, by the late 1800s it was a commercial area filled with slaughterhouses, warehouses and the working classes. The mixture of sought-after brownstone townhouses and warehouses have made it a perfect target for artists priced out of SoHo, and although it's still rough around the edges, many of the quaint streets and buildings have been restored.

It is bounded by 6th Avenue (Avenue of the Americas) in the east, the Hudson River in the west, 16th Street in the south and 29th Street in the north. If you get off the A,

C, E line at 14th Street and walk north on **8th Avenue**, you'll see the main drag of restaurants, shops, bars and gyms. Along the way you'll notice an abundance of Chippendale-type male bodies – the neighbourhood's gay boys, who love to flaunt their pecs in the local nightclubs.

At the corner of 19th stands the **Joyce Theater** (www.joyce.org), famous for dance and its fancy Art Deco building. Just a little further north and you're not only in the **Chelsea Historic District** – the blocks around 9th and 10th Avenues at 20th, 21st and 22nd Streets – but at the heart of the new gallery community that lies between 10th and 12th Avenues.

First port of call should be the **Dia Center for the Arts** (www.diacenter.org), a four-storey, 3,700 sq m (40,000 sq ft) warehouse, which opened in 1987 and still plays a pivotal role in the art world. Other great galleries nearby include **LFL**, **Leslie Tonkonow**, **Max Protetch Gallery**, **303 Gallery** and the **D'Amelio Terras Gallery**. Two blocks north on 24th Street is the 1,950 sq m (21,000 sq ft) **Gagosian Gallery**, **Barbara Gladstone Gallery** and the **Andrea Rosen Gallery**. Photographer Annie Leibovitz's studio is on 26th. Appropriately enough, given the area's new-found propensity for art, it now has its first art museum, the Chelsea Art Museum (page 90), which can be found on West 22nd Street at 11th Avenue.

CHELSEA HOTEL

One of the most infamous of all of New York's hotels, the red-brick **Chelsea Hotel** (or Hotel Chelsea as it is officially known, www.hotelchelsea.com, page 239) is not only still going strong, but is also in the midst of a great revival. Before Sex Pistols frontman Sid Vicious moved in with his girlfriend Nancy Spungen and allegedly killed her, back in the 1970s, famous inhabitants included Mark Twain, Dylan Thomas, William S Burroughs, Arthur Miller and Arthur C Clarke.

Built in 1883 and named a historic landmark in 1966, its lobby walls are covered with plaques commemorating venerated guests and their artworks, while the Spanish **El Quijote** restaurant is famous for its lobster specials.

CHINATOWN AND FIVE POINTS

At a glance: Chinese restaurants * markets * gift shops * Church of the Transfiguration

The sprawling mass that is Chinatown (Map 1) has spread its wings north into the remnants of Little Italy, east into the Lower East Side and south in the Civic Center area. It is also home to the infamous Five Points area, once the most dangerous part of New York city.

Until recently, only history books and tour guides referred to Five Points. The name is derived from the five streets that intersect next to Colombus Park. Originally called Orange, Mulberry, Anthony, Little Water and Cross Streets, they are now known as Bayard, Park, Worth, Mulberry and Baxter.

In the 1820s, a pond graced a lovely area where the rich had their country homes, but they started sub-letting to tanners, who polluted the lake. Attempts to get rid of the dreadful smells from the lake by building a canal down Canal Street failed, and in the end only the poorest came to live in the area, which included freed slaves and immigrant blacks.

Irish immigrants arrived in the 1850s, then Italians and Eastern Europeans in the 1880s. Poverty was rife, and gangs

Chinatown

> ⚡ **BRITTIP**
> Have a game plan when visiting Chinatown – it's so crowded that it's easy to feel daunted by all the hustle and bustle.

flourished to such an extent that the streets were too unsafe for the police to patrol, and at least one person was killed each night. For almost 100 years, Five Points was considered the worst slum in the world and even shocked Charles Dickens. During that time the gangs were schools for criminals and politicians such as Johnny Torrio, Charles 'Lucky' Luciano, Al Capone and Frankie Yale. Paul Kelly set up boxing gyms to teach them how to be gangsters, use guns and extort money. Amazingly, the gangs even produced flyers with their 'services': $100 for the big job (murder), $50 for a slash on the face or $15 for an ear chewed off.

The appalling violence, corruption and history of this era has been brought to life by Martin Scorsese's movie *Gangs of New York*, which starred Leonardo DiCaprio and Daniel Day-Lewis. It genuinely gives a true

BRITTIP

Take advantage of Big Onion's Gangs of New York walking tour (page 84).

insight into the psyche of the early American immigrants.

Fortunately, Chinatown is now a very different place. Many of the overcrowded tenements were pulled down at the turn of the 20th century to build a park. Since then, the Criminal Court Building has also been built nearby, retaining a contact with the area's violent past!

The original Chinese immigrants to New York in the 1850s huddled around Pell Street. Sadly, it was not long before the Tongs, with their extortion rackets, illegal gambling and opium dens, gave the area a new reputation for violence. As a result, the US Government passed the Exclusion Act in 1882, which banned Chinese from entering America.

Canal Street, Chinatown

That all changed in 1965 with the new Immigration Act and a new wave of Chinese immigrants arrived. Very quickly the women in particular were snapped up for poorly paid work in the garment industry, which gradually moved from its old Garment District above 34th Street into Chinatown. In more recent years, there have been more changes, as a new wave of immigrants from the Fujian province of China has once again changed the face of the area. Now many of the well-off Cantonese have moved to Queens and the Mandarin-speaking Fujinese have the upper hand.

The best way to get to Chinatown by subway is to take the A, C, E, J, M, N, Q, R, W, Z, 6 to Canal Street.

At 277 Canal Street at Broadway and up some rickety old stairs you will find Pearl River Mart, Chinatown's idea of a department store, stocking everything from crockery to Buddhas, pretty lacquered paper umbrellas, clothes, shoes and slippers.

Back on the street again, you could be forgiven for feeling a little overwhelmed by the licensed and unlicensed street traders of Chinatown, who sell anything from fake watches to jewellery and handbags. It's often impossible to walk on the pavements, but also dangerous to step too far into the incredibly busy Canal Street!

BRITTIP

You'll have a hard time getting a taxi on Canal Street – they just don't make it into Chinatown that often. Head toward The Bowery and try to hail a taxi as it comes off the Manhattan Bridge, or use the subway stations at Canal and Broadway.

Further down the road, you can get another real insight into the local lifestyle by visiting the **Kam Man** grocery store at 200 Canal Street. It offers a wide range from plucked ducks to squid. Try a bag of Konja, which is filled with deliciously refreshing bite-sized pots of lychee jelly.

Mott Street is the main thoroughfare of Chinatown. Here, along with Canal, Pell, Bayard, Doyers and The Bowery, is a host of restaurants plus tea and rice shops.

South towards Doyers Street you'll find the **Church of the Transfiguration** – one of two so named in New York – which perfectly portrays the changing nature of the immigrant population here. The oldest Catholic church building in New York, it was built in the early 19th century and Padre Felix Varela Morales, a Cuban priest who helped form the Ancient Hibernian Order, preached here. But between 1881 and 1943, no Chinese were allowed into it, apart from some wealthy merchants. It was first used by the Irish immigrants, then the Italians, but is now, finally, used by the Chinese and has services in Chinese. Also worth checking is the Wall of Democracy on Baynard Street, which is festooned with posters and newspaper cuttings that document the changing situation in China.

BRITTIP
It's pointless arriving at Chinatown before 10am as only the local McDonald's will be open.

May May restaurant at 35 Pell Street serves up fabulous dim sum. The chicken and shrimp combo is delicious. Dim sum, incidentally, means the 'little delicacy that will lighten up your heart' – and it certainly does when it's good! Next door is the **Chinese Gourmet Bakery** and **Vegetarian Food Center**, from where you can buy enough ingredients to make your own picnic to eat sitting in the nearby **Confucius Plaza**.

You should try to visit the beautiful **Bowery Savings Bank** on Bowery Street at Grand. When it was built in the 1890s, people liked to save locally and so the bankers tried to create the feeling that their building was a safe place for people to leave their money by making their banks stunningly beautiful inside. The Neo-Classical exterior is an incongruous sight here in Chinatown but it's worth having a peek at it.

DOWNTOWN

At a glance: Wall Street * New York Stock Exchange * Battery Park * Sky Scraper Museum

This is where the history of New York started and where some of the most important financial sites in the world were founded. The Downtown area covers the whole of the Financial District and the Civic Center, stretching from river to river and reaching as far north as the Brooklyn Bridge/Chambers Street (Map 1).

BRITTIP
Look out for people wearing red jackets with red, white and black carts. Employed by the Downtown Alliance, they clean the streets and public areas, are an added level of security and will answer queries on the area.

Today, the winding, narrow streets of the true Downtown – a square mile area south of Chambers Street that stretches from City Hall to the Battery – are a dizzying juxtaposition of colonial-era buildings and towering temples of capitalism. In the beginning, they were the location of some of the most important events in American history. This is where the Bill of Rights was signed, where George Washington was inaugurated as the first president and where millions arrived to begin their search for the American Dream.

Visit www.downtownny.com for more information on free events and services.

THE WALL STREET SHUFFLE
The Dutch were the first to arrive and it was Peter Stuyvesant, New York's first governor, who ordered the building of a wooden wall at the northern edge of what was then New Amsterdam to protect the colonialists from possible attacks from Indians and the British. The name stuck and today it is known as **Wall Street**. This aspect of New York's history is presented in an exhibition in the Ionic-looking **Federal Hall National Memorial** (26 Wall Street, tel 212-825 6888), built on the site of New York's original City Hall. Cross the road into Broad Street and you're at the Neo-Classical entrance to the **New York Stock Exchange** (page 71).

Other fascinating landmarks include the **Federal Reserve Bank** in Liberty Street at Maiden Lane, which stores one-quarter of the world's gold bullion, and the Neo-Gothic **Trinity Church**, where Alexander Hamilton, the country's first secretary of the treasury, was buried after losing a duel. There has been a church on this site since the end of the 17th century and, for the first 50 years after it was built, Trinity was actually the tallest structure in New York.

Just off Wall Street at 25 Broadway is probably one of the poshest post office buildings in the world. Known as the old **Cunard Building**, it was once home to the booking offices of the steamship company in

BRITTIP

The Bowling Green end of Broadway is lined with coffee shops, cafés and pizza parlours. A freshly cooked slice eaten in or taken to go makes a perfect pit stop.

the days before aeroplanes took over the transportation needs of the masses from large liners, and the interior walls of the building are still lined with marble. There are other signs of its former use, too, with murals of ships and nautical mythology around the ceiling.

And it seems only fitting that the former headquarters of John D Rockefeller's Standard Oil Company at 28 Broadway should now be the home of one of New York's newest museums, the **Museum of American Finance** (page 100).

The best subway lines are the 2, 3, 4, 5 to Wall Street.

BOWLING GREEN

Blink and you'll miss this oval of greenery at the end of Broadway. You know you're there by the presence of the Greek revival-style US Customs House, which is now the **National Museum of the American Indian** (page 104) and has the world's largest collection devoted to North, Central and South American Indian cultures. Bowling Green was the site of the infamous business deal between the Dutch colony of New Amsterdam and the Indians, who were conned into selling Manhattan for a bucket of trinkets.

In the 18th century, the tiny turfed area was used for the game of bowls by colonial Brits on a lease of 'one peppercorn per year'. The iron fence that encloses it now is the original and was built in 1771, though, ironically, the once-proud statue of King George III was melted into musket balls for use in the American Revolution.

Here you'll also find the 3,175kg (7,000lb) life-sized **bronze bull**. A symbol of the Financial District's stock market, it appeared overnight outside the New York Stock Exchange in 1989. Now it is a tradition to rub him!

The nearest subways to take you to Bowling Green are the 4, 5 line to Bowling Green or R, W to Whitehall.

BATTERY PARK AND CASTLE CLINTON

Thanks to hundreds of years of landfill, the whole Downtown area is quite different to how it once was. Years ago, State Street houses looked over Upper New York Bay, and Water and Pearl Streets were named because they were at or near the water's edge. The excavation works required to build the deep foundations for the World Trade Center in the 1960s, destroyed by terrorists on 11 September 2001, created enough granite blocks of earth to form 9 hectares (23 acres) of new land, which then became home to Battery Park City and the World Financial Center.

In the Battery Park area, **Castle Clinton** originally stood on an island. Built in 1811 as one of several forts that defended New York harbour, it is now part of Manhattan. It has been an opera house, an aquarium and the original immigration sorting office, dealing with eight million immigrants before the opening of Ellis Island. It is now used as the ferry ticket office.

The opening of a plethora of new shops and cafés and the remodelling of the Battery Park public spaces has given the area a whole new lease of life.

The best subways to take here are the 1, 9 to South Ferry or 4, 5 to Bowling Green.

BATTERY PARK CITY

North-west of Battery Park, you'll find a relatively new area of land known as **Battery Park City**, which is actually the area created by landfill. It's still pretty much a quiet district, though there has been plenty of development. This is home to two of New York's newer museums. The **Museum of Jewish Heritage** (page 102) has been so successful, it already has plans for an extension.

BRITTIP

For more fantastic views of Dame Liberty and the harbour, treat yourself to a drink in the chic bar, Rise, on the 14th floor of the Ritz-Carlton Hotel in West Street (page 225).

At 39 Battery Place is the **Skyscraper Museum** (page 107), which tells the fascinating story of the creation of all those famous buildings. On the southern tip of the 'City' is the recently landscaped **Robert**

Wagner Junior Park with a café, some WCs and street vendors selling food and drink – it is a wonderful place to sit and gaze out at the harbour.

To the north is the **World Financial Center**, which has four tower blocks and a full calendar of fairs and festivals. It's worth coming here for the **Winter Garden** (page 72), a huge, glass-ceilinged public plaza decorated by massive palm trees. From here you can see the fancy private boats docked in **North Cove**.

The nearest subways are the A, C, 1, 2, 3, 9 to Chambers Street (for the World Financial Center) or the 1, 9 to South Ferry (for the museums and park).

EAST OF BATTERY PARK

To see what life was like in 18th-century Manhattan, head for the **Fraunces Tavern Block Historic District**, which has 11 early 19th-century buildings that escaped the fire of 1835. The three-storey Georgian brick house that is home to the **Fraunces Tavern Museum** (page 94) on the corner of Pearl and Broad Streets was built in 1904 and houses an exhibition on the site's history.

A little further north-east along Water Street to the Old Slip, you'll see the tiny **First Precinct Police Station**, which was modelled on an Italian mansion and which has been used for exterior shots for both *Kojak* and *The French Connection*. Fittingly, this is now the permanent home of the **New York City Police Museum** (page 106). Down on the water's edge of South Street is to be the new home of the **Guggenheim's Downtown Museum** project, a Frank Gehry design that will include a water garden, an ice rink and a public plaza. It is expected that the new museum will attract more than three million visitors a year.

BRITTIP

Don't miss the free outdoor concerts at the South Street Seaport Museum (page 109), held almost nightly throughout the summer.

Just off Water Street at 70 Pine Street is the incredibly beautiful Art Deco wedding-cake-shaped **American International Building**. It has one of the most beautiful Art Deco-designed lobbies in New York and visitors are welcome to come inside to have a look.

A little further north at piers 16, 17 and 18, you find yourself in the heart of the **South Street Seaport** (page 66), which has a museum, a shopping and restaurant complex and the 150-year-old **Fulton Fish Market**, open midnight–8am daily.

Best subways to the area are the R, W to Whitehall Street, J, M, Z to Broad Street or the 2, 3 to Wall Street.

CITY HALL PARK AND THE CIVIC CENTER

City Hall Park is right opposite the entrance to Brooklyn Bridge and is also the dividing point between the Financial District and Chinatown. From here you can stroll across the **Brooklyn Bridge** or visit the Neo-Gothic **Woolworth Building** (page 72) on Broadway at Barclay Street, which is likely to be your main reason for swinging by. Check out the lobby's vaulted ceilings and its magnificent mosaics and mail boxes. When it was first built it was the tallest structure in New York and Mr Woolworth paid cash for it!

BRITTIP

There is a farmers' market each Tuesday and Friday (April to December, 8am–6pm) in the City Hall Park where you can buy fresh fruits, vegetables and bread – a great way to create a picnic.

Back in the 1930s, when Prosecutor Dewey decided to target organised crime, he made the Woolworth Building his base and during that time he locked up 15 prostitutes in the building for four months. In the end, he worked out that the prostitutes were controlled by Lucky Luciano and successfully prosecuted him for white slavery. 'Lucky' got 32 years in prison, but lived up to his name by serving just ten before he was pardoned for his efforts on behalf of the American government during the Second World War. Just north of City Hall Park are the **Police Plaza, US Courthouse, New York County**

City Hall

Courthouse and **Criminal Court Building**.

It's useful to note that there is a Lower Manhattan information kiosk in City Hall Park where you can find information on attractions and upcoming events plus maps and directions.

The best subways to take are the R, W to City Hall or the 4, 5, 6 to Brooklyn Bridge/City Hall.

EAST VILLAGE

At a glance: Bohemian cafés and shops * Alphabet City

Forget the picturesque cobbled streets of Greenwich and the West Villages. Once you cross The Bowery (otherwise known as Skid Row) and head up to St Mark's Place you are in the heart of the **East Village** (Map 2) and an area more reminiscent of the Lower East Side than a village and currently back in vogue as one of the coolest neighbourhoods in Manhattan. No matter where you are in New York, it's easy to spot an East Villager – they have long hair and more metal in their face than a jewellery shop window display. You also know when you've entered the neighbourhood by the many tattoo studios, along with boutiques selling punk and leather outfits.

Where Greenwich Village has become upper middle class, the East Village retains its roots as a Bohemian enclave of free-thinkers and non-conformists, though the tramps are gradually being replaced by a more genteel set attracted by newly built apartment blocks and the comparatively reasonable, though not low, rents.

This was once the home of Beat Generation writer Allen Ginsberg (on East 7th Street) and was frequented by Jack Kerouac and other radical thinkers of the 1950s. Amazingly, one of the area's oldest clubs, **CBGB** on The Bowery, is still going strong. The punk-rock club is famous for hosting Blondie, the Ramones, Talking Heads and the Police.

Now the area is most well known for its second-hand shops, which can be found all along 7th Street and 2nd and 3rd Avenues. There's a tiny Little India on 6th Street, where you'll find a row of curry houses, but the most famous eating outlets is the **Yaffa Café** (page 153) on St Mark's Place heading towards Tompkins Square Park.

East 7th Street is home to what is claimed to be New York's oldest pub, McSorley's Old Ale House, which dates back to 1854 and still serves its own beer, while a line of Harley Davidson's on 3rd Street between 1st and 2nd Avenues is evidence of the base of the New York chapter of the Hell's Angels.

Alphabet City, which lies between Avenues A to D towards the East River, is also part of East Village. Once considered a no-go area for tourists, it was predominantly filled with a working class Latino community and had a reputation as the drug-dealing area of the city. These days, the drug problems are largely a thing of the past, and an influx of young professionals has given the area a lift. Its major historical attractions are two churches, San Isidero y San Leandro and Iglesia Pentecostal Camino Damasco, built in an elaborate Spanish-colonial style.

The best subways are the L, N, Q, R, W, 4, 5, 6 to 14th Street/Union Square and the L to 3rd Avenue and 1st Avenue.

GARMENT DISTRICT

At a glance: sample sales * artists and designers

From 34th Street to 42nd Street between 6th and 8th Avenues, you'll find the **Garment District** of New York (Map 3). Having shrunk a little in the past – a lot of work disappeared overseas or moved to the cheap labour available in Chinatown – the area is once again up-and-coming, as designers are now choosing to have their

BRITTIP

Check out the sales section of New York's *Time Out* magazine for up-to-date information on designer sample sales in the Garment District.

clothes manufactured in New York. If you wander around this area – and you may well if you're in search of sample sales – you'll see racks of clothes being pushed around the streets. Some are going to showrooms and warehouses, but as no one manufacturer makes an entire piece of clothing, many of the garments are being shunted from company to company to have different bits sewn on at each place!

GRAMERCY PARK

At a glance: Irving Place * Gramercy Park Hotel * The Players

Two blocks south and two blocks east of the Flatiron Building on East 20th and 21st at **Irving Place** (Map 3) is one of the prettiest squares in New York City (the nearest subway is the 6 to 23rd Street). The park itself was once a swamp but has now been beautifully laid out, though you won't be able to go in unless you are staying with a resident of the surrounding square or at the **Gramercy Park Hotel**.

The most famous building in the neighbourhood is **The Players** at 16 Gramercy Park, a private club created for actors and theatrical types by actor Edwin Booth when Gramercy Park was the centre of the theatre scene. Booth was the greatest actor in America in the 1870s and 1880s and opened the Gothic revival-style house as a club in 1888 so that actors and literary types could meet in private to interact. One tragic event overshadowed the end of Booth's life – his brother John Wilkes Booth assassinated Abraham Lincoln.

GREENWICH VILLAGE

At a glance: Washington Square Park * Bleecker Street * brownstone townhouses * restaurants and boutiques

This is one of the prettiest areas of New York and, although the radical free-thinkers have gone, its quaint cobbled and tree-lined streets, shops and Federal and Greek-style buildings are well worth a visit.

Greenwich Village proper (Map 2) is bounded in the north by 14th Street, in the south by Houston (pronounced 'Howston'), in the east by Broadway and in the west by 7th, where it becomes the West Village, which stretches west to the Hudson River.

When the Dutch first arrived in Manhattan, 'the Village' as it is known in New York, was mostly woodland, but was turned into a tobacco plantation by the Dutch West India Company. Then in the early 1800s people started fleeing from a series of cholera and yellow fever epidemics in the unhygienic Downtown.

However, when the wealthy moved into their 5th Avenue mansions at the end of the 19th century, rents came down and a whole new breed of artists, radicals and intellectual rebels moved in, creating a kind of Parisian Left Bank feel to the neighbourhood. Over the years it has been home to such literary lions as Mark Twain, Edgar Allen Poe, Dylan Thomas, Eugene O'Neill and Jack Kerouac.

Now the writers and artists have largely been forced out by the soaring rents – a tiny two-bed apartment costs at least $2,500 a month and to buy a shoebox of a studio is at

---

GREAT TOURS OF THE VILLAGE

If eating's your thing, then you'll love the **Foods of New York** tour (page 81) of Greenwich Village and West Village, which not only shows you the sights, food shops, restaurants and architectural secrets of the area, but will also give you a chance to taste the foods that are unique to this corner of New York.

Other great tours are the **Literary Pub Crawl** (page 85), which takes you to the watering holes once frequented by literary giants, and **Haunted Greenwich Village** (page 83), which shows you places with a legendary past.

---

least $275,000 – and in their place have come upper middle-class Americans for whom making money is the abiding principle. Yet there is still the sense of a community spirit, many restaurants cater mostly to locals rather than tourists (in New York, only Village restaurants seem filled with people who are in no particular rush) and a great variety of off-Broadway shows and other cultural events can be seen in this neighbourhood.

WASHINGTON SQUARE PARK

If you take the A, B, C, E, F or V subway to West 4th Street and Washington Square, you'll find yourself in what many people consider to be the heart of the Village – and in one of the very few genuine squares in Manhattan. The first thing you'll notice is the Stanford White-designed marble square **Triumphal Arch** at the bottom of 5th Avenue, built in 1892 to commemorate George Washington's inauguration as the first US president.

BRITTIP

Tomoe Sushi on Thompson Street (page 156) looks pretty unappealing from the outside, but has incredible queues. Why? You can get the best sushi in New York here for about a tenth of what it would cost you at Nobu.

You may also become aware of how dingy it all looks and you may be even a little concerned about the 'grungy' nature of many of the people there, but this area is considered 'alternative' rather than dodgy. It's full of locals skating, playing chess and just hanging out, plus students from the nearby **New York University**. It used to be a place where a lot of people took drugs, but that problem is largely in the past.

A little-known fact is that the park was once used by City officials to conduct public hangings until they were moved to Sing Sing penitentiary. Apart from the arch and the people, the other main point of interest in the park is the **Dog Run**. A uniquely New York phenomenon, the idea is that instead of taking your dog for a walk along the roads, you bring them to dog runs where they can literally run around off the lead. It's rather like a parent taking their child to the swings – hilarious and has to be seen to be believed!

North from the park on 6th Avenue between Waverly Place and 9th Street is **Bigelow's Pharmacy**, the oldest traditional chemist in America. Across the street is the beautiful **Jefferson Market Courthouse**, which is now used as a library, and just off 10th Street is one of the most famous rows of mews houses in the Village – **Patchin Place**, which has been home not only to many a writer, including e e cummings and John Reed, but also to Marlon Brando. Also of note on the square is the **Forbes Magazine Building** (page 94), a museum filled with antique toys as well as a signed copy of Lincoln's Gettysburg Address, while the **Church of the Ascension** is an English Gothic Revival church built in 1840 with a mural of the Ascension above the altar by John La Farge.

BLEECKER STREET

Effectively the main drag of the Village, this is one of the best places to be in New York, filled as it is with sidewalk cafés, shops, restaurants and clubs. The corner of Cornelia and Bleecker Streets gives you access to some of the finest food shops and restaurants in Manhattan. To get here, take the 6 to Bleecker Street or B, D, F, V to Broadway/Lafayette Street.

Bleecker Street and 7th

At 259 Bleecker is **Zito's** (page 81) old-fashioned Italian bread shop, which still uses the ovens that were built here in the 1860s and were once used by the whole community. They are particularly famous for focaccia with different toppings, such as onions and olive oil and rosemary, and their prosciutto bread is unique to them.

Next door is **Murray's Cheese Shop** (page 142), with more than 350 cheeses from around the world. Nothing is pre-cut and they have great names such as Wabash Cannonball, Crocodile Tears, Mutton Buttons and Cardinal Sin, a British cows'-milk cheese. They also have 15 different types of olives and sell chorizos, pâtés and breads. Opposite at 260 Bleecker is **Faicco's** (page 142), a landmark shop that has been here since 1900. Its famous range of sausages is made every morning and sold not only to local residents but also to many of the local restaurants. It also sells home-cooked, ready-made meals and offers a huge deli selection.

Around the corner is Cornelia Street, home to four of the best restaurants in the Village. The **Cornelia Street Café** (pages 155 and 198) hosts jazz, readings and other events (from $6 to $11), while **Home Restaurant** specialises in American comfort food with a gourmet twist, **Le Gigot** is a traditional country French restaurant and **Little Havana** offers great Cuban food.

Bleecker Street has two more incredible bakeries with their own seating areas. **Pasticceria Bruno** is run by popular chef Biagio. He produces an amazing range of tarts and mousses for $2 to $3 with names like Kiss Cream, Wildberries, Green Apple and Apricot. The café itself has a lot of atmosphere and old world charm. Next door is **Rocco's** (page 142), run by Rocco, who used to be a head pastry chef at Bruno's until 1972 when he opened his own place here. An entire Italian cheesecake made of ricotta cheese costs just $12.50. The interior is much more modern, with steel-framed chairs, mirrors and more seats than Bruno's.

HAMILTON HEIGHTS

At a glance: City College * Sugar Hill

The Hamilton Heights neighbourhood (Map 6) is up on the high ground north of Morningside Heights and is effectively the middle-class enclave of Harlem. It takes its name from **Alexander Hamilton**, the first secretary of the treasury to the newly formed United States of America. He lived here from 1802 until he was killed in a duel in 1804.

The area is now the home of **City College**, one of the senior colleges in the New York university system. It was founded in the 19th century to educate the children of the working classes and immigrants and used to be known as the poor man's Columbia. It used to be free, but now it charges $3,200 a year, though that is still a lot cheaper than private universities in America, which charge an average of $27,400 per year.

Further north on West 145th Street off Amsterdam is the area known as **Sugar Hill**, which was made famous in the Duke Ellington song 'Take the A Train [to Sugar Hill]'. Now a conservation area, it is filled with beautiful brownstone townhouses, and was dubbed Sugar Hill because life here was considered to be so sweet.

HARLEM

At a glance: jazz * Apollo Theater * Hamilton Heights * Harlem Globe Trotters

Harlem is a huge area that covers a substantial part of the northern reaches of Manhattan above Central Park, though it has various subsections. What we refer to when we use the name Harlem is actually the African-American area, which stretches from 8th Avenue in the west to 5th Avenue in the east and goes north to the East River (Map 6). The area from East 96th Street east of 5th Avenue going up to the East River is **Spanish Harlem**, known as El Barrio and populated largely by Puerto Ricans.

Named after the Dutch town of Haarlem, the area received its first Dutch settlers in the mid-19th century, when it was used as farmland and as an escape from the dust and traffic of Midtown. Better-off immigrant families started moving here following the arrival of the railroad link and the building of attractive brownstone townhouses. Then property speculators, eager to take advantage of the new subway heading for Harlem, started building good-quality homes for the upper middle classes in the early 1900s. But they'd got a little ahead of themselves. A couple of mini depressions and Harlem's distance from Midtown Manhattan put the dampers on hopes of a major middle-class movement into the area.

BRITTIP

Many avenues and streets in Harlem have two names that reflect both historical and more modern influences. For instance, Lenox Avenue is known as Malcolm X Boulevard and 7th Avenue is known as Adam Clayton Powell Junior Boulevard, both named after major African-American activists.

The African-American estate agents spotted a golden opportunity, bought up a whole batch of empty homes cheaply and started renting them out to blacks eager to escape the gang warfare of the West 40s and 50s in Hell's Kitchen and Clinton. This was the beginning of Harlem as the capital of the black world and when African-Americans started migrating from America's southern states, they headed straight here.

BRITTIP

Instead of going to the somewhat touristy Sylvia's Restaurant on 125th, try the M&G Soul Food Diner on West 125th at Morningside Avenue for a truly traditional southern meal to the background sounds of great soul singers (page 180).

And it's no wonder really. Brits are frequently shocked to discover that the blacks may have been freed from slavery by the end of the 19th century, but there was still segregation until the 1960s. Black people were not allowed to sit on the same benches as whites, they had to drink at different water fountains and in church they were forced to wait until after the whites for Communion. When great black musicians such as **Duke Ellington** and **Louis Armstrong** went on tour, they had to stay at black-only hotels and eat at black-only restaurants.

Back in Harlem, at least, there was some semblance of belonging and thanks to the influx of political activists, professionals and artists to the area following the opening of the subway lines between 1904 and 1906, many African-American organisations had sprung up by the early 1920s. They included the **National Urban League**, which helped people who were moving into the area to get training for jobs, and the **White Rose**

Mission, which helped African-American female migrants coming to New York from the South. They were followed by the political Universal Negro Improvement Association and the Union Brotherhood of Sleeping Porters, whose leader Phillip Randolph was at one time considered by the government to be the most dangerous black in America.

THE GLORY DAYS OF HARLEM

The 1920s and 1930s were a great time for the neighbourhood, filled as it was with poets, writers, artists, actors and political activists. The combination of prohibition and great jazz musicians such as Count Basie, Duke Ellington and Cab Calloway made famous nightspots like the Cotton Club attractive to the upper middle classes who came in their droves to enjoy Harlem's speakeasies.

But all this was hardly doing anything for the lot of the average African-American who lived in the area. The speakeasies were strictly for whites only and even W C Handy, who co-wrote a song with Duke Ellington, was not allowed into the Cotton Club to hear it being played for the first time. Then there was the matter of the racism on 125th Street – Harlem's very centre – which runs from Frederick Douglas Boulevard to Malcolm X Boulevard. The white-owned shops and hotels here, which were used by the African-Americans, were staffed by whites and it was impossible for blacks to get anything but the most menial jobs.

BRITTIP

To experience the life and times of Harlem, pick up a copy of *Harlem's Culture: Guide to Great Events*, available at cultural institutions such as the Schomburg Center.

In 1934 Adam Clayton Powell Junior, preacher at the Abyssinian Baptist Church, organised a boycott of these businesses, entitled 'Don't Buy Where You Can't Work'. The campaign was successful and the shops started hiring blacks. You can still see the remnants of those businesses along 125th.

You can start your experience of Harlem with a tour round the Apollo Theater on 125th (page 84), which was the focal point for African-American entertainment between the 1930s and 1970s. Known for its legendary Amateur Night, which is now broadcast on TV, it has launched the careers of Ella Fitzgerald, Marvin Gaye, James Brown and even The Jackson Five.

At the corner of 7th Avenue stands the former Theresa Hotel, now an office block, but which was once considered to be the Waldorf of Harlem. Back in the days of segregation Josephine Baker stayed in the penthouse with its vaulted ceiling and views of both rivers. Malcolm X's Unity organisation was based here in the 1950s and 1960s and, in a show of support for African-Americans, Fidel Castro moved his entire entourage to the Theresa when he came to New York in 1960 for a United Nations conference.

BRITTIP

For soul food, try Miss Maude's Spoonbread, Malcom X Boulevard (Lenox Avenue) at 137th Street or visit Manna's Too at 134th Street (or Manna's at 8th Avenue and West 125th Street) for a great selection of well-priced fresh food and drinks.

A little further down the street is Blumsteins, once the largest department store in Harlem. With its dilapidated frontage and peeling paintwork, it's now hard to imagine this as once being the Macy's of the area.

Another major location in Harlem is up on 135th to 137th Streets between Powell Boulevard and Malcolm X Boulevard. You can either walk from 125th Street or take the 2, 3 subway to 135th Street station. Once there you'll find yourself right outside the Schomburg Center, which chronicles the history of black people in North America, South America and the Caribbean. Opposite is the Harlem Hospital Center where Martin Luther King was operated on after being shot. It was the first hospital in New York to be integrated.

BRITTIP

To experience a gospel choir in action, the place to go is the Abyssinian Church on 138th Street, but you'll need to arrive early because it gets packed. Another great place is the Second Canaan Baptist Church on 110th Street and Lenox Avenue.

A couple of blocks north and you'll find the famous **Abyssinian Baptist Church** at 132 West 138th Street. It was originally founded in 1808, and as the blacks moved from the Lower East Side to Greenwich Village, then up to the West 50s and 60s before finally finding a home in Harlem, the church moved with them. This church was built in 1923 and, with Adam Clayton Powell Junior as its preacher for many years before he became a senator, it was a centre of political activity, particularly in the 1920s.

One block west on 138th and 139th Streets between Powell and Frederick Douglas Boulevards are the four rows of Stanford White houses built in 1891 and known as **Striver's Row** because this is where the middle and upper classes strove to live. The houses were filled by doctors, lawyers, nurses from Harlem Hospital, jazz musicians and politicians such as Malcolm X. Boxer Harry Wills, known as the Brown Panther, lived here. He was paid $50,000 not to fight Jack Dempsey when the mayor banned the fight because he thought a black boxer fighting a white man would lead to riots.

BRITTIP

A terrific variety of tours of Harlem are available from Harlem Heritage Tours (tel 212-280 7888, www.harlemheritagetours.com).

The alleys at the back of these buildings were originally created for parking horses and carriages. Houses were usually built back to back so the alleys are a rarity, but a boon for the current occupants to park their BMWs. You can still see the old signs that say 'Walk your horses' or 'Park your carriages'.

DECLINE AND FALL

Sadly, the good times didn't last long and, from the 1940s to the 1960s, Harlem declined into an urban no-man's land as a result of a lack of government support and racial conflict. The once-fine apartment blocks grew shabbier as landlords were

BRITTIP

If you're concerned about wandering the streets of Harlem by yourself, try either a Big Onion walking tour (page 83) or a Harlem Spirituals bus tour (page 74).

either too unscrupulous or unable to afford to maintain them on the cheap rental income.

Eventually City Hall and certain businesses started investing in the area. In 1976 the city began reclaiming properties abandoned by landlords who couldn't afford to pay their taxes. You can still buy one of these blocks for $1 if you have the $2 million needed to renovate it. Fortunately, many have already been refurbished and, with the influx of banks and even Starbucks, a small but important step towards gentrification is taking place.

For some time the brownstones of *Hamilton Heights* and other local neighbourhoods have been targeted by those trying to escape the substantial rents elsewhere in Manhattan. There have been other developments, too. Former president Bill Clinton has his offices on 125th Street between Lenox and 5th (the one with the huge Gap advert down the side). He's always been a favourite with African-Americans because he did a lot for racial equality and he was invited to move his offices to Harlem from Carnegie Hall. Former baseball star **Magic Johnson** has also been doing much to encourage a sense of pride in the community.

RENAISSANCE

Now many people are predicting a renaissance for Harlem and suggest house prices could sky-rocket within the next few years, though it's unlikely that would help the really poor people. Old nightspots once frequented exclusively by the African-Americans have also been bought up and are being earmarked for renovation, including the *Renaissance Ballroom*, once a neighbourhood institution. Everyone would watch the Harlem Rennies basketball team early in the evening, then clean up to hit the nightclub. It was shut in the 1940s, but is now owned by the Abyssinian Church, which is hoping to renovate it.

Bike tour of Harlem

Another major venue was **Small's Big Apple** jazz club. Its sister establishment, **Small's Paradise**, was a restaurant in the 1930s and 1940s. It was so popular and the dance floor so small that it was said people had to dance on a dime here. It enjoyed a revival from the 1960s and was where Professor du Bois, who once ran the National Association for Advancement of Coloured People, held a birthday party in the 1980s. It closed in the same decade, but is now owned by the Abyssinian Church and there's a chance it may re-open as a tourist centre.

LITTLE ITALY

At a glance: Italian restaurants * street cafés

With its strong ties to Naples and a history of Mafia connections, Little Italy is still seen as a glamorous area of the city by many. The best subway to Little Italy (Map 1) is the N, R, Q, W, 6 to Canal and then walk east to Mulberry, or take the 6 to Spring and walk south. Head along Grand Street towards Mott and Mulberry Streets to **Di Palo's** (page 142), which marks the beginnings of what is left of Little Italy. Di Palo's shop at 210 Grand Street was founded 80 years ago and is still famous for its mozzarella, Italian sausages and salamis. It has its own cheese-ageing room and gets very crowded. A little further on is **Ferrara's** (page 158), the oldest and most popular pastry café in Little Italy.

BRITTIP
Ferrara's in Grand Street, near Mulberry, is a perfect spot for a coffee and pastry break, and you'll find the restrooms on the first floor. You'll also get a real slice of the Italian lifestyle.

Although much smaller now than it was in the 1970s due to a dwindling population, it is still a pleasant few blocks to wander around, particularly for food-lovers, as the delis, packed full of homemade breads, pastas, sausages and cheeses, are legendary. To stop it dwindling further, the Italians struck a deal with the Chinese community to retain **Mulberry Street** between Hester and Kenmare Streets. It's actually an area that was formerly home to Italians from the Naples area of Italy and, as such, it has taken St Gennaro, the patron saint of Naples, as its own saint. Every year in the third week of

September, Italians flock from far and wide to celebrate the **Feast of St Gennaro**. Food carts line Mulberry Street and there is much laughing, dancing and drinking until the early hours of the morning.

BRITTIP
Little Italy is at its finest at the weekend in warm weather when the restaurants put their tables outdoors. Arrive early – around noon – to get a seat outside, or late in the afternoon.

Little Italy's best feature is its wonderful restaurants with outdoor seating where you can watch the world go by while tucking into some great dishes. The restaurants have a reputation for being on the pricey side, but plenty have pasta and pizza specials for a more economical $10.

Just a little bit of gruesome history for you: Da Gennaro on the corner of Mulberry and Hester Streets was the original home of **Umberto's Clam House** (which is now further south on Mulberry). This was a favoured haunt of gangster Crazy Joey Gallo and where he was murdered in 1972 while celebrating his birthday.

Further north at 247 Mulberry between Spring and Kenmare Streets is the former home of the **Ravenlight Club** and Mafia headquarters for John Gotti. He was once known as the Teflon Don because no charges could be made to stick and this was where he made the policemen and judges on his payroll come to pay their respects.

The FBI were so determined to put him away they bugged not only the Ravenlight but also all the parking meters around the streets – but still they got nowhere. Then Gotti's underboss, Sammy Gravano, became a supergrass. He had killed 19 people but got away with all those murders because he did a deal with the FBI that helped them put Gotti away.

LITTLE KOREA

At a glance: Korean restaurants * markets * gift shops

This tiny neighbourhood isn't one of New York's most famous boroughs, but it's expanding rapidly and is a great place to visit for lunch or dinner, thanks to the many excellent restaurants that are packed into West 31st and West 32nd streets.

Empire State Building

Situated in the Herald Square area, next to the Garment District and Chelsea in the west, Little Korea is part of the melting pot of nationalities that have made New York their home. In the 1980s more than a million immigrants, a large percentage from Asia, arrived and took over corners of the city. Bordered by some of New York's major landmarks, this small area lies in the shadow of the Empire State Building, and is only a couple of blocks away from Macy's department store on Sixth Avenue and Pennsylvania Station.

As well as the mouth-watering restaurants, such as **Gam Mee OK** at 43 West 32nd Street and **Han Bat** at 53 West 35th Street (which is open 24 hours Mon–Sun), there are also Korean bookshops, beauty salons and a great supermarket selling all sorts of exotic produce until 2am.

LOWER EAST SIDE

At a glance: Lower East Side Tenement Museum * Delancy/Orchard Streets shopping * bars and restaurants

One of the seedier parts of town that's becoming cool again, the Lower East Side has a fascinating history but is now known for its trendy nightclubs and bargain shopping. The Lower East Side stretches from the East River ostensibly to Chrystie Street (though Chinatown is encroaching) and south from Canal Street to East Houston in the north, while Delancey is its main thoroughfare (Map 2).

The best way to get there by subway is by taking the J, M, Z, F trains to Delancey or Essex Streets.

In many respects the history of the Lower East Side is the history of America's immigration, which in turn has played a pivotal role in the country's development.

◀🇬🇧▶ BRITTIP

The Lower East Side Business Improvement District runs free two-hour walking tours of the historic Orchard Street Shopping District at 11am on Sundays from April to December. Call 866-224 0406 for details.

At one time this was the most densely populated area in the world, with 1,000 inhabitants crammed into a square mile: but more of that later. Almost from the word go, the Lower East Side was a settlement for new arrivals to New York because of its cheap housing and its proximity to where people disembarked. Once these immigrants had established themselves they moved on, leaving space for a new wave of arrivals. Street names such as Essex, Suffolk and Norfolk point to the origins of their first tenants. Since then streets have been named anything from a Kleine Deutschland to a Little Italy or Ireland.

◀🇬🇧▶ BRITTIP

While you're in the neighbourhood, don't miss Katz's Deli (page 158) on East Houston Street at Ludlow Street. It's a real institution.

With each new wave of immigrants came friction between new and old arrivals, which often led to violence. The Protestant English were angry, for instance, when the Roman Catholic Irish built St Mary's on Grand Street in 1828 and burned it down. That led to the formation of the **Ancient Order of Hibernians** in 1830 – the organisation that started the St Patrick's Day parade. The Hibernians rebuilt the church and put walls around the outside. It is still in existence, but now runs a kosher soup service for local Jewish people.

Check out www.lowereastsideny.com for information on events and discounts.

SWEATSHOPS AND TENEMENTS

Other tenants of the early 1800s were relatively well-off Jews from Germany, who eventually moved further north. This was a pattern that was to be repeated again and again with each new wave of immigrants. But perhaps the saddest were the incredibly poor Jewish immigrants who started arriving from Eastern Europe in the 1860s and '70s. They were forced to eke out a miserly existence in sweatshops and live in tenement buildings. Whole families were crowded into 1.8m (6ft) square rooms with no heating or running water and often little light. Visit the **Lower East Side Tenement Museum** (page 97) in Orchard Street for their full story.

During this period **Hester Street** was the main thoroughfare and it was filled with shops and pedlars selling their wares – meat, fruit and vegetables. The pedlars did very well, though, as they paid no tax and had no overheads such as rent. Often they made more than three times as much as teachers did. But the shopkeepers were unhappy with the unfair competition and by the 1930s the city had banned pedlars and created the Essex Market. Famous for its fresh meats, produce and other products, the market has recently been renovated at a cost of $1.5 million. It is open Mon–Fri 8am–6pm.

✠ BRITTIP
The Lower East Side was once known as a mugger's paradise. It's no longer so bad but, as in any city, you still need to be careful.

A NEW DAWN
The main language in Hester Street between the 1880s and 1920s was Yiddish – a mixture of Hebrew, German and Slavic. The local newspaper, called *Forward*, was published in Yiddish and each edition sold 200,000 copies. Now the area is very quiet. There are still many Jews left, but the new waves of immigrants include Puerto Ricans and Latinos from the Dominican Republic.

If you want to see some real action you need to go to **Delancey** and the big shopping area around Orchard and Ludlow Streets. Here you'll find bargain basement products and cutting-edge designer fashions – many young designers have started in the Lower East Side before moving uptown. **Orchard** and **Ludlow** between Delancey and East Houston Streets are also the main drags for the new bars and clubs that have been opening in the area. The best day to experience the Lower East Side is Sunday,

when the market is open and the whole area is buzzing with people. A large chunk of it is still closed on Saturday to mark the Jewish Sabbath, but that is gradually changing due to the arrival of the Latinos.

✠ BRITTIP
For excellently priced and clean accommodation in Lower East Side, stay at the Howard Johnson Express Inn (page 243) on East Houston.

An outstanding sight on Delancey is **Ratner's Dairy Restaurant** at 138 Delancey near Essex Street. Although it's still a dairy restaurant, it's now also home to **Lansky Lounge**, the chic nightspot that celebrates the place where mob boss Meyer Lansky used to hold court. The entrance is at 104 Norfolk Street.

MADISON SQUARE

At a glance: park * churches * New York Life Building

It's a weird but true fact that the ugly Madison Square Garden building, constructed above Penn Station on 33rd Street (pages 70, 195 and 262), is the latest (and probably least attractive) of the four Madison Square Gardens that have been built in New York. But only the first two were, in fact, located at Madison Square (Map 3), which is where Madison Avenue begins and is the site of the recently renovated **Madison Square Park**. Facing the square is Cass Gilbert's **New York Life Building**, which was erected in 1928. In its shadow is **The Little Church Around the Corner** just off 5th Avenue at 29th Street. Its real name is the **Episcopal Church of the Transfiguration** and its stained glass windows commemorate famous actors such as Edwin Booth, who frequented the church at a time when being an actor was not considered to be a very honourable profession. The nearest subways are the N, R, W, 6 to 28th Street.

MEATPACKING DISTRICT

At a glance: fashion boutiques * bars and restaurants * Hotel Gansevoort

The Meatpacking District is to be found in the north-western corner of the West Village, south of West 14th Street to West 12th Street and from West Street to Hudson

Street on the east side (Map 2). The nearest subway is the A, C, E to 14th Street. As the name suggests, the area was originally home to butchers and slaughterhouses for cattle in the 1930s. A handful of warehouses are still used for storing and cutting carcases to be distributed from wholesale markets around the city, but the majority have been abandoned over time and snapped up by eager young entrepreneurs who have used the loft-like spaces for everything from nightclubs to achingly trendy restaurants.

There are some fun hang outs around this area, such as **Hogs & Heifers** (page 189), which is frequented by a mix of motorcycle groups and celebrities. Many women leave their bras on the ceiling as a memento! **Tortilla Flats** in Washington Street on the corner of West 12th Street is a cool, grungy café. While wonderful **Florent** restaurant (page 160) is in Gansevoort Street.

Until recently the area was very edgy and still a hang-out for transvestite prostitutes – as depicted in *Sex And The City* when the man-eating Samantha moved here from the Upper East Side. Now, however, the dark, badly lit cobbled streets and alleyways have slowly been improved and the opening of über cool designer shops from the Brit fashion pack, including Stella McCartney and Alexander McQueen, are all signs that gentrification is well underway and its edgy vibe will soon disappear.

MIDTOWN

At a glance: shopping on 5th Avenue * St Patrick's Cathedral * Radio City Music Hall * Rockefeller Center * Carnegie Hall

Technically Midtown starts at 34th Street, but for the purposes of this area guide, we're starting at the more realistic 42nd Street (Map 3). From this point up to about 59th Street are some of the most beautiful and famous shops, hotels and buildings in the world, both to the east and west and on 5th Avenue itself (page 112). At the northern end of the area, 5th Avenue is lined with marvellous institutions such as **Saks**, **Bergdorf Goodman**, **Tiffany's** (our

BRITTIP

Weird but true, there are few coffee shops or coffee carts on 5th Avenue. If you want a coffee, your best bet is to try one of the side streets leading off to 6th Avenue.

favourite jeweller) and **Trump Tower** (page 72).

Fabulous hotels in Midtown include the media den of the **Royalton** (page 226) and the famous **Algonquin** (page 240). Opposite **St Patrick's Cathedral** (page 74) on 5th Avenue is the main entrance into the **Rockefeller Center** complex of 19 statuesque buildings with the famous ice-skating rink in the middle of its central plaza (page 64). There's so much to do here, from browsing in the shops to checking out the architecture or visiting the beautifully restored Art Deco **Radio City Music Hall** (page 64). Further north on 57th Street is **Carnegie Hall** (page 196).

MIDTOWN EAST

At a glance: Central Station * Chrysler Building * United Nations Building * Waldorf Astoria

The area between 5th Avenue and East River, **Midtown East** (Map 3) has its fair share of New York landmarks. No visit to the city would be complete without seeing the magnificent, marble **Grand Central Station** (page 69) at 42nd Street, which has been restored to its former glory. It may be overshadowed by the **MetLife Building** from the outside, but nothing can detract from its gorgeous interior. The ceiling has been painted to show the sky as seen by God from above.

BRITTIP

The area along East 45th Street between Vanderbilt and Lexington Avenues is packed with food carts selling everything from steak sandwiches to baked potatoes.

To the east is the stunning **Chrysler Building** (page 68) and down by the river is the monolithic **United Nations Building** (page 72); and no visit to Park Avenue would be complete without a drink at the **Waldorf Astoria** (page 222). Out of its many cocktail bars, the lobby bar is best for people-watching with a drink.

UN Building

MIDTOWN WEST

At a glance: Times Square * 42nd Street * Madame Tussauds * Intrepid Sea-Air-Space Museum

TIMES SQUARE AND THE THEATER DISTRICT

If you arrive at **Times Square** (Map 3) by day when all the lights and motion are less distracting, you may actually notice the lack of a square. Like Greeley and Herald Squares, Times Square is no more than a junction where Broadway crosses 7th Avenue. The **Theater District** starts on the boundary with the Garment District at 41st Street, goes north to 53rd Street and is bounded by 6th and 8th Avenues. The best way to get there is to take the 1, 2, 3, 7, 9, N, Q, R, S, W to Times Square/42nd Street.

◄█► BRITTIP

Broadway isn't called The Great White Way for nothing. At night, it's at its magnificent best around Times Square, but the best way to see it is from a few blocks north, where you really can appreciate the glittering beauty of all those neon signs.

The Theater District came into being at the end of the 19th century – previously the theatres were in the Union Square area and then Chelsea – when Oscar Hammerstein I (father of the great lyricist) built his opulent but long-gone Olympia Theater on Broadway between 44th and 45th Streets. Until then, it had been an unfashionable area known as Long Acre Square, housing the city's stables and blacksmiths.

In 1904, when the *New York Times* set up shop in what is now 1 Times Square, the area was renamed in its honour (it's since moved offices to around the corner). That same year a massive fireworks display on New Year's Eve became the precursor to the now famous annual countdown watched by millions of people. The surrounding Theater District, home to the Ziegfeld Follies at the **New Amsterdam Theater**, **Minsky's** and **Gypsy Rose Lee**, blossomed in the 1920s. In fact, so many theatres burst on to the scene that even though many were converted into cinemas in the 1940s, during a clean-up of the burlesque shows by Mayor LaGuardia, 30 theatres still remain.

BAD TIMES COME

Sadly, by the 1960s, Times Square had lost its shine and the economic problems of the 1970s and 1980s compounded the situation. If you've seen Martin Scorsese's film *Taxi Driver*, you'll have some idea of the level of drugs, prostitution and seedy strip joints that crowded the area. Crime rose dramatically and until fairly recently it was not a safe place to be.

Things started to change in the early 1990s, helped by the establishment of the **Times Square Business Improvement District**, which worked hard to clean things up and pay for security guards, and the discovery of an age-old law that prevents sex shops from operating within a certain distance of schools or churches. Since then crime in the area has dropped by 60 per cent and many New Yorkers have even complained of its relative cleanliness. The arrival of the Disney company, which spent millions renovating the New Amsterdam Theater to put on *The Lion King* (page 205), was the last nail in the coffin.

In all honesty, these dirt purists shouldn't fret too much – there is still definitely an edgy vibe to the neighbourhood, while the constant stream of traffic and the grunginess of many visitors stops Times Square from being what some people think of as a squeaky-clean environment.

All the same, it's safe enough for the most part, attracts tenants who pay the same rents as on more elegant 5th and Madison Avenues, and has plenty to offer everyone. New hotels have sprung up and corporate companies have moved into the neighbourhood, including media giants Viacom, MTV, VH-1 studios, ABC TV's *Good Morning America*, Condé Nast Publications and Reuters news service.

◄█► BRITTIP

For dining after the show with a good chance to spot celebs, book into Angus McIndoe, 258 West 44th Street. Tel: 212-221 9222.

There's the huge new **ESPN Zone**, a 3,900 sq m (42,000 sq ft) sports, dining and entertainment complex, **Nasdaq MarketSite** with its massive sign – the largest video screen in the world – and **Madame Tussaud's** (page 63). In between are the **Virgin Megastore** (page 145), the Coco Chanel-style beauty emporium of

Sephora (page 130) and the **World Wrestling Federation** entertainment and dining complex, which includes a restaurant and hot new nightclub. Oh, and, of course, there are the 30 theatres and nearly 50 cinema screens...

HELL'S KITCHEN/CLINTON

Running up the west side of Midtown from 34th Street to 57th from around 8th Avenue to the river is an area known as **Hell's Kitchen**. In the latter part of the 19th century, many poor Irish immigrants settled here, creating a ghetto. They were later joined by blacks, Italians and Latinos and inevitably gangs formed. The big employers were the docks (see *On the Waterfront* starring Marlon Brando for an insight into the lifestyle; although set in Brooklyn, it is equally true of all the dock areas), but when container ships came into play many lost their jobs. Other local industries included slaughterhouses and glue and soap factories.

BRITTIP

If you have an evening out on the World Yacht (pages 78 and 169), you'll find yourself walking through Hell's Kitchen/Clinton in search of a taxi. Adopt 'the New York walk' (walk quickly and confidently) and head east to 7th or 6th Avenues where it's easiest to pick up a cab.

A lot of the gangs were put out of business by the police in 1910, but it remained a scary area until fairly recently. It was renamed Clinton in 1959 to hide its violent past – which is long before Bill came on the scene, so there's no link to the former president. Now a lot of people living there work in the Theater District and it's moving up in the world. 9th and 10th Avenues are full of restaurants, the **Intrepid Sea-Air-Space Museum** (page 95) is on the river and, on the whole, the area is pretty safe until around 11pm.

MORNINGSIDE HEIGHTS

Further north the terrain gets hilly as you reach **Morningside Heights** (Map 6) home to the **Cathedral of St John the Divine** (page 73) and **Columbia University**, one of the most exclusive universities in America where a year's tuition fees, room and board will set you back around $40,000. Even so, it has 20,000 students, of whom 4,000 are undergraduates. This is a beautiful area,

which is bounded by 8th Avenue to the east and West 125th Street to the north.

BRITTIP

A great pit-stop in the Columbia University area is Tom's Restaurant on Broadway at 112th Street (page 180). If you recognise the diner's exterior, that's because it was used in *Seinfeld*.

MURRAY HILL

At a glance: Lutheran Church * Morgan Library

It's a testimony to man's desire to tame his environment that the majority of Manhattan is flat. This is a result of the zoning plans created in the early 19th century, when the streets and avenues were laid out north of Downtown, except for the Village. At the same time, the City flattened the majority of Manhattan except for what is now Morningside Heights and Harlem, as nobody believed anyone would live up there! The only other area that has kept its contours is **Murray Hill** (Map 3), a largely residential neighbourhood for New York's gentry that lies between 5th and 3rd Avenues and 32nd and 40th Streets.

The most famous resident of the area was the multi-millionaire J P Morgan. His son lived in a brownstone on the corner of 37th Street and Madison Avenue, which is now the headquarters of the **Lutheran Church**. J P Morgan lived in a house next door until he had it knocked down to make way for an expansion of his library. Now known as the **Morgan Library** (page 100), it has a unique collection of manuscripts, paintings, prints and furniture, which the financier collected on his trips to Europe. The nearest subways are the 6 to 33rd Street or the 4, 5, 6, 7, S to Grand Central/42nd Street.

The Osbournes at Madame Tussaud's

NOHO

At a glance: boutiques * bars * restaurants

Wedged between Greenwich Village and the East Village is a small section of streets now known as NoHo – North of Houston Street (Map 2). Bounded by Broadway to the west, Bowery to the east, Astor Place to the north and East Houston Street to the south, it's a tiny triangular-shaped area cut off from both of the villages, yet teeming with bars, cafés and shops. The boutiques here are a match for nearby SoHo and some are just as pricey, but for innovative and unique designs they're streets ahead of many areas, with the exception of NoLiTa.

Get here via the 6 subway to Astor Place or Bleecker Street or the F, V, S to Broadway/Lafayette Street.

NOLITA

At a glance: cafés * boutiques * St Patrick's Old Cathedral * Puck Building

NoLiTa stands for North of Little Italy and stretches from Kenmare Street in the south, to Houston in the north and from Crosby Street in the west to Elizabeth Street in the east (Map 2). The best subways to take are the 6 to Spring Street, the F, V, S to Broadway/Lafayette Street and the F, V to 2nd Avenue.

A fairly new part of town, it's filled with funky coffee shops, bars and restaurants. In a very short space of time Elizabeth, Mott and Mulberry Streets have seen a rapid growth in up-and-coming designers. This area was widely regarded as part of Little Italy until recent decades when it started to lose its Italian identity, following the steady relocation of Italian-Americans to outer boroughs.

Thanks to reasonable rents and vacant property, the latter half of the 1990s saw an influx of young urban professionals and it's now acknowledged as a neighbourhood in its own right. Due to the recent regeneration, the area is filled with cosmopolitan cafés, bars and restaurants. There's a also a fashionable, edgy vibe to this cool neighbourhood, which is why it's become a magnet for unique boutiques selling products by up-and-coming designers.

The neighbourhood's most notable historic building is **St Patrick's Old Cathedral**, at the corner of Mott and Prince streets, which was erected in 1815 and rebuilt after a fire in 1868. It was Manhattan's main Catholic cathedral for years until a new St Patrick's was opened in Fifth Avenue in Midtown in 1879. The original St Patrick's Old Cathedral is now used as a parish church and visitors are welcome to take a look around. Another landmark in the area is the **Puck Building** on the corner of Houston and Lafayette streets. The ornate structure, built in 1885, was the original headquarters of the now defunct *Puck* magazine.

SOHO

At a glance: shopping, fashion and beauty * restaurants * hip hotels * New Museum of Contemporary Art * New York City Fire Museum

SoHo means south of Houston, bounded by Lafayette Street at its eastern border, 6th Avenue to the west and Canal Street to the south (Map 2). The best subways are 6, C, E to Spring Street and N, R to Prince Street.

The main drag is on **West Broadway**, though Spring and Prince Streets are major shopping havens, too, and the whole area is reminiscent of Hampstead Village in London. OK, so there are no hills and the roads are wider, but it has the same boutiquey, picturesque, funky design-conscious element.

◀ ▶ BRITTIP

If you're looking for a delicious latte and snack in SoHo, try the aptly named Space Untitled in Green Street between Houston and Prince Streets.

It's hard to imagine the totally trendy and oh-so-expensive SoHo as a slum, yet just over 30 years ago this was the case. Despite the arrival of cutting-edge artists in the 1940s, who'd spotted the great potential of the massive loft spaces once used by manufacturers and wholesalers, the whole area was run down and shabby.

◀ ▶ BRITTIP

Prices tend to be lower than those in more commercial SoHo and the one-off aspect of clothing design is popular with the fashion crowd.

TASTES GOOD TO ME

SoHo is home to a complete first in New York City – a shop that can sell both wine and food. Vintage New York at 482 Broome Street at Wooster Street (212-226 9463) is owned by a vineyard from New York State, which means it can open on Sundays and sell proper alcoholic wine and food together – both of which are otherwise illegal in New York. The true secret to this little gem is that you can get five 1oz tastes of different wines for just $5, which actually works out to be one of the cheapest glasses of wine going in Manhattan! All the wines, incidentally, are from vineyards in the state of New York. Best time to visit Vintage is during the week when there are stools to sit on at the tasting bar.

Then, in the 1960s, those same artists were forced to fight for their very homes when the city decided to pull down all the buildings because they were only supposed to be used for light industry and definitely NOT for living in. The artists successfully argued that the architecture of the cast-iron buildings was too valuable to be destroyed and the whole of SoHo was declared a historic district.

BRITTIP

There is a cracking restaurant just off the beaten track in MacDougal – Provence (page 171) – where you'll get a delicious meal in a romantic setting. For good fare at reasonable prices, locals frequent Jerry's on Prince Street.

In the 1970s, art galleries first started moving into the area and the art boom of the 1980s truly transformed it. In 1992, the Guggenheim opened a downtown site on Broadway at Prince Street. These events coincided with a kind of bubble-bursting feeling for the more cutting-edge artists, especially those who could no longer afford SoHo's sky-rocketing rents. Many have now moved on to Chelsea and TriBeCa, and SoHo has become a wealthy residential neighbourhood occupied by anyone rich enough to afford the large loft spaces that are prevalent.

However, there are still plenty of art galleries – certainly a higher density than most areas of Manhattan – but the nature of the area has changed quite substantially (and we think for the better). Designers, clothes boutiques and dedicated beauty shops have arrived en masse, though the emphasis still lies heavily on style and art in terms of presentation and decor. The Guggenheim has shut up shop to be replaced by **Prada's** stunning flagship store (page 123) but a formidable sense of style remains and can be seen daily at the fashionistas' **SoHo Grand Hotel** haunt (page 226). Coffee shops, bars and restaurants that normal mortals can afford are now in better supply and the beauty boutiques with their wooden flooring, high ceilings and gleaming, glistening displays are wonderful places to get expert beauty advice on the cheap.

BRITTIP

For a well-priced, delicious lunch al fresco, head to the Gourmet Garage on the corner of Broome and Mercer Streets. It has a wonderful deli with ready-made salads to take away.

As well as satisfying the urges of shopaholics, SoHo also has several historic and architectural places of interest too. While MoMA's **New Museum of Contemporary Art** (page 105) is the only remaining art museum in the area, visitors can also get an art fix by hunting out The Broken Kilometer at 393 West Broadway, an installation by Walter De Maria that uses 500 brass rods to play tricks on the viewer's perspective.

Another notable SoHo landmark is **Hunt the Singer Building** at 561 Broadway, a beautiful building that was constructed in 1904 for the sewing machine company. The 12-storey façade is wonderfully ornate, with wrought-iron balconies and graceful arches.

St Patrick's Cathedral

You might also want to check out the **New York City Fire Museum** at 278 Spring Street, which houses a fascinating collection of Manhattan fire-fighting equipment and memorabilia from the 18th to 20th centuries. Children will love the upstairs that houses rows of gleaming original fire engines.

TRIBECA

At a glance: TriBeCa Film Center * TriBeCa Grill * TriBeCa Hotel

TriBeCa (Map 1) like other acronyms, such as SoHo, is a shortening of the area's location. In this case it means the triangle below Canal Street. It is bounded by Canal to the north, Murray to the south, West Broadway to the east and the Hudson River. To get here on the subway, use the 1, 9 to Canal or Franklin Streets or the 1, 2, 3, 9 to Chambers Street.

TriBeCa provides a good idea of what SoHo looked like 20 years ago. With the increasing pressure to find affordable housing, the empty warehouses of TriBeCa were ripe for the gentrification process that has been happening all over New York, including SoHo, the East Village and even the Lower East Side to a certain extent, and the area certainly has its fair share of pretty cast-iron buildings and quaint cobbled streets. Along **Harrison Street** is a row of well-preserved Federal-style townhouses and the area around White Street is particularly picturesque.

In the late 1970s, the former industrial buildings were targeted by estate agents for residential dwellings, but it was not really until the late 1980s that the area became a favourite with artists priced out of SoHo. Now TriBeCa is home to a variety of media and artistic businesses, such as galleries, recording studios and graphic companies.

Its most famous film company, the **TriBeCa Film Center** at 375 Greenwich

Street, which is part-owned by Robert De Niro, has production offices and screening rooms and is used by visiting film-makers. They, of course, frequent De Niro's extremely expensive **TriBeCa Grill** on the ground floor of the building. Visiting film-makers have also been given a boost by the opening of the triangular-shaped **TriBeCa Grand Hotel**, which has its own private screening room.

Now the area is deemed quite hip – being home to Harvey Keitel and Naomi Campbell among others – it has attracted a lot of upper middle-class families, while restaurants and nightclubs are frequented by residents from the nearby Battery Park City. It is also home to the **TriBeCa Film Festival**, which showcases independent movies during the second week of May.

UNION SQUARE

At a glance: Restaurant Row * Luna Park * Flatiron Building

Take the L, N, Q, R, W, 4, 5, 6 to Union Square at 14th Street (Map 2). This area was once pretty run down and overrun with drug pushers and muggers, but now it's one of the trendiest neighbourhoods in New York. The stretch of Park Avenue South between 14th and 23rd Streets is filled with some truly 'hip' eateries and is known as **Restaurant Row**.

◀▷ BRITTIP

The West Hotel Union Square on Park Avenue South at 17th Street is home to Underbar (page 202), one of the most stylish nightclubs in New York.

Along here you'll find **Tammany Hall**, the most corrupt City Hall in New York's history. It was home to Jimmy Walker, ostensibly a popular mayor, but a man who had been elected by the gangsters in the 1920s, which is effectively how organised crime was born in America. The gangsters were impossible to prosecute because they knew all the judges, cops and politicians in New York and virtually lived at Tammany Hall. Walker even had showers installed for them. Eventually, in the face of mounting financial problems in the city, Walker was forced to resign and his successor, Fiorello LaGuardia, decided to go after the gangs.

In the middle of Union Square is **Luna Park** (page 261), a great casual place for a

The Flatiron Building

BRITTIP

Create an instant picnic by buying farm-fresh produce, home-made breads, cheeses and drinks from the Union Square Farmers' Market every Monday, Wednesday, Friday and Saturday.

bite to eat in the summer, with outdoor seating. Further north on Broadway to Madison Square Park, you'll find **Theodore Roosevelt's birthplace** at 28 East 20th Street. It's not the original building, but it does house some great memorabilia from the former president's life (open Wed–Sun 9am–5pm; $3). Just around the corner is the wonderful, triangular **Flatiron Building** (page 69), at the end of what was once known as **Ladies Mile**, the city's most fashionable shopping district along Broadway and 6th Avenue from 14th Street.

UPPER EAST SIDE

At a glance: Museum Mile * shopping on Madison Avenue * Central Park * International Center of Photography

One of the most conservative areas of New York, the **Upper East Side** (Map 4) stretches from Central Park South to 98th Street and is centred on 5th, Madison, Park and Lexington Avenues. It came into being after Central Park was finally completed in 1876 and the rich and famous of the Gilded Era – the Whitneys, Carnegies, Fricks, Vanderbilts and Astors – decided to build their mansions alongside. It was a time when Neo-Classicism was the favourite architectural design, but many of the houses left standing are not the originals as the grandiose properties were built and rebuilt in an ever-more opulent style or replaced with apartment blocks.

BRITTIP

Jim's Shoeshine on East 59th Street between Madison and Park Avenues is a real institution that has existed since the 1930s.

Two things have always remained the same, though. The neighbourhood is known as the Silk Stocking District because of the vast family fortunes represented in the area, and the grand old apartment houses are known as 'white glove' buildings because of the uniforms of the doormen. People still pay a fortune to live there. For instance, Jackie Onassis's former 14-room apartment at 1040 5th Avenue near East 86th Street sold some years ago for a whopping $9 million. The mansion on the corner of East 86th is one of nine once owned by the Vanderbilts. Nearby residents include Michael J Fox and Bette Midler.

If you're serious about designer clothes, then you'll be visiting the designer stores that line **Madison Avenue**. If you're clever you won't buy, just gather information on what's new for when you go rummaging through the designer selections at **Daffy's** or the sample sales (pages 114–115).

This area is also full of museums, with a staggering array to choose from. They range from the world's largest and, arguably, most magnificent – the **Metropolitan Museum of Art** (page 98) – to the jewel of the **Frick Collection** (page 95), housed in the magnate's former mansion. Near to the Frick is the joyous **Whitney Museum of American Art** (page 110), with its emphasis on contemporary art.

WHICH MET'S THE MET?

Traditionally, the Metropolitan Opera House, with its crystal chandeliers and red-carpeted staircases, has been known as the Met. Increasingly, though, the Metropolitan Museum of Art is being referred to by the same moniker, which is causing a certain amount of confusion. It probably depends which establishment you stumble across first. For us, the museum will always be the Met!

Further north is the beautiful-looking **Guggenheim** (page 108), as well as the **Cooper-Hewitt** (page 93), the **Jewish Museum** (page 96) and the **International Center of Photography** (page 95). Finally, up on the borders of East Harlem, populated by Latin Americans, are the **Museum of the City of New York** (page 102) and **El Museo del Barrio** (page 93).

UPPER WEST SIDE

At a glance: AOL Time Warner Center * The Palladium * The Lincoln Center * celebrity houses

Central Park divides the Upper East and West Sides not only geographically, but also in terms of attitude. If the East Side is upper crust, conservative old money, then the West Side (Map 5) is more artistic. It's a vibrant neighbourhood filled with bars, restaurants, shops, museums and, of course, the culture of the Lincoln Center.

The area is now anchored by the amazing new **AOL Time Warner Center**'s twin towers at Columbus Circle, which house a mixture of offices, hotel, shopping and cultural centres. The $1.7-billion complex includes the **Mandarin Oriental Hotel and Spa**, the new home of jazz at the Lincoln Center (pages 194 and 227), broadcast facilities for live transmission of CNN, apartments and **The Palladium**, a massive space for shops, restaurants and entertainment venues (nearest subway is the A, B, C, D, 1, 9 to 59th Street/Columbus Circle). As you navigate the traffic lights to cross the roads at Columbus Circle, you can ponder on the fact that this is where Joe Colombo, the boss of one of the five Mafia families of New York, was shot.

BRITTIP

A new place to take a break is Whole Foods, a huge market selling a dazzling array of prepared foods, on the basement level of AOL Time Warner Center. Either dine at one of the tables there or eat in Central Park across the street.

Up Broadway and left down West 63rd Street you'll find the **Lincoln Center**. This was once filled with the slums that housed poor Puerto Ricans (the setting for the 1961 movie *West Side Story*) until Robert Moses proposed the building of various cultural centres that include the **Metropolitan Opera House**, the **New York State Theater** and **Avery Fisher Hall**. To see more, join one of the popular backstage tours or enjoy the free lunchtime music supplied by visiting jazz and folk bands during the summer months.

BUILT TO LAST

The Upper West Side is well known for its beautiful buildings, including the Beaux Arts **Ansonia Hotel** on Broadway between 73rd and 74th Streets, which has been called home by both Babe Ruth and Igor Stravinsky in its time. Starting on the southern tip of Central Park West, which runs all the way up Central Park, is the Art Deco stunner at No 55, which was used as the setting for the film *Ghostbusters*.

On 67th Street near Central Park West is

the **Hotel des Artistes** that, as the name suggests, was built for the artistic types who used its studios. Over the years it has been home to such celebrities as Noel Coward and Isadora Duncan. Today you can dine at the elegant **Café des Artistes** there (page 179). Back on Central Park West between 71st and 72nd Streets is the yellow façade of the Art Deco **Majestik** apartment house, which was built in 1930.

BRITTIP

Once you cross West 59th Street going north, 8th, 9th, 10th and 11th Avenues become Central Park West, Columbus, Amsterdam and West End Avenues respectively.

This Neighbourhood is particularly favoured by stars of stage and screen who prefer the Big Apple to Hollywood. Many have apartments along Central Park West, where one of the most coveted addresses is the city's first luxury apartment building, the famous **Dakota Building**, which was the first apartment block ever to be built on the Upper West Side in 1884, and was named after the distant territory to indicate its remoteness from anything else on the West

---

BAG YOURSELF A BAGEL

Among the best places for bagels:
Bagelry: 1324 Lexington Avenue between East 88th and 89th Streets on the Upper East Side and many other locations around the city.
Daniel's Bagels: 569 3rd Avenue at 38th Street. This Murray Hill establishment is a favourite of Midtoweners seeking the ultimate bagel, which are displayed in the long counter.
Ess-A-Bagel: 359 1st Avenue at 21st Street.
H&H: 80th Street and Broadway and other locations. Ships bagels worldwide.
Murray's Bagels: 500 7th Avenue at West 12th Street.
Pick-A-Bagel: 200 West 57th Street at 7th Avenue and other locations.
Yonah Schimmel's: 137 East Houston Street between Forsyth and Eldridge Streets in the Lower East Side, near to Katz's Deli. Knishes – pastries stuffed with savoury fillings – are the major speciality here.

Side. Of course, since then it has had a long line of famous inhabitants, including Leonard Bernstein, Judy Garland and Boris Karloff. Its most famous resident of all, **John Lennon**, was gunned down outside the building by a crazed fan in 1980. His widow Yoko Ono still lives here – she owns several apartments – and she donated money to build the Strawberry Fields memorial to the star in Central Park, just across the road.

A couple of blocks north between 73rd and 74th is the Neo-Renaissance style **Langham**, which was built in 1905, and between 74th and 75th is the **San Remo**, built in 1930, where Rita Hayworth died of Alzheimer's in 1987. Residents have included Dustin Hoffman and Paul Simon, and rumour has it that the resident committee turned down Madonna! The **Eldorado**, which Roth also designed on Central Park West, has been home to Marilyn Monroe and Groucho Marx.

Several blocks north, on the corner of 81st Street and Central Park West, stands the elegant **Beresford**. Between these, these grand apartment blocks have housed a huge number of celebrities, including such names as Lauren Bacall, Dustin Hoffman, Steve Martin and Jerry Seinfeld, who bought Isaac Stern's sprawling apartment home.

🇬🇧 BRITTIP

Just a few blocks from the museums is Zabar's (page 143) on Broadway at West 80th Street, the famous food emporium seen in *Friends*, and *Fairway*, on West 75th Street. Both are jam-packed with all the ingredients needed for a picnic in nearby Riverside or Central Parks.

MUSEUM HALF MILE

On Central Park West at 77th Street is the **New York Historical Society** (page 107), which was formed in 1804 and was the only art museum in the city until the opening of the Metropolitan Museum of Art in 1872. It was founded to chronicle New York's history, but still houses the world's largest collection of Tiffany stained-glass shades and lamps and two million manuscripts, including letters sent by George Washington during the War of Independence.

Next door is the real big boy of museums, the **American Museum of Natural History** (page 88), which was the brainchild of scientist Albert Smith Bickmore. It first opened at the New York Arsenal in Central Park in 1869, but by 1874 had moved to these bigger premises. Architect Calvert Vaux, who was also responsible for the Met Museum and largely responsible for Central Park, created the bulk of the building, which has since had a Romanesque-style façade added to its 77th Street side and a Beaux Arts-style frontage on the Central Park West side. This is a favourite museum of ours. It's crammed with well laid-out exhibitions that really bring the world of science, scientific discovery and expeditions to life, while the **Rose Center** and **Big Bang Theater** attract major crowds to see the 13-billion-year history of the universe.

The Upper West Side's Museum Half Mile also includes the **Children's Museum of Manhattan** (page 90) on 83rd Street between Broadway and Amsterdam Avenue, where interactive exhibits keep the wee ones happy.

West 106th Street, at the top end of the neighbourhood, is now known as **Duke Ellington Broadway**. This is where the great musician lived, premiered many of his songs and was buried in 1974. Over 10,000 people came to his funeral and there is a memorial to him on 5th Avenue at West 110th by Central Park's Harlem Meer.

WEST VILLAGE

At a glance: Chumley's * gay community * Christopher Street * restaurants and bars

The West Village, on the other side of 7th Avenue, has an amazingly pretty collection of cobbled streets lined with picturesque homes and trees. These are among some of the oldest remaining houses in New York, many being built in the 1820s and 1850s, and quite a few have the one thing that is so rare in Manhattan – a back garden, albeit tiny. To get here take the 1, 9 to Christopher Street or the A, C, E to 14th Street or the L subway to 8th Avenue.

Christopher Park

FAMOUS SPEAKEASY

On the corner of Bedford Street, number 86 is one of the most famous former speakeasies in New York. Known as **Chumley's** (page 191), it doesn't have its name advertised anywhere outside, but there is a back entrance on Barrow Street that will take you directly into the bar. The front entrance merely has the old grille used for checking over potential customers during Prohibition, and the number 86.

In the old days a dumb waiter took two people at a time to the gambling den upstairs, and the best table in the house was right by the entrance to the cellar, where people could hide if there was a raid. Now Chumley's does fish and chips and shepherd's pie-type food and usually has a roaring fire in the winter, while the walls are still lined with all the book jackets donated by many of the writers who once frequented it.

> ### BRITTIP
> Crossing Bedford is Barrow Street, where you'll find One If By Land, Two If By Sea. It's in the oldest building housing a restaurant in Manhattan, a former carriage house built in 1726. Great food, service and decor. If you're in the mood for a romantic splurge, this is the place. Tel 212-228 0822.

At the corner of **Grove Street** is the oldest wooden house in the West Village. Built in 1822, it's the most exclusive cottage in the area and costs $6,000 a month to rent, but it does have its own little garden: what a bargain! All around Grove Street the houses are covered in a network of vines, which blossom in May and have grown in the area for 150 years.

A MATTER OF RIGHTS

Christopher Street, the main drag of the West Village, is the heart of the gay community and a shopping paradise for antique lovers. **Sheridan Square**, one of the Village's busiest junctions, has been the scene of two major riots. First were the New York Draft Riots of 1863, sparked off by the requirement to join the army for the Civil War. The rich could buy their way out, but the poor had no choice and were fearful they would lose their jobs to the newly freed black slaves.

The second riot is the more famous and is known as the Stonewall Riot. This was sparked in 1969 by the police raiding the Stonewall gay bar and arresting its occupants – an event that frequently occurred at the many gay watering holes in the area. This time the community decided to fight back and, over a period of three nights, the gay community held its ground in the Stonewall as it was surrounded by police. It was the crucial first step made by gay people in standing up for their rights.

Christopher Street is still filled with bars, restaurants and bookstores that are used by gays – though not exclusively – but many members of the gay community have moved on to Chelsea.

YORKVILLE

Between Lexington Avenue and the East River from East 77th to 96th Streets is the working to middle class enclave of **Yorkville** (Map 5) (subway 4, 5, 6 to 86th Street), which has an interesting mix of cultures, singles and families.

> ### BRITTIP
> Fancy the idea of a picnic by the river? Then stop off at The Vinegar Factory in 91st Street (page 143), where you'll find an extensive selection of cheeses, meats, breads and salads, and head for the nearby Carl Schurz Park.

It was originally populated by German-Hungarians, who moved northwards from their first stopping point in the East Village's Thompkins Square with the arrival of Italian and Slavic immigrants. Now, though, you'd be hard-pressed to find the few remnants of German culture, as most left the neighbourhood during the Second World War to avoid anti-German feelings.

> ### BRITTIP
> Do like the locals and head to the cosy DT UT coffee bar on 2nd Avenue between 84th and 85th Streets.

The most famous resident in the area is the mayor, who lives in the official residence at Gracie Mansion (page 69) overlooking the East River and the lovely Carl Schurz Park at East 89th Street.

CHAPTER 3

Getting
Around

When most people talk about New York, they actually mean Manhattan, which is the long, thin sliver of an island in the middle of the four outer boroughs of Staten Island, Queens, the Bronx and Brooklyn.

You'll find diagrammatic maps, such as the one below, dotted throughout the book to help you focus on the basic geography of the area. Once you get the hang of roughly where everything is, you'll find it easier to use the subway and bus maps on the inside front and back covers, and the street maps in the centre pages.

ORIENTATION

Manhattan is 21km (13 miles) long and 3.2km (2 miles) wide for the most part and almost all of it above 14th Street is on the grid system that was introduced quite early on in New York's history. The main exceptions are Chinatown and Greenwich Village, which, like Downtown, had already established its eccentric random arrangement of streets (like ours in the UK) before urban planning and refused to get on the grid system. The other exception is Broadway, which follows an old Indian trail that runs largely north to south on the west side of the island, then cuts across to the east side as it runs down towards Downtown.

Here are a few basic rules about the geography of Manhattan; it is useful to acquaint yourself with them as soon as possible, then you'll be able to walk around with confidence.
➡ Manhattan is divided into three main areas: Downtown, which includes neighbourhoods south of 14th Street; Midtown, the area between 14th and 59th Streets; and Uptown, areas north of 59th Street.
➡ All the roads going across Manhattan east to west are streets and all the roads going north to south are avenues.
➡ The city is divided between east and west by 5th Avenue and all the street numbers begin there. This means that 2 West 57th

Street is just a few steps to the west of 5th Avenue while 2 East 57th Street is just a few steps to the east of 5th Avenue.

🇬🇧 BRITTIP
To New Yorkers, 'downtown' does not mean the city centre, but means south, while 'uptown' means north. You will need to get used to these terms if you are planning to use the subway – which is simpler to use than it looks at first!

➡ Most streets in Manhattan are one-way. With a few exceptions, traffic on even-numbered streets travels east and traffic on odd-numbered streets travels west. Traffic on major 'cross-town' streets – so-called because they are horizontal on the street maps of Manhattan – travels in both directions. From south to north, these include Canal, Houston, 14th, 23rd, 34th, 42nd, 57th, 72nd, 79th, 86th and 96th Streets.
➡ When travelling north to south or vice versa, remember that traffic on York Avenue goes both ways, 1st Avenue goes from south

Areas of New York

BRITTIP

To calculate the distance from one place to another, 20 north-south blocks or 10 east-west blocks equal about 1.6km (1 mile). This rule does not apply to the Financial District or Greenwich Village.

to north, 2nd Avenue goes south and 3rd goes north mostly, though there is a small two-way section. Lexington goes south, Park goes in both directions, Madison goes north and 5th Avenue goes south. Central Park West goes both ways, Columbus Avenue goes south, Amsterdam Avenue north, Broadway goes in both directions until Columbus Circle, after which it continues southbound only to the tip of Manhattan. West End Avenue and Riverside Drive go in both directions.

➡ Numbered avenue addresses increase from south to north.

ARRIVING BY AIR

JOHN F KENNEDY INTERNATIONAL AIRPORT (JFK)
Tel 718-244 4444
www.panynj.gov
JFK is in the borough of Queens and is the best place to enter or leave New York by air. It is 24km (15 miles) from Midtown Manhattan, a journey that will take you 50–60 minutes.

Taxi
The cost of a yellow medallion taxi into town is a fixed rate of $45 (per taxi) as set by the New York Taxi and Limousine Commission (www.nyc.gov/taxi). Bridge and tunnel tolls are extra (around $4 and you can pay at the end of the journey) as is the 15 per cent tip. So think around $50.

Train
The AirTrain JFK (212-435 7000, www.airtrainjfk.com) is a flat $5 enter/exit fare. They run every 4–8 minutes 6am–11pm and will take you to the Howard Beach station from where you connect to the A subway to head into town.

Bus
New York Airport Service Express Bus (Westside & Eastside): Tel 718-875 8200, www.nyairportservice.com. Catch one from the Airport Bus Center. They run 6.15am–

AIRPORT SECURITY
Since 11 September 2001, the relaxed security systems that operated in most American airports have been seriously tightened up. Expect longer queues and subsequent waiting times getting through immigration and baggage checks. Remember that it is prohibited to carry any sharp items in your hand luggage, so make sure you put scissors, tweezers and nail files in your main check-in luggage. You should also be prepared to be asked to open your bags for inspection and to be frisked by a security guard with a hand-held scanner.

11.10pm daily every 15–30 minutes, cost $15 (or $27 round trip) and will drop you off Midtown west or east (serving midtown hotels between 31st and 60th Streets ONLY. Midtown hotels $15 one way, round trip $33).

Trans-Bridge Lines: Tel 1-800 962 9135 or 610-868 6001, www.transbridgebus.com. $17 (one way) $32.30 (round trip) leaving at 3.30, 5.30 and 7pm daily (from terminal 4 to Port Authority Bus Terminal).

Private hire car
Classic Limousine: Tel 1-800-666-4949 or 631-567 5100, www.classictrans.com.

Supersaver by Carmel: Tel 1-800-924-9954 or 212-666 6666, www.carmellimo.com. To Manhattan it costs $40 5am–8pm or $45 8pm–5am.

SuperShuttle: Tel 212-209 7000 (reservations 1-212-258-3826), www.supershuttle.com. A door-to-door minibus service from the airport to your hotel operating 24 hours a day year round. Look for the blue van! Costs $13–22.

NEWARK LIBERTY INTERNATIONAL AIRPORT
Tel 973-961 6000
www.newarkairport.com

Taxi
The journey from Newark to central Manhattan takes around 40 minutes, but add at least 30 minutes in the rush hour. Set taxi fares range from $45 to the Battery Park area to $60 and above to 185th Street. There's a $5 extra charge for all destinations to the east side of Manhattan. For more information contact the Newark Taxi Commission. Tel 973-733 8912, www.nyc.gov/taxi.

Train

AirTrain: Tel 1-888-397 4636, www.airtrainnewark.com. This $415-million link connecting the airport terminals with Newark Liberty International Airport Train Station opened in 2003. You can get to Manhattan from the station by taking an NJ Transit or Amtrak train to New York Penn station, from where you can connect to the city's subways and buses with ease.

Bus

PATH: Tel 800-234 7284, www.pathrail.com. Rapid transit from Newark to Penn station (but you must take a taxi to the bus station from the airport – $14) to stops in Downtown and Midtown Manhattan. Operates 24 hours, fare $1.50.

Olympia Trails Airport Express Bus: Tel 212-964 6233, www.olympiabus.com. Operates between Newark and three Manhattan locations – Penn Station (34th Street/8th Avenue), Port Authority Bus Terminal (42nd Street/8th Avenue) and Grand Central (41st Street between Lexington and Park Avenues). Also operates a hotel shuttle to all Midtown points between 30th and 65th Streets. Departs every 15 minutes, fare $14 (one way) or $23 (round trip) for adults. 12–16-year-olds pay $7 (one way) or $14 (round trip). Kids under 12 ride free (or only pay $4 for hotel shuttle). 4am–1am.

Private hire car and SuperShuttle services: As from John F Kennedy International airport (see page 52).

◀▶ BRITTIP

If you're worried about getting lost in New York, click on to www.hopstop.com for online subway and walking directions around the city.

LAGUARDIA AIRPORT (LGA)

Tel: 718-533 3400
www.panynj.gov
This is the airport you'll probably arrive at if you've taken an internal domestic flight from another state. TWIA, United Airlines and Continental Airlines all operate here. It's situated about 13km (8 miles) from the centre of Manhattan, between Queens and the Bronx.

Taxi

You'll find a clearly marked taxi rank outside the main terminals. Unlike JFK, you pay by the meter rather than a flat rate, and you will also be charged tolls. A basic guide is $25–30 plus tolls ($4-6) and tip, and the journey should take about 20–25 minutes.

Bus

New York Airport Express Bus: Tel 718-875 8200, www.nyairportservice.com. A far cheaper option into town than taxi, taking around 40–50 minutes. The fare costs only $12 (or $21 round trip) and buses run daily 7.20am–11pm, leaving every 30 minutes. To catch your ride into town, follow the Ground Transportation signs out of the terminal and wait at the M60 or Q33 bus stop sign by the curb (serving midtown hotels between 31st and 60th Streets ONLY). Midtown hotels $12 one way, round trip $27).

GETTING AROUND

There are lots of options for getting around Manhattan and the outer boroughs. The yellow cabs that you'll see in abundance are the fastest and most efficient way of getting to a destination, but they're not the cheapest. The subway in New York is easy to use and perfect for people with a limited budget, as well as being under cover when

Areas of Manhattan

METROCARD

The flat fare to travel on the subway is $2. However, you can no longer buy single fares; the cheapest ticket you can now get is the $10 MetroCard. This magnetically encoded card debits the fare when you swipe it through the turnstile in the subway or the farebox on a bus. A $10 card gives you six rides for the price of five and the $20 MetroCard gives you 12 rides for the price of 10. Both of these tickets can be used by up to four people though, so if there are two of you, you only need buy one MetroCard.

You can purchase the cards from subway ticket offices (cash only), vending machines in most subways, from drugstores such as Rite Aid and Hudson News or from the Times Square Visitors' Center at 1560 Broadway between 46th and 47th Streets. Some hotels also sell them at the reception desk.

Unlimited Ride MetroCards include the 1-Day Fun Pass for $7 (which lasts until 3am the following day), the 7-Day card for $24, the 30-Day card for $76 and the 7-Day Express Bus Plus for $41. For more details, phone 1-800-638 7622 or visit www.mta.info.

it's raining. If you'd rather see the sights, then jump on a bus, though progress can be slow in rush hour. Then there's the oldest mode of transport: your feet. Walking around Manhattan is a joyful experience and thoroughly recommended; just don't forget to pack some comfy shoes.

TAXI

No trip to Manhattan would be complete without a ride in a yellow cab. It's the preferred means of transport for many visitors, largely because there are so many about and the fares are reasonable. However, be warned: even though the fares are much cheaper than in London, the cost still mounts up pretty quickly. Fares start at $2.50 and increase 40c every 0.32km(1/5

Cabs in New York

mile) or 20c per minute in stopped or slow traffic, with a 50c surcharge at night (8pm–6am) and $1 in peak hour (Mon–Fri 4–8pm). It's not just the cost of the ride that you have to take into consideration, but the $1 tip to the hotel doorman and the 15 per cent tip to the driver. It can work out as an expensive option if used too often.

In any case, you will need to have a good idea of where you are going and how to get there, as most of the cab drivers in New York are the latest immigrants to have arrived and have very little clue about how to get around the city. The best way to ensure you don't get into any difficulties is to always carry the full address of where you're going, preferably with a map reference too. Fortunately, thanks to the grid system, it is relatively easy to educate yourself about where you are going and so you can give them directions!

➡ First off, never expect the driver to be the kind of chirpy, chatty Cockney character that you're used to in London. Most speak very little English and are not interested in making polite conversation, and many can be downright rude.

➡ Secondly, make sure you get into a taxi heading in the direction that you want to be going. If you are travelling uptown but you're on a road heading downtown, walk a block east or west so you'll be pointing in the right direction. It saves time and money, and if you don't, the taxi driver will know immediately that you're a tourist.

➡ Hailing a taxi is not necessarily as easy as it looks – you have to be aware of the lighting system on the top of the yellow medallion taxis. If the central light is on, it means the taxi driver is working and available. If all the lights are out, it means the driver is working but already has a fare. If the outer two lights or all three lights are on, it means that the taxi driver is off-duty – look carefully and you'll see the words. The best method for actually hailing a cab is to hold out your arm while standing at the kerb.

➡ When you get to a toll, expect the taxi driver to turn around and demand the cash to pay for it, but you are quite within your rights to ask him to add it to your final fare.

➡ Beware of trying to get a cab at around 4pm. Not only is it the approach of rush hour, but it is also when most drivers change shifts, so getting a taxi is well nigh impossible as they don't want to go anywhere but home! If you really need a taxi at this time, be sure to call a car service company.

➡ Do not expect a taxi driver to change any bill larger than $20.

➡ In addition to the medallion on the roof, a legitimate taxi will have an automatic receipt machine mounted on the dashboard so that you can be given an immediate record of your trip.

➡ If you find yourself below Canal Street after business hours or at the weekend, you might have difficulty finding a yellow cab. Your best bet is to phone one of the many companies listed under Taxicab Service in the Yellow Pages. Fares are slightly higher than for the metered cabs, but they are a safer option.

➡ There is no extra charge per person or for luggage, but a licensed taxi won't be able to take more than four people.

➡ Fasten your seatbelt once in the cab. All taxis are now required by law to provide them and passengers in the front seat have to wear them.

CAR SERVICE COMPANIES

When you need to be certain you have a taxi ride to the airport or some other destination, here are the companies you can phone, all of which provide a 24-hour service:

Carmel: Tel 212-666-6666, www.carmellimo.com.

Dial 7: Tel 212-777 7777/1-800-777 8888, www.dial7.com.

Tel-Aviv: Tel 212-777 7777/1-800-222 9888, www.telavivlimo.com.

Tri-State Limousine: Tel (516) 933-4759, toll-free (866) NY-LIMO2, www.tristatelimony.com.

ON THE SUBWAY

The first time you take a look at a subway map of New York, you can be forgiven for thinking you need a degree in the whole system to get anywhere. Plus the signposts –

🇬🇧 BRITTIP

Generally, if you're going downtown, use subway entrances on the west side of the road and if you're going uptown, use subway entrances on the east side. This way you should be heading in the right direction, but do always check before entering.

both outside and inside the stations – can easily be missed.

In addition, the Metropolitan Transportation Authority (MTA) is undergoing a billion-dollar rejuvenation programme of many subway stops and has introduced new, clean trains on to the network, though New Yorkers aren't convinced that will last! On the old subway trains, the conductor would always announce stops and interchanges. These, for the large part, were unintelligible, but the new trains have pre-recorded announcements in a non-New York accent that can be understood.

SUBWAY MAP

There are subway maps on the inside front cover of this book. You can also get hold of free MTA maps in most subways stations, hotel lobbies and information centres.

➡ The subway lines are all indicated on the map by a colour but, unlike the London Underground, the colours are not used in the stations and on the trains. The important bit is the number or letter. Below the name of every stop you will find the letters and numbers of lines that stop there, such as 7, S Grand Central/42nd Street.

➡ When examining a subway map, a number or letter in a diamond means rush-hour service, in a circle it denotes normal service and a square indicates the end of a line. Black and white lines connecting white and black circles indicate a free subway transfer. White circles on coloured lines indicate express stops (express trains skip about three stops for every one that they make).

➡ If the numbers against your destination on the subway map are printed in a lighter tone, they are peak-time only.

RIDING THE SUBWAY

The good news is that New York's subway system is one of the cheapest to ride in the world. Before you can start getting around on the subway you'll need to buy a MetroCard (which also works on buses, see page 57). You can buy these from a booth inside the entrance to the station or from a MetroCard vending machine, which you'll easily spot as they're brightly coloured. The machines accept cash, debit and credit cards. There are two types of ticket, pay-per-use and unlimited-ride.

➡ Don't look for obvious signs indicating a subway; instead look for either the very discreet 'M' signs in blue or the signature red and green glass globes – red means the entrance is not always open and green means it's staffed 24 hours a day.

➡ Before going down a subway entrance, check it is going in the right direction for you – many entrances take you to either 'downtown' or 'uptown' destinations, not both. It means that if you make the mistake of going in and swiping your ticket before you realise you're going in the wrong direction, you will have to swipe your card again to get in on the right side, so you'll end up paying double. The alternative is to travel in the wrong direction until you get to one of the larger subway stations (such as 42nd Street) and then change.

➡ The same rules apply if you're in one of the outer boroughs, but instead of looking for a Downtown or Uptown sign, look for one that says Manhattan.

➡ Some trains are express, meaning they stop only at selected stations. At some stations you have to go down two flights to get to the platforms for express trains, while at others you don't, and it is easy to get on an express train by mistake.

⚡ BRITTIP

Changes to subway schedules often occur at the last minute, so pay attention to posters on subway station walls and any announcements you hear on the platforms.

➡ There are conflicting opinions (hotly debated by the locals) as to whether it is worth waiting for an express. On the plus side, they move quickly, but on the down side you could end up waiting 10 minutes for one, so you won't have saved any time in the end.

➡ There are many different lines going to the same destinations, but they don't all exit at the same place. For example, if you arrive at Fulton Street on the New York subway and head for the exit you can come out at four completely different locations. The Red Line exits at Fulton and William Streets, the Brown Line exits at John and Nassau Streets, the Blue Line exits at Fulton and Nassau Streets, and the Green Line exits at Broadway and John Street – all of which are quite a long way from each other.

➡ The locals consider that the subway is

safe to travel on until around 11pm. After that opinions vary, but when making up your mind to travel do be aware that the subway service after 11pm is generally incredibly slow.

➡ The subway does have one very good point: because the island of Manhattan is largely made up of granite, they did not have to dig as deep as we have to in London to find the really strong foundation level. This means you generally only have to go down one flight of steps to find the line.

➡ If you've been to New York before but not for a few years, bear in mind there have been a few changes to the subway network – and all for the better – thanks to a $17-billion expansion and renovation programme.

➡ The L line runs almost the full width of Manhattan along 14th Street from 8th Avenue in the west to 1st Avenue in the east on its way to Queens. Other stops in Manhattan include 6th Avenue, Union Square and 3rd Avenue.

➡ The S line should not be confused with the shuttle between Times Square and Grand Central Station. It is another good east–west train linking West and East Villages in Greenwich and runs from West 4th Street to Grand Street.

➡ In Manhattan, the new peak-time V line largely runs in conjunction with the F line and includes new stops at 5th Avenue and 53rd Street, as well as Lexington Avenue and 53rd Street.

ON THE BUSES

Travelling by bus is always a little more nerve-wracking because you can never be sure whether you've arrived at your destination, but most people are pretty helpful if asked a direct question. We thought that taking to the buses would be more difficult than travelling by subway, but two of our friends put paid to that notion by going everywhere by bus on their first visit.

FINDING A BUS

Our Manhattan bus map inside the front cover will come in handy as often there are no route maps at the bus stops. However, as a general rule buses run north to south, south to north, east to west or west to east.

➡ You can recognise bus stops by a yellow-painted kerb next to a blue and white sign. Look at the Guide-a-Ride information at the stop, which should show the route and service schedule.

RIDING THE BUSES

⇒ Get on the bus at the front and click in your MetroCard or feed in $2. Exact change is essential – and it must be all in coins as no dollar bills are accepted.

⇒ Although there are bus exits at the back, you can also get off at the front.

⇒ Requesting a stop may be a little confusing. There are no clearly marked red buttons to press; instead there are black strips that run the full length of the bus between the windows or at the back along the tops of the handles. Simply press one of these to request the next stop.

⇒ If the bus says 'Limited Stopping' it means it stops only at major stops, such as the cross-town streets of 14, 23, 34, 42, 50, 57, 68, 72, 79 and 86.

⇒ The main bus routes used by tourists are: M1, which travels from 5th Avenue and Central Park to Madison Avenue; M7, which runs from Union Square to Broadway through the Theater District; and M6, which takes in Carnegie Hall to SoHo.

◀🇬🇧▶ BRITTIP

Our favourite MetroCard is the $20 pass. It offers 12 trips for the price of 10, up to four people can use it at one time and if you transfer to a bus you only have to swipe the ticket once and it will register for everyone. You can also top it up in amounts as small as $5 (page 55).

TOURIST ROUTES

Certain bus routes link key attractions, so if your feet are killing you, jump on one of the following buses to continue your trawl of Manhattan sights shown here in brackets:

M1: 5th Avenue (Central Park), 5th Avenue/84th Street (Metropolitan Museum of Art), 5th Avenue/49th–50th Streets (Rockefeller Centre), Madison Avenue/East 43rd Street (Grand Central Terminal/Chrysler Building).

M6: 7th Avenue/West 57th Street (Carnegie Hall), 7th Avenue/West 42nd Street (Times Square), Herald Square/Broadway (Empire State Building), Broadway/East 8th–9th Streets (Greenwich Village), South Street/Whitehall Street (Battery Park, ferry to Ellis Island and Statue of Liberty).

BY WATER TAXI

For a completely different way of getting around, you can go by water taxi. A commuter service runs around the lower part of Manhattan, but the most useful is a hop on-hop off service designed for sightseeing 1 May–15 October. The three bright yellow catamarans with black and white check are easy to spot and there are six stops from DUMBO to West 44th Street, all easily accessible from the subway and bus stops. The service runs 11am–3pm on weekdays, stopping en route at South Street Seaport, Battery Park, World Financial Center, West Village and Chelsea Piers. At weekends, it runs each hour 11.22am–6.22pm from Hunters Point, stopping at East 34th Street, Schaeffer Landing, Fulton Ferry Landing, South Street Seaport, Red Hook, Battery Park, World Financial Center, Pier 45, West 23rd Street and West 44th Street. The other direction, from West 44th Street, it runs each hour 10.52am–6.52pm. Tickets cost $25 adults, $15 children and seniors.

A Gateway to America Harbor Tour runs every weekend, on the hour 12pm–4pm taking in the Statue of Liberty, the Brooklyn Bridge and Manhattan Skyline. This costs $20 for adults, $18 for seniors and $12 for children 12 and under. For more information, phone 212-742 1969 or visit www.nywatertaxi.com. If you're on a budget or here in winter, check out the commuter route and times.

DRIVING IN NEW YORK

A word of advice: don't even think about it. Most of the streets will be jam-packed, while parking is extremely scarce and astronomically expensive at $8–10 an hour. You can park on the street, but watch out for what is known as alternate-side-of-the-street parking. This means you have to know which day of the week the cleaning truck comes past so you move the car over at the right time. Double parking is common, so it is easy to get boxed in, and frustrated drivers simply get in their cars and honk the horn until the guilty owner moves their car. As one New Yorker told us: 'People do not know how to park here. New Yorkers are not good drivers and are the wildest parkers.'

If you plan to take a trip upstate and wish to do so by car, then there are some dos and don'ts about car hire. Firstly, never hire a car in Manhattan unless you want to pay around $160 a day. Take a ferry to the state

DRIVING TIPS

➡ Most streets in New York are one-way, so be sure to look out for signs before you head down a street.

➡ Drivers have to wear seatbelts by law, as do front-seat passengers and children aged 4–10 in the back.

➡ Speed limits are 30mph around town, 55mph on highways and freeways.

➡ Private parking facilities are available in the city but they cost $25–40 per day.

➡ Illegally parked cars will be towed away and there's a $150 fine plus $15 per day to be paid. Collect your car from Pier 76, West 38th Street at 12th Avenue (Midtown West). Tel 212-971 0772. It's open 24 hours a day Mon–Sat.

of New Jersey and hire a car from there for around $85 for a medium-sized car with unlimited mileage. Secondly, don't consider hiring a car in the summer or at weekends because that's what most New Yorkers will be doing and they'll be difficult to come by. Cars are also snapped up in the autumn when New Yorkers like to go to see the autumn foliage.

CAR HIRE

If you do decide to take the plunge and drive around the city, there are a number of car hire companies to choose from. Most are

BRITTIP

Overtaking is permitted on the inside and outside lanes of interstate highways, so if you're driving to Manhattan from one of the airports, be sure to use both of your wing mirrors to look for passing cars.

based at the major airports, so you can simply pick them up when you arrive. Prices vary enormously, from a one-day rental costing from $90 to a week rate of $225–300. Remember that to rent a car you'll need to be over 25, have a valid driver's licence, have your own insurance and some photo ID. You'll also need to have a credit card (or very large cash deposit) to be able to rent a car and most rental companies add sales tax of around 8.6 per cent.

Car hire companies

Alamo: Tel 1-800-462 5266, www.alamo.com.

Argus Rentals: Tel 212-372 7266, www.argusrentals.com.

Avis: Tel 1-800-331 1212, www.avis.com.

Dollar: 1-800-800 3665, www.dollar.com.

Hertz: Tel 800-654 3131, www.hertz.com. Independent (and often cheaper) car rental companies: www.carrentalexpress.com.

FINDING A WC

It's worth raising this subject early as you'll probably be spending quite a lot of time walking around and you could easily get caught out. It is wise to know that public lavatories are thin on the ground in New York. In addition, subway loos – if they are actually open – are dangerous and unhygienic. It is considered impolite to use the word 'toilet'; in America a public toilet is always the 'restroom'.

So you're in the middle of Greenwich Village, you're desperate, and you don't want to pay through the nose for a beer so you can use the bar's facilities. What do you do? We have it on good authority from those New Yorkers in the know that you can go to the following places:

Barnes & Noble: This is a chain of bookstores that offers restrooms because the company wants people to treat the stores as public meeting places.

Department stores: The restrooms are hidden away and you have to ask where they are; this is to deter street people from using them.

Government buildings: Try places like the United Nations, though you'll have to go through a security check.

Hotels: The restrooms are usually on the ground floor or you can ask.

Lincoln Center: There are ten 'stalls' open to the public, close to the entrance.

McDonald's and Burger King: Unisex toilets that are usually clean and modern because they are built to the company's spec rather than the typical New York building spec.

Public libraries: They all have public loos.

Restaurants: Some have signs saying 'For customers only', but if you ask authoritatively enough and look okay, they'll probably let you use them.

Statue of Liberty: In the gift shop.

CHAPTER 4

What to See and Do

There is so much to see and do in the city that never sleeps that it can all feel a bit daunting when you first step out of your hotel, guide book in hand. Therefore it's a good idea to make a plan of what you'd really like to see before you're back on the plane and heading home. The major sights are often the number one priority – especially for the first-time visitor – so, to make your life a little easier, we have indicated the location of each of the following sights. It would be advisable to read Chapter 2 first so you get a good feel for each of the neighbourhoods and that way you can make the most of your time by planning your days in specific areas of the city. For instance, if you plan to see the Empire State Building, bear in mind it is deep in the heart of the 34th Street shopping district. The section entitled Orientation (page 51) will also help you make sense of the streets of New York and get to know the intricacies of the grid system and the distances involved. Having said all of that, do make sure you leave a little time in your schedule for simply wandering. Even if it's only for a couple of hours, the feeling of walking along the streets of New York like a local and discovering a charming café or cool local shop as yet unearthed by a guidebook is marvellous.

PART ONE – THE SIGHTS

This section gives you our Top Five must-see sights, plus all the major sights in New York. You can either visit them under your own steam or take advantage of the many and varied tours that are listed in the second part of this chapter.

BRITTIP
Security at many sights and buildings has been tightened following the tragic events of 11 September, so allow extra time for this when planning your schedules.

A–Z of SIGHTS

CENTRAL PARK
Think of New York and Central Park is likely to spring to mind. It's the New Yorkers' playground and a wonderful place to spend time during your stay. For a complete description of the park and all its facilities, see pages 257–260.

TOP FIVE SIGHTS
There are plenty of exciting things to see and do in New York, but some are simply unmissable, particularly if you're visiting for the first time. Below is our definitive guide to the top sights, and whatever else you do when you are in the city, these are the ones you mustn't miss:

Central Park: pages 257–260

Ellis Island Immigration Museum: with Statue of Liberty (page 60)

Empire State Building: 34th Street (page 61)

Statue of Liberty: ferry from Battery Park (page 60)

Times Square: Midtown West (page 66)

The Chrysler Building

ELLIS ISLAND IMMIGRATION MUSEUM AND THE STATUE OF LIBERTY

Battery Park

☎ 212-269 5755

🖰 www.circlelinedowntown.com

🚗 Statue of Liberty and Ellis Island Ferry, which leaves every 20–30 minutes from Gangway 5 in Battery Park 8.30am–4.30pm. Subway 1 to South Ferry, 4, 5 to Bowling Green

🕐 9am–5pm

$ $11.50 adults, $9.50 seniors, $4.50 children (4–12), under 3s free. Credit cards accepted.

The Statue of Liberty (www.nps.gov/stli), one of the biggest attractions in New York, is reached by a ferry, which also takes you to the Ellis Island Museum where you learn the immigration story of America. Ferry tickets are sold at Castle Clinton, the low, circular brownstone building in Battery Park (open 8.30am–4.30pm). Luggage, including backpacks, is not permitted and the security checks can take up to an hour.

◀🇬🇧 BRITTIP

Don't spoil your day of sightseeing by missing the boat. The last boat leaves from Liberty Island at 6.15pm and Ellis Island at 6.30pm in summer and the museum closes at 5pm.

The Statue of Liberty originally came to New York in 1886, as a gift from France. You can enjoy the panoramic views from the observation deck, about 16 storeys above ground, and tour the museum in the pedestal. A limited number of time passes are available for an 'insider's view' into this work of art (www.statuereservations.com). The rest of the statue will continue to be off-limits, however, including the statue's interior spiral staircases, but you can stroll along the promenade above the star-shaped former fort on which the statue and its pedestal rise some 30 storeys above the harbour.

The Statue of Liberty café is extremely small and there are simply not enough loos. There is space to eat outside, but not very much. At Ellis Island, however, you'll find plenty of WCs on all the different levels, a large café and a huge amount of outdoor seating that looks right out over to the

Statue of Liberty

Statue of Liberty and the skyscrapers of Lower Manhattan.

The Ellis Island Immigration Museum (www.ellisisland.com) is the most visited museum in New York, particularly beloved by crowds of Americans who want to see where their immigrant ancestors arrived. In use from 1892 to 1954, it 'processed' up to 10,000 immigrants a day. Each person was examined and then interviewed to find out if they could speak English. An unfortunate 2 per cent were turned away.

Visitors follow the immigrants' route as they entered the main baggage room and went up to the Registry and then the Staircase of Separation. Poignant exhibits include photos, video clips, jewellery, clothing, baggage and the stark dormitories.

TICKET TO RIDE

The CityPass is an excellent way to avoid long queues and save money if you visit at least three of the participating attractions. These are the American Museum of Natural History, the Empire State Building and New York Skyride, the Intrepid Sea-Air-Space Museum, the Guggenheim Museum, the Museum of Modern Art and a harbour tour with the Circle Line. You can buy a CityPass from any of the attractions, which will save you queuing again. Prices are $53 (a $56 saving on normal admission prices) for adults and $44 for 6–17s. Call 208-787 4300 or you can buy online at www.citypass.com.

The Immigrant Wall of Fame lists half a million names, including those of the grandfathers of Presidents Washington and Kennedy.

🇬🇧 BRITTIP

When leaving the Statue of Liberty to go on to Ellis Island DO NOT get on the ferry that takes you to New Jersey. That is on the left. It IS clearly signposted, but it is very easy to get disorientated!

This is a great museum and well worth allocating a good portion of your day to. All the films and the guided tour are free. The Ranger Tours last 45 minutes and leave at regular times throughout the day (times posted in the information booth). At 2pm there is a re-enactment of a board of inquiry, which decides an immigrant's fate. Immigrants tell their stories in the movie *Island of Hope, Island of Tears*, which runs

🇬🇧 BRITTIP

The tour, film and play on Ellis Island are free, but you need to get tickets for each of them from the information desk (just to the left on your way in). Busiest times are obviously just after a boat has arrived, so try to be the first off the ferry and head straight for the desk.

FREE SIGHTS AND ATTRACTIONS

Cathedral of St John the Divine: Upper West Side/Morningside Heights (page 73)
Central Park: (pages 257–260)
Federal Reserve Bank: Financial District (page 68)
Gracie Mansion: Upper East Side (page 69)
Grand Central Station: Midtown East (page 69)
New York Public Library: Midtown (page 70)
Rockefeller Center: Midtown (page 64)
South Street Seaport: Financial District (page 66)
Staten Island Ferry: Battery Park (page 66)
Times Square: Midtown West (page 66)
The Winter Garden: Battery Park City (page 72)
Woolworth Building: Civic Center/Financial District (page 72)

frequently in two theatres. Free tickets are available at the desk. Audio tours are available for $6.

The museum is very well laid out, has lots of benches everywhere and is so big it never feels too crowded. There is a cashpoint (ATM) in the corridor on the way to the café, which is on your right as you enter the building. The café is a little pricey but you could bring your own picnic and sit outside and enjoy the fabulous views.

EMPIRE STATE BUILDING
34th Street
- ✉ 350 5th Avenue between 33rd and 34th Street
- ☎ 212-736 3100
- 🖐 www.esbnyc.com
- 🚇 Subway B, D, F, Q, N, R, V, W to 34th Street
- ⏱ 8am–2am, last lifts go up at 1.15am; be sure to bring ID
- $ $18 adults, $16 seniors and youth (12–17), $12 children (6–11), under 5s free. Tickets can be bought online.

It is hard to believe that the Empire State, which was for almost 40 years the world's tallest building, was nearly not built at all. Just weeks after its building contract was signed in 1929, the Wall Street Crash brought the financial world to its knees. Fortunately, the project went ahead and was even completed 45 days ahead of schedule, rising to 443m (1,454ft) in 1931. The lobby interior features Art Deco design incorporating rare marble imported from Italy, France, Belgium and Germany. It is, once again, New York's tallest building, and

The Empire State Building

BRITTIP

Fancy a coffee when you're in the Empire State Building? To avoid the pricey snack bars, get back down to ground level and visit Starbucks next door.

one of the world's most recognisable from movies, most recently, the remake of *King Kong*.

There are two observation decks, one on the 86th floor and another on the 102nd floor, which costs an extra $15 to visit but gives the most fabulous, if dizzying, views. Your best bet is to arrive as early in the morning as possible to avoid long waits for tickets. Weekends, of course, get really crowded. Once you reach the glass-walled viewing deck on the 86th floor you can enjoy some fabulous views of Manhattan and the outer boroughs and really get your bearings. Those who lack the stomach for heights can catch the view live through ESB TowerCams on the concourse. If you like you can hire the ESB Audio Tour for $7. You buy your tickets on the concourse level below the main lobby, but don't have to use them on the same day.

BRITTIP

If you've a CityPass booklet (page 60), you can avoid the ticket queues at the Empire State Building. Walk straight past the crowds on the ground floor and turn right to go up one flight.

The **New York SkyRide** is on the second floor and is open seven days a week 10am–10pm. It simulates a thrilling flight around the skyscrapers and bridges of New York. Entrance $18 adults, $14 youth (12–17) and $13 seniors and children (5–11). For a combined New York Skyride and Empire State Building ticket, the prices are $38 adults, $24 seniors, $26 youth and $24 for children. Tel 212-279 9777 or buy online www.skyride.com.

BRITTIP

While the Empire State is covered in scaffolding, as it was at the time of going to press, the best views are to be had from the Top of the Rock at the Rockefeller Center.

GROUND ZERO – WORLD TRADE CENTER MEMORIAL FOUNDATION
Financial District
- 120 Liberty Street, between Greenwich and Church Streets
- 212-227 7722/212-393 9160 ext 138
- www.groundzero.nyc.ny.us/www.build thememorial.org/www.tributenyc.org
- Subway N, R, W to Cortlandt Street; 1, 9 to Rector Street
- Mon, Wed–Sat 10am–6pm; Tues 12–6pm; Sun 12–5pm
- $ $10 suggested donation

After a lengthy public consultation, in 2002 the Lower Manhattan Development Corporation (LMDC) began a worldwide search for a suitable design concept for the 6.5-hectare (16-acre) former World Trade Center site. There were 400 submissions from around the globe, which were whittled down to seven and exhibited at the Winter Garden. More than 100,000 visitors saw the exhibition– generating 8,000 comments– and another eight million looked at the plans on the internet. Finally, after three public meetings, Studio Daniel Libeskind's Memory Foundations design was chosen in early 2003.

Originally, Libeskind planned to divide the 'superblock' formed by the World Trade Center into four parts. His plan included a sunken memorial site on the spot where the Twin Towers had stood, and around the memorial he envisioned five irregularly shaped towers, of which the tallest would be a 541m (1,776ft) towering spire of glass called the Freedom Tower.

Eventually, Libeskind redesigned the towers to be slimmer, taller and squarer, in order to provide more office space. Then, the

Ground Zero

site developer brought in architect David Childs, who changed Libeskind's glass Freedom Tower into a larger, heavier building but retained the spire. Wind turbines will harness the wind and generate the building's energy. The occupied portion will be 60 storeys high. The 1,776ft Freedom Tower is expected to open in 2010.

In January 2004, a jury chose Michel Arad's memorial design, Reflecting Absence, which differed from Libeskind's. It includes a forest of trees planted throughout a plaza around the footprints of the Twin Towers; reflecting pools deep within the footprints, with constantly falling water to mark the voids; exposure of the bedrock-and-slurry wall to reveal the scale of the site and the disaster; and chambers for unidentified remains of the dead, as well as relics of the disaster. Peter Walker, a Californian landscape architect, is designing a park on the broad, open street-level plaza.

Santiago Calatrava, designer of the transportation hub, has incorporated Libeskind's Wedge of Light feature. His steel-and-glass train station will allow a shaft of light to fall between its wings without a shadow each year on 11 September between the hours of 8.46am, when the first plane hit, and 10.28am, when the second tower collapsed, in perpetual tribute to altruism and courage.

BRITTIP

Always carry water around with you whether you are sightseeing or shopping. No matter what the weather, it is incredibly easy to get dehydrated. Take a small bottle and refill along the way.

The design concept is being built in several phases, and includes better street and pedestrian layouts, better connections between subway and PATH train systems, easily accessible shops and restaurants at street level, particularly along Fulton and Church Streets, plus better bus and car

NEW YORK PASS

As well as the CityPass, the New York Pass offers discounted entry to over 40 sights and also gives discounts and extras at a range of shops and restaurants and for some tours, plus free access to the subway and buses. One day costs $65, phone 877-714 1999 or visit www.newyorkpass.com.

parking. There will be a mix of office space, shops and other amenities including a Performing Arts Center. As part of the first phase of development, the Tribute WTC Visitor Center opened in 2006 with exhibits, programmes and unique personal walking tours with survivors or those who were involved in the rescue mission. The memorial and museum are scheduled to open in 2009.

MADAME TUSSAUD'S
Times Square
- ✉ 234 West 42nd Street between 7th and 8th Avenues
- ☎ 800-246 8872
- ⌐ www.nycwax.com
- 🚇 Subway A, C, E, S to Port Authority or 1, 2, 3, N, B, D, F, Q, R to Times Square/42nd Street
- ⊙ Open daily throughout the year. Sun–Thurs 10am–8pm. Fri–Sat 10am–10pm
- $ $29 adults, $26 senior, $23 children, under 4s free

London's famous waxworks has been spreading its wings around the globe and has recently opened attractions in Las Vegas, Hong Kong, Amsterdam and this one in New York. If wax models (extremely well done) are your thing or you have the kids in tow, it is worth visiting this sight in the heart of New York's Times Square as the celebs portrayed reflect personalities associated with the city, such as Woody Allen, Leonard Bernstein, Jacqueline Kennedy Onassis, John D Rockefeller, Yoko Ono, Donald Trump, Andy Warhol and former mayor Rudolph Giuliani among others. Kids and teenagers will get to see all their favourite stars, from Michael Jordan to Tom Cruise.

NBC TOURS
Rockefeller Center/Midtown
- ✉ Lobby level of 30 Rockefeller Plaza at 49th Street between 5th and 6th Avenues
- ☎ 212-664 7174 tickets, 212-664 3700 information
- ⌐ www.nbcuniversalstore.com
- 🚇 Subway B, D, F, V to 47th–50th Streets/Rockefeller Center
- ⊙ Mon–Thurs 8.30am–4.30pm every 30 minutes, Fri and Sat 9.30am–5.30pm every 15 mins, Sun 9.30am–4.30pm every 15 mins
- $ $18.50 adults, $15.50 seniors and children (6–12), no children under 6. For a small extra fee, combine with Rockefeller Center Tour (page 64)

WHAT TO SEE AND DO

BRITTIP

You can no longer get tickets for TV shows by sending away for them, but you can join the crowd outside the Today Show's walled studio Mon–Fri 7am–10am at 49th Street and Rockefeller Plaza. For other TV shows you can attend, visit www.nycvisit.com. Click on 'Visitors' and 'Things to Do'

You get a 1 hour 10 minute look behind the scenes at NBC, the major television network headquartered in New York, including a peek at some of its most famous studios such as 1A – home of the *Today Show*. You'll be shown around by an NBC Page – some of these characters have gone on to become famous entertainment personalities.

RADIO CITY MUSIC HALL
Midtown

✉ 1260 6th Avenue at 50th Street
☎ 212-247 4777/212-307 7171 to order tickets
🖐 www.radiocity.com
🚗 Subway B, D, F to 50th Streets/ Rockefeller Center
🕐 Tours daily 11am–3pm
$ $17 adults, $14 seniors, $10 under 12s.

While you're at the Rockefeller Center you won't want to miss out on this fabulous building, which has been fully restored to its original Art Deco movie palace glory and is utterly beautiful. This is where great films such as *Gone With The Wind* were given their premieres and it has the largest screen in America. Make a point of visiting the loos – they have a different theme on each floor, from palm trees to Chinese and floral. There are even cigar-theme loos for the boys. The one-hour Stage Door Tour takes you around the whole building and you get to meet a Rockette.

BRITTIP

Buy your ticket for the Radio City Music Hall in the morning to find out what time your tour is, as it is well worth planning your day around. Alternatively, you can now see it as part of the Rockefeller Center Tour.

ROCKEFELLER CENTER
Midtown

✉ Midtown at 5th Avenue – West 48th to West 50th Streets between 5th and 6th Avenues
☎ 212-632 3975
🖐 www.RockefellerCenter.com
🚗 Subway B, D, N, F, V, W, R, 1 to 47th-50th Streets/Rockefeller Center
🕐 Tours Mon–Sat 11am–5pm, Sun 10pm–3pm every 2 hours, departing from the NBC experience store (see page 63)
$ Tour $12 adults, $10 seniors and children (6–12), no children under 6. Reservations are necessary on 212-664 7174

Built in Art Deco style in the 1930s, this was named after the New York benefactor whose fortune paid for its construction. As well as Radio City Music Hall, it houses opulent office space, restaurants, bars, shopping on several levels and even gardens. To help you find your way round the 19 buildings, collect a map at the lobby of the main building (30 Rockefeller Center). The central plaza, a restaurant in summer, is turned into an ice rink in winter, and a massive Christmas tree with 8km (5 miles) of fairy lights draws huge crowds.

You can either wander around the plaza or take the one-hour Rockefeller Center Tour. This takes in The Channel Gardens, Radio City, the ice rink, NBC and more, while giving an insight into the Center's history, architecture and more than 100 pieces of artwork that create the world's most amazing public collection of Art Deco.

BRITTIP

Lovers of the Metropolitan Museum shops can get their fix at one of its branches in the heart of the Rockefeller Center. It's just off the main plaza by the ice rink.

In November 2005, the Top of the Rock observation deck was reopened on the 70th floor at 30 Rockefeller Plaza, offering visitors spectacular 360-degree views of the city. The observation deck, first opened in 1933, has been redeveloped into a 55,000 sq ft, multi-level complex with state-of-the-art features such as new transparent safety glass panels that allow completely unobstructed views of the city's landmarks. It's open 365 days of the year 8am–midnight and costs $17.50 adults, $16 seniors, $11.25 children. Call

CLOWNING AROUND NEW YORK

Circuses lay on their death-defying extravaganzas and even backstage activities for children in the city, mostly arriving in spring. Some of those most popular with families are:

BIG APPLE CIRCUS

Midtown West

✉ 505 Eighth Avenue, 19th floor; venues vary
☎ 212-268 2500 or 800-899 2775 toll free
🖱 www.bigapplecircus.org
$ $14 and upwards

A not-for-profit, totally family-friendly circus that has been operating since the 1970s. In spring 2007, it appeared at Cunningham Park in Queens.

CIRQUE DU SOLEIL

Midtown West

✉ Madison Square Garden, 7th Avenue at 32nd Street
☎ 212-465 6741 (info); 212-307 7171 (ticketmaster)
🖱 www.cirquedusoleil.com
🚇 Subway A, C, E, 1, 2, 3, 9 to 34th Street/Penn Station
🕐 Annually 6 November–6 January (until 2010)
$ Check website for prices

This magical, world-famous animal-free circus is perhaps the most popular with parents. Wintuk, its fantastical new 90-minute show, sees 50 performers weave circus acts, breathtaking theatrical effects and memorable songs into an enchanting tale of a boy in the Arctic, waiting for the arrival of snow.

RINGLING BROS AND BARNUM & BAILEY CIRCUS

Midtown West

✉ Madison Square Garden, 7th Avenue at 32nd Street
☎ 212-507 8900
🖱 www.ringling.com
🚇 Subway A, C, E, 1, 2, 3, 9 to 34th Street/Penn Station
$ $12 upwards from TicketMaster 212-307 7171 or go through www.ticketmaster.com for a 10 per cent saving for weekday matinees

An extremely popular circus, America's original and most famous company keeps children and adults glued to their seats with a triple extravaganza of thrilling high-energy acts taking place in three rings at once each spring in Madison Square Garden. There's a special all-access tour an hour before the performance to learn circus skills, become circusfit™ and meet the animal stars.

UNIVERSOUL CIRCUS

Midtown West

✉ 510 Whitehall Street, Atlanta; venues vary
☎ 800-316 7439 or book through TicketMaster on 212-307 7171, www.ticketmaster.com
🖱 www.universoulcircus.com
$ $10 upwards

For thrills with a difference, try this African-American troupe, which provides death-defying circus acts to hip-hop, R&B and salsa music. Catch them at The Wollman Rink in Brooklyn's Prospect Park in spring or playing at the Bronx and Queens.

212-698 2000 or visit www.topoftherock nyc.com to reserve tickets or take it in as part of the hour-and-a-half Art and Observation tour new in 2007 for $20, which departs every two hours from 10am Mon–Sun. Call 212-664 3700 for more information. All tours depart from the NBC Experience Store at 30 Rockefeller Plaza across from the *Today Show* studio.

BRITTIP

If you want to do the NBC Studio Tour and the Rockefeller Center Tour, save yourself a bit of cash by buying a combination ticket for $23.45 through the call centre on 212-6647174.

WHAT TO SEE AND DO

SOUTH STREET SEAPORT
Financial District
- ✉ Water Street to the East River between John Street and Peck Slip
- ☎ (212) SEA-PORT/ (212) 748-8600 museum
- ⌂ www.southstreetseaport.com
- 🚇 Subway A, C, J, M, Z, 2, 3, 4, 5 to Fulton Street/Broadway Nassau
- ⏲ Museum Apr–Sept Tues–Sun 10am–5pm, Nov–Mar Fri–Mon 10am–5pm.
- $ Free. Museum $8 adults, $6 seniors and students, $4 children (5–12).

You don't have to go into the South Street Seaport Museum (page 109) to get a feeling of the maritime history of the city – the ships are all around you. So are the shops. The Seaport is a rare New York approximation of a typical American shopping mall. Most shops are open Mon–Sat 10am–9pm, Sun 11am–8pm, and there are dining options at all prices, indoors and out, some with a view of the Brooklyn Bridge. The port was previously home to the 150-year-old Fulton Fish Market, but this has now been moved to the Bronx.

🇬🇧 BRITTIP
Taste & Tour – New York in Five Flavours www.nycvisit.com/tastetoursearch has suggestions of mouthwatering pitstops in the five neighbourhoods near key sights.

South Street Seaport

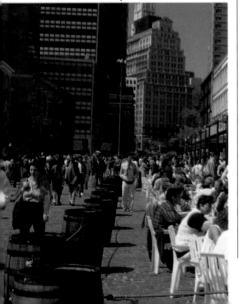

STATEN ISLAND FERRY
Battery Park
- ✉ Ferry Terminal, 1 Whitehall Street at South Street
- ☎ 718-815 2628
- ⌂ www.siferry.com
- 🚇 Subway 4, 5 to Bowling Green; R, W to Whitehall Street, 1 to South Ferry, J, M, Z to Broad Street
- $ Free

Probably the best sightseeing bargain in the world, this free ferry between Whitehall Street in Lower Manhattan and St George on Staten Island, passes close to the Statue of Liberty and gives dramatic views of Downtown and the bridges and skyscrapers of Lower Manhattan. Runs regularly 24 hours a day and takes 25 minutes for the crossing. Since 2004, three new ferries have been designed to capture the feel of the old-style ferries.

TIMES SQUARE AND THE THEATER DISTRICT
Another iconic area of New York and a must-see place. Full details of what to see and do here are given in Chapter 9 Theatre and Film.

THE OUTER BOROUGHS

BRONX ZOO
A wonderful zoo that combines conservation and ecological awareness with Disney-style rides and a children's zoo. Further details are given on page 273.

HISTORIC RICHMOND TOWN AND ST MARK'S PLACE, STATEN ISLAND
The two top historical sites on Staten Island, both give a unique insight into the New York of yesteryear. Further details are given on pages 279 and 280.

NEW YORK BOTANICAL GARDEN
Home to the Bronx River Gorge, it not only gives a fascinating insight into the geological history of New York, but also has acres and acres of beautiful gardens. Further details are given on page 266.

AMAZING ARCHITECTURE

Whether you have an interest in architecture or not, you won't fail to appreciate just how beautiful many of the buildings of New York are. The fact that Manhattan is an island has been key to so many of the designs over the last 200 years: when space is a premium the

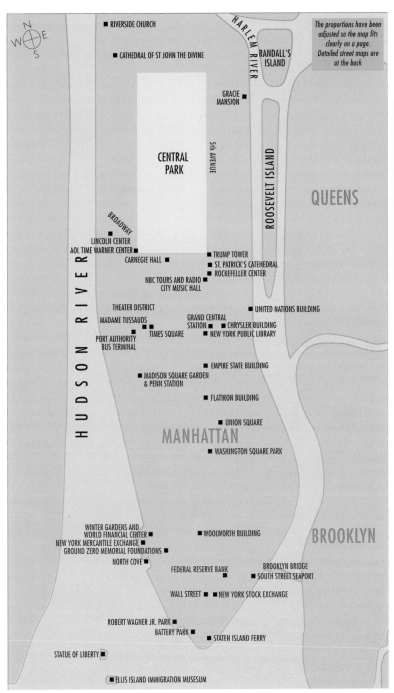

Major sights in Manhattan

TOP ZOOS FOR THE FAMILY

Like many sights in New York, the zoos here are larger-than-life affairs and a great choice for families – visit www.newyorkcityzoos.com for an idea. Bronx Zoo is famous worldwide, but those below are also ideal entertainment for children if you happen to be in the neighbourhood:

Bronx Zoo and Wildlife Conservation Society (see page 273)

Children's Zoo and Wildlife Center, Central Park (see page 259)

Prospect Park Zoo, Brooklyn (see page 270)

New York Aquarium, Coney Island, Brooklyn (see page 272)

only way to go is up. New York gave the world skyscrapers and it's these soaring buildings that have given the city its sensational skyline that is recognised the world over.

BROOKLYN BRIDGE

This Gothic creation was considered one of the modern engineering feats of the world when it was completed in 1883 after 16 long years of construction, and at the time was both the world's largest suspension bridge and the first to be built of steel. It was also the first bridge to link the two separate cities of New York and Brooklyn, making it now only a 10-minute taxi ride to travel between them.

BRITTIP

To hear the dramatic story of how the bridge was built while walking over it, take Big Onion's Brooklyn Bridge & Brooklyn Heights tour (www.bigonion.com).

The original engineer, John A Roebling, died even before the project began and his son, who took over, had to oversee the building from his Brooklyn apartment after being struck down by the bends. In all, 20

Brooklyn Bridge

people died during the construction of the bridge. Take the A or C train to High Street station and stroll back along the walkway to see some incredible views of the Downtown skyscrapers or the 4,5 or 6 to Brooklyn Bridge/City Hall station. It's a mile (1.8km) to walk across it and the most magical walk is from Brooklyn to Manhattan as the sun goes down over the stunning city skyline.

CHRYSLER BUILDING

Midtown East
- ✉ 405 Lexington Avenue at 42nd Street
- ☎ 212-682 3070
- 🚇 Subway S, 4, 5, 6, 7 to Grand Central/ 42nd Street
- ◷ 7am–6pm, lobby only
- $ Free

Opened in 1930, this was William van Alen's homage to the motor car. At the foot of the Art Deco skyscraper are brickwork cars with enlarged chrome hubcaps and radiator caps. Inside see its marble and chrome lobby and inlaid-wood elevators. Its needle-like spire is illuminated at night and the building vies with the Empire State for the most stunning.

BRITTIP

Just across the way from the Federal Reserve Bank is probably the poshest McDonald's in the world at 160 Broadway. It has doormen, a chandelier and a grand piano upstairs.

FEDERAL RESERVE BANK

Financial District
- ✉ 33 Liberty Street between William and Nassau Streets
- ☎ 212-720 6130
- 🖰 www.ny.frb.org
- 🚇 Subway 2, 3, 4, 5, A, C, J, M, Z to Fulton Street/Broadway-Nassau Street
- ◷ Mon–Fri 9.30am–3.30pm, by tour only
- $ Free

Yes, this really is the place where billions of dollars' worth of gold bars are stashed (as stolen by Jeremy Irons in *Die Hard 3*) on behalf of half the countries of the world, and where money is printed. Security, as you can imagine, is tight, but you can still do a free one-hour tour that takes you deep into the underground vaults, Mon–Fri at 9.30am, 10.30am, 11.30am 1.30pm and 2.30pm providing you book at least five days in advance. Your name will be placed on a computer list, but the minimum age is 16. Passport or picture identification is essential.

WHAT TO SEE AND DO

FLATIRON BUILDING
Flatiron District
✉ 175 5th Avenue between 22nd and 23rd
Streets
☎ 212-477 0947
🚇 Subway F, V, N, R, 6 to 23rd Street
🕐 Lobby open office hours
$ Free
The Renaissance palazzo building was the
first-ever skyscraper when it was completed
in 1902 and is held up by a steel skeleton
covered in white terracotta. Its name refers
to its unusual triangular shape. It is set at
the windiest crossroads of the city where 5th
Avenue crosses Broadway and in the 19th
century had to be policed as local New York
men hung around here to catch a glimpse
up ladies' skirts as they blew up around their
ears!

GRACIE MANSION
Yorkville
✉ Carl Schurz Park, 88th Street at East End
Avenue
☎ 212-570 4751
🖱 www.historichousetrust.org
🚇 Subway 4, 5, 6 to 86th Street
🕐 Tours Tues, Wed, Thurs pm; phone ahead
to reserve
$ $7 adults, $4 seniors, under 12s free
Built by the shipping tycoon, Archibald
Gracie in 1799, this mansion is the last of
the elegant country homes that once lined
Manhattan's East River shore. Dinner guests
here were the likes of Alexander Hamilton
and Joseph Bonaparte. It later became the
first home of the Museum of the City of
New York and then official residence of the
mayor. Now, the 'People's House', once
visited by Nelson Mandela, offers 45-minute
tours on Wednesdays at 10am, 11am, 1pm
and 2pm by reservation only (212-570 4773)
that take you through the mayor's living
room, a guest suite and smaller bedrooms.
The best part, though, is the view down the
river.

GRAND CENTRAL STATION
Midtown East
✉ East 42nd Street and Park Avenue
☎ 212-340 2345
🖱 www.grandcentralterminal.com
🚇 Subway S, 4, 5, 6, 7 to Grand Central/
42nd Street
🕐 Daily 5.30am–1.30am
$ Free
Even if you're not going anywhere by train,
this huge, vaulted station, which was

✚ BRITTIP
If you go to Grand Central
station on a Friday at 12.30pm,
you can go on a free tour sponsored
by the Grand Central Partnership (tel
212-883 2420, www.grandcentral
partnership.org). Meet in the
sculpture court of the Whitney
Museum at Altria. On Wednesdays at
12.30pm, the tour is given by The
Municipal Arts Society (tel 212-935
3960, www.mas.org). Meet at the
Center info booth on the main
concourse, with a suggested
donation of $10.

opened in 1913, is well worth a visit. A
$196-million, two-year renovation
programme completed in the 1990s saw the
ceiling once again twinkle with the stars and
astrological symbols of the night skies, and
the chandeliers, while the marble balusters
and clerestory windows gleam in the main
concourse.

The Grand Central Map, picked up from
the information booth on the main
concourse will lead you to a Mediterranean
restaurant, Michael Jordan's Steakhouse NYC
and a cocktail lounge, Cipriani Dolci,
modelled on a Florentine palazzo. The lower
level dining concourse offers inexpensive
meals and takeaways, while main floor
shopping outlets include Banana Republic,
Godiva chocolates and Aveda. Among eating
and shopping opportunities, take in a visit to
the New York Transit Museum Gallery and
Store, with exhibitions of transit
memorabilia, and to The Vanderbilt Hall, the
former main waiting room, which stages
entertainment. Complete your trip to this
elegant edifice by tucking in at the Oyster
Bar & Restaurant.

Grand Central Station

MADISON SQUARE GARDEN'S ALL ACCESS TOUR

34th Street

- ✉ 4 Pennsylvania Plaza at 33rd Street and 7th Avenue
- ☎ 212-465 MSG1/6741 (information); 212-307 7171 (ticketmaster)
- ⌐ www.thegarden.com
- 🚇 Subway A, C, E, 1, 2, 3, 9, D, F, B, V, N, Q, R, W to 34th Street/Penn station
- $ $17 adults, $12 children (12 and under), one-hour tours operate every day, every 30 minutes, 11am–3pm.

This is the round building that sits right on top of Penn station and the entrance is on 7th Avenue at 33rd Street. It occupies the site of the original Pennsylvania station, an architectural masterpiece that was even more beautiful than Grand Central Station, but which was razed in the 1960s. (One good thing came out of its destruction, though: the creation of the Landmarks Preservation Commission, which has helped to protect many buildings and areas in New York from developers.)

Madison Square Garden's arena is 10 storeys tall, covers 3.24 hectares (8 acres) and is famous for its circular ceiling, which is suspended by 48 bridge-like cables. Every year it hosts 600 events from concerts to boxing, wrestling, basketball and hockey, bringing in five million people. Its most famous residents are the New York Knickerbockers basketball team (known as the Knicks), the New York Rangers ice-hockey team and the New York Liberty women's pro basketball team.

Below the arena are the theatre, exhibition centre, box office and two club restaurants. Incidentally, this is actually the fourth Madison Square Garden building. The first two were built at Madison Square on the site of the current New York Life Building; the third was built on 8th Avenue between 49th and 50th Streets, where the

New York Public Library

Worldwide Plaza stands. This building opened in 1968 with a gala featuring Bob Hope and Bing Crosby.

During the course of the one-hour behind-the-scenes tour, you will hear about its 125-year history, see the inner workings and the Walk of Fame, and gain access to the locker rooms of both the Knicks and the Rangers.

MORRIS–JUMEL MANSION

Harlem

- ✉ Roger Morris Park, 65 Jumel Terrace at 160th Street
- ☎ 212-923 8008
- ⌐ www.morrisjumel.org
- 🚇 Subway C to 163rd Street
- ◷ Wed–Sun 10am–4pm, closed Mon and Tues
- $ $4 adults, $3 seniors, students and children, free for children under 12; various tours offered (for groups over 12) $5 adults, $3.50 seniors, students and children

Built by British colonel Roger Morris in 1765, this is the oldest house in Manhattan. It was confiscated by George Washington in 1776 and briefly used as his war headquarters until the Brits kicked him out of New York. Charles Dickens visited it, too. Tours are offered every Saturday at noon (register in advance), and family programmes include free art workshops during school holiday times.

NEW YORK PUBLIC LIBRARY

Midtown

- ✉ Fifth Avenue at 42nd Street
- ☎ 212-930 0830
- ⌐ www.nypl.org
- 🚇 Subway B, D, F, V, 7 to 42nd Street
- ◷ Tues–Wed 11am–7.30pm, Thurs–Sat 10am–6pm, Sun 1–5pm, closed Mon
- $ Free

Opened in 1911, this is one of the best examples of the city's Beaux Arts architecture and the largest branch public library in the world. Inside you'll find more than 8.5 million volumes on 140km of shelving guarded by the twin marble lions of Patience and Fortitude. Despite this mammoth collection, members can tap what they're looking for into a computer and get it in just 10 minutes. Take a tour at 11am or 2pm Tues–Sat and 2pm Sun to check out the murals by Richard Haas in the Periodicals Room, the fabulous white marble Astor Hall and the cathedral-like main reading room

FILM LOCATIONS

New York is one of the most filmed and photographed cities in the world, which is one of the reasons why we feel we know it so well. Many of the most popular films and TV series around the globe have been set in the city, so here's a taster of locations to visit, ranging from the famous to the plain weird. For an organised tour of Manhattan's locations, turn to page 80. For TV locations see boxes on pages 74 and 76.

Annie Hall: The roller coaster next to where Alvy Singer (Woody Allen) grows up is the one on Coney Island. Lots of other scenes from this classic 1977 movie starring Allen and Diane Keating are shot all over the city.

Breakfast at Tiffany's: Audrey Hepburn immortalised 5th Avenue's most famous jewellery store in this 1961 film (727 5th Avenue at 57th Street. Tel 212-755 8000, www.tiffany.com).

Home Alone 2: Lost in New York: The hotel where Macaulay Culkin fights off the baddies is The Plaza, but sadly it has now been made into condos.

Love Story: Ali MacGraw and Ryan O'Neal's ice-skating scenes were filmed in Central Park.

Maid in Manhattan: Jennifer Lopez and Ralph Fiennes filmed scenes in the Roosevelt Hotel (East 45th Street at Madison Avenue. Tel 212-661 1200, www.theroosevelthotel.com).

Men in Black II: A scene from the Will Smith blockbuster was filmed in the Art Deco eatery Empire Diner (210 10th Avenue at 22nd Street. Tel 212-243 2736, www.empire-diner.com).

Serendipity: You can reconstruct Kate Beckinsale and John Cusack's elevator race at the Waldorf-Astoria Hotel (301 Park Avenue at 50th Street. Tel 212-355 3000, www.waldorf astoria.com) where the film's couple meet, split and reunite.

Sleepless in Seattle: Meg Ryan and Tom Hanks fall for each other at the top of the Empire State Building (350 5th Avenue between 33rd and 34th Street. Tel 212-736 3100, www.esbnyc.com).

When Harry Met Sally: The canteen scene where Meg Ryan fakes an orgasm in front of Billy Crystal was filmed at Katz's Delicatessen (205 East Houston Street at Ludlow Street. Tel 212-254 2246, www.katzdeli.com).

Sex And The City: For the legions of fans out there with box sets of DVDs who still emulate the fabulous lifestyles of the *Sex And The City* girls, New York is one big set. Take an organised tour around the girls' haunts, from Jimmy Choos, to The Monkey Bar to The Little Church Around the Corner and the Magnolia Bakery or take some of the girls' shopping tips (see page 79).

where Leon Trotsky once read under the same brass lamps. The steps up to the library are a suntrap during the day and serve as a meeting place. Alternatively, they make a great place for a sandwich or drink stop.

◀▶ BRITTIP

Visit the library on a Monday afternoon from June to August (Tuesdays if it rains) and you can enjoy free outdoor movies and other events at Bryant Park (page 260).

NEW YORK STOCK EXCHANGE
Financial District

✉ 20 Broad Street at Wall Street
☎ 212-656 3000
🖰 www.nyse.com
🚇 Subway 6, 4, 5 to Wall Street; J, M, Z to Broad Street
🕐 Not open to the public at present

Amazing fact: the stock exchange was founded by 24 brokers meeting beneath a tree; now more than 1,300 members crowd on to the building's trading floor where over two billion shares change hands on busy days. This Neo-Classical building that represents the heart of capitalism is an interesting place to visit, although for the foreseeable future, due to security concerns, it is closed to the public. For now, a taste of the frenetic activity within can be seen from watching the traders scurrying around the crowded pedestrian-only streets. For the inside story, such as tickertape from the morning of the big crash, head to The Museum of American Finance a few blocks away (see page 100).

New York Stock Exchange

SEAGRAM BUILDING
Midtown
- ✉ 375 Park Avenue at 53rd Street
- ☎ 212-572 7000
- 🚇 Subway 6 to 51st Street
- ⏲ Open weekdays 9–5pm, tours Tues 3pm

The New York City mile's only Mies Van Der Rohe building, and widely recognised as one of the finest architectural skyscrapers in the world. It ignited a passion for plazas that you can still see in New York today. If you want to splash out, have dinner there in the much praised The Four Seasons restaurant (www.fourseasonsrestaurant.com) designed by Philip Johnson.

TRUMP TOWER
Midtown
- ✉ 725 Fifth Avenue between 56th and 57th Streets
- ☎ 212-832 2000
- 🖰 www.trumptower.com
- 🚇 Subway F, N, R, Q, W to 57th Street
- ⏲ Building daily 8am–10pm; shops Mon–Sat 10am–6pm, Sun noon–5pm
- $ Free

Donald Trump's monument to opulence includes an extravagant pink marbled atrium with waterfalls and plenty of cafés, restaurants and upmarket shops. The glitzy residences at the top can't be visited, but a glimpse of them could be seen in Trump's reality TV show The Apprentice, filmed in the tower. This is not to be confused with Trump International Hotel and Tower at Columbus Circle.

UNITED NATIONS HEADQUARTERS
Midtown East
- ✉ 1st Avenue between 42nd and 48th Street
- ☎ 212-963 8687 for tour reservations
- 🖰 www.un.org/tours
- 🚇 Subway 4, 5, 6, 7 to Grand Central/42nd Street
- ⏲ Mon–Fri 9am–4.45pm, Sat and Sun 10am–4.30pm (not at weekends Jan and Feb)
- $ $13 adults, $9 seniors, $8.50 students, $7 children (5–14). No children under 5.

You can't miss this building; the epicentre of global peace, where world leaders meet and international issues are discussed, is heralded by a colourful array of flags from 192 member states. Tours of the General Assembly, the Economic and Social Council and other areas every half hour last around 45 minutes. Despite its fame, this is not the most exciting tour in the world! The lovely Reclining Figure by Henry Moore and the Peace Bell from Japan, among the objects on display around the building may be more tantalising. If you send a postcard from here it will be with its own stamp, being in an international zone.

WINTER GARDEN AT THE WORLD FINANCIAL CENTER
Battery Park City
- ✉ 200 Vesey Street at West Street
- ☎ 212-417 7000
- 🖰 www.worldfinancialcenter.com
- 🚇 Subway E or PATH to World Trade Center, 2, 3, 4, 5, A, C, J, M, Z to Chambers Street; R, W to City Hall, 1 to Rector Street

The World Financial Center is actually the main focal point for the northern end of Battery Park City, a strip of land running down the west side of Lower Manhattan from Chambers Street to South Park. It was created from landfill from the digging work required to build the foundations for the World Trade Center. The World Financial Center has a complex of four office towers, but is most famous for the beautiful glass-roofed Winter Garden that looks over the boats moored in North Cove. Filled with palm trees, it houses upscale shops including Ann Taylor, Godiva Chocolates and Banana Republic and holds free events outdoors in summer. Check the website for schedules.

◀🇬🇧▶ BRITTIP
The Winter Garden is not just a pretty place to enjoy a drink or two; it also holds a series of free concerts and fairs.

WOOLWORTH BUILDING
Civic Center/Financial District
- ✉ 233 Broadway at Park Place
- 🚇 Subway 2, 3 4 to Park Place; N, R to City Hall
- ⏲ Weekdays 9–5pm
- $ Free

There is no official tour of the city's second skyscraper, soaring 55 storeys above Broadway and now referred to as the 'Mozart of skyscrapers'. It was built in 1913 at a cost of $13.5 million and it's worth sneaking a look inside the lobby of one of New York's most magical and flamboyant interiors, with extravagant marble walls, bronze filigree and glass-tiled ceiling. The outside is pretty wild, too, with gargoyles and flying buttresses under a pyramid-shaped roof. Incidentally, one-time shop assistant F W Woolworth's building was derided as a 'cathedral of commerce' when it opened, but the 'five and dime' store millionaire took this as a compliment. Just to prove a point, he can be spotted as a sculpture in the lobby, counting out his money.

RELIGIOUS BUILDINGS

CATHEDRAL OF ST JOHN THE DIVINE
Upper West Side/Morningside Heights
- ✉ 1047 Amsterdam Avenue at 112th Street and Amsterdam Avenue
- ☎ 212-316 7540 (info); tours 212-932 7347
- 🖱 www.stjohndivine.org
- 🚇 Subway 1 to 110th Street
- 🕐 Mon–Sat 7am–6pm, Sun 7am–7pm (July and August closes at 6pm). Public tours Tues–Sat 11am, Sun 1pm, at least four services a day
- $ Free, tours by arrangement

The world's largest Gothic cathedral has one of the world's biggest rose windows with 10,000 pieces of glass. Even more amazing are the main bronze doors, which weigh 3,000 tonnes each and are opened only for an official visit by the bishop. An Episcopal church built in 1892, its grounds cover 4.9 hectares (12 acres) of land and include a school and accommodation for the clergy. It has a capacity to seat 3,000 people, but because it holds so many art and performing art events it has chairs rather than pews. At the back of the cathedral behind the main altar are seven different chapels, which represent different countries in Europe and are used for weddings, christenings and the services.

BRITTIP
The Cathedral of St John the Divine is blessed with plenty of loos if you get caught short!

One of the highlights of the cathedral's calendar is the Feast of Assisi when real animals, including an elephant and a llama, are ceremonially taken up to the altar to be blessed by the cathedral clergy. Inspired by St Francis of Assisi, whose life exemplified living in harmony with the natural world, the feast usually takes place on the first Sunday in October. On Saturdays 10am–noon, families can join a Medieval Arts Workshop, which includes stone carving, weaving and sculpting.

GRACE CHURCH
Union Square
- ✉ 802 Broadway at 10th Street
- ☎ 212-254 2000
- 🖱 www.gracechurchnyc.org
- 🚇 Subway N, R, L, 4, 5, 6 to Union Square
- 🕐 Winter services Sun 9am, 11am, 6pm, Wed 6pm; summer services Sun 1pm, 6pm, Wed 6pm
- $ Free

A beautiful example of the Gothic Revival period that was occurring in the city when this was built by James Renwick in 1846, when he was only 23 years old! Grace Church was something of a society church and is still known for its Choir of Men and Boys established in the late 1800s. It is as pretty inside as out with Pre-Raphaelite stained-glass windows and a marvellous mosaic floor. The original wood steeple was replaced by marble in 1888, and it is a landmark on the skyline if you gaze along Broadway from Downtown. Tours take place on the first Sunday of the month after the 11am service.

BRITTIP
It is appropriate to tip your guide around 15 per cent of the cost of the ticket, if you are happy with the service you received.

St Patrick's Cathedral

FRIENDS

Although most of the filming was actually done in California, the many *Friends* series, starring Jennifer Aniston and co, were set in New York. There are some locations you may recognise: the place where Ross and Rachel consummated their relationship was filmed in one of the old-school dioramas in The American Museum of Natural History (page 88); and Central Perk Café where the six friends meet every day was based on Manhattan Café, now Grille, in West Village. Tel 212-888 6556, www.portfinogrille.com.

RIVERSIDE CHURCH
Morningside Heights

✉ 490 Riverside Drive at 120th Street
☎ 212-870 6700
🖰 www.theriversidechurchny.org
🚇 Subway 1 to 116th Street

Famous for having the world's largest tuned bell and its Carillon Concerts on Sundays at 10.30am, 12.30pm and 3pm. There's a free weekly tour starting at 12.15pm straight after the Sunday service or by reservation for a small fee for groups of five or more. You can also go for the great views of Upper Manhattan and the Hudson River. Nearby is the Union Theological Seminary at West 120th and Broadway. Woody Allen uses this façade in many of his movies.

ST PATRICK'S CATHEDRAL
Midtown

✉ 14 East 51st Street between 50th and 51st Street (entrance 5th Avenue)
☎ 212-753 2261
⇦ Subway 6 to 51st Street; E, V to 5th Avenue/53rd Street
◷ Daily 7.30am–8.30pm
$ Free

The seat of New York's Roman Catholic Archdiocese, the cathedral was begun in 1857 and the stained-glass windows weren't completed until l930. However, the magnificent results have definitely been worth the wait. Check out the Great Bronze doors, The Rose Window and the Pieta statue in the Lady Chapel.

◀┃▶ BRITTIP
The steps leading up to St Patrick's create a perfect picnic spot for a lunch or snack stop.

PART 2 –
TOUR NEW YORK

Time is a precious commodity when visiting New York, so you need to make sure that any tour you take pays for itself both financially and in terms of time. Your choice of tours will depend on whether it is your first or second visit or you are a regular. Newcomers need to get their bearings and two ways of doing this are to take a boat tour and a bus tour. The boat trip goes in a semi-circle around Manhattan from Midtown on one side to Midtown on the other; the bus tour, such as Gray Line's Manhattan Essential New York tour, is known as New York 101 (101 being slang for a first-year university course) because it covers so much of the city in one day. An alternative is the New York Visions tour, which takes a lot less time, is cheaper and is generally more fact filled.

Bus tours are useful when you want to visit an area such as Harlem or the Bronx, but are unsure of your personal safety, in which case the Harlem Spirituals/New York Visions tours are your best bet. Then there are helicopter tours, which will certainly give you breathtaking views, but won't show you the full ins and outs of each area.

◀┃▶ BRITTIP
If you take a tour of New York, you are likely to hear the word 'stoop'. This is taken from a Dutch word by original settlers and refers to the steps up to a townhouse, such as a brownstone – another New York term, this time for much sought-after townhouses, though they are as likely to be made out of grey stone as brown.

The reality is that the best way to see New York, get to know the city and find those interesting nooks and crannies is on foot, which possibly explains why the Big Onion Walking Tours are so popular – or it could be that they are just so darned good – and why so many people take advantage of the Big Apple Greeters, who can show you any area or sight you wish to visit. There is also a wide choice from bike tours to gangland tours and a reasonable selection of food tours.

The following categories of tour have been put in alphabetical order for ease of use. Within each category, what we consider are the most important or useful tours have been put first.

AIR TOURS

LIBERTY HELICOPTER TOURS
Chelsea
- ✉ VIP Heliport, West 30th Street and Hudson River
- ☎ 212-967 6464 or 800-542 9933 toll free
- 🖱 www.libertyhelicopters.com
- 🚇 Subway A, C, E to 34th Street/Penn Station
- ⏲ Daily 9am–9pm

This is a fantastic, if pricey, way to see New York, and perfect if you're looking for a once-in-a-lifetime experience. There are lots of tours to choose from, such as the Taste of New York, Lady Liberty, both $69 each for 5–7 minutes and, if you really want to push the boat out, there's the Romance Over Manhattan tour that lasts for 15 minutes and costs $849 for private hire of the whole helicopter, maximum four people.

BIKE TOURS

BIKE THE BIG APPLE
- ☎ 201-837 1133 or 877-865 0078 toll free
- 🖱 www.bikethebigapple.com
- $ $65-75 includes bike rental for tours and helmet rental.

Licensed guides take you through a variety of neighbourhoods, to see both historic and hip sides of the city. The five main tours include The Ethnic Apple Tour through Queens, Bike and Bite Brooklyn Tour, The Sensational Park and Soul tour travelling from Central Park to Harlem, Secret Streets – from High Finance to Chinatown, and The Brooklyn Bridge and Skyline at Twilight Bike Tour. Tours can be customised to your interests and are taken at a gentle pace.

CENTRAL PARK BICYCLE TOURS AND RENTALS
Colombus Circle
- ✉ 59th Street and Broadway
- ☎ 212-541 8759
- 🖱 www.centralparkbiketour.com
- 🚇 Subway A, B, C, D, 1, 2 to Columbus Circle/59th Street
- $ $40 adults, $20 children (15 and under) includes bike rental for tours; bike rental only is $20 for two hours, $25 for 3 hours and $40 all day.

A two-hour bike tour of Central Park from April to November starting at 10am, 1pm and 4pm daily and 9am and 11am on summer weekends, which includes stops at the Shakespeare Garden, Strawberry Fields, Belvedere Castle and other sights, plus bike rentals for your own use. Other tours on offer include a Central Park Picnic Tour, and at weekends the Central Park Movie Scenes Tour and the 3½-hour Manhattan Island Bike Tour.

✚ BRITTIP
Once you have your bike, don't feel you have to cycle everywhere you go because you can take bikes on the subway. A list of bike rental shops and cycle events can be found on www.bikenewyork.org.

THE HUB
SoHo
- ✉ 73 Morton Street between Hudson and Greenwich Streets
- ☎ 212-965 9334
- 🚇 Subway A to Canal
- $ $7 hour, $35 for 24 hours

Tandems, mountain, cruiser, recumbents and electric bikes, along with standard types.

Liberty Island from a helicopter

METRO BICYCLES
Upper West Side and Upper East Side
- ⊠ 96th Street at Broadway and 87th Street at Lexington
- ☎ 212-766 9222
- ⌐ www.metrobicycles.com
- 🚇 Subway 1, 2, 3, A, C, B, D to West 96th Street; 4, 5, 6 to East 87th Street
- ◷ Daily 9.30am–6.30pm.
- $ $7 hour, $35 for 24 hours, helmets $2.50

If you want to check out the Upper West Side along the river or the Upper East side, rent from here. Rentals include hybrid models. Metro have seven shops in convenient locations such as Eastside Bicycles, 1311 Lexington Avenue at 88th Street (212-427 4450) Central Park and Canal Street Bicycle Shop at 417 Canal Street between 6th Avenue and Grand Street in Chinatown (212-334-8000). Check the website links for hours, bikes for hire and other locations.

BRITTIP
Rent your bike from Canal Street Bicycle Shop and head off to the Financial District, where the streets are usually almost deserted on a Sunday.

PEDAL PUSHER BIKE SHOP
Central Park
- ⊠ 1306 Second Avenue at East 69th Street
- ☎ 212-228 5592 or 877-257 9437 toll free
- ⌐ http://pedalpusherbikeshop.com
- 🚇 Subway 6 to Hunter College/E 68th Street
- ◷ Fri–Mon 10am–6pm, Wed 10am–7pm, Thurs 10am–8pm, closed Tues
- $ $5.99 hour, $24.99 for a day, $29.99 for 24 hours, helmet and lock $2.50 each

This is perhaps the cheapest bike hire in New York City and comes highly recommended by Bike The Big Apple for those who want to go

Pony cab

it alone. Just five blocks away from Central Park, it is handily located for a whirl around New York's backyard. Types of rentals include road, hybrid, mountain and three-speed.

HUB STATION/PONY PEDICAB
SoHo
- ⊠ 517 Broome Street at Thompson Street
- ☎ 212-254 8844
- 🚇 Subway C, E to Spring Street; N, R to Prince Street
- ◷ Open Tues–Sun 11am–7pm
- $ $15 for 30 minutes, $30 for 1 hour

Technically not bicycles, but three-man tricycles or 'pedicabs' (one 'driver' to pedal and two passengers!). So amazing-looking that even seen-it-all-before New Yorkers stop to stare. That may be a little off-putting for some, but I found them an excellent way to see SoHo without breaking into a sweat or breaking the bank! You may even be able to hail one of these after the theatre in the Times Square area. Don't forget to tip – 'drivers' earn their money! In good weather only. You can either reserve in advance and arrange a meeting point or turn up at the hub. You get $5 off with NYTAB's NYCard (page 23).

THE SOPRANOS
Most of the locations for this ultra-popular series are shot in New Jersey, a short bus ride from main Manhattan. For a more comprehensive tour, see page 80.

Pizzaland: 260 Belleville Turnpike, North Arlington, NJ (www.pizzalandpizza.com), can be seen in the opening sequence of every episode as Tony Soprano drives past it on his way home.

Satin Dolls: 230 State Route 17 South, Lodi, NJ. (tel 201-845 6494, www.satindollsnj.com), is a real-life dancing club where scenes for the Bada Bing Club are filmed.

BOAT TOURS

ADIRONDACK, CLASSIC HARBOR LINE
Chelsea Pier
- ⊠ Pier 59, 18th Street at Hudson River
- ☎ 646-336 5270 or 212-209 3370 to book
- ⌐ www.sail-nyc.com
- 🚇 Subway A, C, E to 8th Avenue/14th Street
- ◷ End April–end October
- $ Tickets $40–$50 for sails, $75 for Sunday brunch sails

A sail on this three-masted replica of a 19th-century schooner is unforgettable. It sails from Chelsea Pier to Battery Park, allowing you the chance to catch a glimpse of Ellis Island and the Statue of Liberty, Governor's Island and Brooklyn Bridge, while sipping your complimentary glass of wine.

Otherwise, you can opt for a brunch cruise on the 80ft 1920s-style yacht *Manhattan* from March to end of December. Both offer sunset and city lights cruises, too.

CIRCLE LINE
West Midtown
✉ Pier 83, West 42nd Street at Hudson River
☎ 212-563 3200
🖰 www.circleline42.com
🚗 Any subway to 42nd Street, then transfer to an M42 bus heading west
$ From $19 adults, $11 children; combo packages available

Choose from a three-hour full island cruise, $29.50 adults, $16.50 children, $25 seniors or a two-hour semi-circle or sunset/harbour lights cruise, $25 adults, $14 children, $21 seniors. Or you can take a summer music cruise, a full-day cruise to Bear Mountain ($45 adults, $40 seniors and $30 for children 12 and under) or a 1½-hour Liberty Island cruise ($20 adults, $17 seniors and $12 children) May–Oct.

Alternatively, you can go for a spin on *The Beast*, a speedboat that takes you on a quick and memorable 30-minute tour. Sights fly by as you reach a speed of 64kph (45mph) and stop at the Statue of Liberty for photos. May–Oct daily on the hour noon–dusk ($18 adults, $12 children, seniors $18).

🇬🇧 BRITTIP
Special value packages combining cruises and even sights such as Top of the Rock or the Empire State Building with a cruise are only available from the Circle Line Box Office at Pier 83. Check www.circleline42.com for combos and savings.

NY WATERWAY
Financial District
✉ Pier 78 at West 38 Street and 12th Avenue or Pier A at West St and Battery Place
☎ 800-533 3779
🖰 www.nywaterway.com

🚗 Any subway to 42nd Street, transfer to M42 bus heading west
🕐 A few cruises operate year round, most April–Dec
$ Harbour cruise prices from $23 adults, $19 seniors and $13 children, without service charge, and baseball cruises from $18 adults and $14 children under 12, no service charge; children under 3 free on both.

🇬🇧 BRITTIP
The harbour cruises are very informative and give a great insight into Manhattan and beyond, but it can sometimes be hard to hear the commentary from the upper deck. If you want to hear everything, it's probably best to stay inside.

Offers a wide variety of sightseeing options all year round, including New York harbour cruises to Downtown and Midtown. There is also an Architecture, a History and a Riverkeeper Kids' Cruise for families, as well as evening cruises with on-board entertainment. Also available in the summer are day trips to Sandy Hook Beach and, for baseball fans, cruise packages that include a round-trip sail on the *Yankee Clipper*, tickets, souvenirs and the ubiquitous hot dog.

Views from the Circle Line Ferry

BATEAUX NEW YORK
Chelsea
- ✉ Pier 61 at Chelsea Piers on West 23rd Street
- ☎ 212-727 2789 or 866-817 3463 (toll-free)
- ⌁ www.spiritcitycruises.com
- 🚇 Subway C, E, 1, 9 to 23rd Street, transfer to B23 cross-town bus heading west
- $ Brunch ticket around $60 without alcoholic drinks, dinner around $120, $5 tax excluded

Indulge in a dinner (7.30–10.30pm daily) or brunch (noon–2pm) while cruising around Lower Manhattan (note: boarding an hour earlier).

WORLD YACHT DINNER CRUISES
Midtown West
- ✉ Pier 81 at West 41st Street and Hudson River
- ☎ 212-630 8100
- ⌁ www.worldyacht.com
- 🚇 Any subway to 42nd Street, then transfer to M42 bus heading west
- ◷ April Thurs–Mon, May–Dec daily for dinner; board at 6pm, sail 7–10pm
- $ From around $100, depending on the season/day of the week

With four-course menus created by a selection of New York's best chefs, linen tablecloths, live music, a dance floor and world-class videos, this is an upmarket experience you are sure to enjoy. The cruise lasts three hours and also provides spectacular views of the harbour. Note that the dress code is smart and that jackets are required, so make sure you allow yourself plenty of time to put on your glad rags.

⚑ BRITTIP
Be one of the first to take the city's only land and water sightseeing tour, The New York Splash Tour (www.newyorksplashtours.com), aboard a special amphibian aquabus. The hour-long tour splashes out of Times Square and gives views of the city skyline from the Hudson River. Don't worry, you won't get wet!

The Chrysler Building

BUS TOURS

HARLEM SPIRITUALS/ NEW YORK VISIONS
Midtown
- ✉ 690 8th Avenue between West 43rd and West 44th Streets
- ☎ 212-391 0900 or 800-660 2166 toll free
- ⌁ www.harlemspirituals.com or www.harlemheritagetours.com
- 🚇 Subway A, C, E, 1, 2, 3, 7, 9, S, N, Q, R, S, W, B, F, D, V to 42nd Street/Times Square
- $ Varies, see below

One of the most reputable tour companies in New York, the guides are highly qualified, great founts of knowledge and very friendly, while the buses are modern and comfortable with the all-important air-conditioning. Tours by the Harlem Spirituals include:

Harlem Gospel Tour: A combined walking (though not too far!) and riding tour of Harlem (Sun and Wed), during which you attend a church service, hear a gospel choir and have the option of having lunch or brunch at a soul food restaurant. Prices are $49 adults/$89 with meal, $35 children (5–11)/$69 with meal. Tours Sun 9.30am–1.30pm, Wed 9am–1pm.

Soul Food and Jazz: A chance to relive the heyday of Harlem, thanks to the return of jazz to the area. This combines a walking and riding tour through Harlem's historical sites with a soul food meal and the chance to see a jam session at a local jazz club. Tours are available Mon, Thurs and Sat 7pm–midnight and cost $125 for adults and children (5–11).

BRITTIP

In case you're wondering what you'll be served as soul food, this traditional African-American cuisine consists of spicy ribs, fried fish and chicken, cornbread and sides such as okra and black-eyed peas.

The **New York Visions Manhattan Sightseeing Tour New York New York:** An excellent four-hour introduction to all the major sights including Times Square, Central Park, Rockefeller Center, Greenwich Village, SoHo, Little Italy, Chinatown and the Wall Street area. Tours Mon, Thurs and Sat 9.30am. Prices are $49 adults, $35 children. Pay extra $65/45 (adults/children) and you also get tickets for the ferry to the Statue of Liberty and Ellis Island Immigration Museum (you'll be dropped off at Battery Park) plus an MTA Fun Pass for 24-hour use on the subways and buses (page 54).

GRAY LINE NEW YORK SIGHTSEEING

West Midtown

✉ 777 8th Avenue between 47th and 48th Streets
☎ 212-445 0848/800-669 0051 toll free
⌂ www.graylinenewyork.com
🚇 Subway C, E to 50th Street
🕐 Daily 8.30am–5pm
$ Varies, see below; prices are with $5 online booking discount

The oldest sightseeing bus company in New York, it has much to offer, although the average tour guide gives very little information in comparison with the New York Visions tours. Still, if you don't want to be overwhelmed by information on your first visit to New York, then try the **Classic New York Tour** ($79 adults, $57 children (5–11). A double-decker bus tour with hop-on, hop-off stops, it includes the ferry to the Statue of Liberty and Ellis Island, a ticket to the Empire State Building and a ticket to South Street Seaport Museum. It comes with the 48-hour **All Loops Tour**, which runs around Downtown, Midtown, uptown and Brooklyn and at night with 50 stops. You can do as few or as many as you like, so you can spend as long as you want in each area, giving you plenty of flexibility. A three-day Super Saver Combo, combines the NYC Official Heritage Tour with the All Loops Tour for $112/$88. The newest hottest tours include **The Essential New York**, which takes you to the

Top of the Rock, the UN Headquarters and the Statue of Liberty/Ellis Island for $95/$66, a two-hour **In a New York Minute Package**, which includes a ticket to the Empire State, and a Lady Liberty harbour cruise for $68/$48. If you just want to hop on and off, The All Loops Tour gives you 48 hours for $44/$34 if you book online.

The **NYC Showbiz Insiders Tour** ($74 online) is a six-hour daily extravaganza giving a behind-the-scenes look at New York's TV and Broadway shows. Starting from the Blue Diamond Theater you'll take the Stage Door Tour at Radio City Music Hall and lunch at Planet Hollywood. The tour ends with a private performance given by a current Broadway actor and the opportunity for some photos and autographs.

ON LOCATION TOURS

Upper East Side
☎ 212-209 3370
⌂ www.sceneontv.com

The best company in New York for fun and informative bus tours around the sights and attractions seen in two of the city's most famous shows, *Sex And The City* and *The Sopranos*, plus a general TV and movie tour and a walking tour of Central Park movie sites. Details are as follows:

Sex And The City

✉ Meet by the Pulitzer Fountain on 5th Avenue at 58th Street
🚇 Subway 4, 5, 6, to 59th Street/Lexington Avenue; N, R, W to 5th Avenue
🕐 Daily 11am and 3pm, Sat–Sun 10am, 11am and 3pm
$ $37 (plus $2 ticket fee)

Here's a chance to check out the stomping grounds of the girls from *Sex And The City* even now the show has ended. During the three-hour bus tour, which includes over 40 locations, you'll visit D&G in SoHo, where Carrie shopped for shoes, and the New York

Gray Line sightseeing

Holy Trinity Lutheran Church – as seen in *Ghostbusters*!

Sports Club where Miranda worked out, plus bars such as O'Neil's and Tao where Carrie, Samantha, Charlotte and Miranda did their flirting. Most important of all, you'll get some behind-the-scenes scoop on the show and the actors. This is a really fun experience, which gets into the spirit of the show and gives everyone plenty of browsing and chatting opportunities. You'll also get to eat a cupcake from the famous Magnolia Bakery, though be warned: they are incredibly sweet! By the end, you should be fluent in *Sex And The City*-speak and know your Manhattan Guy (a genetically mutant strain of single man that feeds on Zabar's and midnight shows at Angelika) from your Trysexual (someone who will try everything once) or a 'We' Guy (a man who refers to your potential future relationship by using 'we' statements such as 'we' can cook etc, thus faking a future with you to get what he wants in the present). This tour is busy, so book at least a week in advance.

THE SOPRANOS

- ✉ Bus departs from the 'Button' statue on 7th Avenue at 39th Street
- 🚇 B, D, F, V to 42nd Street; N, Q, R, S, W, 1, 2, 3, 7, 9, S to Times Square
- 🕐 Sat and Sun 2pm
- $ $40 (plus $2 ticket fee)

Get the shakedown on a tour of 40 sites used in *The Sopranos* including Satriale's Pork Store, the cemetery where Livia Soprano is buried, the Bada Bing nightclub and the diner where Chris was shot. The four-hour tour also includes a guide to New Jersey Mafia-speak, a stop for cannolis (traditional Italian pastries) and six other stops along the way. The tours tend to sell out quickly, so reserve your place as far in advance as possible.

TOUR NEW YORK TV AND MOVIE SITES

- ✉ Bus departs from Ellen's Stardust Diner, 1650 Broadway at 51st Street
- 🚇 Subway 1, 9 to 50th Street; N, W, R to 49th Street
- 🕐 Daily at 11am
- $ $34 (plus $2 ticket fee)

Takes you to over 40 different locations from over 60 TV shows and movies such as *Friends*, *You've Got Mail*, *Ghostbusters*, *The Bill Cosby Show*, *Will & Grace* and Woody Allen's *Manhattan* in around three hours. This is updated as new movies come out, so it now has sites from *Hitch*, *The Devil Wears Prada*, *The Interpreter* and *The Apprentice*. The restaurant used in *Spider-Man* was the latest to be added, at the time of going to press.

CENTRAL PARK MOVIE TOUR

- ✉ Meet at the entrance to Central Park, 59th Street between 5th and 6th Avenues
- 🚇 Subway N, R to 5th Avenue
- 🕐 Fri 3pm, Sat noon
- $ $15 (plus $2 ticket fee)

Take some snaps of the Boathouse Café seen in *When Harry Met Sally* and *Sex And The*

City, check out Tavern in the Green that featured in *Ghostbusters* and feed pigeons in the park à la Macaulay Culkin in *Home Alone 2*, The Bandshell from *Breakfast at Tiffany's* plus many more choice spots in the park. This walking tour takes two hours and, for the novelty, you could do it by bike (see page 75).

🇬🇧 BRITTIP
Pace yourself. There's no point in trying to pack so much into your day that you arrive back at your hotel exhausted with your head spinning. Less can often be more!

FOOD TOURS

ENTHUSIASTIC GOURMET
Chinatown
- ✉ 245 East 63rd Street
- ☎ 646-209 4724
- 🖰 www.enthusiasticgourmet.com
- 🕙 10am and 2pm. Different days for different tours; check website for times and availability
- $ $45 per person, reservations necessary

The Chinatown Discovered Tour explores the neighbourhood's grocery stores, meat and fish markets and produce stands for three hours. If you're still hungry, head for Jing Fong Restaurant (20 Elizabeth Street, 212-964 5256) for some of the best dim sum in NYC. There are lots of other gourmet tours to be enjoyed, such as the kosher NY Nosh, and a taste of Hispanic, Jewish, Chinese and Italian on The Melting Pot. Tours are personal, with a maximum of eight people.

FOODS OF NEW YORK
Greenwich Village
- ✉ 4th Floor, 9 Barrow Street, meet near 6th and Bleecker Street
- ☎ 212-209 3370/917-408 9539
- 🖰 www.foodsofny.com
- 🕙 Daily, year round 11am–2pm (but varies so check website)
- $ $40 per person

🇬🇧 BRITTIP
In the unlikely event you still feel peckish after the Foods of New York tour, head back to Fish at 280 Bleecker Street where you can have six oysters and a glass of wine or beer at the bar for an unbelievable $8.

A great-value three-hour tour, considering the amount of food you eat along the way, and with a friendly atmosphere as they take a maximum of 16.

In Greenwich Village you'll stop to sample the wares of Zito's old-fashioned bread shop and Murray's famous cheese shop and you'll end up at Vintage New York on Broome Street, where you get the chance to taste five wines from New York State. As well as all you'll learn about the food of New York, especially of the Italian community, you'll gain hints about architecture and properties in the Village and visit a real speakeasy. Alternatively, you can choose to go on a tour of the Chelsea Gourmet Market and the West Village Meatpacking area (Thurs–Sun) or Central Greenwich Village and Soho tour (Fri and Sat). Not surprising that it won Citysearch's Best City Tour 2007.

SAVORY SOJOURNS
Chelsea
- ✉ 155 West 13th Street
- ☎ 212-691 7314 or 888-9SAVORY toll free
- 🖰 www.savorysojourns.com
- $ $95–190

For a unique insight into the fine foods and culinary skills of some of New York's finest restaurants, Savory Sojourns promises to give you an insider's guide to New York's best culinary and cultural destinations followed by a great slap-up meal. Some even include a cookery lesson and can last around four hours. Areas covered include Upper East Side, Chinatown, Little Italy, Soho, Lower East Side, Greenwich Village, Flatiron and Chelsea Market, Financial District, Hell's Kitchen, The Bronx, Brooklyn and Harlem. They also offer a whole range of other tours from exclusive customised shopping trips with fashion industry experts to unique behind-the-scenes tours of New York's art scene and evenings of jazz and gourmet dining. If you don't like the sound of any of these, you can request your own.

The Wall Street Bull

INSIDER TOURS

Some of the most interesting New York tours are led by residents who have unique inside perspectives that they are willing to share on everything from shopping to a haircut. Here is a fascinating selection:

KRAMER'S REALITY TOUR
West Midtown

- ✉ The Producer's Club, 358 West 44th Street between 8th and 9th Avenues
- ☎ 212-268 5525 or toll free 1800 KRAMERS/572 6377
- ⌁ www.kennykramer.com
- 🚗 Subway A, C, E to 42nd Street/Penn Station
- ⏲ Sat noon, Sun (on holiday weekends) noon; check site for winter availability
- $ $37.50 plus $2 service charge

The real Kramer behind the *Seinfeld* character has come out of the woodwork and invented his own three-hour tour based on all the *Seinfeld* spots in the city. Kenny Kramer will answer questions, share backstage gossip and the real-life incidents behind the show. Book early as this tour sells out weeks in advance. It starts from The Producers Club Theater, 358 West 44th Street between 8th and 9th Avenue, a short walk from Times Square.

MYSTICAL WORLD OF HASSIDIC JEWS
Brooklyn

- ✉ Chassidic Discovery Welcome Center, 305 Kingston Avenue
- ☎ 718-953 5244
- ⌁ www.jewishtours.com
- 🚗 Subway 3 to Kingston Avenue
- ⏲ Sun 10am–1pm for individuals or Sun–Fri for groups
- $ $36 adults, $18 children (12 and under); three-hour tour includes a kosher deli lunch

---

Chassidic Discovery Welcome Center

BRITTIP
It's easy to get to the Chassidic Discovery Welcome Center by the 3 train (the red line). Allow an hour from Midtown. The subway exit is right by the synagogue and you simply walk a few yards up Kingston Avenue to two brown doors just by a bookshop. There is no dress code, but it would be inappropriate for a woman to turn up in a sleeveless top.

The Lubavitcher Jews in Crown Heights, Brooklyn, are focused on sharing what they have with the outside world, providing a unique opportunity to get an insight into a Chassidic community. Guided by Rabbi Beryl Epstein, a person with a charming manner and great sense of humour, you'll hear about the history of the Hassidic Jews; visit the synagogue to learn about some of the Jewish customs and traditions; watch a scribe working on a Torah scroll; and see the Rebbe's library, a Matzoh bakery and a Hassidic art gallery. A real insight into a fascinating culture.

BRITTIP
The Kingston Avenue subway stop for the Chassidic tour is just one away from Eastern Parkway, the stop for the Brooklyn Museum (page 267) and the Botanic Garden (page 266) – both great places to visit on a Sunday afternoon.

ROCK 'N' ROLL WALKING TOUR
East Village

- ☎ 212-696 6578
- ⌁ www.rockjunket.com
- ⏲ Mon–Fri by appointment; Sat 1pm
- $ Tickets $25

Die-hard rockers and liggers Bobby Pinn and Ginger Ali lead these fun tours around East Village's legendary punk, rock and glam nightspots. Rock Junket also does tours of Union Square and the West Village and artist-specific tours for the Beatles and Bob Dylan.

BRITTIP
If you're feeling peckish after your Rock Junket tour, www.rock junket.com's NYC Guide has a list of cool joints serving food for $10.

Columbia University Library

WALKING TOURS

ADVENTURE ON A SHOESTRING
- ✉ 300 West 53rd Street
- ☎ 212-265 2663
- 🚇 Varies depending on area
- ⏰ Every day, rain or shine
- $ $5

The 'granddaddy' of walking tours, Adventure has been going strong for nearly 45 years, offering two-hour tours of many Manhattan neighbourhoods, as well as outlying areas that are less familiar to tourists, such as Astoria, the Greek section of the borough of Queens, and Hoboken, a new artists' centre in New Jersey. Two of the most popular tours are Haunted Greenwich Village and Hell's Kitchen. Theme tours, such as those based on Marilyn Monroe's New York and Jacqueline Kennedy Onassis's New York are also favourites.

ALLIANCE FOR DOWNTOWN NEW YORK
Financial District
- ✉ Tours start at the steps of the US Custom House, 1 Bowling Green
- ☎ 212-606 4064
- 🚇 www.downtownny.com
- 🚇 Subway 4, 5 to Bowling Green
- ⏰ Thurs and Sat, noon

Just turn up to take this free 90-minute Wall Street Walking Tour exploring the birthplace of New York, including the Customs House, Trinity Church, Wall Street and the Stock Exchange, among others. The Alliance has been doing much work on sprucing up the entire district and employs red-hatted security staff/cleaners who are there to help you find your way around.

BIG ONION WALKING TOURS
Brooklyn
- ✉ 476 13th Street, Brooklyn, NY 11215
- ☎ 212-439 1090
- 🚇 www.bigonion.com
- ⏰ Jun–Aug Wed–Sun, Sept–May Thurs–Sun, 1pm; always call after 9.30am on the morning of your tour to verify the schedule as it will change if the weather is bad
- $ $15 adults, $12 seniors, $10 students

Amazingly informative ethnic, architectural and historic walking tours, which you can just turn up to (apart from the multi-ethnic eating tour, which needs to be reserved). Led by American history graduates, they're not for the faint-hearted – you'll be on your feet for a full two hours – but they are informative and gem packed. Tours are offered on a rotating basis and begin in different spots. Call the main number or check the website to see what's on the schedule. Options include the East Village, Central Park, Gay New York, Financial District, Gramercy Park and Union Square, Greenwich Village, Historic Lower Manhattan, Historic TriBeCa, the Jewish Lower East Side, Presidential New York, Revolutionary New York, Roosevelt Island, SoHo and NoLiTa and the Upper East Side. 'Big Onion' was the nickname given to New York in the 19th century by non-New Yorkers who believed it smelled of the immigrants' heavily spiced cooking!

The Original Multi-ethnic Eating Tour: Meet on the corner of Essex and Delancey Streets in front of Olympic Diner. Subway J, M, Z to Essex Street; F to Delancey Street.

> **BRITTIP**
> Some Big Onion tours can get a little crowded. If so, make sure you stand as close to the guide as possible to hear their pearls of wisdom and you'll still get good value for money.

This is one of the more popular tours, which covers the Lower East Side, Chinatown and Little Italy, and it is offered frequently. You pay a $5 supplement for nosh, which includes delicious spicy tofu, mozzarella and Italian sausage, chicken and shrimp and vegetarian dim sum, plus other

WHAT TO SEE AND DO

BRITTIP
If you need to visit the loo before you start this tour, head for the McDonald's diagonally opposite the meeting point.

food favourites of the locals, all eaten outdoors in the streets. The tour also provides a good way to get an insight into areas you may find confusing to wander around on your own.

It gives a fascinating insight into the history of the area and what modern-day life is like – for instance, what was once a very high-density Jewish area is now populated by Puerto Rican immigrants; and before the Jews and Chinese, there were the English, Irish and Italians.

You'll end the tour deep in the heart of Chinatown outside a vegetarian food centre and the Chinese Gourmet Bakery. It may be good to stop for a drink before you head off to the nearest subway stations at Canal Street, where you have the choice of the A, C, E, J, M, N, Q, R, W, 6 lines to take you just about anywhere in Manhattan.

Historic Harlem Tour: Meet at the Schomburg Center at 135th Street and Lenox Avenue. Subway 2, 3 to 135th Street. A brilliant way to get to know a major chunk of Harlem, its history, politics and modern-day life through the eyes of a history graduate.

BRITTIP
For a cheap and delicious meal before the Harlem tour, head for Mannas at 486 Lenox Avenue at 134th Street (www.mannas restaurants.com). After the tour you'll find yourself outside the Apollo Theater. Just a few metres east is a clean McDonald's with TVs on one wall (and a loo on the opposite side).

You'll hear about Martin Luther King and other African-American activists, local literary salons and gospel churches. You'll learn about the old neighbourhood joints of the Renny and Savoy, how the Apollo Theater and Cotton Clubs were only open to rich white folk looking for an 'authentic black' experience, the campaign to allow black people to work in the shops they bought their food and clothes from, Striver's

Metropolitan Life Insurance Company

Row, the architecture and the old black pressure groups, two of whose buildings now house beauty parlours.

The 'Official' Gangs of New York Tour: Meet on the south-east corner of Broadway and Chambers Street at City Hall Park, Sun 1pm. Subway 1, 2, 3, 9, A, C, E to Chambers Street, R, W to City Hall.

This very popular tour is (like the movie of the same name) inspired by Herbert Asbury's

---

GREETINGS FROM THE BIG APPLE
It's certainly a novel idea and it's also a winner – the Big Apple Greeters are ready to take you on a personalised and entirely customised tour of any part of New York any day of the week and it costs absolutely nothing. The idea is simple: New Yorkers who are proud of their neighbourhoods and have some spare time will spend between two and four hours with you. They will take you round any area you like and help you do just what you want to do, be it shopping, sightseeing or eating and drinking, rain or shine. Just make your request at least 10 working days (preferably three–four weeks) in advance and confirmation will be awaiting you upon your arrival at your hotel. The service is entirely free and no Big Apple Greeters worth their salt will take a tip, but I found that it was no problem to get them to agree to letting me pay for a spot of brunch or lunch, and they're well worth it. Tel 212-669 8159, email visitrequest@bigapplegreeter.org, www.bigapplegreeter.org.

1927 classic book *The Gangs of New York*, and Martin Scorsese's film, which explores every aspect of the city's dark and brutal gang culture that had its centre at Five Points.

◄►◄ BRITTIP

A 21st-century version of the audio walking tour is available any time you want by mobile phone from Talking Street (877–870 TOUR/8687, www.talkingstreet.com). The sultry tones of Sigourney Weaver will show you around Lower Manhattan and the World Trade Center. Other tours include Lower East Side and Staten Island Ferry.

Led in conjunction with Miramax Films, the tour paints a vivid and detailed picture of life for the immigrants in the 1800s and includes stops at Paradise Square, Murderer's Alley and other sites associated with Bill 'The Butcher' Poole, William Tweed and the police and draft riots. Before you get too carried away with any notions of glamour, just bear in mind that the area then was so unsafe that the police refused to go anywhere near it. There was at least one murder a night and ordinary people were so scared of leaving their tenements they even buried their dead in their buildings.

JOYCE GOLD HISTORY TOURS OF NEW YORK
Chelsea
- ✉ 141 West 17th Street
- ☎ 212-242 5762
- 🖥 www.nyctours.com
- ⏱ Various starting times for two–three hours, no reservations needed
- $ $15

Specialists in unusual, in-depth weekend forays into 30 of the city's distinctive neighbourhoods all led by Joyce herself. Fascinating tours include the East Village, culture and counter-culture, Downtown graveyards, Greenwich Village highlights, Colonial New York and Noshing Manhattan.

LITERARY PUB CRAWL
West Village
- ✉ Meet at the White Horse Tavern, 567 Hudson Street at 11th Street
- ☎ 212-613 5796
- 🖥 www.bakerloo.org/pubcrawl
- 🚇 Subway 1, 9 to Christopher Street
- ⏱ Sat 2pm

$ $15 adults; $12 students/seniors
Tour four pubs in the Village area that attracted writers, poets and artists, among them Dylan Thomas, Ernest Hemingway, John Steinbeck, e e cummings, Jack Kerouac, Jackson Pollock and Frank McCourt.

MUNICIPAL ART SOCIETY
Midtown
- ✉ 457 Madison Avenue between at 51st Street
- ☎ 212-439 1049
- 🖥 www.mas.org
- 🚇 Subway 6 to 51st Street
- $ $15

Walking tours taking in both historic and architectural sites, focusing on skyscrapers in different neighbourhoods, as well as tours around Staten Island. Well-run, informative and very enjoyable. Telephone or visit the website for more information.

SUSANSEZ NYC WALKABOUTS
Bronx
- ☎ 917-509 3111
- 🖥 www.dbsystemsgroup.com/susansez
- 🚇 Subway various starting points
- $ $30–40

Walking tours off the beaten track in Manhattan and the outer boroughs, the Bronx and Queens led by native New Yorker Susan Birnbaum including curiosities such as the Knitting Crawl Walkabout and Pushcarts to Funky Swank, around the Lower East Side.

TALK–A–WALK
- ✉ Floor 10, 30 Waterside Plaza, NY 10010
- ☎ 212-686 0356
- $ $9.95

These walking tour guides on cassettes are an excellent way to learn about the city. It's best to order them before you leave home and they will be posted to you. There is a choice of four, each looking at the history and the architecture of historic Downtown.

Rose Center at the Natural History Museum

BRIT'S GUIDE AWARDS FOR SIGHTSEEING TOURS

Best overview of city:
By bus: New York Visions (page 79)
By boat: Circle Line (page 77)
Best walking tours:
The Big Onion (page 83)
Best for thrills:
The *Beast* speedboat (page 77)
Liberty Helicopter Tours (page 75)
Most eye-opening experiences:
The Mystical World of Hassidic Jews (page 82)
Best for foodies:
Foods of New York around Greenwich Village and Chelsea Gourmet Market (page 81)
Best for free:
Big Apple Greeters (see page 84)
Best for romance:
Bateaux New York dinner cruises around Manhattan (page 78)
Best TV show tours:
Sex and the City (page 79)
Kramer's Reality Tour (page 82)
Most offbeat:
Hub Station/Pony Pedicabs (page 76)
Best musical tours:
Harlem Gospel Tour (page 78)
Soul Food And Jazz (page 78)

TYING THE KNOT IN NEW YORK

If you're thinking about getting married in the city, then you've picked a top spot, because the Big Apple is one of the most popular places for Brits to marry abroad thanks to an abundance of romantic venues.

WHERE TO WED

There's no shortage of exceptional places to marry in New York, but it's best to get it all booked before you go. Most upmarket hotels will accommodate weddings, so be sure to contact the ones we've listed in our accommodation section (Chapter 11) for some of the best in town.

BRITTIP

To get a better grasp of all the great NYC wedding venues check out the Great Places Directory at www.greatplacesdirectory.com, for ceremony and reception locations.

As well as hotels, other places you may want to investigate include Gotham Hall (1356 Broadway at 36th Street, 212-244 4300, www.gothamhallevents.com), a historic landmark in Midtown Manhattan that is a great venue for occasions such as weddings, holding from 25 to more than 1,000 guests. There's also **The Lighthouse** and **Pier Sixty** at Chelsea Piers (23rd Street at 12th Avenue, 212-336 6144, www.pier sixty.com) for an intimate affair to remember. Or how about *New York Aquarium* (610 Surf Avenue at West 8th Street, Coney Island, Brooklyn, 718-265 FISH, www.nyaquarium.com) for a more unusual location?

For an outdoor ceremony, the obvious place is Central Park, and it's not as tricky to organise as you might imagine. The Central Park Conservancy (212-310 6600, www.centralparknyc.org) grants the permits for wedding ceremonies and photography in venues throughout the park, including the lovely Conservatory Garden and Shakespeare Garden.

THE KNOW-HOW

For all the legal aspects of a wedding in New York, such as the minimum age, documentation and costs, contact the NYC Marriage Bureau (City Clerk of New York in Manhattan), Municipal Building, 1 Center Street, 2nd Floor South, NY 10007. Tel 212-669 8090, www.nycmarriagebureau.com.

TOP FIVE PLACES TO PROPOSE

Just in case you haven't got down on one knee yet, here are some of the most idyllic spots to ask for her (or his) hand:

- Top of the Empire State Building before sunset (page 61)

- By the boating lake in Central Park (page 266)

- In a helicopter flying over the city (page 75)

- The penthouse suite of the Four Seasons (page 226)

- A $10,000 Martini at the Algonquin Hotel (page 240) – it's a mix of vodka, vermouth, olive and ice, except that the ice is a sparkling diamond from the hotel's jeweller!

CHAPTER 5

Museums and Galleries

New York has some of the best-known museums and galleries in the world, so it's little wonder that some tourists come to the Big Apple just to visit these major attractions. Among the names that you are most likely to be familiar with are the Metropolitan Museum of Art (the Met), the Solomon R Guggenheim Museum, Whitney Museum of Modern Art and the Museum of Modern Art (MoMA). Most of the major museums are located around a specific area of the city called the Museum Mile, which stretches along 5th Avenue on the Upper East Side north to 89th Street.

As befits a city that is famed for regenerating itself, none of the museums sits on its laurels. There is a constant wave of refurbishment and renewal, as well as cutting-edge exhibitions that inspire people to keep returning. In 2003, the American Museum of Natural History spent $25-million updating its Milstein Hall of Ocean Life using state-of-the-art technology, and MoMA reopened in 2004 after a multi-million-dollar refurbishment and expansion, in a much-praised new building designed by architect Yoshio Taniguchi. The Museum of Jewish Heritage and the Morgan Library both reopened in 2006 after extensive refurbishment. Highlights of the cultural calendar in the first half of 2007, for example, included *Annie Leibovitz: A Photographer's Life, 1990–2005* at the Brooklyn Museum, an examination of Gold at the American Museum of Natural History from pre-Colombian jewellery to Olympic medals and Doug Aitken's *sleepwalkers* was projected on the façades of the Museum of Modern Art.

On top of this, a raft of new museums have opened, including the American Folk Art Museum, the Chelsea Art Museum, the Annette Green Museum dedicated to the history of perfumes, the Jewish Children's Museum in Brooklyn and the National Cartoon Museum (formerly the International Museum of Cartoon Art), which opened in 2007 in the Empire State Building as the largest museum of cartoon art in the world.

The biggest events of 2007 were the opening of the New Greek and Roman Galleries in an entire wing of The Metropolitan Museum of Art in April and the new Elizabeth A Sackler Centre for Feminist Art, which opened at The Brooklyn Museum in March. The National Sports Museum, the first ever museum dedicated to sports, will add to the new openings in April 2008.

Of course, it does mean there is a lot to choose from and, especially if you're on your first visit to New York, you'll want to ensure you don't waste any time. It should also be noted that many cultural institutions in New York go to great lengths to make themselves family friendly, so don't let having youngsters in tow put you off visiting.

A–Z OF MUSEUMS

AMERICAN FOLK ART MUSEUM
Midtown
- ✉ 45 West 53rd Street between 5th and 6th Avenues
- ☎ 212-265 1040
- 🖱 www.folkartmuseum.org
- 🚇 Subway E, V to 5th Avenue/53rd Street; B, D, F, V to 47th–50th Streets, Rockefeller Center
- ⏲ Tues–Sun 10.30am–5.30pm, except Fri 10.30am–7.30pm, closed Mon
- $ $9 adults, $7 students and seniors, under 12s and members free; free Fri after 5.30pm

The first entirely new museum building in New York since 1966, the museum's

---

American Museum of Natural History

TOP FIVE MUSEUMS

Here are the *Brit's Guide* favourites. They cover a broad spectrum, from the history of New York City to art and the world's amazing natural history, and each is a true delight in itself.

American Museum of Natural History: page 88

Intrepid Sea–Air–Space Museum: page 95

Metropolitan Museum of Art (The Met): page 98

Museum of Modern Art (MoMA): page 101

Solomon R Guggenheim Museum: page 108

$18 million structure was designed by award-winning architects Tod Williams and Billy Tsien. This new museum provides an excellent opportunity to get to grips with American folk art. It also gives an insight into America's history and cultural heritage from the perspective of these arts. The temporary exhibition *Gilded Lions and Jeweled Horses: The Synagogue to the Carousel* runs October 2007–23 March 2008.

AMERICAN MUSEUM OF NATURAL HISTORY
Upper West Side

✉ Central Park West at 79th Street
☎ 212-769 5100
🖱 www.amnh.org
🚇 Subway B, C to 81st Street/Museum of Natural History; 1, 9 to 79th Street
🕐 10am–5.45pm daily
$ Suggested price $14 adults, $10.50 students and seniors, $8 under 13s. The most comprehensive package, which includes the space shows, IMAX films and special exhibitions, costs $30 adults, $23 seniors and students and $19 children.

Like the Metropolitan, this is an epic of a museum, best seen in parts rather than attempting the whole (although you'll save money if you do!). It provides an

American Museum of Natural History

entertaining and amazingly detailed yet comprehensive overview of life on Earth and beyond, and has undergone an enormous amount of growth and redevelopment over the last few years.

One of its most famous permanent exhibitions is the **Milstein Hall of Ocean Life**, given a $25-million redesign in 2003 using the latest marine technology and a $15-million donation by museum trustee Irma Milstein and her husband Paul. Using the hall's massive blue whale as its centrepiece, lights, video and sound effects create the illusion of being immersed in the ocean to provide a breathtaking view of life under the sea.

Other permanent exhibits include the dinosaur collection, the $50-million gem collection including the famous Star of India blue sapphire, the Native American section and the seven continents. Much fun is to be had using the many interactive computer exhibits, for instance, to travel back in time in order to trace the roots of evolution.

In addition to the main museum, there is the **Rose Center for Earth and Space** – a spectacular museum within a museum housed in glass, which incorporates the newly revamped **Hayden Planetarium** as its centrepiece. This is the place to come to learn about both the inner workings of Earth and the outer reaches of the universe. The **Big Bang Theater** gives a dramatic recreation of the first minutes of the origins of the universe and is found inside a 26.5m (87ft) wide sphere that appears to float in a glass-walled ceiling.

Here you will also find the **Space Theater**, billed as the most technologically advanced in the world, which shows incredibly realistic views of outer space. The two films are *Passport to the Universe*, in which Tom Hanks narrates an amazing journey from Earth to the edge of the universe, and *The Search For Life: Are We Alone?*, narrated by Hollywood star Harrison Ford, which takes you on an incredible journey in a search of the answers.

The **IMAX Theater** also shows a wonderful range of breathtaking movies

🇬🇧 BRITTIP

Some museums offer free or half price entry late afternoon/evenings on Fridays (see list on page 94). It's worth checking for if you are on a budget.

BRITTIP

Avoid the restaurants at the American Museum of Natural History and head round the corner to Pizzeria Uno in Columbus Avenue at 81st Street (page 181) where you'll find far more friendly-family fare at excellent prices.

examining different aspects of life on earth.

Don't miss the **Butterfly Conservatory**, full of stunning tropical butterflies, which is open every year from the beginning of October to the end of May. Walk among the lush vegetation and flowering plants to see some of the 500 free-living butterflies, but do remember it's 27°C (80°F) inside, so leave your coat in the cloakroom.

Each weekend it offers workshops and astronomy programmes for children from 4 upwards, and in the Discovery Room, open weekdays 1.30pm–5.10pm and weekends 10.30am–1.30pm and 2.15–5.10pm, children from 5 to 12 can have a hands-on, behind-the- scenes look at science. There's also a **Gateway Storytime** on Monday mornings 10.30am and 11.15am, which is free with admission. Teenagers will be enthralled with SonicVision, a digitally animated alternative music show on Friday and Saturday evenings at the Hayden Planetarium from 7.30pm and 8.30pm and *A Field Trip to the Moon*, when the ground shakes beneath them on a thrilling rocket launch simulation at 10am on Wednesdays. Science and nature programmes are offered on weekdays to children 2½ years to 10, and the museum offers themed day camps on everything from frogs to robotics.

BRITTIP

If you take the B or C train to 81st Street you can go straight into the American Museum of Natural History from the subway. Just follow the tiled signs in the mosaic wall to avoid the crowds, heat or cold.

Check out the website first to see which activities will be available during your visit to the city. The museum also runs field trips, such as bird watching, bug (insect) hunts or flower inspections in the adjacent Central Park.

AMERICAN MUSEUM OF THE MOVING IMAGE
Queens

It's only a short trip to Queens and worth a visit here if you are into films. See page 275.

ASIA SOCIETY
Midtown East

- ✉ 725 Park Avenue at 70th Street
- ☎ 212-288 6400
- ⌖ www.asiasociety.org
- 🚇 Subway 6 to 68th Street/Hunter College, F to 63rd Street/Lexington Avenue
- ⏲ Tues–Sun 11am–6pm, Fri 11am–9pm, closed Mon
- $ $10 adults, $7 seniors, $5 students, under 16s free; free Fri 6–9pm

Founded in 1956 by John D Rockefeller III with his collection of Asian art, in 2006 the society celebrated its 50th birthday. It aims to build an awareness of the 30 Pan-Asian countries, which include Japan, New Zealand, Australia and the Pacific Islands. To this end it runs films, lectures and seminars in conjunction with its exhibitions and even has a regular schedule of Asian musicians who play at the museum. Daily guided tours of exhibitions are Tues–Fri 12.30pm and 2.30pm, Fri also 6.30pm, Sat 12.30pm, Sun 2.30pm (although 12.30pm and 6.30pm tours are suspended from 4th July to Labor Day, first Monday in September).

BROOKLYN CHILDREN'S MUSEUM

New York's first children's museum, it has a great programme of events and workshops and is particularly worth the trip if you are on a family holiday. See page 267.

BROOKLYN MUSEUM

One of the largest museums in the world and the oldest art museum in the country, it underwent a facelift in 2004 to become the most visitor-friendly museum in the Big Apple. It is easy to reach in Brooklyn, if you have the time to plan it into your schedule. See page 267.

Mosaic art on the MTA subway

BRILLIANT MUSEUMS FOR ALL THE FAMILY

New York is fantastic when it comes to providing exciting and engaging museums and museum activities for children. They not only have plenty of dedicated children's museums, but also many of the major New York museums put their wealth of resources to great use by offering fabulous events and activities that both entertain and educate children from as young as four right up to teens. Below are some of the best:

Children's Museums:

Adult Museums:

CARNEGIE HALL/ROSE MUSEUM
Midtown
- ✉ 2nd Floor, 154 West 57th Street
- ☎ 212-903 9629
- 🖰 www.carnegiehall.org
- 🚇 Subway A B, C, D, 1 to Columbus Circle, N, Q, R, W to 57th Street/7th Avenue, E to 7th Avenue
- ◷ Daily 11am–4.30pm, closed in summer
- $ Free

In 1991, the Rose Museum opened as part of Carnegie Hall's 100th anniversary celebrations. On the First Tier level of Carnegie Hall, the museum houses special temporary exhibitions, as well as a permanent collection of over a century's worth of photographs, letters, musical quotes and Carnegie Hall archival material, from programmes to unique memorabilia, including items from the famous names that have walked through 'the house that music built.'

CHELSEA ART MUSEUM
Chelsea
- ✉ 556 West 22nd Street at 11th Avenue
- ☎ 212-255 0719
- 🖰 www.chelseaartmuseum.org
- 🚇 Subway C, E to West 23rd Street
- ◷ Tues–Sat noon–6pm, except Thurs noon–8pm, closed Sun and Mon
- $ $6 adults, $3 seniors and students, free for children under 16

In the heart of Chelsea's new gallery district, this new medium-sized, three-storey museum provides a venue for abstract work by artists who have not been exhibited in New York before and for mid-size travelling shows from Europe and smaller American museums. It is also the new home of the Miotte Foundation, which is dedicated to the conservation of Informal Art (abstract) works by Jean Miotte, who has had a studio in SoHo since 1978.

🇬🇧 BRITTIP
Be prepared to prove you're a student if you want to make the most of discounted admissions to the museums.

CHILDREN'S MUSEUM OF MANHATTAN
Upper West Side
- ✉ The Tisch Building, 212 West 83rd Street between Broadway and Amsterdam Avenue
- ☎ 212-721 1234
- 🖰 www.cmom.org
- 🚇 Subway 1 to 79th or 86th Street, B, C to 81st Street
- ◷ Tues–Sun 10am–5pm, closed Mon; call or check the website for summer and school holiday hours
- $ $9 adults and children, $6 seniors, infants under 1 free

🇬🇧 BRITTIP
After you've explored CMOM, cross the street for a light snack and drinks at Café Lalo (212-496 6031, www.cafelalo.com), which serves up great cakes and is featured in the Meg Ryan and Tom Hanks movie *You've Got Mail.*

The CMOM is entirely dedicated to children under the age of 10. This is a fabulous place and almost worth a visit even if you don't

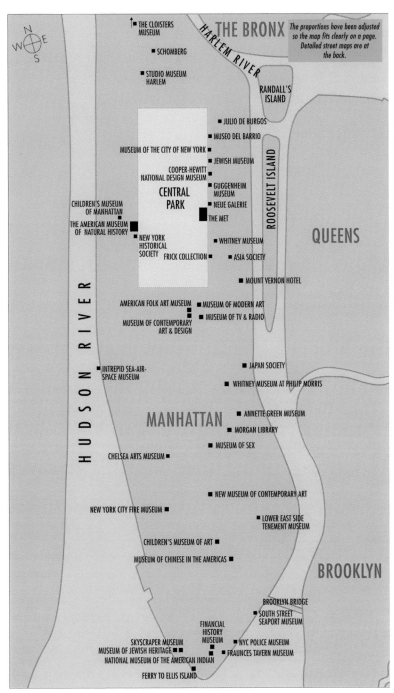

Museums in Manhattan

BRITTIP

Many museums are closed on national holidays, such as Thanksgiving Day on the fourth Thursday of November. Be sure to check first before you make your trip.

have kids. Its mission statement is to inspire children and their families to learn about themselves and our culturally diverse world through a unique environment of interactive exhibits and programmes.

They certainly achieve it with their inspiring exhibits. Past exhibits have included the zany and fun-filled **Body Odyssey**, which showed children just what they're made of. In May 2007, **Gods, Myths and Mortals** was launched and will stay for 18 months, designed to introduce six to ten-year-olds to the exciting world of ancient Greece, with original artefacts and replicas of figures such as the Trojan Horse, multimedia experiences, games and hands-on interactive stations.

Current exhibits include **Playworks** from birth to 4 years where children feed alphabet letters to a talking baby dragon, drive a city fire truck, paint on a 6ft (1.8m) art wall or crawl through a challenge course. Weather-permitting, in the spring and summer **City Splash** allows all ages to play with water, whether it be racing boats down a zigzag stream or painting a masterpiece with water.

The Cloisters Arcade

CHILDREN'S MUSEUM OF THE ARTS
Little Italy

- ✉ 182 Lafayette Street between Broome and Grand Streets
- ☎ 212-941 9198
- 🖰 www.cmany.org
- 🚇 Subway N, R to Prince Street, B, D, F, Q to Broadway/Lafayette Street; 6 to Spring Street
- ◷ Wed, Fri and Sun noon–5pm, Thurs noon–6pm, closed Mon and Tues
- $ $8, free for infants under 1 and seniors

Under 7s can have an artistic ball with art computers, an art playground and a giant floor-to-ceiling chalkboard at this place, which is more like a giant playroom than a museum. There are also regular performing arts workshops led by local artists. A visit here is the perfect way to combine a shopping trip to SoHo for you with fun for the kids!

THE CLOISTERS
Washington Heights

- ✉ Fort Tyron Park, Fort Washington Avenue at Margaret Corbin Plaza
- ☎ 212-923 3700
- 🖰 www.metmuseum.org
- 🚇 Subway 1, 6 to 86th Street
- ◷ Mar–Oct Tues–Sun 9.30am–5.15pm, Nov–Feb Tues–Sun 9.30am–4.45pm
- $ Suggested donation $20 adults (includes free same-day admission to the Metropolitan Museum of Art (page 98), $15 seniors and $10 students, under 12s free with an adult

Rockefeller cash allowed the Metropolitan Museum to buy this beautiful red-tiled Romanesque-style building 70 years ago. Now it is purely devoted to medieval art and architecture, including five cloisters – hence the name – some from ruined French monasteries, dating from the 12th to the 15th centuries. It is stunning to look at and houses some really exciting exhibits, probably the most famous being the Unicorn Tapestries, woven in Brussels in the 1500s. Tours Tues–Fri 3pm, Sun noon are included in the price of admission and an audio guide or podcast is available. There are also gallery talks, films and medieval concerts in the wonderful 12th-century chapel from Spain.

The Cloisters has a series of free workshops for children aged from 4 to 12, on the first and third Saturday of the month 1–2pm. Subjects include medieval feasts and celebrations and stories from the Middle Ages.

BRITTIP

It's a long way north to The Cloisters, so make the most of your time by combining it with a walking tour of Harlem (page 84).

COOPER-HEWITT NATIONAL DESIGN MUSEUM

Upper East Side

- ✉ 2 East 91st Street at 5th Avenue
- ☎ 212-849 8400
- ⌂ www.cooperhewitt.org
- 🚇 Subway 4, 5, 6 to 86th or 96th Street
- ⏱ Tues–Thurs 10am–5pm, Fri 10am–9pm, Sat 10am–6pm, Sun noon–6pm
- $ $12 adults, $9 students and seniors; under 12s free

The only American museum devoted entirely to historic and contemporary design, the Cooper-Hewitt's international collection covers everything from applied arts and industrial design to drawings, prints, textiles and wall coverings. Take time to look at the exterior of the building itself, which was designed in a Georgian style for tycoon Andrew Carnegie and at the time was a triumph of modern engineering.

DAHESH MUSEUM OF ART

Midtown East

- ✉ 580 Madison Avenue between 56th and 57th Streets
- ☎ 212-759 0606
- ⌂ www.daheshmuseum.org
- 🚇 Subway 4, 5, 6 to 59th Street, F, Q, N, R, W to 57th Street, E, V to Fifth Avenue, A, B, C, D, 1, 9 to Columbus Circle
- ⏱ Tues–Sun 11am–6pm; open until 9pm on first Thurs of each month, closed Mon
- $ $10 adults, $6 students, $8 seniors, free children under 12 and first Thurs of month 6–9pm

BRITTIP

The stylish Café Opaline on the mezzanine, overlooking Madison Avenue, in the Dahesh Museum of Art is a good place for a snack or afternoon tea (2.30–5.30pm) with city views.

Established in 1995, Dahesh is the only museum in America solely dedicated to 19th and 20th-century European art. It occupies three storeys of architect Edward Larrabee

Barnes's black granite IBM building. Dahesh was a Lebanese writer and philosopher known as Salim Achi; his collection of over 3,000 works of art was moved to the US in 1975 from Beirut because of unrest.

EDWYNN HOUK GALLERY

Lower East Side

- ✉ 4th Floor, 745 5th Avenue between 57th and 58th Streets
- ☎ 212-750 7070
- ⌂ www.houkgallery.com
- 🚇 Subway N, R, W to 5th Avenue/59th Street
- ⏱ Tues–Sat 11am–6pm
- $ Free admission

A delightful gallery for photography enthusiasts with both vintage and contemporary prints on display and for sale from the likes of Man Ray, Henri Cartier-Bresson and Annie Leibovitz.

EL MUSEO DEL BARRIO

Spanish Harlem

- ✉ Heckscher Building, 1230 5th Avenue at 104th Street
- ☎ 212-831 7272
- ⌂ www.elmuseo.org
- 🚇 Subway 6 to 103rd Street, 2, 3 to 110th Street/Lenox Avenue
- ⏱ Wed–Sun 11am–5pm, closed Mon and Tues
- $ Suggested donation $6 adults, $4 students and seniors, under 12s free with an adult

Opened in 1969 by a group of Puerto Rican parents, teachers and artists, it houses 8,000 objects of Caribbean and Latin American art from pre-Colombian times to date. Exhibits include musical instruments, miniature houses, dolls and masks, as well as posters, paintings and sculptures. Every January it stages the Three Kings' Day Parade with lively music, colourful costumes and a theatre programme.

Fraunces Tavern Museum

ELLIS ISLAND IMMIGRATION MUSEUM
Battery Park

The most visited museum in New York, this is worth dedicating a good portion of the day to, combining it with the Statue of Liberty nearby (see page 60).

FORBES MAGAZINE GALLERIES
Financial District

- ✉ 62 Fifth Avenue at 12th Street
- ☎ 212-206 5548
- 🖰 www.forbesgalleries.com
- 🚗 Subway A, B, C, D, E, 1, 9 from West to 14th Street, or 4, 5, 6, N, R from East to 14th Street
- ⏲ Tues–Sat 10am–4pm, except Thurs (group tours only), closed Sun and Mon
- $ Free

The Forbes Magazine Galleries at the magazine's headquarters showcase The Forbes Collection of home and business furnishings, decorative accessories, gifts, jewellery, books, toy boats, miniature soldiers, the Monopoly game, presidential manuscripts and fine art.

FRAUNCES TAVERN MUSEUM
Financial District

- ✉ 54 Pearl Street at Broad Street, 1st and 2nd floors
- ☎ 212-425 1778
- 🖰 www.frauncestavernmuseum.org
- 🚗 Subway J, M, Z to Broad Street; 4, 5 to Bowling Green; 1, 9 to South Ferry
- ⏲ Tues–Fri 12am–5pm, Sat 10am–5pm
- $ $4 adults, $3 children and seniors, under 6s free

Ellis Island Immigration Museum

GETTING IN FREE

No charge is made for admission to the following museums, so they make a great addition to your itinerary:

Carnegie Hall/Rose Museum: (page 90)

Forbes Magazine Galleries: (page 94)

National Museum of the American Indian: (page 104)

Schomburg Center for Research In Black Culture: (page 107)

Whitney Museum of American Art at Philip Morris: (page 110)

In addition to this, many museums offer times – usually on a Friday – when you can get in free or pay a voluntary donation of whatever you wish:

American Folk Art Museum: 5.30–9pm Friday (page 87)

Asia Society: 6–9pm Friday (page 87)

Frick Collection: after 6pm on certain Fridays (page 95)

International Center of Photography: 5–8pm Friday (page 95)

Jewish Museum: 5–8pm Thursday (page 96)

When New York was (briefly) capital of America, the Fraunces Tavern housed the Departments of Foreign Affairs, Treasury and War and was where George Washington delivered his famous farewell speech to his officers. Now, nestled among the skyscrapers of the Financial District, this 18th-century Georgian building, along with four adjacent 19th-century buildings, houses a fine museum dedicated to the study of early American history and culture. Among the collection of artefacts, paintings, drawings and documents from the revolutionary era is a lock of Washington's hair and one of his false teeth. Although well preserved, it is New York's oldest surviving building and an awful lot of restoration work has been done to keep its 1783 façade. Guided tours need to be booked in advance.

◀🇬🇧 BRITTIP

Don't miss the cosy restaurant at the Fraunces Tavern Museum. It serves lovely food in a stately tourist environment.

FRICK COLLECTION
Midtown East

✉ 1 East 70th Street at 5th Avenue

☎ 212-288 0700

🖰 www.frick.org

🚇 Subway 4, 5, 6 to 68th Street

🕐 Tues–Sat 10am–6pm, Sun 11am–5pm, closed Mon

$ $15 adults, $10 seniors, $5 students; pay what you wish 11am–1pm on Sundays; admission includes ArtPhone audio guide

Henry Clay Frick (1849–1919) was a fascinating man who, obsessed with making money, built up a massive fortune with the Carnegie Steel Company. His sole interest outside the business was art and, as his wealth grew, so did his fabulous collection of European art, which he hung in his palatial mansion on 5th Avenue. Despite having a reputation as an ungenerous man, he bequeathed both the pictures and his mock-18th century European mansion to the public when he died.

There are 16 galleries displaying this priceless collection of masterpieces from the 14th to 19th centuries, including some of the best-known paintings by the European masters. Unusually, the pictures aren't displayed by period or style, but in the way that Frick would have hung them in his home, giving an insight into the lives of New York's rich in the Gilded Age. The Fragonard Room shows the large Fragonard paintings, as well as 18th-century furniture and porcelain. Paintings by Holbein, El Greco, Titian and Bellini are in the Living Room, while in the sky-lit West Gallery you'll find landscapes by Constable and portraits by Rembrandt, as well as a collection of rare Limoges enamels.

INTERNATIONAL CENTER OF PHOTOGRAPHY
Midtown

✉ 1133 Avenue of the Americas at 43rd Street

☎ 212-857 0000

🖰 www.icp.org

🚇 Subway B, D, F, V to 42nd Street

🕐 Tues–Thurs 10am–6pm, Fri 10am–8pm, Sat and Sun 10am–6pm, closed Mon

$ $12 adults, $8 students and seniors, under 12s free; voluntary contribution Fri 5pm–8pm

The ICP is a school and a museum. It houses some excellent exhibitions, such as legendary photographer Larry Clark's work, as well as a permanent collection that consists of more than 100,000 photographs from famous photographers spanning decades. It has a large body of work by Henri Cartier-Bresson and some original prints by Weegee, who photographed crime scenes and New York nightlife in the 1930s and 1940s. Film screenings, artists' talks and lectures are on offer, as well as a store selling some stunning prints.

INTREPID SEA-AIR-SPACE MUSEUM
Clinton

✉ USS *Intrepid*, Pier 86, west end of 46th Street at the Hudson River

☎ 212-245 0072

🖰 www.intrepidmuseum.org

🚇 Subway A, C, E, N, Q, R, S, W, 1, 2, 3, 7, 9 to 42nd Street, then the M42 bus to 12th Avenue

🕐 Closed for renovation and refurbishment until October 2008

A thoroughly enjoyable museum around a ship berthed on the Hudson River, which appeals to all ages. All the staff are very friendly and there are former members of the crew around the ship who are happy to give an insight into its history and life on board. *Intrepid* was one of 24 Second World War US aircraft carriers and, despite incidents of serious damage to these ships, none of them was ever sunk. *Intrepid*'s worst moment came on 25 November 1944, when two kamikaze pilots hit the ship five minutes apart, killing 69 men and seriously injuring 85 others.

Intrepid Sea-Air-Space Museum

MUSEUMS AND GALLERIES

BRITTIP
The only way to see the submarine at *Intrepid* is on a tour and long queues build up very quickly, so get there early and see it before anything else.

The second plane exploded on the hangar deck and the ship burned for about six hours, but *Intrepid* made it back to America for repairs and returned to the war. Stories of life on board are told by veterans at film screenings throughout the ship and there are also plenty of hands-on exhibits such as 'Kamikaze: Day of Darkness, Day of Light' to keep children happy. One of the best exhibits is the F-18 navy jet flight simulator, which costs an extra $5 but is great fun. The museum also exhibits the British Airways Concorde. The Museum is currently closed for refurbishment until October 2008.

JAPAN SOCIETY
Midtown East
- ✉ 333 East 47th Street between 1st and 2nd Avenues
- ☎ 212-832 1155
- 🖰 www.japansociety.org
- 🚇 Subway E, V to Lexington Avenue/53rd Street; 6 to 51st or 42nd Street
- ⏱ Tues–Thurs 11am–6pm, Fri 11am–9pm, Sat and Sun 11am–5pm, closed Mon
- $ $12 adults, $10 students and seniors, under 16s free

The perfect place to feed your yearnings for all things Japanese, from textiles and modern photography to historical ceramics, paintings, glass and metalworks. The ideal combination of Zen and now, away from the Samurai swords and kimonos, its traditional Japanese garden is a Zen-like space with calming waterfall, reflecting pool and bamboo garden. The Society, which celebrated a century of existence in 2007, also has Japanese traditional and contemporary arts performances, films and lectures.

Jewish Museum

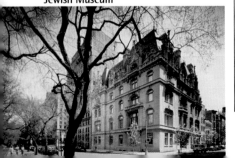

JEWISH MUSEUM
Upper East Side
- ✉ 1109 Fifth Avenue at 92nd Street
- ☎ 212-423 3200
- 🖰 www.thejewishmuseum.org
- 🚇 Subway 4, 5, 6 to 86th Street
- ⏱ Sat–Wed 11am–5.45pm, Thurs 11am–8pm, closed Fri
- $ $12 adults, $10 seniors, $7.50 students, children under 12 free. Free on Saturdays.

The largest Jewish museum in the Western Hemisphere, the Jewish museum, set in a chateau-style residence, lays on impressive annual exhibitions. The core exhibit is called Culture and Continuity: The Jewish Journey and sets out how the Jewish people have survived through the centuries and explores the essence of Jewish identity. Many of the objects were actually rescued from European synagogues before the Second World War. It covers 4,000 years of history with an emphasis on art and culture both ancient and modern. Audio guides, including a family gallery guide, are free with admission. As well as talks, performances and films, there's a free drop-in arts and crafts session for children aged 3 upwards from 1pm–4pm every Sunday and live music every Thursday during the summer.

BRITTIP
Treat yourself to delicious kosher cuisine at the Jewish Museum's trendy Café Weissman (closed on Fridays).

JEWISH CHILDREN'S MUSEUM
This specialist museum has its home in child-friendly Brooklyn. See page 271.

JULIA DE BURGOS LATINO CULTURAL CENTER
Spanish Harlem
- ✉ 1680 Lexington Avenue between 105th and 106th Street
- ☎ 212-831 4333
- 🚇 Subway 6 to 110th Street
- ⏱ Tues–Sat noon–6pm, Thurs 1–7pm
- $ Free

Another excellent location to see works by Latino artists, named in honour of the woman considered to have been the greatest poet in Puerto Rico. Around the museum, look out for pavement artwork by James de la Vega, a young local artist.

LOWER EAST SIDE TENEMENT MUSEUM

Lower East Side

✉ 108 Orchard Street between Broome and Delancey Streets

☎ 212-431 0233

🖰 www.tenement.org

🚍 Subway F to Delancey Street; B, D to Grand Street; J, M, Z to Essex Street

🕑 Visitor Center open Mon 11am–5.30pm, Tues–Fri 11am–6pm, Sat and Sun 10.45am–6pm; the museum can only be visited via a tour, best to book in advance

$ $15 adults, $11 students and seniors for one-hour tour; 2 Ticket Combo: $23 adults, $16 students and seniors; 3-ticket combo: $32 adults, $22 students and seniors. Under 5s free.

After they had gone through Ellis Island, what happened to many of those millions of immigrants? They ended up in tenements on the Lower East Side of New York, and this is the museum that tells their poignant stories. You'll get the chance to see four re-created apartments in a typical, five-storey tenement, giving a good insight into the living conditions of the seekers of the American Dream.

BRITTIP

Before you take one of the walking tours at the Lower East Side Tenement Museum, it is well worth watching the slide show and film.

The museum consists of several tenement houses – essentially America's first public housing, predating almost every housing law in the US – that are accessible only via the tours. These houses contain several apartments, faithfully restored and complete with furniture and clothes. It's a must-see in order to understand not only this neighbourhood, which continues to function as a launching pad for fresh generations of artists and retailers, but also the American success story.

The tour **Piecing It Together: Immigrants in the Garment Industry** examines the life of the Polish Levine family, who ran a garment shop in their apartment in the early 1900s, plus the stories of other immigrants involved in the garment industry from the 1930s to the present day. The tour **Getting By: Weathering the Great**

Depressions of 1873 and 1929 focuses on the German-Jewish Gumpertz family in the 1870s and the Sicilian-Catholic Baldizzi family in the 1930s and how they forged new lives for themselves in America.

The best tour for children is the 45-minute **Confino Living History Tour**, which aims to bring history to life. The apartment re-creates the life of the Sephardic-Jewish Confino family from Kastoria in Greece in 1916. Teenager Victoria Confino welcomes visitors as if they were newly arrived immigrants and she were teaching them how to adapt to life in America. Along the way you can touch any items in the apartment, try on period clothing and foxtrot to music played on an authentic wind-up Victrola.

BRITTIP

Holiday-time tours at the Lower East Side Tenement Museum sell out quickly, so book as far in advance as possible.

Kitchen conversations after selected tours are where participants get a chance to share thoughts and explore thoughts arising from the tours over a drink and a snack. If you have time, the Lower East Side Stories walking tour operated by the museum is an eye-opening look at past and present in this fascinating neighbourhood.

Lower East Side Tenement Museum

MUSEUMS AND GALLERIES

TOP FIVE GALLERIES FOR MODERN ART

New York is a hotbed of artistic talent so if you want to pick up some original work while you are there, or just look at some, here are five places to head for.

Andrew Kreps Gallery: Chelsea
- ✉ 525 West 22nd Street
- ☎ 212-741 8849
- ⊕ www.andrewkreps.com.
- 🚇 Subway 23rd Street
- ⊙ Tues–Sat 10am–6pm

An innovative band of work on display from artists including Ruth Root and Roe Ethridge.

Deitch Projects: SoHo
- ✉ 18 Wooster Street between Canal and Grand Streets
- ☎ 212-343 7300
- ⊕ www.deitch.com
- 🚇 Subway N, R, W to Prince Street; B, D, F, V to Broadway/Lafayette Street
- ⊙ Tues–Sat noon–6pm
- $ Free

Jeffrey Deitch's gallery is worth a peep if you are in SoHo – a second gallery has opened at 76 Grand Street. Focusing on large-scale installations, and sometimes live spectacles, by contemporary artists (including Yoko Ono) working in all kinds of media, it's not as scary as it sounds.

Gagosian Gallery: Chelsea
- ✉ 555 West 24th Street between 10th and 11th Avenues
- ☎ 212-741 1111
- ⊕ www.gagosian.com
- ⊙ Tues–Sat 10am–6pm
- $ Free

An excellent, vast gallery that opened in 1999, it has featured exhibitions of work by the likes of Damien Hirst.

Maccarone Inc: Lower East Side
- ✉ 630 Greenwich Street
- S 212-431 4977
- ⊕ www.maccarone.net
- 🚇 Subway 1, R, W to Rector Street
- ⊙ Wed–Sun noon–6pm
- $ Free

Spread over four floors, this cool gallery run by Michele Maccarone features work by up-and-coming local and European artists.

Projectile Gallery: 57th Street
- ✉ 3rd floor, 37 West 57th Street between 5th and 6th Avenues
- ☎ 212-688 1585
- 🚇 Subway F to 57th Street. N, R, W to 5th Avenue/59th Street.
- ⊙ Mon–Sat noon–6pm.
- $ Free

A darling of the art world since it opened in 1998, it features work by hotter than hot young artists.

MERCHANT'S HOUSE MUSEUM
East Village
- ✉ 29 East 4th Street between Lafayette and Bowery Streets
- ☎ 212-777 1089
- ⊕ www.merchantshouse.com
- 🚇 Subway 6 to Astor Place
- ⊙ Thurs–Mon 12pm–5pm, closed Tues and Wed
- $ $8 adults, $5 students and seniors, children under 12 free

Built in 1832, this was home to prosperous merchant Seabury Tredwell and his family for over 100 years and is the city's only preserved 19th-century home, complete with original furnishings and decor, and a resident ghost!

METROPOLITAN MUSEUM OF ART
Upper East Side
- ✉ 1000 5th Avenue at 82nd Street
- ☎ 212-535 7710
- ⊕ www.metmuseum.org
- 🚇 Subway 1, 6 to 86th Street
- ⊙ Tues–Thurs, Sun 9.30am–5.30pm, Fri and Sat 9.30am–9pm, closed Mon; no pushchairs on Sun
- $ Suggested price $20 adults, $10 students and $15 seniors, under 12s free with an adult, same-day entrance to The Cloisters (page 92) is included in the price

New York is filled with fine museums, yet this really is the mother of them all and you could easily spend a well-paced day here.

Metropolitan Museum of Art

But with 5,000 years of art – around two million pieces – from all Continents spread over two million sq ft, it's best to admit that you won't be able to see it all in one visit: and therein lies your perfect excuse to return to the city! If you can, visit the website in advance to get a good feel for the layout. Think about what you really want to see and write out a list of priorities, allowing a reasonable amount of time to absorb what each gallery has to offer. Make sure you visit the new Greek and Roman Galleries opened in April 2007 which, with 5,400 objects taking up an entire wing, are the talk of the town.

BRITTIP

Don't miss the Metropolitan's fabulous Roof Garden café filled with sculptures on the fifth floor for stunning views of Central Park, open May–early Sept or take some air in the Ming-style meditative Chinese garden in Astor Court, built with handmade tools by Chinese craftspeople.

A good place to start is with an aspect of American culture, which you will find in the **American Wing**, where there is a wonderful collection of Tiffany's along with US arts and crafts and glorious Neo-Classical sculptures in the garden court. It's one of the Met's most popular areas, with three floors and 25 rooms filled with more than 1,000 paintings by American artists, 600 sculptures and 2,500 drawings. The two real musts are the **Egyptian Art** exhibits and the **Temple of Dendur**, which was built by Egypt to thank the American people after the US helped rescue monuments threatened by the Aswan Dam. Other greats include the **Greek** and **Roman** displays, the **Japanese** and **Chinese** exhibits and the **medieval** art.

BRITTIP

If visiting the Met on Friday or Saturday, you can chill out over cocktails to free live classical music in the Balcony Bar in the afternoon.

The wonderful thing about this museum is that you can wander around by yourself, hire an audio guide for the day ($7 adults, $5 under 12s), which you can use in any order you choose, or bag a free podcast, and

THE MET FOR FAMILIES

This magnificent museum uses various means to make its resources as accessible to children as possible – for free – and provides printed gallery guides and museum hunts at the **Uris Information Desk** on the ground floor near the 81st Street entrance. A whole series of workshops and programmes is available both through the week and at weekends. For exact times and dates, check out the calendar section of the website or call 212-570 3961. Programmes include:

Art Evenings for Families: Conversation and sketching help visitors aged from 6 to 12 to explore the museum's art collection. Sat 6pm–7pm.

Art Mornings for Families: An art adventure through conversation and sketching offered to 5 to 12 year olds and their parents on weekday mornings throughout the summer.

Hello Met!: Children from 5 to 12 and their families are given a stimulating introduction to the Met's encyclopaedic collection through sketching its masterpieces. Sun 2pm–3pm.

Look Again!: The history, meaning and cultural aspects of art in the museum are explored through chats, drawing and, from time to time, performances for children from 5 to 12 (plus an adult) on Sat, Sun, 11am–12.30pm, 2pm–3.30pm.

Start With Art at the Met: Children aged 3 to 7 (plus an adult) meet at the Uris tiered seating area to explore art at the Met through storytelling, sketching and games. Tues and Thurs 2.30pm–3.30pm, Wed 3.30pm–4.30pm, Fri 4pm–5pm, Sat 10am–11am.

take advantage of a plethora of free tours, talks, and films.

The hour-long Museum Highlights tour leaves from the Great Hall at 2.30pm. Check the calendar on the website in advance for information on the one-hour gallery talks or lectures, which focus on either a special exhibition or one of the permanent collections and films. You do not need to make reservations except for the Saturday afternoon film. The highlight of the programme is **Sunday at the Met** at 3pm, a combination of lectures, film, performances and discussion.

BRITTIP

Child Magazine has recently recognised the Met as the second most family-friendly museum in the US.

MORGAN LIBRARY
Midtown East
✉ 225 Madison Avenue at 36th Street
☎ 212-685-0008
🖰 www.morganlibrary.org
🚗 Subway 6 to 33rd Street, 4, 5, 6, 7 to Grand Central

The Morgan reopened in spring 2006 after a three-year $102 million major expansion and renovation to its already fabulous palazzo-style 1902 building. The glass and steel pavilions designed by Renzo Piano doubled the exhibition space for its fabulous collection which, having started as the private collection of banker, Pierpont Morgan, includes medieval and Renaissance manuscripts; drawings and prints from the 14th century onwards, including: works by Rubens, Degas, Blake and Pollock; ancient Middle Eastern seals and tablets; and original handwritten music manuscripts by Bach, Beethoven, Brahms and Schubert. It also has a new reading room and a central court in the style of an Italian Piazza and offers daily tours, concerts, lectures and films.

Morgan Library

MOUNT VERNON HOTEL MUSEUM AND GARDEN
Upper East Side
✉ 421 East 61st Street between 1st and York Avenues
☎ 212-838 6878
🖰 www.mvhm.org
🚗 Subway 4, 5, 6, N, R to 59th Street/Lexington Avenue
🕐 Tues–Sun 11am–4pm; Tues 6–9pm in summer; closed Aug and some holidays
$ $8 adults, $7 students and seniors, under 12s free

An amazing structure that dates back to the colonial era, this was once the coach house of the daughter of America's second president, John Adams. Dating back to the early 18th-century, it is one of the seven oldest buildings in Manhattan and has been lovingly restored by the Colonial Dames of America who will sometimes be on hand to talk about the furnishings in the house and the park at the back.

MUSEUM OF AMERICAN FINANCE
Lower Manhattan
✉ 48 Wall Street
☎ 212-908 4110
🖰 www.financialhistory.org
🚗 Subway 2, 3, 4, 5 to Wall Street; J, M, to Broad Street, 1, R , W to Rector Street,
🕐 Closed until October 2007
$ Suggested donation $2

Founded in 1998, this museum moved into the former headquarters of the Bank of New York on Wall Street in October 2007, with the banking hall as its new exhibition space, traces the growth of the world's largest financial superpower. It has the largest public museum archive of financial documents in the world and exhibits include rare $100,000 bills. Wow!

MUSEUM OF ART AND DESIGN
Midtown
✉ 40 West 53rd Street between 5th and 6th Avenues
☎ 212-956 3535
🖰 www.madmuseum.org
🚗 Subway E, V to 5th Avenue, B, D to 7th Avenue. N, R to 49th Street
🕐 Daily 10am–6pm, Thurs 10am–8pm
$ $9 adults, $7 students and seniors, under 12s free; pay what you wish Thurs 6pm–8pm

Along with the neighbouring American Folk Art Museum, this museum, formerly known

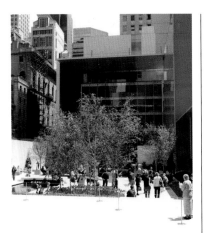

MoMA

as the American Craft Museum, gives a perfect insight into American arts and crafts. It has everything from wood and metal to clay, glass and fibre. In 2006, it revealed plans for a $60 million renovation of the building at 2 Columbus Circle to be its new home from Spring 2008, complete with floor-to-ceiling windows on the ground floor and zigzagged windows on the upper floors.

MUSEUM OF CHINESE IN THE AMERICAS

Chinatown
- ✉ 2nd floor, 70 Mulberry Street on the corner of Bayard Street
- ☎ 212-619 4785
- 🖰 www.moca-nyc.org
- 🚇 Subway N, R, Q, W, J, M, Z and 6 to Canal Street
- 🕐 Tues–Sun noon–6pm
- $ $2 adults, $1 seniors, students and children, under 12s free; Fri free

A fascinating little museum tucked away on the first floor of the community centre. It contains photographs and personal belonging, and talks are given on the history of Chinese immigrants to both North and South America.

MUSEUM OF MODERN ART (MoMA)

Midtown
- ✉ 11 West 53rd Street between 5th and 6th Avenues
- ☎ 212-708 9400
- 🖰 www.moma.org
- 🚇 Subway E, V to 5th Avenue/53rd Street

- 🕐 Sat, Sun, Mon, Weds, Thurs 10.30am–5.30pm, Fri 10.30am–8pm, closed Tues
- $ $20 adults, $16 seniors, $12 students, under 16s free with an adult; Fri 4pm–8pm, pay what you wish

Founded in 1929 by three private citizens including Abby Rockefeller, this was the first museum to devote its entire collection to the modern movement. Since then it has retained its pioneering sense of the new, and was the first museum to see architecture, design, photography and film as art forms. The museum's collection started with a gift of eight prints and one drawing, and dates from the 1880s to the present day and now encompasses more than 150,000 works.

The new-look MoMA opened in November 2004 after a much-praised redesign by Yoshio Taniguchi in time to celebrate its 75th anniversary. The new building, with a stunning atrium and high-ceilinged galleries, is a work of art itself and occupies over 58,000 sq m (630,000 sq ft).

🇬🇧 BRITTIP

For a treat, dine in The Modern, an Alsatian-inspired restaurant, which was recently awarded three stars by *The New York Times.*

If you only have a day, head off with your free audio guide to the fabulous Paintings and Sculpture galleries on two floors. Many of the icons of modern and contemporary art are housed here, including Van Gogh's 'The Starry Night', Monet's 'Water Lilies', Picasso's 'Les Demoiselles' and Andy Warhol's 'Gold Marilyn Monroe'. The photographic galleries are second on most people's list and have exhibits from famous names such as Henri Cartier-Bresson and Man Ray. Films are screened every evening in the two cinemas (cost included in the entrance fee, though you need to get a special ticket to reserve your place) and afternoons and evenings at weekends. Free gallery talks are given Wed–Monday 11am and 1.30pm, plus 6.30pm Fri.

🇬🇧 BRITTIP

The most child-friendly time at the MoMA is July when the Ford Family Programs mean a whole host of weekend activities from Storytime in the Sculpture Garden to Tours for Tweens.

The Family Programs at the MoMA introduce children and their parents to the world of modern art through guided walks, art workshops, artist talks and film screenings. Grab a free Family Activity Guide at the entrance and call 212-708 9805 or email familyprograms@moma.org for a list of scheduled activities. MoMA has dedicated websites for children to familiarise themselves with the art before coming. Five to 8-year-olds can click on www.moma.org/destination and older children can visit http://redstudio.moma.org.

Free Gallery Talks are run for different ages from the museum lobby on Sat and Sun 10.30am–11.15am. Pre-register as early as possible as they are very popular and spaces sell out. They include:

Tours for Fours: Themed sessions for 4-year-olds

A Closer Look for Kids: A look at modern masterpieces and cutting edge contemporary art for 5 to 10-year-olds

Tours for Tweens: Gallery activities, sharing of ideas and opinions about modern and contemporary art for those between 11–14

Other programmes include:

Family Art Workshops: Children (ages vary by date) and their parents explore artworks in the museum, then create their own art in a hands-on workshop

You can just turn up for the **Family Films** shown Sat noon–1pm and for 'tweens' at 2pm. The Abby Aldrich Sculpture Garden is a good place to go for a bit of fresh air and a run around.

MUSEUM OF THE CITY OF NEW YORK
Spanish Harlem
- ✉ 1220 5th Avenue at 103rd Street
- ☎ 212-534 1672
- ⌂ www.mcny.org
- 🚇 Subway 6 to 103rd Street
- ⊙ Tues–Sun 10am–5pm, closed Mon
- $ Suggested donation $20 families, $9 adults, $5 seniors, students and children; under 12s free

🏴 BRITTIP
The Museum of the City of New York is very relaxed about defining your family. Groups can buy a family ticket here even if they are not related.

The entire breadth of New York's history and the people who played parts in its development are celebrated in this fascinating museum, which received The Hundred Year Association of New York's Gold Medal Award in 1982 in recognition of its outstanding contribution to the city. Prints, photographs, paintings, sculptures and even clothing and decorative household objects are used to tell the story of New York City. The museum is particularly noted for its Broadway memorabilia and has period rooms from famous homes such as the bedroom of philanthropist John D Rockefeller, as well as gritty photographs showing the harsh realities of the Depression. The new multimedia presentation that opened in its major renovation and extension in 2006 making the span of history accessible is a good place to start.

MUSEUM OF JEWISH HERITAGE: A LIVING MEMORIAL TO THE HOLOCAUST
Battery Park City
- ✉ 36 Battery Place, Battery Park City
- ☎ 646-437 4200 info; 646-437 4202 tickets
- ⌂ www.mjhnyc.org
- 🚇 Subway 1 to South Ferry; R, W to Whitehall Street; 4, 5 to Bowling Green, J, M, Z to Broad Street
- ⊙ Sun-Tues, Thurs 10am-5.45pm, Wed 10am-8pm, Fri 10am-5pm, and eve of Jewish holidays 10am-3pm, closed Sat and Jewish holidays
- $ $10 adults, $7 seniors, $5 students, under 12s free; free for all Wed 4pm–8pm

🏴 BRITTIP
Before entering the Museum of Jewish Heritage, take a look at the six-sided shape of the tiered roof, a symbolic reminder of the six million who died in the Holocaust and of the Star of David.

Joy, tradition, tragedy and unspeakable horror are the powerful themes of this museum, which tells the moving story of 20th-century Jewish life from the perspective of those who lived it. Created as a living memorial to the Holocaust, it puts the tragedy into the larger context of modern Jewish history and includes 24 original films that feature testimonies from Steven Spielberg's Survivors of the Shoah Visual History Foundation, as well as the museum's own video archive. A family guide to the museum is available and a programme of family events, concerts, lectures and performances is on offer.

BRITTIP
It is worth renting an audio guide at the Museum of Jewish heritage, narrated by Meryl Streep and Itzhak Perlman, cost $5.

MUSEUM OF SEX
Madison Square Park
✉ 233 5th Avenue at 27th Street
☎ 212-689 6337
🖰 www.museumofsex.org
🚇 Subway 6, N, R to 28th Street
🕐 Sun–Fri 11am–6.30pm, Sat 11am–8pm
$ $14.50 adults, $13.50 students and seniors. Minimum age 18 and IDs will be checked

Times Square may have been cleaned up, but the prostitutes are back in Manhattan in force at New York's most audacious museum. Not for the fainthearted, the inaugural exhibition examined how New York City transformed sex in America by exploring the histories of prostitution, burlesque, birth control, obscenity and fetish. This and other exhibitions use selections such as blow-up dolls and bawdy house coins from private and public collections never shown before and if you're in any doubt as to whether this is the museum for you, just bear in mind that some of the material was once confiscated and classified as obscene.

BRITTIP
Special package holiday breaks that include a ticket to this museum are available for guests staying at the nearby Gershwin Hotel. Check out www.gershwin hotel.com for details.

The main collections of the museum include serious works of art by contemporary artists and a massive collection of film, videos, magazines, books and artefacts acquired over 20 years by Ralph Whittington, the former curator of the Library of Congress. Blow-up dolls never had it so good! Clearly the entrance fee is designed to put off casual thrill-seekers and the museum strictly enforces the minimum age requirement. Despite the subject matter, it is a serious institution with an important message about past and present sexual subcultures and our modern attitudes to sex and sexuality.

MUSEUM OF TELEVISION & RADIO
Midtown
✉ 25 West 52nd Street between 5th and 6th Avenues
☎ 212-621 6600
🖰 www.mtr.org
🚇 Subway E, V to 5th Avenue/53rd Street; B, D, F, V to 47th–50th Streets/Rockefeller Center
🕐 Tues–Sun noon–6pm, Thurs noon–8pm, closed Mon
$ $10 adults, $8 students and seniors, $5 under 14s

In addition to the exhibits, the museum also has a daily programme of screenings in two

Madison Square Park

MUSEUMS AND GALLERIES

cinemas and two presentation rooms as well as guided tours. Pick up a copy of the schedules in the lobby on your way in. You can also make an appointment with the library to check out the museum's collection of over 120,000 radio and TV programmes covering more than 85 years before accessing them on the custom-designed database. You won't miss the building – it looks like a giant antique radio set!

NATIONAL ACADEMY OF DESIGN
Midtown

- ✉ 1083 5th Avenue at 89th Street
- ☎ 212-369 4880
- 🖰 www.nationalacademy.org
- 🚗 Subway 4, 5, 6 to 86th Street
- ⏱ Weds, Thurs noon–5pm,; Fri–Sun 11am–6pm, closed Mon and Tues
- $ $10 adults, $5 students and seniors, children free

Both a museum and a design school of fine art, it has the largest collection of 19th and 20th-century American art in the country, comprising more than 5,000 works. Museum tours every Friday at 2pm ($5 per person).

THE NATIONAL CARTOON MUSEUM
Midtown

- ✉ Looking for premises to relocate at time of going to press, check website for updates
- 🖰 www.cartoon.org

The former International Museum of Cartoon Art renamed itself and was relocating to the Empire State Building in 2006, but it proved too expensive. Its collection is now holed up in Connecticut while it seeks permanent New York premises. With over 200,000 original cartoons, 10,000 books and 1,000 hours of animation, it is the largest collection in the world. Highlights include the very first drawings Walt Disney made of Mickey and Minnie Mouse.

National Museum of the American Indian

NATIONAL MUSEUM OF THE AMERICAN INDIAN
Bowling Green/Financial District

- ✉ George Gustav Heye Center, US Custom House, 1 Bowling Green between State and Whitehall Streets
- ☎ 212-514 3700
- 🖰 www.americanindian.si.edu
- 🚗 Subway 4, 5 to Bowling Green; 1, 9 to South Ferry
- ⏱ Daily 10am–5pm, Thurs 10am–8pm
- $ Free

The first museum dedicated entirely to Native American history, art, performing art and culture housed in one of America's finest Beaux Arts Buildings, designed by Cass Gilbert. The collection includes fabulous leather clothing, intricately beaded headdresses, sashes, hats and shoes, explaining the white man's influence on Indian culture, as well as their own centuries-old traditions. Despite the size and grandness of the beautiful building, it has only 500 pieces on display and thus seems quite small. However, it is very well laid out and the explanations of each piece have usually been given by Native Americans. It also has a lively programme of events such as plays, music and dance performances, lectures and crafts workshops and daily film screenings on contemporary Native American life, one especially designed for families.

NATIONAL SPORTS MUSEUM
Lower Manhattan

- ✉ 26 Broadway at the base of the Canyon of Heroes, at the starting point for the ferry to the Statue of Liberty and Ellis Island
- ☎ 212-837 7950
- 🖰 www.thesportsmuseum.com
- 🚗 Subway 1 to South Ferry, 4, 5 to Bowling Green

This first ever dedicated sports museum, with interactive exhibitions and multimedia displays on sports across the ages and throughout the world is expected to open in April 2008, delayed from its original opening date of November 2006. It is developed at a cost of $93 million in the former Cunard Passenger Ship Line building, it brings together exhibits and memorabilia from over 50 single sports halls of fame, museums and organisations across the US. Sports buffs will enjoy seeing the prestigious Heisman Trophy, awarded to some of the most notable athletes of the 20th Century and it includes

Museum Mile Festival

a progressive Women's Hall of Fame, initiated by Billie Jean King and a sports-themed eatery. Check the website for up-to-date information.

NEUE GALERIE MUSEUM FOR GERMAN AND AUSTRIAN ART
Upper East Side

✉ 1048 5th Avenue at 86th Street
☎ 212-628 6200
🖰 www.neuegalerie.org
🚇 Subway 4, 5, 6 to 86th Street at Lexington Avenue; B, C to 86th Street at Central Park West
🕐 Sat, Sun, Mon, Thurs 11am–6pm, Fri 11am–9pm, closed Tues and Wed
$ $15 adults, $10 students and seniors. Under 12s not permitted, under 16s only with an adult

◀▶ BRITTIP
While you're on the Museum Mile, take a pit stop at the fabulous Sabarsky Café in the Neue Galerie, which is open every day except Tuesday. Catch a classical music performance on Wednesday and Thursday afternoons or Friday evenings.

Founded by the late German Expressionist art dealer Serge Sabarsky and chairman of the MoMA board Ronald S Lauder, the 'New Gallery' exhibits fine and decorative arts of Germany and Austria from the first half of the 20th century, on two floors. Think Klimt, Klee and Kandinsky. A real bonus is the building itself – a wonderful Louis XIII-style

Beaux Art landmark once the home of Mrs Grace Vanderbilt. Check out the new Klimt painting, purchased in 2006 for $135 million, the most expensive painting ever sold.

NEW MUSEUM OF CONTEMPORARY ART
Chelsea

✉ 235 The Bowery, Lower East Side
☎ 212-219 1222 (at time of going to press)
🖰 www.newmuseum.org

When they say 'contemporary', they really mean it. All the works exhibited are by living artists, often looking at social issues through modern media and machinery.

The *new* New Museum of Contemporary Art will open in late 2007. Designed by cutting-edge Japanese architects, SANAA, their stunning seven-storey white tower – a stack of rectangular boxes shifted off axis in different directions dressed in silvery metal and punctuated by skylights – was named

◀▶ BRITTIP
At the beginning of June, don't miss the wonderful Museum Mile Festival (tel 212-606 2296, www.museummilefestival.org). On the first Tuesday of the month all nine museums along 5th Avenue – including the Met – are free to the public. The road is closed and the traffic is replaced by live bands, street entertainers and outdoor art activities for children.

one of the top architectural projects of the year in 2003 and is the first museum constructed in Downtown Manhattan in over a century. It will house a theatre, library, learning centre and café, as well as rooftop terraces where you can gaze out on the New York skyline. Check the website for details on visiting.

NEW YORK CITY FIRE MUSEUM
West SoHo
- ✉ 278 Spring Street between Varick and Hudson Streets
- ☎ 212-691 1303
- ⌂ www.nycfiremuseum.org
- 🚇 Subway 1, 9 to Houston Street; C, E to Spring Street
- ⊙ Tues–Sat 10am–5pm, Sun 10am–4pm, closed Mon
- $ $5 adults, $2 students and seniors, $1 under 12s

Technically not a children's museum, though the bright shiny engines are an undoubted hit with youngsters and the young at heart. Housed in the old quarters of Engine 30, here you will find artefacts and fire engines depicting 200 years of city fire-fighting.

NEW YORK CITY POLICE MUSEUM
Bowling Green/Financial District
- ✉ 100 Old Slip between South and Water Streets
- ☎ 212-480 3100
- ⌂ www.nycpolicemuseum.org
- 🚇 Subway 4, 5 to Bowling Green; 2, 3 to Wall Street; 1, 9 to South Ferry/Whitehall
- ⊙ Mon–Sat 10am–5pm, closed Sun
- $ Suggested donation $5 adults, $3 seniors, $2 age 6–18, under 6s free

Opened in January 2000, this museum portraying the 160-year history of the NYPD in the Downtown area is a little corker. It is now permanently housed in the former 1st

Wall Street

BRIT'S GUIDE MUSEUM AWARDS

Most unmissable museum:
Metropolitan Museum of Art (page 98)

Most hands-on museums:
American Museum of Natural History (page 88)
Intrepid Sea-Air-Space Museum (page 94)
Children's Museum of Manhattan (page 90)

Most audacious museum:
Museum of Sex (page 107)

Most amazing museum building:
Solomon R Guggenheim (page 108)

Most unattractive museum building:
Whitney Museum of American Art (page 110)

Most fun bijou museum:
Museum of the City of New York (page 102)

Most tear-jerking museums:
Lower East Side Tenement Museum (page 97)
Museum of Jewish Heritage (page 102)

Precinct building, the oldest cop shop in New York. Highlights include the Mounted Unit – one of the oldest and most prestigious within the NYPD – and the K-9 dog unit. In addition to over 10,000 items of police memorabilia – a line-up of guns, uniforms and badges – there's even the Tommy gun with its original violin case that was used to kill mobster Frankie Yale. Plus, you can have a go at playing detective yourself in the interactive crime scene area. View the NYPD Hall of Heroes, which now has a memorial to the 23 policemen and women who lost their lives in the attack on the World Trade Center in 2001. June 2007 saw the opening of a new exhibition, Policing a Changed City, looking at how the NYPD has used new technology and intelligence gathering to fight crime and terrorism.

NEW YORK CITY TRANSIT MUSEUM
Brooklyn Heights
A great little museum that is particularly popular with children. See page 271.

NEW YORK HALL OF SCIENCE
Queens
A great science museum with demonstrations. See page 276.

NEW YORK HISTORICAL SOCIETY
Upper West Side
- ✉ 170 Central Park West at 77th Street
- ☎ 212-873 3400
- ⌂ www.nyhistory.org
- 🚇 Subway B, C to 81st Street; 1 to 79th Street
- 🕙 Tues–Sun 10am–6pm
- $ $10 adults, $5 students and $7 seniors, under 12s free

When this jewel was formed in 1804 it was the only art museum in the city until the opening of the Metropolitan Museum of Art in 1872. The Historical Society was founded to chronicle New York's history and is home to the world's largest collection of Tiffany stained-glass shades and lamps, two million manuscripts, including letters sent by George Washington during the War of Independence, a lock of his hair and his camp bed. Recent additions include The History Responds exhibition, which contains artefacts and evidence collected from the 11 September attacks.

THE NOGUCHI MUSEUM
The Japanese sculptor's art can be seen at this museum in Queens (see page 277).

P.S. 1 CONTEMPORARY ART CENTER
Long Island City, Queens
A ground-breaking modern art museum. See page 277.

QUEENS COUNTY FARM MUSEUM
Floral Park, Queens
A fun, working historical farm with hayrides. See page 277.

SCHOMBURG CENTER FOR RESEARCH IN BLACK CULTURE
Harlem
- ✉ 515 Malcolm X Boulevard at 135th Street
- ☎ 212-491 2200
- ⌂ www.schomburgcenter.org
- 🚇 Subway 2, 3 to 135th Street
- 🕙 Tues–Sat 10am–6pm, closed Sun and Mon, tours by appointment
- $ Free

Established in 1926 by Arthur Schomburg, this museum under the umbrella of the New York Public Library has more than five million items including books, photographs, manuscripts, art works, films, videos and sound recordings that document the historical and cultural development of black people in the United States, the Caribbean, the Americas, Afric, Europe and Asia over 400 years of migration.

✚ BRITTIP
To see the Schomburg Center at its best, phone or check out the website in advance to find out about film screenings and jazz concerts.

The research unit is open to anyone, while there are exhibitions on art dating back to the 17th century that include masks, paintings and sculptures. Incidentally, the corner of Malcolm X Boulevard, where the Schomburg sits, was once home to Harlem's Speaker's Corner where people used to come and talk about their political beliefs and organisations.

SKYSCRAPER MUSEUM
Battery Park
- ✉ 39 Battery Place
- ☎ 212-968 1961
- ⌂ www.skyscraper.org
- 🚇 Subway 4, 5 to Bowling Green; 1, R, W to South Ferry/Whitehall Street
- 🕙 Wed–Sun 12–6pm
- $ $5 adults, $2.50 seniors and students

In a new home since 2004, this is one of New York's most apt museums, celebrating as it does the city's rich architectural heritage and examining what historic forces and which individuals shaped the different skylines of its past. Through exhibitions,

Schomburg Center

programmes, publications and walking tours, the museum offers a fascinating insight into how individual buildings were created, complete with detailed information about how the contractors bid for the work, what was involved and how the building work was executed, all with comprehensive photographic illustrations.

Since 1997, the museum has presented exhibitions in temporary spaces – two vacant banking halls on Wall Street in the heart of New York's historic Financial District – including Downtown New York, Building The Empire State and Big Buildings. The exhibitions are surprisingly moving as they manage to convey the very real human sacrifices and energy put into creating these incredible edifices. Most moving of all was its recent homage to the Twin Towers, which marked the entire 30-year history of the World Trade Center. In its current space is a Ground Zero Viewing Wall.

SOLOMON R GUGGENHEIM MUSEUM

Upper East Side

- ✉ 1071 Fifth Avenue at 89th Street
- ☎ 212-423 3500
- ⌐ www.guggenheim.org
- 🚇 Subway 4, 5, 6 to 86th Street
- ⏱ Sat–Wed 10am–5.45pm, Fri 10am–7.45pm, closed Thurs
- $ $18 adults, $15 students and senior citizens, under 12s free. Fri 5.45pm–7.45pm by donation.

The Guggenheim Museum in New York is probably best known for its beautiful spiral-shaped, space age building, which was designed by 'organic' architect Frank Lloyd Wright. Considered one of the greatest

---

THE INSIDE STORY

If you haven't much time, try a one-hour tour of museums. From January to March and July to September, the **Insider's Hour** gives you a quick peek around the most diverse art collections and interactive exhibits. Participating institutions include the Metropolitan Museum of Art (page 98), Lower East Side Tenement Museum (page 97), Intrepid Sea-Air-Space Museum (page 94), American Museum of Natural History (page 88), Museum of Modern Art (page 101), Museum of Jewish Heritage (page 102) and National Museum of the American Indian (page 104).

---

architectural achievements of the 20th century, it is one of the youngest buildings in the city to be designated a New York City landmark. Walk by it at night if you get the chance, to see the glass layers in its shell-like façade lit up like a rainbow. It has been under restoration since 2005 but should be complete by the end of 2007, in time for its 50th Anniversary in 2009.

It houses one of the world's largest collections of Kandinsky, as well as works by Chagall, Klee, Picasso, Cézanne, Degas, Gauguin and Manet. It also has Peggy Guggenheim's entire collection of cubist, surrealist and abstract expressionist art and impressive temporary exhibitions.

◄ ► BRITTIP

It's best to take the elevator to the skylight at the top of The Guggenheim and wind down the central spiral ramp that passes works by major artists from the mid-19th to the 21st century.

Audio tours and free tours by the museum staff, gallery talks and screenings are included in the price of admission. Every second Sunday, the Guggenheim offers interactive family tours for 5–10-year-olds from 10.30am–noon ($15 per family, call 212-423 3587 to preregister), as well as a series of fascinating paid-for workshops They include Digital Workshops for both 7–11-year-olds and 14–18-year-olds, who get real hands-on experience exploring The Shapes of Space exhibition to weeklong art mini-camps in summer. The museum installed A Year with Children 2007: Selected Works from Learning through Art in May.

Solomon R Guggenheim Museum

South Street Seaport Museum

◀◀▶ BRITTIP

Check out the Guggenheim's sculpture gallery for some of the best views of Central Park.

SONY WONDER TECHNOLOGY LAB

✉ Sony Plaza, 56th Street and Madison Avenue
☎ 212-833 8100
🖳 www.sonywondertechlab.com
🚗 Subway E, V to 5th Avenue, F to 57th Street, 4, 5, 6, N, R to 59th Street
🕐 Tues–Sat 10am–5pm, Sun noon–5pm, closed Mon
$ Free, but you must book your time in advance

A technology museum with four floors of interactive exhibits with robots and lots of hi-tech entertainment, adults will love playing here as much as kids. Reservations only though, so book well in advance.

SOUTH STREET SEAPORT MUSEUM

Financial District
✉ 12 Fulton Street at South Street
☎ 212-748 8600
🖳 www.southstseaport.org
🚗 Subway A, C to Broadway/Nassau Street; 2, 3, 4, 5, J, Z, M to Fulton Street
🕐 Summer (Apr–Oct) Tues–Sun 10am–6pm; winter (Nov–Mar) Fri–Sun

10am–noon galleries only, noon–5pm galleries and ships. Mon 10am–5pm galleries only.
$ $8 adults, $6 seniors and students, $4 children (5–12) including all tours, films, galleries and museum-owned ships. Discounted entrance on winter Mon.

A sprawling mass of galleries, 19th-century buildings, a visitors' centre and a selection of ships in imposing warehouses built in 1813, gives an insight into life in the olden days of New York. This world-class museum along the East River offers walking tours around this historic area, so full of sailors and their ships in the 19th century, it was called the 'street of sails'. It is also the venue for a series of free outdoor summer concerts held almost nightly.

STUDIO MUSEUM IN HARLEM

Harlem
✉ 144 West 125th Street between 7th and Lenox Avenues
☎ 212-864 4500
🖳 www.studiomuseum.org
🚗 Subway A, B, C, D, 2, 3, 4, 5, 6 to 125th Street
🕐 Wed–Fri noon–6pm, Sat 10am–6pm, Sun noon–6pm, closed Mon–Tues
$ $7 adults, $3 students and seniors, under 12s free

Works of art by African-American artists in a beautiful space. The photographic archive gives a fascinating glimpse into Harlem history and lectures, children's programmes and a film festival combine to fulfil its mission to be the major centre for African-American art.

VAN CORTLANDT HOUSE MUSEUM

The Bronx
Fascinating former family plantation estate-turned museum. See page 274.

Whitney Museum

WHITNEY MUSEUM OF AMERICAN ART
Upper East Side

✉ 945 Madison Avenue at 75th Street
☎ 212-570 3676 or 1-800-WHITNEY
🖰 www.whitney.org
🚗 Subway 6 to 77th Street
🕐 Wed, Thurs 11am–6pm; Fri 1–9pm; Sat, Sun 11am–6pm, closed Mon and Tues
$ $15 adults, $10 students, under 12s free; first Friday of every month 6–9pm pay what you wish, plus musical performances

The Whitney may be housed in one of the most ghastly looking buildings in the world – a series of grey, granite cubes designed by Marcel Breuer – but it has the world's leading collection of 20th-century American art. Yet it all came about almost by accident. Gertrude Vanderbilt Whitney offered her entire collection to the Metropolitan but was turned down, so she decided to set up her own museum. As a result, in 1931, the Whitney was founded with a core group of 700 art objects.

Subsequently, the museum's holdings have been greatly enriched by other purchases and the gifts of other major collectors. It now has a permanent collection of 15,000 works including paintings, sculptures, drawings, prints, photographs and multimedia installations and is still growing.

⚓🇬🇧 BRITTIP
If arriving in even-numbered years (2008), check out the Whitney Biennial, the most significant showcase for contemporary art in America.

As well as the wide range of artists in its collection, the Whitney has huge bodies of works by artists such as Alexander Calder, Edward Hopper, Georgia O'Keefe, Gaston Lachaise and Agnes Martin. It mounts cutting-edge exhibitions, recently Summer of Love: Art of the Psychedelic Era, which finished in September 2007.

Although the Midtown branch (opposite) is known for exhibitions of works by contemporary artists, the main museum still likes to mount cutting-edge exhibitions.

To make the most of your visit, you can take an audio tour or join one of the free daily exhibition tours by museum staff.

The Museum Store in the basement, next to Sarabeth's restaurant, is filled with funky and colourful gifts. There's some great stuff for kids including soap crayons that will wash off baths and tiles and colourful blocks of soap that can be moulded into sculptures.

The Whitney has worked hard to make itself accessible to young children. Free activity guides are provided for families to introduce children and adults to selected works of art and encourage new ways of learning about art together through interactive gallery tours and hands-on activities. **People, Places and Spaces** is the Whitney's family audio guide to works from the Whitney's permanent collection and is included with the admission fee.

Family activities held on select Saturdays. **Look Out Sketch Tours** session from 10.30–11.30am for children aged 6–8 and 7–12 explores different themes through sketching activities. It is best to reserve a place by calling. **Family Fun! Workshops** from 10am–noon feature gallery tours and art projects for children aged 5–10 and their families. Registration is necessary. **Whitney Wees** for families with children aged 4–5 are an interactive experience of looking and sharing and run from 10am–11am and also on select Wednesdays 3pm–4pm.

WHITNEY MUSEUM OF AMERICAN ART AT ALTRIA
Midtown

✉ 120 Park Avenue at 42nd Street
☎ 917-663 2453
⇦ Subway S, 4, 5, 6, 7 to 42nd Street/Grand Central
🕐 Mon-Fri 11am–6pm, Thurs 11am–7.30pm. The Sculpture Court Mon-Sat 7.30am–9.30pm, Sun 11am–7pm
$ Free

The Midtown branch of the Whitney, in the pedestrian plaza opposite Grand Central Station, is devoted to exhibitions of the work of individual contemporary living artists. Lunchtime gallery tours are offered at 1pm and regular artist talks. It also produces Performance on 42nd, an ongoing series of free music, dance, theatre and performance art that you can just turn up to.

CHAPTER 6

Shopping and Beauty

For many people, New York is synonymous with shopping. Yes, there are jaw-dropping buildings, amazing museums and exciting nightlife, but when it comes down to it, New York City is one of the best places in the world to indulge in a spot of retail therapy. You can get a taste of fantastic American service at the fabulous and famous department stores, and shop until you drop for cheaper CDs, clothes, shoes and cameras. Although the city does have some real American malls, like the one at the South Street Seaport, it is better known for its many boutiques.

The distinct atmosphere of each New York neighbourhood is reflected in the type of shopping available there. The upper section of 5th Avenue in the Midtown area is where you will find all the best department stores and other posh shops. Even posher – exclusive, actually – is Madison Avenue, which is where the top American and European designers are based, such as Prada, Valentino and Versace.

BRITTIP

If you like to be ahead of the pack fashion-wise then make a beeline for 30 Vandam (212-929 6454), a boutique store in SoHo that showcases 50 handpicked designers that you may not have heard of now, but you will in the future.

The Villages are excellent for boutique shops that tend to open late but stay open late, too. In **Greenwich Village** you'll find jazz records, rare books and vintage clothing and the **West Village**'s tree-lined streets are full of fine and funky boutiques and popular restaurants that cater to a young, trendy crowd. On the major shopping streets of Bleecker, Broadway and 8th, you'll find everything from antiques to fashion and T-shirt emporiums. There are plenty of up-and-coming designers and second-hand shops in the **East Village**. Try 9th Street for clothes and 7th for young designers.

The **Flatiron District** around 5th Avenue from 14th to 23rd Streets is full of wonderful old buildings that are brimming with one-of-a-kind shops and designer boutiques. **SoHo** has lots of boutiques selling avant-garde fashion and art, plus restaurants and art galleries, all housed in handsome cast-iron 1850s buildings. West Broadway is the main drag, but other important shop-lined streets include Spring, Prince, Green, Mercer and Wooster. High-profile recent openings include Prada and Earl Jeans.

In **TriBeCa** you will find trendsetting boutiques such as the fantastic Issey Miyake flagship store, art galleries and restaurants in an area that combines loft living with commercial activity.

Last but not least is the **Lower East Side**, which is to bargains what Madison Avenue is to high-class acts. Many of the boutiques offer fashion by young designers – some of whom go on to open outlets in the posher areas – and famous-name gear at huge discounts. This whole area reflects the immigrant roots of New York and stands out as a bargain hunter's paradise particularly when the market is open on Sundays. Orchard Street from Houston to Delancey Streets is well known for leather goods, luggage, designer clothes, belts, shoes and fabrics. Ludlow Street is famous for trendy bars, and boutiques filled with clothes by flourishing new designers.

agnès b

TOP FIVE SHOPPING TIPS

If you're on a really tight schedule, call ahead and book appointments with the **personal shoppers** at major stores. They're very helpful and their service is absolutely free. Bargain! Call Macy's on 212-560 3618, Bloomingdale's on 212-705 2000 and Saks on 212-940 4650.

You have a right to a **full refund** on goods you return within 20 days with a valid receipt unless the shop has signs saying otherwise. Always check, though, especially if the item is in a sale.

Call in advance for **opening hours**. Smaller shops downtown – in SoHo, the Villages, Financial District and Lower East Side – tend not to open until noon or 1pm, but are often open as late as 8pm. Many are also closed on Mondays.

You can **avoid sales tax** if you arrange to have your purchases shipped outside of New York State – a facility that is available at larger stores and those that are more tourist orientated.

Watch out for 'Sale' signs on the Midtown section of 5th Avenue in the streets 30s and 40s. Here most of the shop windows are filled with signs that say 'Great Sales!', 'Going Out Of Business!' – yet they have been around for years and are still going strong. In fact, most of what is on sale there can be bought cheaper elsewhere and with a guarantee.

DEPARTMENT STORES

The big department stores in New York City are reliable places to buy good quality, brand-named merchandise at fair prices. These stores usually sell a variety of men's, women's and children's clothing, including designer label items. You can also expect to find cosmetics, small appliances, electronics and household goods. Department stores usually hold end-of-season clearance sales with significant price reductions. Most of the following are in the Midtown area either in or near 5th Avenue. Standard opening times are Mon–Fri 10am–8pm, Sat 10am–7pm, Sun noon–6pm.

BRITTIP

The voltage system is different in America, so any plug-in electrical goods will not work properly in the UK without an adaptor.

5TH AVENUE

Bergdorf Goodman: 754 5th Avenue at 57th Street. Tel 212-753 7300, www.bergdorfgoodman.com. Subway N, R, W to 5th Avenue/59th Street; F to 57th Street.
An air of understated elegance pervades every department – not surprising, given that it has been around for generations. This department store is not only still going strong, but it is also positively booming and has even opened a Bergdorf Goodman Men on the opposite side of the street. Well-known for its classic, high-end, high-priced fashion, homewares and accessories, the

store has recently expanded its offer to include items for a younger (although still affluent!) clientele.

BRITTIP

The only major department store NOT open on a Sunday is Bergdorf Goodman, but it's still well worth a visit on any other day.

Henri Bendel: 712 5th Avenue at 55th Street. Tel 212-247 1100, www.henribendel.com. Subway E, V to 53rd/5th Avenue.
This is a very small department store that's perfect for fashionistas as there are lots of very cool clothes on four compact, easy-to-get-around floors. Bendels, as the style set call it, has Missoni, Matthew Williamson, Michael Kors and Colette Dinigan, but also Street of Shops, which is a set of exclusive in-store boutiques for the likes of Diane Von Furstenberg, and Femmegems Design-Your-Own Gemstone jewellery. There are also accessories, such as hats, hosiery, casual wear lingerie and to top it all Frederic Fekkai – one of NY's top hair stylists – opened a salon on the fourth floor in February 2006.

Lord and Taylor: 424 5th Avenue at 39th Street. Tel 212-391 3344, www.maycompany.com. Subway B, D, F, V to 42nd Street; 7 to 5th Avenue.
A New York shopping institution that started in 1826, with good service and prices far cheaper than Saks, it's great for highlighting American designers. The store is famous for its animated Christmas window displays.

Macy's

Saks Fifth Avenue: 611 5th Avenue at 50th Street. Tel 212-753 4000, www.saksfifthavenue.com. Subway E, V to 5th Avenue/53rd Street.
One of the finest shopping experiences in New York, it also has fabulous views of the Rockefeller Center and is right next door to St Patrick's Cathedral. Saks is a classic and has all of the big names. There's also a fabulous beauty area on the ground floor where you can have a personal consultation and makeover and it now also boasts an Elizabeth Arden Red Door Salon and Spa. There are lots of extras here that make for a truly A-list shopping trip, from wardrobe consultations for men and women, a complimentary package delivery to local hotels and even a taxi and limo service.

BRITTIP
Go for brunch, lunch or afternoon tea at Cafe SFA at Saks for impressive views of the city while you dine. Open Mon–Sat, 11am–5pm (Thurs until 7pm).

Takashimaya: 693 5th Avenue between 54th and 55th Streets. Tel 212-350 0100. Subway N, R to 5th Avenue; 4, 5, 6 to 59th Street.
The New York branch of this hugely expensive Japanese store, filled with truly gorgeous things laid out in a six-storey townhouse building. A must-visit for anyone that adores Japanese clothing, homewares and gifts, and if you want an elegant spot for tea visit The Tea Box, a café in the basement of Takashimaya, which has a superb range of teas and a great selection of teapots to buy.

MEATPACKING DISTRICT
Jeffrey: 449 West 14th Street between 9th and 10th Avenues. Tel 212-206 1272. Subway N, R to 5th Avenue/59th Street.
A boutique department store sounds like an oxymoron, but this little gem, on the edge of the gritty up-and-coming Meatpacking District is packed full of tremendously hip clothes and accessories. It attracts A-list celebrities – note the limousines waiting at the front – and great labels like Dries Van Noten and Balenciaga. The women's shoe department is one of the best in New York.

MIDTOWN–34TH STREET
Macy's: Herald Square at 151 West 34th Street, 6th Avenue and Broadway. Tel 212-695 4400, www.macys.com. Subway B, D, F, N, Q, R, V, W to 34th Street.

BRITTIP
Macy's is the venue for the Thanksgiving Day Parade, Fourth of July Fireworks and a Spring Flower Week in April.

You can get pretty much anything you require, provided you are prepared to hunt, as this is a beast of a gigantic store, filling as it does an entire city block and soaring up ten floors. There are lots of entrances and it's easy to get lost in here, so it's best to select a time and place to meet in-store if you're with a group. If you enter from the Herald Square side, you'll find the Visitors' Center on the mezzanine level up to your left. Here you can pick up a discount card for international shoppers that entitles you to 11 per cent off most goods. Along the way you'll pass the delightful Metropolitan Museum Shop. A favourite area with Brits is the jeans department and, of course, the beauty counters that throng the ground floor. If you're with children, head for the seventh floor where all their needs are catered for, along with the only McDonald's inside a department store in New York. Don't miss the coffee shops, restaurant and food store run by Cucina & Co (page 143).

UPPER EAST SIDE

Barneys: 660 Madison Avenue at 61st Street. Tel 212-826 8900, www.barneys.com. Subway N, R, W to 5th Avenue; 4, 5, 6 to Lexington. Open 10am–8pm every weekday.

A truly up-to-the-minute fashion outlet, this store is filled with all the top designers and a good selection of newer ones. There isn't really a Brit equivalent; the nearest would be Harvey Nichols, but it doesn't come close. It has eight floors of fashion where there's everything from big-name designers to more obscure, but very hip, small labels. There is a branch called Coop on 18th Street in Chelsea, and another one at the World Financial Center in Downtown, but this is the $100-million megastore. Treat yourself to a trip to the Image Studio if you've got the time and money to get a whole new look before heading home. Don't miss it!

◢◣ BRITTIP

If you plan to be in New York in August or March, get on down to the Barneys Warehouse Sale – call ahead for locations or check www.barneys.com.

Bloomingdale's: 1000 3rd Avenue between 59th and 60th Streets. Tel 212-705 2000, www.bloomingdales.com. Subway 4, 5, 6 to 59th Street; N, R to Lexington Avenue.

This is probably the most famous of all 5th Avenue's department stores. You can't go wrong with anything you buy from here, and if you spend over $50, claim your free gift from the brand-new state-of-the-art visitors' centre. You can also have a hotel package delivery with every $250 purchase, there's currency exchange and you can even buy theatre and Metro Cards here! A truly glitzy shop filled with all the right designers, you can now also sample its delights at the new SoHo branch (page 122).

◢◣ BRITTIP

Weekdays before lunchtime are the least crowded time to visit Bloomingdale's and the lower floors tend to be more crowded than the upper floors.

DISCOUNT STORES

Burlington Coat Factory: 707 6th Avenue at 23rd Street. Tel 212-229 1300, www.burlingtoncoatfactory.com. Subway F, V at 23rd Street. Area: Flatiron.

A retail dream for the fashion-conscious and a proper New Yorker's secret. It's a continual designer overstock sale and it does carry more than just coats. There's lots of casual womenswear and menswear, plus formal apparel from names like Calvin Klein, Ralph Lauren, Michael by Michael Kors and DKNY. There are some golden periods, such as the arrival of AG Jeans selling for around one-third of their original price, but you won't know what's in until you hit the rails.

Century 21: 22 Cortlandt Street between Church Street and Broadway. Tel 212-227 9092, www.c21stores.com. Subway 1, 2, 4, 5, A, C to Fulton Street/Broadway Nassau. Area: Financial District.

Excellent discounts on everything from adults' and children's clothing to goods for the home. Arrive early or mid-afternoon to avoid the lunchtime rush.

Daffy's: 462 Broadway (corner Grand). Tel 212-334 7444, www.daffys.com. Subway J, M, Q, W, 2, 6 to Canal Street. Area: SoHo.
335 Madison Avenue at 44th Street. Tel 212-557 4422. Subway S, 4, 5, 6, 7 to 42nd Street/Grand Central. Area: Midtown East.
1311 Broadway at West 34th Street. Tel 212-736 4477. Subway B, D, F, N, Q, R to 34th Street. Area: 34th Street.
125 East 57th Street between Lexington and Park Avenues. Tel 212-376 4477. Subway 4, 5, 6 to 59th Street; N, R, W to Lexington Avenue. Area: Midtown East.

You'll find an amazing range of designer stock from all over the world at all four outlets of this famous discount store, and a hunt could result in a real bargain.

Filene's Basement: 620 6th Avenue between 18th and 19th Streets. Tel 212-620 3100, www.filenesbasement.com. Subway F, V, L to 6th Avenue/14th Street. Area: Union Square.

Part of the Boston-based bargain-basement company, which is one of the country's oldest off-price chains. There's also an outlet on Broadway at West 79th Street in the Upper West Side.

TAXES AND ALLOWANCES

US taxes: Be aware that local taxes will be added to the cost of your purchases when you pay at the till, so don't get too carried away by the often seemingly very low price tags. New York sales tax is around 4 per cent, though it has now been dropped on clothes and shoes costing under $110, while New York state tax is 4 per cent.

UK allowances: Your UK duty-free allowance was raised from £145 to £340 in 2006 and, given the wealth of shopping opportunities, you're likely to exceed this, but don't be tempted to change receipts to show a lesser value as, if you are rumbled, the goods will be confiscated and you'll face a massive fine. In any case, the prices for some goods in America are so cheap that, even once you've paid the duty and VAT on top, they will still work out cheaper than buying the same item in Britain.

Duty can range from 3.5 to 19 per cent depending on the item: for example, computers are charged at 3.5 per cent, golf clubs at 4 per cent, cameras at 5.4 per cent and mountain bikes at a massive 15.8 per cent. You pay this on goods above £145 and then VAT of 17.5 per cent on top of that. Keep your eye on the newspapers though, as the Chancellor has been pushing for a higher allowance for some time and wants the European Union to raise the figure to a more reasonable £1,000 – enough for more than a couple of iPods!

Duty free: Buy your booze from US liquor stores – they're better value than the airports – but remember your allowance is only 1 litre of spirits and two bottles of wine.

Gabay's Outlet: 225 1st Avenue between 13th and 14th Streets. Tel 212-254 3180, www.gabaysoutlet.com. Subway F, V, L to Ave 1.
An East Village gem offering high-end designer fashion at seriously discounted prices. Its shoes and bags are coveted by the fashion pack and often include Manolo, Christian Louboutin and Tod's.

INA: 21 Prince Street between Thompson and Spring Streets. Tel 212-334 9048. Subway C, E to Spring Street; N, R, W to Prince Street. Area: NoLiTa.
A designer resale stock that changes daily and offers discounts of 30–50 per cent per item. You'll be able to get your hands on plenty of model cast-offs, from Manolo shoes to Prada.

Loehmann's: 101 7th Avenue between 16th and 17th Streets. Tel 212-352 0856, www.loehmanns.com. Subway 1, 9 to 18th Street. Area: Chelsea.
A five-storey building filled with bargains – typically 30–65 per cent off – for men and women. Head straight to the top floor for designer labels such as Donna Karan, Calvin Klein and Versace. The other floors feature accessories, bags, clothing and shoes all at great prices.

Pearl River Mart: 477 Broadway between Broome and Grand Streets. Tel 212-431 4770, www.pearlriver.com. Subway R, W at Prince Street. Area: SoHo.
It's moved from its grungy location in Chinatown to a more fashion-conscious location in SoHo, but its Asian-inspired clothes and homewares are still bargain basement prices. Pick up paper lanterns, bamboo blinds, satin slippers, chopstick and rice bowl sets and mandarin-collared jackets for low, low prices.

BRITTIP
To find out about more bargain outlets before you go, log on to http://gonyc.about.com/od/shopping/tp/discount_shop.htm.

SHOPPING TOURS
Arrange a shopping tour of everything from Saks 5th Avenue to little boutiques in SoHo. They're lots of fun, really good value and a must-do for any shopaholic. **Pamela Parisi's Tightwad Treks** aim to have you dressing like a diva on a tight budget. Call her on 516-735 2085, www.theeleganttightwad.com. Rebecca Merritt of **Shop Gotham** will help you get under the city's skin with shopping trips around areas like SoHo and NoLiTa, speed shop the big department stores and get huge discounts in the Garment Center. Call 212-209 3370, www.shopgotham.com. Tours cost from $30.

BRITTIP
If you don't want to go on an organised shopping tour, create your own using the Shopping Walking Tour Map at http://gonyc.about.com.

FASHION

You can find everything in New York from top designers to up-and-coming newcomers. The main shopping areas for fashion are the Upper East Side (for posh), SoHo (for designer), the East Village and Lower East Side (for cheap designer). Call ahead for opening times as many shops do not open until late – but they stay open later in the evening.

CHELSEA

Balenciaga: 542 West 22nd Street at 11th Avenue. Tel 212-206 0872, www.balenciaga.com. Subway C, E to 23rd Street.
The New York flagship store of this popular womenswear label often spotted on the backs of supermodels such as Kate Moss.

Barney's Co-op Store: 236 West 18th Street between 7th and 8th Avenues. Tel 212-593 7800. Subway 1, 2 to 18th Street.
An abundance of edgy, funky styles and accessories for men and women, it's one of the best stores in New York.

Camouflage: 139–141 8th Avenue at 17th Street. Tel 212-691 1750. Subway A, C, E to 14th Street.
Designer menswear store that offers the highlights of the season from labels like Michael Kors, Etro and Marc Jacobs.

Comme des Garcons: 540 West 22nd Street between 10th and 11th Avenues. Tel 212-604 0013. Subway C, E to 23rd Street.
Japanese designer Rei Kawakubo's stark designs are worn by fashion's elite, and the high prices reflect that.

St Mark's Place, East Village

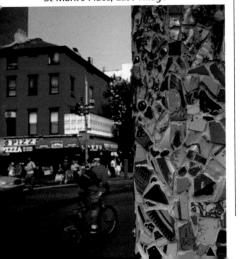

BEST FOR BRIDES

If you're a bride-to-be on the look-out for your dream dress during your trip to the Big Apple, make a beeline for **Kleinfeld** (110 West 20th Street. Tel 212-229 0203, www.kleinfeldbridal.com). This venerable institution has just moved to a new location in the Chelsea neighbourhood and features the world's largest selection of wedding dresses from American and European designers. There's also **Kleinfeld Bridesmaids**, Loft (270 West 38th street, 212-398 5255) to check out if you're travelling with friends. You'll find almost 400 samples in every style, size and fabric imaginable.

If you've got money to burn then you'll also want to make a trip to the Upper East side to visit the **Vera Wang Bridal Salon** (991 Madison Avenue, 212-628 3400, www.verawang.com). The queen of wedding gowns is renowned the world over for her amazing creations and boasts customers such as Sharon Stone. **Saks Fifth Avenue** (see page 113) has an exclusive bridal salon while you'll find less pricey gowns at RK Bridal (318 West 39th Street between 8th and 9th Avenues, www.rkbirdal.com).

EAST VILLAGE

A Cheng: 443 East 9th Street at 1st Avenue. Tel 212-979 7324, www.achengshop.com. Subway L to 1st Avenue.
A mix of smart and street styles from this trendy designer.

Eileen Fisher: 314 East 9th Street between 1st and 2nd Avenues. Tel 212-529 5715, www.eileenfisher.com. Subway L to 1st Avenue.
Casual, maintenance-free clothing that travels anywhere. Lots to choose from, such as T-shirts, jackets, skirts and the co-ordinating colour palettes make matching up items a dream. Lots of other outlets around the city, including SoHo and Midtown East.

Enelra Lingerie: 48 East 7th Street. Tel 212-473 2454. Subway F, V to 2nd Avenue.
Madonna's haunt 20 years ago. Now worth checking out at Halloween when the window displays feature items like full-length latex devil outfits!

Himalayan Vision: 127 2nd Avenue at 7th Street. Tel 212-254 1952. Subway 6 to Astor Place.

Tibetan-style dresses, silk skirts, trousers, tops and hand-knit hats from around $40 can be found in this serene shop.

Jill Anderson: 331 East 9th Street at 1st Avenue. Tel 212-253 1747. Subway 6 to Astor Place.
The sweeping coat-dresses and girly slips are in keeping with the bohemian vibe of the artsy East Village.

Suzette Sundae: 182 Avenue near 11th Street. Tel 212-777 7870, www.suzettesundae.com. Subway L to 1st Avenue.
Lady-like dresses crossed with punk rock is the name of the game at this wonderfully named store. There's a private-label collection hanging alongside pieces from hot designers of the moment.

Trash and Vaudeville: 4 St Mark's Place between 2nd and 3rd Avenues. Tel 212-982 3590. Subway 6 to Astor Place.
Fitting out rock stars like Iggy Pop since the early 1980s, you'll get the East Village look in no time if you step into this punk/grunge paradise. Here you'll find outrageous rubber dresses and shirts, black leather outfits and

plenty of studded gear and footwear to match.

GREENWICH VILLAGE
American Apparel: 712 Broadway at Washington Place (and 12 other outlets in New York). Tel 212-383 2257, www.american apparel.net. Subway N, R to 8th Street.
Stocks a huge selection of slogan T-shirts.

Bang Bang Boutique: 53 8th Street near Broadway. Tel 212-475 8220, www.bang bang.com. Subway 6 to Astor Place.
Fun, way-out clubbing and party gear for men and women.

Patricia Field: 10 East 8th Street between 5th Avenue and University Place. Tel 212-254 1699. Subway A, C, E, F, V, S to West 4th Street.
Once only famous for her outrageous club clobber, Patricia is the designer who created all the fashion for the *Sex And The City* girls. So if you want to emulate Carrie, Mia or Lizzie, then come here to stock up on cool bags and jewellery worn by the cast.

Untitled: 26 West 8th Street between 5th and 6th Avenues. Tel 212-505 9725. Subway A, C, E, F, V, S to West 4th Street.
Contemporary clothing and accessories from exclusive New York designers as well as the likes of Vivienne Westwood.

LOWER EAST SIDE
Alfie Rivington Club: 158 Rivington Street at Clinton Street. Tel 212-3758128. Subway J, M, Z to Essex Street.
A very cool menswear shoe store specialising in trainers with the air of a gentlemen's club; think dark red carpets and low, black leather sofas against the wood-panelled walls. The shoes are displayed in individually lit cubby-holes and there are more behind locked glass cupboards. This is where to shop if you want the very latest designs, way before your friends are likely to even hear about them. Be warned: they get new arrivals each week and don't restock here, so if you see something you like, buy it!

Edith and Daha: 104 Rivington Street at Ludlow Street. Tel 212-979 9992. Subway F to Delancey Street.
This pair of womenswear designers make a

BRITTIP
For info on sample sales in the Lower East Side area, go to www.lowereastsideny.com.

SHOPPING AND BEAUTY

TOP FIVE MOST WANTED AMERICAN LABELS

East Village
Mark Montano: 434 East 9th Street between 1st Avenue and Avenue A. Tel 212-505 0325. Subway 6 to Astor Place.

Drew Barrymore, Johnny Depp and Kate Moss are all fans of the funky designer who uses bright, often vintage, fabrics to create designs with style.

SoHo
Earl Jeans: 160 Mercer Street between Houston and Prince Streets. Tel 212-226 8709, www.earljean.com. Subway N, R to Prince Street; 6 to Spring Street.

Self-taught California designer Suzanne Costas has not only created jeans that actually fit women, but also made them sexy, too. Her ultra-low-slung jeans have been the definitive favourites of stars like Cameron Diaz and Kate Moss.

Marc Jacobs: 163 Mercer Street between Houston and Prince Streets. Tel 212-343 1490, www.marcjacobs.com. Subway N, R to Prince Street.

The darling of supermodels and superwomen, such as movie director Sophia Coppella, Jacobs' style is minimalist and luxurious.

Upper East Side
Calvin Klein: 654 Madison Avenue at 60th Street. Tel 212-292 9000, www.calvinklein.com. Subway N, R to Lexington Avenue; 4, 5, 6 to 59th Street.

CK's leading outlet seems to have enjoyed as much attention from the designers as the clothes themselves!

Donna Karan: 819 Madison Avenue between East 68th and 69th Streets. Tel 212-861 1001, www.donnakaran.com. Subway 6 to 68th Street.

A leading American designer who is best known for her elegant, simple outfits for women. The floating staircase is worth popping in for.

maximum of only 12 copies of each item, so you're pretty much guaranteed not to meet anyone else wearing your cool dress or skirt. A nice touch is that you can watch the clothes being created at the back of the shop.

Nova USA: 100 Stanton Street at Ludlow Street. Tel 212-228 6844. Subway J, M, Z, F to Delancey Street.
Great for basic but brilliant sportswear, Cameron Diaz and Helena Christensen are just two of the many women who stock up on these casually cool bits of kit when they're in Manhattan.

Earl Jeans

MEATPACKING DISTRICT
Alexander McQueen: 417 West 14th Street between 9th Avenue and Washington Street. Tel 212-645 1797, www.alexander mcqueen.com. Subway A, C, E to 14th Street, L to 8th Avenue.
British fashion guru who made his name at Givenchy before designing for Gucci. The clothes are way out and very expensive.

An Earnest Cut & Sew: 821 Washington Street at Gansevoort Street. Tel 212-242 3414, www.earnestsewn.com. Subway A, C, E to 8th Avenue.
High-end denim label Earnest Sewn's opened its first stand-alone store in 2005 and it has been a major hit with trendy young New Yorkers. The major hook here is its customising – you can have pockets, buttons or zips tweaked and fabric added to ensure you get a genuine one-off garment. The service takes two hours and costs $300–350.

Diane von Furstenberg: 385 West 12th Street between Washington Street and West Side Highway. Tel 646-486 4800, www.dvf.com. Subway A, C, E to 8th Avenue.

Flagship store of the queen of the classically sexy silk jersey wrap dress. The dramatic shop, with its draped changing rooms, is worth a visit in its own right.

Stella McCartney: 429 West 14th Street. Tel 212-255 1556, www.stellamccartney.com. Subway A, C, E to West 14th Street.

The famous daughter of a Beatle moved on from shaking up fashion at Chloe to designing under her own label to great acclaim. Her first store in this cool district sees the likes of Liv Tyler and Gwyneth Paltrow when they are shopping in town.

◀🇬🇧▶ BRITTIP

If you long to wear Armani but don't have the bank balance to match, then hunt out one of five AIX Armani Exchange stores in Manhattan, which offer the label's chic, well-made clothes at a fraction of the cost of Armani – www.armani exchange.com. Stores are at 645 and 656 5th Avenue, Time Warner Center (10 Columbus Circle), 129 5th Avenue and 568 Broadway.

MIDTOWN

Alice + Olivia: 80 West 40th Street at 6th Avenue. Tel 212-840 0887, www. Subway B, D, F, V to 42nd Street.

Situated in Midtown West around Bryant Park, this is the place to stock up on latest trends, such as shift dresses and 1960s-inspired minidresses. Has some cute handbags, too.

BOSS Hugo Boss: 717 5th Avenue at 56th Street. Tel 212-485 1800, www.hugo boss.com. Subway N, R to 5th Avenue.

Flagship store of this fashionable menswear label. It has a wide range of the brand's goodies, from sharp suits to coveted watches.

Burberry: 9 East 57th Street between 6th and Madison Avenues. Tel 212-407 7100, www.burberry.com. Subway 4, 5, 6 to 59th Street.

The opening of this fabulous flagship store reflects the resurgence of the great British classic as a trendsetting force in recent years. There's something for everyone here – men, women, teenagers and even children since the introduction of the new tots' clothing line.

Chanel: 15 East 57th Street between 5th and Madison Avenues. Tel 212-385 5050, www.chanel.com. Subway E, V to 5th Avenue.

The enduring French label offers you the chance to buy all the classics from $1,000 suits to quilted handbags and, of course, the famous No 5 perfume.

Gianni Versace: 647 5th Avenue between 51st and 52nd Streets. Tel 212-317 0224, www.versace.com. Subway E, V to 5th Avenue/53rd Street.

A beautiful shop, housed in the former Vanderbilt mansion, selling beautiful clothes for the rich and famous.

Gucci: 685 5th Avenue at 54th Street. Tel 212-826 2600, www.gucci.com. Subway E, V to 5th Avenue/53rd Street.

So you may not be able to afford anything on display, but it's essential to know what 'look' you are trying to achieve when you browse through the copy-cat shops downtown.

Lacoste: 575 Madison Avenue near 56th Street. Tel 212-750 8115, www.lacoste.com. Subway 6 to 51st Street. Also at 608 5th Avenue and 134 Prince Street.

The alligator-logo polo shirts are a classic item to snap up while you're in the Big Apple.

Levi's: 536 Broadway, between Prince and Spring Streets. Area: SoHo. Tel 646-613 1847, www.levi.com. Also at 750 Lexington Avenue. Area: Upper East Side.

If you've ever had trouble finding a pair of jeans that fit you perfectly, come here to be measured and have your jeans custom-made and sent to you.

Lingerie & Company: 1217 3rd Avenue at 70th Street. Tel 212-737 7700. Subway 6 to 68th Street.

A user-friendly shop for a wide choice of gorgeous undies.

Lulu Guinness

. MIDTOWN SHOPS FOR ACCESSORIES

. Veneta: 699 5th Avenue between 54th and 55th Streets. Tel 212-371 5511, www. ttegaveneta.com. Subway E, V to 5th Avenue/53rd Street.
Who wouldn't covet the gorgeous soft leather, logo-free handbags offered at this Italian designer store.

Ferragamo on Madison: 655 Madison Avenue at 52nd Street. Tel 212-759 3822. Subway V to 5th Avenue.
The largest Ferragamo store in the world has an amazing 23,000-plus shoes as well as handbags, scarves and ties.

Jimmy Choo: 645 5th Avenue at 51st Street. Tel 212-593 0800, www.jimmychoo.com. Subway E, V to 5th Avenue/53rd Street.
Originally part of Jimmy's upscale ready-to-wear 'chain' of stores – think London, Paris, Los Angeles and New York – the designer has sold up most of his shares and gone back to his couture clients. Now the thongs (flip-flops), slingbacks and skinny high-heeled shoes are designed by his neice Sandra Choi, but still remain the favourites of celebs like Madonna and Sarah Jessica Parker. A pair of women's shoes are upwards of $450. Men's loafers, sneakers and thongs start at around $300.

Manolo Blahnik: 31 West 54th Street between 5th and 6th Avenues. Tel 212-582 3007. Subway E, V to 5th Avenue/53rd Street.
Anyone serious about their shoe collection wouldn't miss this Mecca for celebs. In fact, Manolo has even designed the SJP – an ankle-strapped stiletto named after Sarah Jessica Parker.

Roger Vivier: 750 Madison Avenue at 65th Street. Tel 212-861 5371, www.rogervivier.com. Subway F at Lexington Avenue/63rd Street.
The designer who gave the world chrome-buckle, square-toe flats in the 1960s, worn by Catherine Deneuve in cult film *Belle de Jour*, has finally opened a store. Marlene Dietrich and our very own Queen Elizabeth II have all stepped out in Vivier's creations, which until now have been available in Saks Fifth Avenue. Pop in to marvel at the salon even if you can't afford the shoes, as the furniture was designed to complement the footwear and the interior decoration is modelled on Vivier's luxurious home, complete with a Picasso sketch.

Liz Claiborne: 650 5th Avenue at East 52nd Street. Tel 212-956 6505, www.lizclaiborne.com. Subway 6 to 51st Street; E, F to Lexington Avenue.
Career and sportswear with plenty of style for women.

NOHO

Avirex Cockpit Store: 652 Broadway between Bleecker and Bond Streets. Tel 212-925 5456, www.avirex.com.
Great for flight and varsity jackets.

Urban Outfitters: 628 Broadway between Houston and Bleecker Streets. Tel 212-475 0009, www.urbanoutfitters.com. Subway F, V, S to Broadway/Lafayette Street; 6 to Bleecker Street.
The last word in trendy, inexpensive clothes. Also has vintage urban wear. There's one in London now so it's not as special as it used to be, but still worth a visit for its mix of hip clothes, accessories, toys and other whatnots.

NOLITA

Calypso Christiane Celle: 280 Mott Street between East Houston and Prince Street. Tel 212-965 0990, www.calypso-celle.com. Subway 6 to Spring Street.
A French boutique with a Caribbean influence, this shop is filled with designs from Christiane Celle. There's a riot of sexy silk slip dresses, tie-dye tops and cute beaded cardigans. Her newest store is at 654 Hudson Street in the trendy Meatpacking District.

Maverick: 262 Mott Street near Prince Street. Tel 212-965 1150. Subway 6 to Spring Street.
Rebecca Romero's store is full of feminine pieces perfect for an uptown look. Think floral-print pencil skirts and pinstripe shirt dresses.

Selvedge: 250 Mulberry Street near Prince Street. Tel 212-219 0994. Subway 6 to Spring Street.

CLOTHES SIZES

Clothes sizes for men and women are one size smaller in America, so a dress size 10 in the US is a size 12 in the UK, a jacket size 42 is a UK 44. But it's the opposite with shoes – an American size 10 is our size 9. For men the sizing is similar: a size 36 suit in the US is also a size 36 in the UK, while shoes are one size smaller in the UK – a US size 10 is a UK size 9. Children sizes vary: an American size 4 is a British size 20.

Known as a laboratory for denim, it sells everything from funky reproductions of cult classics like 501s through to the Levi's Red collection.

Tracey Feith: 209 Mulberry Street between Spring and Kenmare Streets. Tel 212-334 3097. Subway 6 to Spring Street.
Tucked away in the hip NoLiTa, here you can get a dress made to order if you've $550 to burn. Just remember, Sarah Jessica Parker wore one of Feith's red and blue silk creations in *Sex And The City*.

SOHO

Adidas Originals Store: 136 Wooster Street near Prince Street. Tel 212-673 0398, www.adidas.com. Subway C, E to Prince Street.
If you have a penchant for old-school trainers and sportswear, then this is the place to head for.

agnès b: 103 Greene Street between Spring and Prince Streets. Tel 212-925 4649, www.agnesb.com. Subway N, R to Prince Street.
Superb designs for women and children here – simple but stunning and beautifully cut.

Anna Sui: 113 Greene Street between Prince and Spring Streets. Tel 212-941 8406, www.annasui.com. Subway N, R to Prince Street.
Get the glamour-with-a-hint-of-grunge look with Anna's dresses, skirts, blouses, boots and scarves. The small collection for men includes trousers, shirts and jackets from the outrageously loud to the quite positively restrained.

A.P.C.: 131 Mercer Street near Prince Street. Tel 212-966 9685, www.apc.fr. Subway N, R to Prince Street.
Men's and women's Euro-hip functional city clothes, such as shirt dresses, crisp shirts and jackets and trench coats, sold in a trendy loft space.

A Uno: 198 Spring Street near Thompson Street. Tel 212-343 2040. Subway C, E to Spring Street.
Edgy sportswear and versatile women's clothing.

Banana Republic: 552 Broadway between Spring and Prince Streets. Tel 212-925 0308, www.bananarepublic.com. Subway N, R to Prince Street.
A classy and reputable chain, famous for classic clothing in feel-good fabrics such as cashmere, suede, velvet and soft cotton at affordable prices. Nevertheless, the best buys are in the frequent sales.

Betsey Johnson: 138 Wooster Street between Houston and Prince Streets. Tel 212-995 5048, www.betseyjohnson.com. Subway C, E to Spring Street; N, R to Prince Street.
A wonderful presentation of a combination of party and working clothes that are thrilling to wear.

⊞ BRITTIP

SoHo is the place to take a trip to if you're looking for quirky, one-off clothing that you can be sure no one back home will have. Its streets are lined with boutique designer shops and have stores from some of the world's leading designers.

Bio: 29 Prince Street near Elizabeth Street. Tel 212-343 3006, www.bio-nyc.com. Subway B, D, F, V to Broadway and Lafayette Street.
Owner Au Vu stocks fabulous suits and matching coordinates for well-heeled city women who want to look professional but fashionable.

Manolo Blahnik

Bloomingdale's: 504 Broadway between Spring and Broome Streets. Tel 212-729 5900, www.bloomingdales.com. Subway N, R to Prince Street.
Aimed at Lower Manhattan's trendy set, this brand-new, six-level SoHo branch of the world-famous store offers something for everyone, with plenty of different designer lines.

Burberry: 131 Spring Street between Greene and Wooster Streets. Tel 212-925 9300, www.burberry.com. Subway C, E to Spring Street.
Don't miss this younger, hipper outlet of the super trendy British company for rainwear, leather, trench dresses, bags, shoes and casual wear.

Catherine Malandrino's: 468 Broome Street at Greene Street. Tel 212-925 6765, www.catherinemalandrino.com. Subway 6 to Spring Street.
The designer's own sexy French knitwear in block colours stands alongside more tailored knitted skirts and jackets.

Club Monaco: 520 Broadway at Spring Street. Tel 212-941 1511, www.clubmonaco.com. Subway 6 to Spring Street.
Once a Canadian company offering high fashion at high street prices, Ralph Lauren loved it so much he bought it.

Curve: 83 Mercer Street at Spring Street. Tel 212-966 3626. Subway 6 to Spring Street.
This recently opened womenswear boutique is a great place to head for wardrobe classics, such as the little black dress, albeit with a designer label price tag. There's also top quality bags, jewellery and shoes and a

same-day-delivery service if you're going for a big shop and don't want to cart bags around.

D&G: 434 West Broadway between Prince and Spring Streets. Tel 212-965 8000, www.dolcegabbana.it. Subway N, R to Prince Street.
Shop for jeans, suits, bags and dresses to a background of (loud) pop music. *Sex And The City*'s Carrie's favourite shop!

Earl Jeans: See page 118.

Helmut Lang: 80 Greene Street near Prince Street. Tel 212-925 4519, www.helmutlang.com. Subway C, E to Spring Street; N, R to Prince Street.
A stark, white gallery-like space that contrasts well with the designer's dark creations for men and women. It's pricey, think $500 upwards, but items like tuxedo jackets and shoes are exquisite.

Hotel Venus: 302 Bowery. Tel 212-966 4066, www.patriciafield.com.
One of Patricia Field's outlets. Her trendsetting club and streetwear are so outrageous they attract a large following among the drag queen and stripper crowd. But don't let that put you off if you fancy a corset, fake fur coat, bodysuit or bikini that's completely OTT. Patricia, by the way, is now known for dressing Sarah Jessica Parker of *Sex And The City*.

J Crew: 99 Prince Street between Mercer and Greene Streets. Tel 212-966 2739, www.jcrew.com. Subway N, R to Prince Street.
American-style men's and women's clothes plus shoes and accessories.

Keiko: 62 Greene Street between Spring and Broome Streets. Tel 212-226 6051, www.keikonewyork.com. Subway N, R to Prince Street.
Designer swimwear for all tastes – and you may recognise the odd supermodel shopping here.

Le Sportsac: 176 Spring Street between West Broadway and Thompson Streets. Tel 212-625 2626, www.lesportsac.com. Subway C, E to Spring Street.
Beloved of Japanese trendoids and US out-of-towners, not to mention Brit hipsters, Le Sportsac offers great nylon bags in every style, size, colour and pattern and they're reasonably priced, too. Worth a visit as the range isn't available in the UK.

Marc Jacobs: See page 118.

Bloomingdales

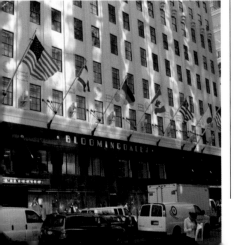

Operations: 60 Mercer Street at Broome Street. Tel 212-334 4950. Subway N, R to Prince Street.
The quirky work-style clothing, like red trucker jackets with black elbow patches, hang off meat hooks, while the changing rooms are industrial-sized freezers.

Phat Farm: 129 Prince Street between West Broadway and Wooster Street. Tel 212-533 7428, www.phatfarmstore.com. Subway C, E to Spring Street.
If you're into hip-hop baggies, you'll find everything you need here.

Philosophy di Alberta Ferretti: 452 West Broadway near Prince Street. Tel 212-460 5500, www.philosophy.it. Subway C, E to Spring Street.
The younger, more affordable line from top designer Alberta Ferretti.

Pleats Please: 128 Wooster Street at Prince Street. Tel 212-226 3600, www.pleatsplease.com. Subway N, R to Prince Street.
Issey Miyake's tightly pleated skirts, tops, scarves and trousers can be found here.

◀▣▶ BRITTIP

A great place for a pit stop is the Universal News and Café Corp (tel 212-965 9042, www.universalnewsusa.com) at 484 Broadway between Broome and Grand Streets, where you'll not only be able to find a snack, but also to check out their range of 7,000 magazine titles!

Prada New York Epicenter: 575 Broadway at Prince Street. Tel 212-334 8888, www.prada.com. Subway N, R, W to Prince Street.
Art is the byword of this incredible $40 million flagship store for Prada. Once the Guggenheim's SoHo museum, the two-level space has been designed by architect Rem Koolhaas and includes a zebrawood 'wave' in the entry hall and shoe display steps that can be converted into auditorium seating. Other neat design elements include dressing rooms behind a wall that switches from translucent to transparent (be warned!) and clothes suspended from the ceiling in metal cages. And therein lies one of the main drawbacks of the store from a punter's point of view. Prada's entire collection is to be found here, yet all the empty areas make

Park Avenue, Upper East Side

people feel as if there isn't that much to buy. On top of that, the store has taken being cool so seriously that the staff are positively frosty. Deal with them by either telling yourself that you earn a lot more than they do, or as one woman put it: 'You can have fun by asking the sales people for things from the storage rooms and keep them running!'

Sean: 132 Thompson Street near Prince Street. Tel 212-598 5980, www.seanstore.com. Subway 1, 9 to Houston.
A superb range of menswear for work and play at low prices, from colourful shirts to wool sports jackets.

Stüssy Store: 140 Wooster Street between West Houston and Prince Streets. Tel 212-274 8855, www.stussy.com. Subway N, R to Prince Street.
Everything you could want if you're after a West Coast look.

TRIBECA

Buffalo Chips Boot Company:
426 Washington Street near Vestry Street. Tel 212-965 0300. Subway 1, 9 to Franklin Street.
Pop star Sheryl Crow is just one of the celebrities who have got in touch with their inner cowgirl and gone on a spending spree at this cowgirl-kitsch store. Cowboy boots, handmade leather pants and Western shirts are just some of the fun items on offer.

Rival: 225 Hudson Street near Canal Street. Tel 212-929 7222, www.225hudson.com (still under construction). Subway 1, 9 to Canal Street.

SHOPPING AND BEAUTY

TOP FIVE STORES FOR MENSWEAR

Ascot Chang: 7 West 57th Street between 5th and 6th Avenues. Tel 212-759 3333, www.ascotchang.com. Subway F to 57th Street.
Known as New York's finest shirt-maker, the store also makes suits and overcoats, too. It's a real investment buy as Ascot Chang items don't date and last for ever – but they are pricey. If you're not feeling flush, there are off-the-rack pieces, too, from shirts to pyjamas.

Brooks Brothers: 666 5th Avenue at 53rd Street. Tel 212-261 9440, www.brookbrothers.com. Subway E, V at 5th Avenue.
Something for every man at this all-American flagship store. There are hundreds of outfits, plus accessories to check out and a made-to-measure service. A very famous American label known for its preppy and Ivy League type customers, it offers a great range of luxurious suits, shirts and jackets along with cashmere sweaters, polo shirts and blazers. This is the place to come if you're looking for sophisticated menswear with a unique American style.

Duncan Quinn: 8 Spring Street between Bowery and Elizabeth Streets. Tel 212-226 7030, www.duncanquinn.com. Subway C, E to Spring Street.
For those that believe exciting clothes shopping isn't just for women. This menswear treasure is packed full of brightly patterned suits, ties and shirts all expertly crafted. There are also some excellent shoes on offer.

Sean John: 475 5th Avenue at East 41st Street. Tel 212-220 2633, www.seanjohn.com. Subway B, D, F, V to 42nd Street.
Lots of sportswear for the hip-hop look, but plenty of other bits to ensure you look cool even at special occasions, such as white linen suits and pink polo shirts. There's also toiletries, ties, watches and belts for a complete bling style.

Tom Ford: 845 Madison Avenue at 70th Street. Tel 212-359 0300, www. Subway 6 at 66th Street/Hunter College.
A one-stop shop for stylish men everywhere, the man who made Gucci sexy again rolled out this store in April 2007 and it's a big hit. The ground floor stocks three-piece suits, colognes and dress shirts in 350 colours. Upstairs, via a velvet-lined lift, there's a made-to-measure service and three private rooms where you can have items customised, from shirts and ties to tennis shorts and even pyjamas. Lots of lovely accessories, too, such as sunglasses and cufflinks.

Skatewear for grown-ups best describes this store, which is packed full of great labels such as Burton and Oliver Spence. Best of all, you don't have to be under 18 to get the attention of staff; customer service here is excellent, even if your days of whizzing along on a snow or skateboard are well behind you.

Steven Alan: 103 Franklin Street between Church Street and West Broadway. Tel 212-343 0692, www.stevenalan.com. Subway 1 to Franklin Street.
A small but perfectly formed boutique filled to the rafters with up-and-coming designers such as Kayatone Adeli's cute disco top and Daryl K's hipster trousers.

Tribeca Issey Miyake: 119 Hudson Street at North Moore Street. Tel 212-226 0100, www.isseymiyake.com. Subway 1, 2 to Franklin Street.
The new Prada store got the old Guggenheim Museum space in SoHo: Issey Miyake got Frank Gehry, the architect of the amazing Guggenheim Museum in Bilbao. Now serious shoppers mingle with art buffs that come to see the titanium tornado that swirls through this two-storey, 279sq m (3,000sq ft) boutique, plus art by Gehry's son Alejandro. Fortunately, the purpose of the shop (sorry, but that's what it is) has not been forgotten and the entire Issey collection is here including the Pleats Please, Haat, A/POC and fragrance lines. What's more, the staff are actually helpful. A truly wonderful experience – especially if you can afford $1,600 for a shirt. Otherwise, wait for the sales!

UPPER EAST SIDE

Allegra Hicks: 1007 Madison Avenue at 78th Street. Tel 212-249 4241, www.allegrahicks.com. Subway 6 at 77th Street.
Loved by the jet-set, Bahamas-based Hicks has injected some of her summer style into

this brand-new store. As well as her signature beachwear, think brightly coloured bikinis and one-pieces, as well as lots of bold, printed kaftans, high-waisted trousers, knits and floaty empire-line dresses.

Anne Fontaine: 687 Madison Avenue near 62nd Street. Tel 212-688 4362, www.annefontaine.com. Subway 4, 5, 6 to 59th Street.
The place in New York to snap up the perfect white shirt.

Betsey Johnson: 1060 Madison Avenue. Tel 212-734 1257, www.betseyjohnson.com. Subway 6 to 77th Street.
Eclectic mix of rock chick chic and artsy boudoir designs.

Billy Martin's Western Wear: 220 East 60th Street. Tel 212-861 3100, www.billymartin.com. Subway 6 to 68th Street.
Everything for the posh cowboy.

Calvin Klein: See page 118.

Cantaloup: 1036 Lexington Avenue at 74th Street. Tel 212-249 3566. Subway 6 to 77th Street.
This candy-coloured boutique is a magnet for trendspotters, thanks to its display rails filled with edgy designers such as True Religion.

D&G: 825 Madison Avenue between 68th and 69th Streets. Tel 212-249 4100, www.dolcegabbana.it. Subway 6 to 68th Street.
Shop for jeans, suits, bags and dresses to a background of (loud) pop music.

Diesel: 770 Lexington Avenue at 60th Street. Tel 212-308 0055, www.diesel.com. Subway N, R to Lexington Avenue 4, 5, 6 to 59th Street.
A massive store in which you'll find everything from denim to vinyl clothing, shoes and accessories.

Donna Karan: See page 118.

Emporio Armani: 601 Madison Avenue between 57th and 58th Streets. Tel 212-317 0800. Subway N, R to 59th Street.
Armani's line for younger people.

Giorgio Armani: 760 Madison Avenue at 65th Street. Tel 212-988 9191, www.giorgioarmani.com. Subway 6 to 68th Street.
A huge boutique that sells all three of Armani's lines. Come here to find well-tailored classics.

Nicole Farhi: 10 East 60th Street near Madison Avenue. Tel 212-223 8811, www.nicolefarhi.com. Subway 4, 5, 6 to 59th Street.
Elegant, simple designs for men and women. It also sells homeware.

Prada: 841 Madison Avenue at 70th Street. Tel 212-327 4200, www.prada.com. Subway 6 to 68th Street.
Check out the season's look before you head for the bargain basement stores.

Ralph Lauren: 867 Madison Avenue at East 72nd Street. Tel 212-606 2100, www.polo.com. Subway 6 to 68th Street.
Worth a visit just to see the store – it's in an old Rhinelander mansion and is decorated with everything from Oriental rugs to riding whips, leather chairs and English paintings. The clothes are of excellent quality too.

WEST VILLAGE
Claudine: 19 Christopher Street at Waverly Place. Tel 212-414 4234. Subway 1 to Christopher Street.
Website www.handbag.com named this the top store in NY to spot new trends. It's a delightful boutique run by fashionista Kyung Lee, with welcoming scented candles, soft music and pretty prints on the wall. The stock's pretty good too, with a mix of casual and formal collections from up-and-coming New York and LA designers. Many of the items are handmade one-offs, so there's lots of potential for bagging outfits no one else has. A good shoe selection, too.

D&G

Darling: 1 Horatio Street at 8th Avenue. Tel 646-336 6966. Subway A, C, E to 14th Street.
Ann French Emonts fills this small boutique with her own designs plus choice pieces from other top-notch womenswear designers. Thursday nights are popular as the store stays open until 10pm and customers are offered champagne while they browse.

Girlshop: 819 Washington Street between Little West 12th and Gansevoort Streets. Tel 212-255 4985, www.girlshop.com. Subway A, C, E to 14th Street.
Fun, stylish clothes and accessories from lesser-known designers.

Lulu Guinness: 394 Bleecker Street between 11th and Perry Streets. Tel 212-367 2120, www.luluguinness.com. Subway A, C, E to 14th Street; L to 8th Avenue; 1, 2 to Christopher Street.
Our own home-grown Brit girl Lulu, who started out in Notting Hill, West London, has established herself in the Big Apple. Her vintage-inspired accessories include embroidered and appliquéd bags and purses. If you think you can get it all in the UK, think again. Lulu's produced some fab bags just for New Yorkers.

VINTAGE FASHION

EAST VILLAGE

Cronick Valentine: 324 East 9th Street between 1st and 2nd Avenue. Tel 212-228 7767, www.cronickvalentine.com. Subway L to 1st Avenue.
Vintage T-shirts rush out of this store, along with accessories like luggage and ties. As an added extra, you can bring in your old T-shirts and have them made into a handbag, cuff, iPod holder or even a duvet cover, from $50 to $150.

BRITTIP

For the complete lowdown on what New York has to offer shoppers, log on to www.newyork metro.com/shopping, which gives comprehensive listings by neighbourhood or store type.

Love Saves The Day: 119 2nd Avenue at East 7th Street. Tel 212-228 3802. Subway 6 to Astor Place.
Currently in the process of moving the store, so be sure to ring up before you make your way to check out the objects of real retro

---

TOP FIVE PLACES TO GET YOUR CLOTHES MADE-TO-MEASURE

Frida's Closet: Carroll Gardens, 296 Smith Street, Brooklyn. Subway F, G, 2, 3, 4, 5 to President Street. Tel 718-855 0311, www.fridascloset.com.
An amazing store run by Sandra Paez who has based her shop on the style of inspirational Mexican artist Frida Kahlo; think long peasant skirts, soft blouses and gorgeous leather bags. Dresses, skirts and blouses are custom made for you in the shop.

Lee Anderson: 23 East 67th Street between 5th and Madison Avenues. Tel 212-772 2563. Subway 4, 5, 6 to 68th Street.
This is where the businesswomen of New York go to get their classic suits, separates and eveningwear. You can have your order custom made or choose off-the-rack if time is short.

Mary Adams: 138 Ludlow Street between Stanton and Rivington Streets. Tel 212-473 0237, www.maryadamsthedress.com. Subway F, J, M, Z at Delancey Street/Essex Street.
A fascinating shop bursting with dresses full of lace, ruffles, satin and feathers. You'll feel like you've stepped into the Moulin Rouge wardrobe and you can even get your own custom-made creation to wow your friends back home.

Piccione: 116 East 57th Street (2nd floor) between Park and Lexington Avenues. Tel 212-421 2828. Subway 4, 5, 6 to Lexington Avenue/59th Street.
The Italian master of tailoring will make made-to-measure suits for men and women using the finest cloths from the best mills in the world. Be warned: prices start from around $3,000 and deliveries can take five weeks.

Ripplu: 575 5th Avenue between 46th and 47th Streets. Tel 212-599 2223, www.rippllu.com. Subway S, 4, 5, 6, 7 to 42nd Street/5th Avenue.
Nip and tuck too scary and expensive? Never fear, your prayers for a better bod have been answered courtesy of Ripplu, the New York women's secret lingerie store. Their custom made bras and pants miraculously lift and reshape those wobbly bits; they even offer free alterations.

desire such as biker jackets last worn by fans of Evil Knievel or Barry Sheene. As well as clothes, there are gems such as 1950s *Playboy* magazines and hardback manuals of John Travolta's work-out routines for *Saturday Night Fever*.

Tokio: 7 East 7th Street between 1st and 2nd Avenues. Tel 212-353 8443, www.tokio7.com. Subway 6 to Astor Place; N, R to 8th Street.
Plenty of vintage and downtown designer gear to choose from here. Particularly good collection of Japanese designers.

Tokyo Joe: 334 East 11th Street between 1st and 2nd Avenues. Tel 212-473 0724. Subway 6 to Astor Place.
The pre-worn designer offerings are advertised on a blackboard outside the shop every day.

Village Scandal: 19 East 7th Street between 2nd and 3rd Avenues. Tel 212-460 9358. Subway 6 to Astor Place.
A must-visit for vintage addicts as this retro store is packed full of cool hats and accessories from floppy Bianca Jagger-esque designs to trendy bucket caps. It's open until midnight.

GREENWICH VILLAGE
Stella Dallas: 218 Thompson Street between Bleecker and West 3rd Streets. Tel 212-674 0447. Subway A, C, E, F, V, S to West 4th Street.
An amazing vintage shop full of girly chiffon and other items.

LOWER EAST SIDE
Foley + Corinna: 114 Stanton Street at Essex Street. Tel 212-529 2338. Subway F, V to Lower East Side/Second Avenue.
Sexy, edgy, girly clothing tucked away in a spacious boutique that has become a magnet for uptown girls and celebs looking for something different. There's a great range of vintage shoes that line the floors under the racks of silk tops and Harlowe dresses. It's a wide mix of vintage and new clothing, plus accessories like handbags and jewellery, and it's all exceptional.

MEATPACKING DISTRICT
Cherry: 19 Eighth Avenue between West 12th and Jane Streets. Tel 212-924 1410. Subway A, C, E to 14th Street.
A cool vintage shop, which stocks all manner of goodies and shoes dating back as far as the 1940s. It's popular for its one-of-a-kind pieces such as a cute Pucci top or Versace

gown. You'll also find lots of fab accessories, from sunglasses to headscarves. Be sure to leave at least a couple of hours, for serious shoppers have been known to disappear for an afternoon in this vintage Mecca.

NOLITA
Screaming Mimi: 382 Lafayette Street between 4th and Great Jones Streets. Tel 212-677 6464, www.screaming mimis.com. Subway N, R to NYU 8th Street.
Everything from polyester dresses to denim shirts and tropical prints from the 1960s. There are also jewellery, sunglasses and other accessories, plus a home department upstairs in which to browse.

BRITTIP
If you need shoe repairs while you're in NY, go to Angelo Shoe Repair at 666 5th Avenue (lower level) at 53rd Street. Tel 212-757 6364, open 7am–6.30pm.

SOHO
Transfer International: 594 Broadway, Suite 1002, between Prince and Houston Streets. Tel 212-941 5472, www.transfer ny.com. Subway N, R to Prince Street.
Specialises in Gucci, Prada, Chanel and Hermès – one of the best places to buy post-worn designer clothes and accessories. They also carry agnès b and Betsey Johnson.

TRIBECA
Geminola: 41 Perry Street near 7th Avenue. Tel 212-675 1994, www.geminola.com. Subway 1, 9 to Christopher Street.
Owner Lorraine Kirke travels the world for vintage fabrics, then reworks and dyes them to create gorgeous and unique clothing. Skirts from $165 and accessories and belts from Afghanistan and handbags from India at around $295.

BRITTIP
The Americans still measure in feet and inches – good news for older Brits.

UPPER EAST SIDE
BIS Designer Resale: 1134 Madison Avenue between 84th and 85th Streets. Tel 212-396 2760, www.bisbiz.com. Subway 4, 5, 6 to 86th Street.
For those that like a designer label but don't have the cash to splash, there is a shopping

JEWELLERY

Want a true sparkler? Then look no further than the 47th Street Diamond District where the little gems are traded, cut and set. More than 2,600 independent businesses are to be found in a single block between 5th Avenue and the Avenue of the Americas (6th Avenue). Many have booths in jewellery exchanges such as the World's Largest Jewellery Exchange at 55 West 47th Street (tel 212-719 5235, www.jewelry55exchange.com). Jack of Diamonds (52 West 47th Street, tel 212-869 7272, www.jackofdiamondsintl.com) has everything from loose diamonds and strings of pearls to watches.

Chelsea

DVVS: 263A 19th Street near 8th Avenue. Tel 212-366 4888, www.dvvs.com. Subway C, E to 23rd Street.
Modern, unusual jewellery from contemporary designers. Prices range from around $1,000 to $2,000.

Lower East Side

Daniel Espinosa: 250 Elizabeth Street near Houston Street. Tel 212-966 4999, www.danielespinosa.com. Subway F, V to 2nd Avenue.
Individual, handmade pieces that range from $80 to $2,000.

Midtown

Agatha: 611 Madison Avenue at 58th Street. Tel 212-758 4301, www.agatha.fr. Subway 4, 5, 6 to 59th Street.
Affordable, fashionable trinkets, $200 or less, like charm bracelets and chunky necklaces.
Asprey: 723 5th Avenue at 56th. Tel 212-688 1811, www.asprey.com. Subway N, R to 5th Avenue.
Pricey, bling-bling jewellery beloved of stars, not least because boho Brit Jade Jagger now has a hand in its designs.
Graff: 721 Madison Avenue near 64th Street. Tel 212-355 9292, www.graffdiamonds.com. Subway 6 to 68th Street.
Some of the best diamonds that you're ever likely to come across are here, to suit every type of price range, from tiny 1-carat to 100-carat yellow diamonds.
H Stern: 645 5th Avenue near 51st Avenue. Tel 212-688 0300, www.hstern.net. Subway E, V to 5th Avenue.
One of New York's most prestigious jewellers.
Tiffany & Co: 727 5th Avenue. Tel 212-755 8000, www.tiffany.com. Subway N, R to 5th Avenue.
Few can resist popping in to sneak a look at the store that featured so highly in the classic film *Breakfast at Tiffany's* starring Audrey Hepburn. If you can't afford the $2,000-plus diamond necklaces and bracelets, you can always fork out for a $100 keyring.

SoHo

Fragments: 116 Prince Street between Greene and Wooster Streets. Tel 212-334 9588, www.fragments.com. Subway A, C, E to Spring Street.
A hit with the fashion crowd keen to snap up the works of between 60 and 100 designers that are on sale at any one time.
Jane Eadie: 248 Elizabeth Street at Houston Street. Tel 212-334 7975, www.janeeadie.com. Subway B, D, F, V to Broadway/Lafayette Street.
A brand-new arrival on the New York gems scene, this tiny boutique is a breath of fresh air, packed with statement jewellery from around the world including Argentina, Brazil and Italy. Ideal for someone who wants to stand out from the crowd but not pay thousands of dollars for the privilege; A studded bronze and topaz cocktail ring is around $579.

God. BIS is jammed with pieces that have only been worn once or sometimes never, from barely worn Manolos to Chanel quilted jackets. Stock is stored by items, such as shoes or skirts, but if you're after a specific label, such as Gucci, the staff will show you what's available. You may be beaten to some of the best bits by die hard fans who log on to the store's eBay site to snap up bargains. Prices are around 50 per cent of the original value, but while you're saving, don't forget that still means many 3-figure price tags.

Tiffany & Co.

UNION SQUARE
Cheap Jack's: 303 5th Avenue at East 31st Street . Tel 212-777 9564, www.cheap jacks.com. Subway N, R, W to 28th/34th Streets.
A huge selection, but on the pricey side, despite the name!

UPPER EAST SIDE
Gentlemen's Resale: 322 East 81st Street between 1st and 2nd Avenues. Tel 212-734 2739, www.resaleclothing.net. Subway 6 to 77th Street.
Top-notch designer suits at a fraction of the original price.

BEAUTY STORES AND SPAS
Everyone knows New York is the place to find fabulous fashion bargains, but not so well known are the great beauty buys to be had, too. In the first instance, most make-up – particularly the gorgeous American brands such as Philosophy, Hard Candy, Benefit and Laura Mercier – is a lot cheaper in the Big Apple. The exceptions are the 'prestige' French brands such as Décleor, Christian Dior and Chanel, which are generally cheaper in the UK (they have to be imported to America).

Most brands have dedicated stores in Manhattan, the majority around SoHo and its environs of NoLiTa, north SoHo and West Village.

BEAUTY STORES

MIDTOWN
Mary Quant Colour Concept Store: 520 Madison Avenue at 53rd Street. Tel 212-980 7577, www.maryquant.co.uk/ny.htm. Subway 6 to 51st Street.
Groovy cosmetics brand from the queen of 1960s cool. It's cheap and cheerful and comes in daisy-plastered packaging.

Sephora: 597 5th Avenue between East 48th and 49th Streets. Tel 212-980 6534, www.sephora.com. Subway B, D F, V to 47th–50th Streets/Rockefeller Center.
The Rockefeller Center is home to the flagship Manhattan Sephora store packed with beauty products and smelling like a perfumery.

SOHO
To get to SoHo use either the N, R subway lines to Prince Street or the 6, C, E to Spring Street.

Aveda: 233 Spring Street between 6th Avenue and Varick Street. Tel 212-807 1492, www.aveda.com.
As befits the beauty line entirely based on the gentle and nurturing Ayurvedic system, this is a tranquil setting in which to choose your favourite hair and skincare products. Made from natural plant and flower extracts, Aveda's holistic approach is carried through all products including the make-up ranges and massage oils.

BRITTIP
Stores in SoHo tend to open some time between 10am and noon and stay open until 7pm Mon–Sat, while most open from noon to 6pm on Sundays.

5S: 98 Prince Street between Greene and Mercer Streets. Tel 212-925 7880.
A make-up and skincare line by Japanese company Shiseido, the products reflect the ancient philosophies of the islands and are organised into five senses of well-being including energising and nurturing.

Face Stockholm: 110 Prince Street at Greene Street. Tel 212-966 9110, www.facestockholm.com.
Fans of the cosmetic company can go mad in this glittery emporium, filled as it is with the full range of colours and brushes. You can have your make-up done here or take a lesson. Phone for an appointment or just drop in.

BRITTIP
Tracie Martyn is considered by many to be the best facialist in New York, using a massage technique that some – including Liv Tyler and Kate Winslet - say can leave you looking 10 years younger. Tel 212-206 9333, www.traciemartyn.com.

Fresh: 57 Spring Street between Lafayette and Mulberry. Tel 212-925 0099, www.fresh.com.
Soaps, lotions and potions with lovely fragrances based on natural ingredients from the Boston-based company. It even has a *Memoirs of a Geisha* collection, inspired by the film.

Kiehl's: 109 3rd Avenue between 13th and 14th Streets. Tel 212-677 3171, www.kiehls.com.
One of New York's most famous establishments, the crowds still flock to this emporium in the Union Square area for its luxurious moisturisers and lip balms.

MAC: 113 Spring Street between Greene and Mercer Streets. Tel 212-334 4641, www.maccosmetics.com.
As with many of the beauty boutiques in SoHo, the wonder of this flagship store for MAC is as much in the architecture, lighting and displays as in the products. In fact, it's such a wonderful place, it has become a big favourite with celebs such as Britney Spears, Gwyneth Paltrow, kd lang and Alanis Morissette.

It sells all MAC products including the MAC Pro range used by make-up artists on fashion shows and movie shoots, which are available in only a few of their outlets around the globe.

During your visit, you can either plump for a 45-minute makeover for $40, complete with useful tips, or turn up with nothing but foundation on your face and let the artists finish off your make-up for free.

Make-Up Forever: 409 West Broadway between Prince and Spring Streets. Tel 212-941 9337, www.makeupforever.com.
A French line specialising in ultra-bright colours, thanks to the triple pigment formula used in all its lipsticks and eyeshadows. This is a funky little shop decked out to look like the make-up area of a film set. The well-trained staff are happy to advise on colours and products, while a $50 makeover is redeemable against purchases, including the company's best-selling silicon-based foundation.

SCO: 5th Floor, 584 Broadway near Prince Street. Tel 212-966 3011, www.scocare.com. Subway N, R to Prince Street.
Stands for Skin-Care Options, of which there are many. Lots of custom-blended concoctions including face products and sun blocks.

Sephora: 555 Broadway between Prince and Spring Streets. Tel 212-625 1309, www.sephora.com.
One of many New York outlets of this pristine, clean French beauty chain, which has become a sure-fire hit, thanks to its incredibly broad range, sparkling presentations and low-key staff who can provide plenty of help and advice when requested. This is the best place to get your favourite American brands such as Benefit, Hard Candy, Nars and Philosophy.

Shu Uemura: 121 Greene Street between Prince and Houston Streets. Tel 212-979 5500, www.shuuemura-usa.com.
Like MAC, Shu Uemura is another make-up range much loved by industry professionals, thanks to its quality and texture. The Japanese cosmetics company, based on Eastern philosophies, is famous for its colour and tools – this is the place to come for everything to do with make-up from brushes to eyelash curlers.

A quiet space, the boutique has an open, friendly atmosphere that makes browsing here a delight. You can also get a free 30-minute make-up lesson from one of the professional make-up artists on Thurs and Fri 11am–5pm, Sat 11am–1.30pm. The Saturday lessons are very popular, though – they are usually booked up a month in advance – so go in the week.

UPPER EAST SIDE

Face Stockholm: 687 Madison Avenue at 62nd Street. Tel 212-207 8833, www.facestockholm.com. Subway 4, 5, 6 to 68th Street.
Another outlet of the fab beauty company. You'll also find another one of these boutiques on the Upper West Side at 226 Columbus Avenue between 70th and 71st Streets (tel 212-769 1420).

Sephora

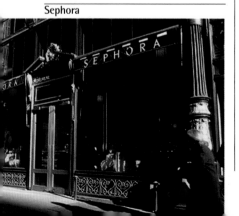

Fresh: 922 Madison Avenue between 73rd and 74th Streets. Tel 212-396 4545, www.fresh.com. Subway 6 to 68th Street. A Boston-based company specialising in beauty products made from natural ingredients such as honey, milk, soy, sugar and even Umbrian clay. Other branches can be found at 388 Bleecker Street in West Village (tel 917-408 1850), 1367 Third Avenue (tel 212-585 3400) and 872 Broadway (tel 212-477 1100).

L'Occitane: 1046 Madison Avenue at 80th Street. Tel 212-639 9185, www.loccitane.com. Subway 6 to 77th Street.
Ultra-luxurious bath and beauty products from the famous French company. Also branches at 510 Madison at 52nd Street and 1288 Madison at 92nd Street.

WEST VILLAGE

Aedes de Venustas: 9 Christopher Street near 6th Avenue. Tel 212-206 8674, www.aedes.com. Subway 1, 9 to Christopher Street.
Sublime emporium where you can pick up almost impossible-to-find skincare products.

HAIR

MIDTOWN

Borja Colour Studios: 118 57th Street near Park Avenue. Tel 212-308 3232. Subway 4, 5, 6 to 59th Street.
Excellent cuts, highlights and colours as well as a good reputation for eyebrow shaping. Treat yourself to a consultation over a glass of wine.

Crisca Salon: 21 East 51st Street at Madison Avenue. Tel 212-759 4743. Subway E, V to Lexington Avenue.
Unisex salon that's been going for years, mainly because the prices are low and the standards high. The decor isn't all singing and dancing, but there are wall televisions

BRITTIP

For the best shave a man can have in New York take a seat and join the queue in one of three The Art of Shaving Barber shops (Tel 305-593 0667, www.theartof shaving.com) located around the city. You can get every type of shave imaginable, including a hot, straight-edged Royal Shave, at these Victorian-style outlets.

and a good stack of magazines to read while you wait for your colour to set.

The Ouidad Salon: Fourth Floor, 37 West 57th Street between 5th and 6th Avenues. Tel 212-888 3288, www.ouidad.com. Named after the owner, this hair salon specialises in cutting and styling curly hair. In fact, they take curly hair so seriously you won't be allowed in without it! The dedicated team spends up to four hours styling and taming your locks and the salon has its own range of products. This new premises has the feel of a SoHo loft, with faux snakeskin couches to boot.

SOHO

To get to SoHo use either the N, R subway lines to Prince Street or the 6, C, E to Spring Street.

Devachan: 2nd Floor, 558 Broadway between Prince and Spring Streets. Tel 212-274 8686, www.devachansalon.com. Small salon where celebs come to get perfect locks and an amazing scalp massage. It also doubles as a spa.

Frédéric Fekkai: 394 West Broadway at Broadway. Tel 212-888 2600, www.frederic fekkai.com. Subway B, D, F, V to Broadway/Lafayette Streets; 6 to Spring Street.
A more relaxed vibe to the uptown salon, this latest branch to open in SoHo is already proving a big hit, particularly as you can get your make-up done here, too. Open until 9pm Thurs and Fri.

Prive: The Soho Grand, 310 West Broadway between Canal and Grand Streets. Tel 212-274 8888.
Home of Laurent D, who looks after Gwyneth's hair when she's in town. His haircuts start at around $200.

WEST VILLAGE

Avalon Salon & Day Spa: 271 West 4th Street at Perry Street. Tel 212-337 1966. Subway 1 to Christopher Street/Sheridan Square.
A popular local salon that is a world away from snooty 5th Avenue. Friendly staff, lots of cutting stations and excellent products, such as Keratase and Aveda, guarantee you'll walk away happy.

Gemini Salon & Spa: 547 Hudson Street between Perry and Charles Street. Tel 212-675 4546. Subway 1, 9 to Christopher Street. If you have wild, untameable hair or you just want your locks to be sleeker, then book an appointment to test out this salon's patented Opti-smooth straightening treatment for yourself.

NAILS

MIDTOWN
50th Street Madison Nail: 44 East 50th Street at Madison Avenue. Tel 212-754 2277. Second-floor salon that isn't going to break the bank, with prices far lower than its neighbours. Look for Panini Totz Deli at street level; the sign for the nail salon is above it.

Blooming Nails: 812 2nd Avenue between 93rd and 94th streets. Tel 212-876 2445. Long-lasting manicures and pedicures that are easy on the plastic. Four nail stations and three pedicure stations, plus a back room for waxing.

Pinky Nail Fifty Six Corp: 240 East 56th Street. Tel 212-446 9553. A fab chain of nail salons where manicures start at $10 and pedicures at $20. This location is particularly well known for its cleanliness and friendliness.

SOHO
Jin Soon Natural Hand & Foot Spa: 56 East 4th Street between Bowery and 2nd Avenue. Tel 212-473 2047. Subway F, V to Lower East Side/2nd Avenue.
When in town, actress Julianne Moore always books a full foot treatment with Jin Soon Choi. Expect rose petals and botanicals with the ultra pampering $30 pedicure – a basic manicure costs just $15. The tiny NoLiTa spa became such a Mecca for celebs and those wanting perfect hands and feet that a second, larger, Jin Soon Spa has been established in the West Village at 23 Jones Street between Bleecker and West 4th Streets. Tel 212-229 1070. Check out the 'floating room' where gorgeous orange silk hangs over a small pond.

Rescue Nail Spa: 21 Cleveland Place between Kenmare and Spring Streets. Tel 212-431 3805, www.rescuebeauty.com.

◀︎🇬🇧 BRITTIP
For excellent manicures with no frills for just $5, head to the East Village where a plethora of salons dot the streets of Marks Place and 2nd Avenue. Generally New Yorkers pay around $25 for a manicure or a pedicure.

Subway 6 to Spring Street.
Famous for intensive treatments, this nail specialist also has an outlet in NoLiTa at 8 Centre Market Place between Grand and Broome Streets (tel 212-431 0449) and 2nd Floor, 32 Gansevoort Street, between Greenwich and Hudson Streets (tel 212-206 6409).

UPPER EAST SIDE
Bloomie Nail Corp: 1320 Madison Avenue at 92nd Street. Tel 212-426 5566. Subway 6 to 96th Street.
Another city-wide nail chain where no appointments are necessary (see also Pinky's, opposite), here you can have anything from your basic manicures to paraffin pedicures and massages.

Charming Nails: 212 East 87th Street at 3rd Avenue. Tel 212-987 7239.
A fashionista's secret, who knows that you get spa-quality results for budget prices here.

UPPER WEST SIDE
Fashion 74 Nails: 303 Amsterdam Avenue at 74th Street. Tel 212-799 5252.
Where those in the know get their nails done – even, it's rumoured, other spa owners!

PERFUMES

MIDTOWN
Bond No 9 New York: 680 Madison Avenue at 61st Street. Tel 212-838 2780. Subway 4, 5, 6 to 59th Street.
Delicious scents with witty names like Chelsea Flowers, Gramercy Park and Madison Soirée. Or you can have your own custom blended. Branches also at 897 Madison Avenue (tel 212-794 4480) and 9 Bond Street (tel 212-228 1940).

Caswell-Massey: 518 Lexington Avenue at East 48th Street. Tel 212-755 2254, www.caswellmassey.com. Subway 6 to 51st Street.
An apothecary founded in 1752 that once provided perfumes for George Washington and Dolly Madison. Today it continues to make a glorious range of floral scents such as freesia, lilac and rose. You can buy gift sets or individual bottles.

UPPER EAST SIDE
Caron: 675 Madison Avenue near 61st Street. Tel 212-319 4888. Subway 4, 5, 6 to 59th Street.
The complete range of glitzy, crystal-bottled Caron fragrances, from $80 upwards, can be bought here.

SPAS

CHELSEA

Nickel: 77 8th Avenue at 14th Street. Tel 212-242 3203, www.nickelspanyc.com. Subway A, 9, A , C, E to 19th Street.

One of the only men-only spas in the city – in a chic, two-storey haven – offering a wide range of treatments from massages (from $60) to facials and waxing. Book at least four weeks in advance.

Sam-C Spa and Margolin Wellness Center: 2nd Floor, 166 5th Avenue at 21st Street. Tel 212-675 9355.

A doctor-meets-spa centre in Chelsea, owned and run by chiropractor Dr Margolin and celebrated masseur Sam-C. Famous treatments include the hydrotherapy tub in which you are immersed in a large, very hot tub of pulsating water while a therapist massages your head and applies cold compresses, and the Sam-C Massage, a unique, intensive body massage. Other treatments include chiropractic, reflexology, acupuncture, body scrubs, steam shower and mud wraps.

TOP FIVE NEW SPAS IN NEW YORK

Downtown

Delluva Vinotherapy Day Spa: 152 Franklin Street at Varick Street. Tel 212-937 7757, Subway 1 to Franklin Street.

Recently opened spa using cosmetics based around grapes (vinotherapy), currently in vogue in the beauty world thanks to their anti-aging properties. Pop in to try the skin-nourishing signature blend facial of the relaxation body wrap, an ideal way to recover from any jet lag.

Meatpacking District

G Spa & Lounge: Hotel Gansevoort (see page 229).

Situated in the lower level of this chic hotel, which transforms into a VIP hot spot lounge after 9pm. By day you enjoy treatments such as the signature hot stone massage or 45-minute fitness facial in one of three red-lit compartments, or you can opt to have your treatment in a cabana on the hotel's wonderful roof top. You can even get your hair chopped at the Hiro Haraguchi satellite salon that lies just past the spa's laser-lit steam room. Très chic.

Midtown

Lather Spa: 127 East 57th Street at Lexington Avenue. Tel 212-644 4449. Subway 4, 5, 6 to 59th Street.

Formerly the Greenhouse Spa, this three-storey space has now been relaunched as the Lather line's first US store. Check in on the street-level floor where you'll also get your robe and rubber clogs. The relaxation area is great; all white with a skylight and a wall covered with plants and flowers. There are eight pedi-stations for hands and feet, and a further 15 treatments rooms for facials, massages and body treatments using concoctions of fruits, plants and herbs from around the world. There are men's treatments here, too.

Ohm Spa: 7th floor, 260 Fifth Avenue at 28th street. Tel 212-481 7892. Subway N, R, W to 28th Street.

Aiming to be the antithesis of overly feminine spa design , owners Jonathan Ho and Kathy Yan have come up with clean lines and a gender neutral palette of blue and brown, the message being that men are welcome here, too. As you'd expect, the treatments are similarly straightforward, including massages that target certain muscle groups that give you problems and facials from Dermalogica and Plantogen. You can watch movies on flat-screen TVs while you have a manicure or pedicure.

Tribeca

Tribeca MedSpa: 114 Hudson Street at Franklin Street. Tel 212-925 9500. Subway 1 at Franklin Street.

Lots of therapies on the menu dedicated to getting rid of wrinkles. There are four treatment rooms, including one for Injectables, such as Botox and Restalyne, which are only given by licensed professionals. If you want something less heavy, there are Medi-Pedis plus Titan skin-tightening and rejuvenation laser treatments. It's rumoured that Robert DeNiro is both the landlord and a customer.

MIDTOWN

Affinia Wellness Spa: 125 East 50th Street at Lexington Avenue (The Benjamin Hotel). Tel 212-715 2517, www.affinia.com. Subway 6, 5 to 51st Street.
A tiny but perfect spa where you can have candlelit massages, hot-salt body scrubs and self-tanning treatments. Also at Oasis Day Spa, Affinia Dumont, 150 East 34th Street. Tel 212-545 5254.

Avon Center Spa: 6th Floor, Trump Tower, 725 5th Avenue between 56th and 57th Streets. Tel 212-755 2866.
An incredible space and a wonderful opportunity to enter the spanking Trump Tower for a face and body treatment. Eliza Petrescu is famous for her eyebrow waxings, so book early.

Bliss 57: 3rd floor, 19 East 57th Street between 5th and Madison Avenues. Tel 212-219 8970, www.blissworld.com. Subway N, R to 59th Street.
Sarah Jessica Parker's favourite spa, which also sells its own skincare range, BlissLabs. Hangover herbie, anyone?

Elizabeth Arden Red Door Salon & Spa: 691 5th Avenue at 54th Street. Tel 212-546 0200, www.reddoorspas.com. Subway E, V to 5th Avenue/53rd Street.
For the ultimate beautifier, nothing beats the Pomegranate Warm Stone Facial, which promises to firm up skin and deflect damage-inducing free radicals in a trice, with the help of a pomegranate paste.

Georgette Klinger Salon: 501 Madison Ave between 52nd and 53rd Streets. Tel 212-838 3200, www.georgetteklinger.com. Subway 6 to 51st Street; E, V to 5th Avenue/53rd Street.
Georgette is one of New York's most famous facialists and the foundation of her work is

purification. Each facial is comprehensive and tailor-made for individual needs, starting with a thorough skin analysis. Deep cleansing and steaming rid the skin of underlying impurities, a gentle massage adds skin tone and individualised face masks finish off the refining process.

Green Tea Nail & Spa: 141 West 35th Street between Broadway and 7th Avenue. Tel 212-564 6971. Subway A, C, E to 34th Street/Penn Station.
Nestled in the 34th Street district right next to Macy's is this large Japanese spa in which you are served antioxidant-rich green tea in a clean, minimalist environment. Treatments include waxing, facials, manicures, pedicures and massages. For the perfect pick-me-up-in-an-instant opt for the 10-minute neck massage for $10.

J Sisters International: 35 West 57th Street at 6th Avenue. Tel 212-750 2485, www.jsisters.com. Subway N, Q, R, W to 57th Street.
Family-run beauty centre famous for its extremely thorough Brazilian waxes. You can also have your make-up, nails and hair done here.

La Prairie Spa: The Ritz Carlton Hotel, 50 Central Park South at 6th Avenue. Tel 212-521 6135, www.ritzcarlton.com. Subway F, N, R, Q, W to 57th Street.
An extremely high-end spa beloved by celebrities. The Caviar Firming Facial is the signature treatment and rings in at around $260 a go.

Physical Advantage: Penthouse, 139 East 57th Street at Lexington Avenue. Tel 212-460 1879. Subway 4, 5, 6 to 59th Street.
This isn't the type of spa where you're going to get reiki and reflexology; it's a no-nonsense massage centre often patronised by professional athletes and dancers. The ideal place if you want a treatment without the frills.

SOHO

To get to SoHo, use either the N, R subway lines to Prince Street or the 6, C, E to Spring Street.

Acqua Beauty Bar: 7 East 14th Street between 5th Avenue and Union Square West. Tel 212-620 4329, www.acquabeautybar.com.
This hip beauty parlour in the ultra trendy Union Square area offers a full menu of nail, body and face treatments from just $12 for

Kiehl's

a manicure and $60 for a Bye Bye Eye Bags facial – or splash out on the works for $150!

Amore Pacific: 114 Spring Street between Mercer and Greene Streets. Tel 212-966 0400, www.amorepacific.com.
A feng shui-influenced spa that uses Korean AP products and where you can have a massage according to your elemental disposition: wood, metal, earth, water or fire.

Bliss Soho: 2nd Floor, 568 Broadway between Houston and Prince Streets. Tel 212-219 8970, www.blissworld.com.
One of New York's most famous spas, this is the place where you can get it all and in the fastest possible time. You can have a manicure at the same time as your facial and even an underarm wax, too. Therein lies its down side though – for some, it can seem too swift and impersonal.

Inspiration – a Rose Alcido Day Spa: Suite 1116, 1133 Broadway between 25th and 26th Streets. Tel 212-243 0432, www.rosealcido.com.
A teeny space that's become famous for Rose's signature Golden-Spoon facial. Following a full facial, two hot spoons are used to massage the face, giving an intense, penetrating treatment.

BRITTIP
The best anti-ageing facial in the Big Apple is the Intense Pulsed Light treatment at Shizuka spa in Midtown East (7 West 51st Street, 6th Floor. Tel 212-644 7400, www.shizukany.com).

John Masters Organic Spa: 77 Sullivan Street between Spring and Broome Streets. Tel 212-343 9590, www.johnmasters.com.
Outstanding full-body massages and facials for those who like to ensure all aspects of their life are organic.

Ling Skin Care: 191 Prince Street at Sullivan Street. Tel 212-982 8833, www.lingskincare.com.
Not big on pampering, so don't expect scented candles, white fluffy robes and feng shui, but extremely good facials from $115 that are considered the best in town by some New Yorkers, including the salon's celebrity clientele.

Maximus Soho: 15 Mercer Street between Grand and Canal Streets. Tel 516-333 4083. Subway A, C, E, N, Q, R, W to Canal Street.

SoHo

Treatment rooms that change colour every few seconds for mood enhancement is just one of the reason's to visit this lovely, water-centric spa.

The Mezzanine Spa at Soho Integrative Health Centre: 62 Crosby Street between Broome and Spring Streets.
Tel 212-431 1600, www.mezzaninespa.com.
Dr Laurie Polis founded this tiny spa at her office. Body treatments include volcanic mud therapy, while the Diamond Peel involves suction and microcrystals to exfoliate the face.

Monique K Skin Care: 345 East 9th Street between Avenues A and B. Tel 212-673 2041, www.moniquek.com/facials.
For an excellent deal on superb facials, head to this East Village hideaway. Owned by Monique K, once head facialist at the famous Georgette Klinger Salon (page 134), you get the same quality facials at much better prices.

Oasis Day Spa: 2nd Floor, 108 East 16th Street between Irving Place and Union Square East. Tel 212-254 7722, www.oasisdayspanyc.com. Subway L, N, Q, R, W, 4, 5, 6 to Union Square/14th Street.
Get off the beaten track for a truly relaxing experience at one of New York's best-kept secrets. Here you'll escape all elements of hustle and bustle in a sweet-smelling space where you are given your own massage slippers and a comfy robe. Fab therapies include a deep-penetrating Lava Stone Massage for $100, or an exquisite facial with customised face mask and warm hand mitts for $95.

TOP FIVE SPAS FOR MINOR COSMETIC SURGERY

You're visiting one of the leading cities in the world for beauty treatments, including minor cosmetic surgeries such as laser eye treatment or Botox. Many tourists even combine a long weekend of shopping with a trip to a clinic so that they can return to the UK looking 10 years younger!

If you're considering a minor treatment, make sure that the spa or beauty centre is registered, book well in advance as they tend to get booked up quickly, and be sure to have a consultation prior to any treatment so that you understand exactly what you're getting. Below are five highly rated spas regularly used by New Yorkers, from celebrities to Upper East Side ladies who lunch.

Midtown

Sleek New York: 800B 5th Avenue at 61st Street. Tel 212-521 3100, www.sleekmedspa.com. Subway 4, 5, 6 to 59th Street.
Nurses, practitioners and dermatologists are on hand at this no-nonsense clinic to treat a wide variety of skin issues, from wrinkles to spots. Treatments include glycolic peels, Botox, microdermabrasion, beta for acne, and laser hair removal.

Smooth Synergy: 686 Lexington Avenue at East 57th Street. Tel 212-397 0111, www.smoothsynergy.com. Subway 4, 5, 6 to 59th Street.
Laser hair and tattoo removal, microdermabrasion, Botox, vein therapy and glycolic peels are just some of the many treatments on offer at this highly regarded spa.

Upper East Side

Ajune: 1294 3rd Avenue at 74th Street. Tel 212-628 0044, www.ajune.com. Subway 6 to 77th Street.
Experts in laser wrinkle reduction, collagen implants and Botox, all administered in a tranquil setting with slate floors and wooden features.

Dr Ronald Sherman/Trish McEvoy Skincare Centre: 4th Floor, 800A 5th Avenue at 61st Street. Tel 212-758 7790. Subway N, R to 5th Avenue.
Laser hair removal, Botox and skin cancer examinations can be had at the make-up guru and top dermatologist's skincare Mecca.

Howard Sobel Skin & Spa: 960 Park Avenue at 82nd Street. Tel 212-288 0060, www.drsobel.com. Subway 4, 5, 6 to 86th Street.
Award-winning specialists in Botox treatments.

Prema Nolita: 252 Elizabeth Street between Houston and Prince Streets. Tel 212-226 3972. Subway 6 to Spring Street.
Thought to be the smallest spa in town, Celeste Induddi and her two partners have just one treatment room, but sell their own Prema line plus celeb faves Jurlique and Anne Semonin.

SoHo Sanctuary: 3rd Floor, 119 Mercer Street at Princes Street. Tel 212-334 5550, www.sohosanctuary.com.
Fabulous massages in this mellow favourite of the fashion pack. There are also yoga and Pilates classes, plus a steam room.

ANTIQUES AND FLEA MARKETS

In balmy weather, nothing beats strolling through the treasure trove of antiques, collectables and one-off pieces at any of New York's outdoor markets or in some of the unusual individual shops.

CHELSEA

Adrian Ruehl: 9th Avenue at Gansevoort Street. Tel 212-242 2576, www.adrianruehl.com (currently under construction). Subway 1, 2, 3, A, C, E to 14th Street; L to 8th Avenue.
Packed full of 19th-century European antiques from chandeliers to candlesticks.

Chelsea Antiques Building: 110 West 25th Street between 6th and 7th Avenues. Tel 212-929 0909. Subway F, V to 23rd Street.
This 12-storey building houses 90 galleries of antiques and collectables with merchandise ranging from Japanese textiles to vintage phonographs and radios.

The Garage: 112 West 25th Street between 6th and 7th Avenues. Tel 212-647 0707. Subway F, V to 23rd Street.
The Garage is exactly that – a two-storey parking garage that transforms into another bustling venue at the weekend.

The Showplace: 40 West 25th Street. Tel 212-741 8520. Subway F, V to 23rd Street.
An indoor extension of the outdoor market (open at weekends only), with a small café downstairs.

EAST VILLAGE

Irreplaceable Artefacts: 216 East 125th Street between 2nd and 3rd Avenues. Tel 212-777 2900.
An excellent selection of actual architectural bits and bobs.

GREENWICH VILLAGE

Alan Moss: 436 Lafayette Street near Astor Place. Tel 212-473 1310, www.alanmossny.com. Subway 6 to Astor Place.
Glass gems and interesting lighting from the mid-20th century.

HELL'S KITCHEN

Annex/Hell's Kitchen Flea Market: 39th Street between 9th and 10th Avenues. Tel 212-243 5343, www.hellskitchenfleamarket.com. Subway A, C, E or 1, 2, 3, 9 to 34th/42nd Streets. Now includes The Annex, America's most famous outdoor market, where celebrities browse through vintage clothing, furniture, pottery, glassware, jewellery and art. Get there early for the best finds. Weekends only.

MADISON SQUARE

Old Print Shop: 150 Lexington Avenue between East 29th and East 30th Streets. Tel 212-683 3950, www.oldprintshop.com. Subway 6 to 33rd Street.
This is the place to search out Americana up to the 1950s.

MIDTOWN EAST

Lillian Nassau: 220 East 57th Street between 2nd and 3rd Avenues. Tel 212-759 6062, www.lilliannassau.com. Subway 4, 5, 6 to 59th Street.
Come here for art nouveau lamps and glassware, especially original Tiffanys.

Manhattan Arts & Antiques Center: 1050 2nd Avenue between East 55th and East 56th Streets. Tel 212-355 4400, www.the-maac.com.
Subway 4, 5, 6, to 59th Street; F, N, R, W to Lexington Avenue.

SOHO

Coconut Company: 131 Greene Street near Prince Street. Tel 212-539 1940. Subway N, R to Prince Street.
A fascinating, eclectic mix of 19th and 20th-century antiques, from photographs and books to coffee tables.

The SoHo Antiques Fair: Broadway and Grand Street.
Antiques and collectables all year round.

BRITTIP

Check out www.fleamarket guide.com for a list of flea markets, what they sell and special fairs and events around the city.

TRIBECA

Antiqueria Tribeca: 129 Duane Street near Broadway. Tel 212-227 7500, www.antiqueria.com. Subway 1, 2, 3, 9, A, C to Chambers Street.
Filled with French Art Deco pieces, from furniture to accessories. Often some lovely Lalique and Murano glass items to be found.

Burden & Izett Ltd: 180 Duane Street near Houston Street. Tel 212-941 8247, www.burdenandizett.net. Subway 1, 2, 3, 9, A, C to Chambers Street.
Extremely pricey, high-end, one-of-a-kind pieces of furniture to gaze at in awe.

UPPER EAST AND WEST SIDES

Green Flea Market: Greenwich Avenue at Charles Street between West 10th and 11th Streets on Saturdays 10am–5.30pm and Columbus Avenue between West 76th and 77th Streets on Sundays 10am–5.30pm. Tel 212-239 3025, www.greenfleamarkets.com. Subway 1, 9 to 79th Street; B, C to 77th/81st Street.
Antiques, collectables, bric-a-brac, handmade pottery and discount clothing in this indoor and outdoor market.

SoHo street market

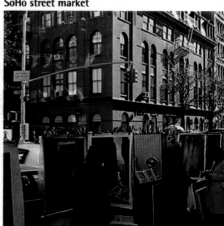

BOOKS

Books are big business in New York and book readings are a popular form of entertainment. For a real slice of the New York lifestyle, there are a number of places that specialise in readings: **The Drawing Center** (35 Wooster Street between Grand and Broome Streets, tel 212-694 0910, www.drawingcentre.org) gives readings related to the exhibitions; **The Poetry Project** at St Mark's Church (131 East 10th Street, tel 212-674 0910, www.poetry project.com) has three evening readings a week, Mon and Wed 8pm, Fri 10.30pm.

The 92nd Street Y (1395 Lexington Avenue, tel 212-414 5500, www.92y.org) has a great series of lectures and readings, as does **The Dia Center for the Arts** (548 West 22nd Street, tel 212-989 5566, www.diacenter.org). Also check out **Barnes & Noble** (page 139) and **192 Books** (below) for more.

CHELSEA

192 Books: 912 10th Avenue between 21st and 22nd Streets. Tel 212-255 4022, www.192books.com. Subway C, E to 23rd Street.
A good range of art and literature titles as well as a large children's section. The atmosphere in this bright, airy shop is very comfortable, with reading tables and comfy chairs to help you relax. There are weekly readings here.

EAST VILLAGE

Alabaster Bookshop: 122 Fourth Avenue at 12th Street. Tel 212-982 3550. Subway 4, 5, 6, L, N, Q, R, W at 14th Street, Union Square.
Only one used bookstore remains on what was once book row. Owner Steve Crowley is still there with a great array of paperbacks that are around half the cover price, to rare photography books by the likes of Lou Reed, locked in ornate wood cabinets. There are carts to trawl through on the sidewalk, too.

Times Square Toys 'R Us

St Mark's Bookshop: 31 3rd Avenue on the corner of 9th Street. Tel 212-260 7853, www.stmarksbookshop.com. Subway 6 to Astor Place.
An excellent bookstore with a broad range of books. The bulletin board in the front gives details of local literary events.

GREENWICH VILLAGE

Shakespeare & Co: 716 Broadway at Washington Place. Tel 212-529 1330, www.shakeandco.com. Subway N, R to 8th Street; 6 to Astor Place. This is an excellent bookstore. Unlike many a Barnes & Noble, where the staff sometimes don't appear to recognise joined-up writing, all the assistants here are graduates and will be genuinely helpful.

MIDTOWN

Rizzoli: 31 West 57th Street between 5th and 6th Avenues. Tel 212-759 2424, www.rizzoliusa.com. Subway N, R, W to 5th Avenue/59th Street; F to 57th Street. This trendy store has a good stock of art, fashion and design publications and is popular with those in the media and with design students.

MIDTOWN EAST

Argosy: 116 East 59th between Park and Lexington Avenues. Tel 212-753 4455, www.argosybooks.com. Subway 4, 5, 6, F, N, R to 59th Street.
The best book shop in New York if you're looking for rare, hard-to-find books. There are seven storeys of out-of-print publications, antiques, maps, autographs and letters to browse through. Beware, though: you can easily lose an afternoon engrossed in here.

Borders Books & Music: 461 Park Avenue at 57th Street. Tel 212-980 6785, www.bordersstores.com. Subway N, R to Lexington Avenue; 4, 5, 6 to 59th Street. Excellent outlet for books, CDs, videos and more obscure books, too. A few other megastores throughout the city.

Urban Centre Books: 457 Madison Avenue, between East 50th and East 51st Streets. Tel 212-935 3595, www.urbancenterbooks.org. Subway 6 to 51st Street; E, F to 5th Avenue. Housed in the pretty Villard Houses, this bookstore is a treasure trove for anyone interested in architecture and buildings.

NOLITA

Tower Books: 383 Lafayette Street at 4th Street. Tel 212-228 5100. Subway B, D, F, Q to Broadway/Lafayette; 6 to Bleecker Street.

A wide range of contemporary fiction and a huge magazine section.

WEST VILLAGE

Biography Bookshop: 400 Bleecker Street at West 11th Street. Tel 212-807 8655. Subway 1, 2, 3 to 14th Street. A massive selection of biographies covering all genres.

Bookleaves: 304 West 4th Street near Bank Street. Tel 212-924 5638. Subway 1, 2, 3 or A, C, E or L to 14th Street. Just what you imagine a New York bookstore to be like: dusty, quiet and tucked away in a neighbourhood and offering a fabulous selection of everything from paperbacks to out-of-print pricey tomes.

Three Lives Bookstore: 154 West 10th Street off 7th Avenue. Tel 212-741 2069, www.threelives.com.
A delightful shop with a charming ambience, known for attentive staff with encyclopaedic knowledge. Specialises in literary fiction, poetry and design books, as well as memoirs.

UNION SQUARE

Barnes & Noble: 105 5th Avenue at 18th Street. Tel 212-675 5500, www.bnnewyork.com. Subway L, N, R, 4, 5, 6 to 14th Street/Union Square.
This is the original store of one of the largest chains of bookstores in America and, as well as a massive selection of books, it also sells CDs and videos. Barnes & Noble is responsible for putting many independent bookstores out of business, but is well worth a visit. Many branches have coffee shops and seating areas for you to look through books before buying. You'll see branches everywhere.

Books of Wonder: 18 West 18th Street at 5th Avenue. Tel 212-989 3270, www.booksofwonder.net. Subway 1 at 18th Street.
Top place in New York to go for children's books, limited editions and art from children's literature. There are rare collector's editions through to picture pop-ups, and as many adults flock here as kids. There's a storytelling time if your brood ranges from 3 to 6-years-old every Sunday at noon.

◀ ▶ BRITTIP

If shopping's sapping your energy and you're feeling in need of a sugar rush, tuck into some of the delicious desserts and pastries at the Cupcake Cafe in Books of Wonder.

Strand Book Store: 828 Broadway at 12th Street. Tel 212-473 1452, www.strandbooks.com. Subway L, N, R, Q, W, 4, 5, 6 to 14th Street/Union Square. This whole area used to be famous for antiquarian bookshops, but the Strand is the only one left. The store has over two million second-hand and new books on any subject you'd care to name – all at around half the published price.

CHILDREN

MIDTOWN

The Disney Store: 711 5th Avenue between 55th and 5th Streets. Tel 212-702 0702, www.worldofdisney.com. Subway E, F to 5th Avenue. Also at 218 West 42nd Street. Tel 212-302 0595. Subway 1, 2, 3, 9, N, R to Times Square/42nd Street.
If it comes with a pair of ears, then you'll find it here!

FAO Schwarz: 767 5th Avenue at 58th Street. Tel 212-644 9400 ext. 4242, www.fao.com. Subway N, R to 5th Avenue. The most famous children's store in the world, it's not only huge but is also an entertainment centre in its own right, with oversized displays that take your breath away, plus every conceivable toy your child could want.

◀ ▶ BRITTIP

If you stay at the Ritz-Carlton Hotel in Battery Park City, you'll be entitled to a 10 per cent discount at FAO Schwarz.

Hershey's Times Square: 48th Street and Broadway. Tel 212-581 9100, www.hersheys.com/discover/timessquare. Subway N, R, S, 1, 2, 3, 7, 9, A, C, E to 42nd Street/Times Square.
The Cadbury's of America now has a massive chocolate haven in Times Square. Enter (at your peril) under the 65m (215ft) tall, 18m (60ft) wide giant Hershey bar to find every kind of Hershey sweet under the sun, as well as clothing, toys and giant chocolate greetings cards.

Toys R Us: 1514 Broadway between 44th and 45th Streets. Tel 212-225 8392, www.toysrus.com. Subway N, Q, R, S, W, 1, 2, 3, 7 to Times Square.
In the heart of the rejuvenated Times Square district, this three-storey, glass-enclosed building is home to an 18m (60ft) Ferris

wheel, a giant roaring dinosaur and a life-size Barbie townhouse. If you are here with kids, it's a must-see.

WEST VILLAGE

Gepetto's Toy Box: 10 Christopher Street between Gay Street and Greenwich Avenue. Tel 212-620 7511. Subway 1, 9 to Christopher Street.
A great antithesis to the bright, brash modern toy stores. Here you'll find beautiful, traditional handmade toys, such as rocking horses and mobiles.

DRINK

CHELSEA

Chelsea Wine Vault: 75 9th Avenue at Chelsea Market. Tel 212-462 4244, www.chelseawinevault.com. Subway A, C, E to 14th Street.
More than 3,000 labels to choose from. Take advantage of the fun free tastings – mainly at weekends (see website).

BRITTIP

Don't be fooled by the bottles of wine you may see in food shops in New York. They are either non-alcoholic or low alcohol as it is illegal for food stores to sell wine. However, this doesn't apply to beer.

EAST VILLAGE

Astor Wines & Spirits: 399 Lafayette Street at 4th Street at the corner of Astor Place. Tel 212-674 7500, www.astorwines.com. Subway 6 to Astor Place; R, W to 8th Street.
Stocks a wide range of wines and spirits.

LOWER EAST SIDE

Schapiro's Winery: 120 Essex Street, The Essex Street Market, www.schapiro-wine.com. Subway J, M, Z, F to Essex/Delancey Street.
The Schapiro family has been running this winery since 1899 and it's decorated with old casks and bottles. It's the city's only kosher wine and spirits warehouse and sweet wine is made on the premises. There is a free tasting tour Sun at 2pm.

MIDTOWN EAST

Park Avenue Liquor Shop: 292 Madison Avenue between 40th and 41st Streets. Tel 212-685 2442, www.parkaveliquor.com. Subway 4, 5, 6, 7 to Grand Central/42nd Street.

Specialises in Californian wines and European bottles. Discounts are given with bulk purchases.

Schumer's Wine & Liquor: 59 East 54th Street between Park and Madison Avenues. Tel 212-355 0940. Subway E, F to Lexington Avenue; 6 to 51st Street.
With a great range of American and European wines, it also stocks a good selection of spirits and champagne.

SOHO

Vintage New York: 482 Broome Street at the corner of Wooster and SoHo Streets. Tel 212-226 9463, www.vintagenewyork.com. Subway 6 to Spring Street.
SoHo is home to a complete first in New York City – a shop that can sell both wine and food. The reason is because it is owned by a vineyard from New York State, which means it can open on Sundays and sell alcoholic wine and food together – both of which are otherwise illegal in New York. All the wines come from New York State vineyards and five tastes cost just $5. It also houses a wine bar open in the evening with over 200 wines by the glass and a creative, delicious menu.

UNION SQUARE

Union Square Wine and Spirits: 33 Union Square West between 16th and 17th Streets. Tel 212-675 8100, www.wineaccess.com/store/unionsquarewines. Subway 4, 5, 6, L, N, Q, R, W to Union Square.
More than 4,000 wines, good prices and the staff know their wines.

UPPER EAST SIDE/YORKVILLE

Best Cellars: 1291 Lexington Avenue at 87th Street. Tel 212-426 4200, www.bestcellars.com. Subway 4, 5, 6 to 86th Street.
One of the best-value stores in the city for fine wines under $10. Free tastings every weekday 5pm–8pm, Sat 2pm–4pm paired with food from top new chefs are even better value!

Sherry-Lehmann: 679 Madison Avenue between 61st and 62nd Streets. Tel 212-838 7500, www.sherry-lehmann.com. Subway 4, 5, 6 to 59th Street.
The most famous wine shop in New York. A huge selection and well situated for that Central Park picnic.

UPPER WEST SIDE

Acker, Merrall & Condit Wine Merchants:
160 West 72nd Street between Broadway
and Columbus. Tel 212-787 1700,
www.ackerstore.com. Subway 1, 2, 3, 9 to
72nd Street.
America's oldest wine store – it opened in
1820 – is well worth a visit for its vast
selection of wines from around the world
that range in price from a couple of dollars
to more than $20,000.

BRITTIP
You can only buy wine and
spirits from liquor stores, which
do not sell mixers or even beer!

ELECTRONICS

Have a clear idea of what you're looking for
before buying – pick up a copy of Tuesday's
New York Times to check out prices in the
science section first. Of course, you can
always find electrical items at really cheap
prices in the Chinatown stretch of Canal
Street, but you won't get a guarantee.

CHELSEA

Adorama: 42 West 18th Street near 6th
Avenue. Tel 212-741 0052,
www.adorama.com. Subway 1, 9 to 18th
Street.
Six floors that cover all your photographic
needs, from disposable cameras through to
$10,000 professional snappers. In addition, it
offers a range of other services including
creating digital prints for 20 cents each.

BRITTIP
National electronics chain Best
Buy (tel 888-237 8289,
www.bestbuy.com) sells a wide
variety of gadgets and gizmos from
speakers to stereos plus games, CDs
and computers at really competitive
prices. They can be found at locations
throughout the city including 60
23rd Street in Chelsea (tel 212-366
2373) and 1280 Lexington Avenue at
86th Street, Upper East Side (tel
917-492 8870).

MADISON SQUARE

Fotografica: 124 West 25th Street between
6th and 7th Avenues. Tel 212-929 6080.
Subway F, V to 23rd Street.
A vast stock of used camera equipment at

trade prices. Owner Ed Wassel will be happy
to order anything not in stock.

MIDTOWN

Datavision Computer Video: 445 5th
Avenue near 39th Street. Tel 212-689 1111.
Subway 7, B, D, F, V to 42nd Street/5th
Avenue.
You'll find whatever techie treat you desire,
from laptops to iPod accessories, in this
cramped but comprehensive store.

Harvey Electronics: 2 West 45th Street at
5th Avenue. Tel 212-575 5000. Subway B, D,
F, V to 42nd Street/Bryant Park.
Not bargain basement prices, but specialists
where you are guaranteed great products
and deals. Stocks a good selection of top
brands such as Fujitsu and Pioneer.

34TH STREET–PENN STATION

B&H Photo & Video: 420 9th Avenue
between West 33rd and West 34th Streets.
Tel 212-444 6615, www.bhphotovideo.com.
Subway A, C, E to 34th Street/Penn Station.
A massive three-storey, block-long store that
stocks every conceivable piece of electronic
imaging, audio, video and photo equipment
you've ever heard of. All the staff are
professionals in their own right and really
know their onions. They're helpful, too,
which is why this emporium is an excellent
place to go for everyone from novices to
professionals.

Willoughby's: 136 West 32nd Street
between 6th and 7th Avenues. Tel 212-564
1600, www.willoughbys.com. Subway B, D, F,
Q, N, R, V, W, 1, 2, 3 to 34th Street.
Reputedly the world's largest collection of
cameras and all things audio, but the service
isn't brilliant so make sure you know what
you want before you go.

Toys 'R Us

FOOD

CHELSEA

Chelsea Market: 75 9th Avenue between 15th and 16th Streets. Tel 212-243 6005, www.chelseamarket.com. Subway A, C, E, L to 14th Street and 8th Avenue.
You'll find everything you need here for a gourmet feast, from fishmongers and bakers to wine merchants, and even florists for table decorations. Check out Buon Italia for great cheeses, sauces and all manner of Italian fodder and Amy's for breads you never dreamed of. An instant picnic!

CHINATOWN

Asia Market: 71 Mulberry Street between Canal and Bayar Streets. Tel 212-962 2020. Subway 6, J, M, N, Q, R, W, Z to Canal Street. The tightly packed Asia Market is loved by chefs and residents alike. There's everything here from canned curries to dried cuttlefish and dozens of varieties of noodles; every staple of Thai, Malaysian and Indonesian cuisine under one roof.

GREENWICH VILLAGE

Take the subway A, C, E, F, V, S to West 4th Street for a whole area of foodie shops.

Aphrodisia: 264 Bleecker Street between 6th and 7th Avenues. Tel 212-989 6440. A huge selection of bulk herbs, spices, teas and potpourri.

> ### 🇬🇧 BRITTIP
> If you'd like a taste of the foods sold in some of the shops in Greenwich Village, go on the Foods of New York tour, which also introduces you to great restaurants in the area (page 81).

Balducci's: 155A West 66th Street, near the Lincoln Center just west of Broadway. Tel 212-653 8320, www.suttongourmet.com. One of the most famous gourmet food emporiums in New York. You can find everything from fresh vegetables and fruit to edible flowers and hung game.

Faicco's Sausage Store: 260 Bleecker Street between 6th and 7th Avenues. Tel 212-243 1974.
A landmark Italian speciality food shop established in 1900, it is known for its own sausages that are made daily (and sold to many of the neighbouring restaurants), its home-made mozzarella cheese, again made

Bagel vendor

daily, plus rice balls made with three cheeses and rolled in breadcrumbs. Other specialities include prosciutto balls, potato croquettes, fried ravioli and stuffed breads.

Murray's Cheese Shop: 254 Bleecker Street between 6th and 7th Avenues. Tel 212-243 3289, www.murrayscheese.com.
The owner travels all over the world to bring back a fascinating selection of more than 350 cheeses with amazing names such as Wabash Cannonball, Crocodile Tears, Mutton Buttons and Cardinal Sin, a British cow's milk cheese. They also sell olives, chorizos, pâtés and breads and you may even catch a cookery class.

Pasticceria Bruno: 245 Bleecker Street between 6th and 7th Avenues. Tel 212-242 4959, www.brunobakery.com.
An Italian-French bakery run by one of the top 10 pastry chefs in New York. It does miniature and large fruit tarts, mousses, cookies, sorbets, ice-cream cakes and home-made chocolates, and you can sit down to try any of them with a nice cup of tea or coffee.

Rocco's: 243 Bleecker Street between 6th and 7th Avenues. Tel 212-242 6031, www.roccospastry.com.
Famous for its fresh cannolis (an Italian pastry filled with cream), it sells large and small sizes of everything from Italian cheesecakes to chocolate, hazelnut and lemon cakes. You can eat in, too, with a cup of delicious coffee.

LITTLE ITALY

Di Palo's: 206 Grand Street at Mott Street. Tel 212-226 1033. Subway J, M, N, Q, R, W, Z, 6 to Canal Street.
One of the last remaining Italian speciality food stores in Little Italy, it was founded 80

years ago and is particularly famous for its mozzarella and Italian sausages and salami. It even has its own ageing room for cheeses.

LOWER EAST SIDE
Russ & Daughters: 179 East Houston Street between Allen and Orchard Streets. Tel 212-475 4880, www.russanddaughters.com. Subway F to 2nd Avenue.
Along with Katz's Deli (page 158), this is one of the most famous outlets in the Lower East Side. Established in 1914, it sells every possible kind of fish, caviar, pickled vegetables and bagels.

SOHO
Dean & Deluca: 560 Broadway at Prince Street. Tel 212-226 6800. Subway N, R, Q, W to Prince Street.
Gourmets love the fresh bread, cheese, coffee beans and other delicious foods on sale at this SoHo secret.

34TH STREET
Cucina & Co: In the Cellar at Macy's (page 113), 151 West 34th Street, 6th Avenue and Broadway. Tel 212-868 2388, www.rapatina.com/cucinaCoMacys. Subway B, D, F, N, Q, R, V, W to 34th Street.
One of the most fabulous grocer's markets in New York, now famous for its supplies of lobster and caviar.

UPPER EAST SIDE/YORKVILLE
Martine's Chocolates: 400 82nd Street off 1st Avenue. Tel 212-744 6289, www.martineschocolates.com. Subway 6 to 86th Street.
If you're not on a diet, drool over the rich Belgian choccies, which take up to three days to make. Chocolate heaven!

The Vinegar Factory: 431 East 91st Street between York and 1st Avenues. Tel 212-987 0885. Subway 4, 5, 6 to 86th Street.
One of the most famous markets in the city. Here you'll find stacks of cheeses, meats, breads, salads and cakes – in fact, everything you need to create a perfect picnic.

UPPER WEST SIDE
Zabar's: 2245 Broadway at 80th Street. Tel 212-787 2000, www.zabars.com. Subway 1, 2 to 79th Street.
Just about the most famous food store in New York and also considered to be one of the finest. It has a tremendous range of cheeses, fresh fruit and veg, meats, fish and bagels. In fact it's so famous it's even been featured in *Friends*.

HOMEWARE
CHELSEA
Authentiques Past & Present: 255 West 18th Street at Eight Avenue. Tel 212-675 2179. Subway 1 to 18th Street.
A must-visit for lovers of interiors from the 1950s and '60s. The long attic-style room is like a time capsule stocking fab American glass, barware, kitchen items, lamps and lots of cool kitsch items.

MIDTOWN
Crate & Barrel: 650 Madison Avenue at 59th Street. Tel 212-308 0011, www.crateandbarrel.com. Subway 4, 5, 6 to 59th Street.
Fashionable, funky furniture, accessories, kitchen and tableware for incredibly low prices. There's also another branch in SoHo at 611 Broadway at Houston Street.

SOHO
Anthropologie: 375 West Broadway at Spring Street. Tel 212-343 7070, www.anthropologie.com. Subway C, E to Spring Street.
One of our favourite shops selling gorgeous boudoir items, such as silk quilts, Venetian-style mirrors and night stands, in an airy loft-like space. There's also a collection of stylish women's clothes on sale with the same thrift-store, trendy feel.

Broadway Panhandler: 477 Broome Street between Greene and Wooster Streets. Tel 212-966 3434, www.broadwaypanhandler.com. Subway N, R, W to Prince Street.
All things for the kitchen, from the latest gadgets to classic pieces such as steel saucepans and Alessi toasters. There are hundreds of items to choose from and it's a must-visit for any domestic gods or goddesses when in town. Famous chefs often give in-store demonstrations.

Taxis are a good way to get around

UPPER EAST SIDE

Charlotte Moss: 20 East 63rd Street at Madison Avenue. Tel 212-308 3888, www.charlottemoss.com. Subway 4, 5, 6 at 59th Street.
Newly opened gorgeous townhouse filled with expensive items you'll want to snap up for your own home, from doorknobs to stools and even the bedroom floor.

Laytner's Linen and Home: 237 East 86th Street at 2nd Avenue. Tel 212-996 4439, www.laytners.com. Subway 4, 5, 6 to 86th Street.
Come here to buy some luxurious high thread-count linen to take home.

UPPER WEST SIDE

Avventura: 463 Amsterdam Avenue at 82nd Street. Tel 212-769 2510. Subway A, 9 to 79th Street.
Contemporary tableware, from cocktail and champagne glasses to Deruta dishes.

MUSIC STORES

CHINATOWN

Gigantic Brand: 59 Franklin Street between Broadway and Lafayette Streets. Tel 212-966 2361. Subway 6, J, M, N, Q, R, W, Z at Canal Street.
A cool mix of concepts including an area dedicated to indie CDs, some from the Gigantic record label and some staff favourites, plus another section dedicated to independent feature and documentary DVDS. Throw in a wall at the back showing work from emerging artists and some edgy fashion labels from unheard of overseas designers and you've discovered a very hot place to visit.

The Trump Building

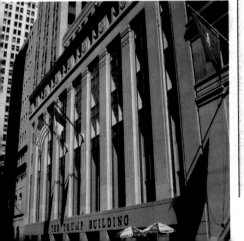

EAST VILLAGE

A-1 Records: 439 East 6th Street at Avenues A. Tel 212-473 2870. Subway F, V at Lower East Side, Second Avenue.
Geared towards those still interested in vinyl, with a focus on soul, jazz, hip-hop and an ever-changing assortment of house and dance. You can listen to records in store before you buy.

Downtown Music Gallery: 342 Bowery between East 2nd and East 3rd Streets. Tel 212-473 0043, www.downtownmusic gallery.com. Subway 6 to Astor Place.
Jazz aficionados love this specialist shop with its wide selection of records and CDs to search through. Live performances take place Sun 6pm.

Sounds: 20 St Mark's Place between 2nd and 3rd Avenues. Tel 212-677 2727. Subway 6 to Astor Place.
The place to visit if you want to buy the latest popular tracks from well-known artists at very competitive prices.

FINANCIAL DISTRICT

J&R Music World: 33 Park Row between Ann and Beekman Streets. Tel 212-238 9000, www.jr.com. Subway A or C to Broadway/ Nassau Street.
Check out the weekly ads in the New York Post and Village Voice to get an idea of what's on offer. The store also sells jazz, Latin and pop music.

GREENWICH VILLAGE

Bleecker Bob's Golden Oldies Record Shop: 118 West 3rd Street at MacDougal Street. Tel 212-475 9677, www.bleecker bobs.com. Subway A, B, C, D, E, F, V to West 4th Street.
Whatever sounds you're into, you'll find something to satisfy your tastes. Choose from thousands of jazz, rock, punk and R&B vinyls and now CDs and DVDs, too.

Tower Records: 692 Broadway at 4th Street. Tel 212-505 1500, www.tower records.com. Subway N, R, W to 8th Street.
An excellent range of CDs and tapes. Around the block on Lafayette Street is the knockdown Tower Clearance shop.

SMOKER'S CORNER

If you still haven't managed to quit, the best shop to buy your ciggies from is a chain of chemists called Duane Reade – the New York equivalent of our Boots. Check www.duanereade.com for locations.

Newstand

MIDTOWN
Virgin Megastore: 1540 Broadway between 45th and 46th Streets. Tel 212-921 1020, www.virginmega.com. Subway 1, 2, 3, 9, N, Q, R, S, W to 42nd Street.
Just like the ones in the UK, only this is even bigger and better, with an even wider variety of CDs, records, DVDs, games, T-shirts and posters. It's always worth checking out the website before you visit the city, as the store often has high-profile pop stars performing there to promote a new release.

UPPER WEST SIDE
Tower Records: 1961 Broadway at 66th Street. Tel 212-799 2500, www.towerrecords.com. Subway 1, 9 to 66th Street/Lincoln Center.
The Lincoln Center branch also has an excellent range of CDs and tapes.

SPECIALITY AND GIFT SHOPS
CHELSEA
IS: 136 West 17th Street between 6th and 7th Avenues. Tel 212-620 0300. Subway A, C, E, 1, 9 to 14th Street.
A designer stationery store with a distinctly hip edge.

MIDTOWN
Midtown Comics: 2nd floor, 200 West 40th Street at 7th Avenue. Tel 212-302 8192, www.villagecomics.com. Subway 1, 2, 3, 7, N, Q, R, S, W to Times Sq/42nd Street.
A two-storey comic emporium with bags of back issues running up and down the length of the store. 500,000 volumes are available, from Japanese manga to Spiderman.

UPPER EAST SIDE
E.A.T. Gifts: 1062 Madison Avenue at 80th Street. Tel 212-861 2544. Subway 6 to 77th Street.
You can hardly move for the shelves that are tightly packed with every conceivable gift,

from gadgets to trinkets, a lot of it fun stuff for kids.

WEST VILLAGE
Alphaville: 226 West Houston Street at Varwick Street. Tel 212-675 6850. Subway 1 to Houston Street.
Nostalgia lovers and design geeks need to make a stop at this unique store and gallery, which offers an excellent range of mid-century vintage toys and posters. Original Mr Potato Heads sit in their original packaging next to 1950s rocket-shaped water pistols. Movie buffs will want to part with their cash for the vintage film posters and covet the iconic action figures from film and TV.

Flight 001: 96 Greenwich Avenue between Jane and West 12th Streets. Tel 212-691 1001, www.flight001.com. Subway 1, 2, 3, 9 to 14th Street.
A travel accessories shop that looks like a sleek 1960s airport lounge, it stocks fabulously cool carry-on items such as digital cameras, spray-on vitamins and WAP-activated global travel guides. It also has practical but funky luggage.

MXYPLYZYK: 125 Greenwich Avenue at West 13th Street. Tel 212-989 4300, www.mxyplyzyk.com. Subway 1, 2, 3, 9 to 14th Street.
Kitschy-cool gifts and whatnots including Devil Ducks (with horns – glow-in-the-dark or plain red) and tractor-seat stools for when you're tired of serious shopping.

Tea and Sympathy: 110 Greenwich Avenue between 12th and 13th Streets. Tel 212-989 9735, www.teaandsympathynewyork.com. Subway 1, 2, 3, 9 to 14th Street.
Filled with all things the Brit abroad loves, this is a combination of a shop and café offering sausage rolls, fish and chips and 'proper' tea. Liz Hurley orders food for her fashion shoots, David Bowie had his 50th birthday bash here and Kate Moss and Rupert Everett are regulars.

WOODBURY COMMON PREMIUM OUTLETS
It's no exaggeration to say that shopaholics from around the world call in at this American colonial-style village that's just a 1½-hour bus ride away from Manhattan. With more than 220 discount shops, it's the equivalent of paradise. For ordinary folk, it's still a wonderful place to make useful and fun purchases. Midweek is the quietest time to visit.

WOODBURY COMMON SHOPPING

✉ 498 Red Apple Court, Central Valley
☎ 1-845 928 4000
🖰 www.premiumoutlets.com/woodburycommon
🕐 Mon–Sat 10am–9pm, Sun 10am–8pm (check the website for seasonal and holiday hours)

Upon arrival by Gray Line (tel 800-669 0051), you'll be dropped off close to the tower entrance where you'll also find the information office, pushchairs (essential with a young child on a hot day), lockers, telephones, cashpoints and WCs.

Pick up a copy of the full-colour Shopping Guide (or download one from the website before you go) and in the centre you'll find a map with the five different sections in different colours. The colour coding is carried throughout the village, so as you walk around you can work out which area you are in by the colour of the apple above each shop sign.

The information tower is in the main red section, called Red Apple Court, which is largely dedicated to designer boutiques; to its south is Evergreen Court, home to many lifestyle stores; to the north of Red Apple Court is the Food Court and then Bluebird Court. To the left from the main entrance is the purple Grapevine Court.

Filled with the most upscale designer shops, Grapevine Court is serious droolsville territory and the first port of call for Japanese shoppers, who tend to be known as

Goochers thanks to their love of Gucci. Here you'll find Betsey Johnson, Chanel, Christian Dior, Fendi, Giorgio Armani General Store, Hugo Boss, Missoni, Nieman Marcus Last Call, Off 5th – Saks Fifth Avenue, La Perla, Valentino and the Thyme To Eat Restaurant. The Cosmetics Company Store here has great deals on many brands including Clinique, Estée Lauder, Bobbi Brown, MAC, Prescriptives and Origins.

Big names in Red Apple Court include A/X Armani Exchange, Burberry, Brooks Brothers, Carolina Herrera, Donna Karan/DKNY, Escada, Giorgio Armani, Gucci, Liz Claiborne, Polo Ralph Lauren, Salvatore Ferragamo and Versace.

Good shops that you should make a beeline for in the Bluebird Court are Claire's Accessories, Bombay Outlet, OshKosh B'Gosh, Perfumania, Puma, LeSportsac, Bebe and Nike Factory Store.

In the Evergreen Court you will discover other great stores such as Lancôme – The Company Outlet, Timberland, the Zegna Outlet Store, Benetton, Banana Republic, Reebok and Claiborne Menswear.

SALES TIMES

You can save even more money on your favourite labels by heading to Woodbury at sales times. Before you go, visit www.premiumoutlets.com/woodburycommon to check out the next sales date – there's usually one a month. However, the big sales times coincide with all the American holidays including 4 July, Memorial Day, President's Day, Labor Day Weekend, Columbus Day and the day after Thanksgiving (page 256).

Best time of all, though, is around Christmas, when some of the biggest savings are to be had – along with the biggest crowds, so arrive early!

◀🇬🇧▶ BRITTIP

Take the weight off your slingbacks and make the most of the free trolley that tours Woodbury – but bear in mind they only run on weekends. Trolley stops are shown in the Shopping Guide.

STAYING NEAR WOODBURY COMMON

The Orange County Bed & Breakfast Association offers shop-and-stay packages. Tel 800-210 5565, www.new-york-inns.com.

Woodbury Common

CHAPTER 7

Restaurants

N ew York is a city of extremes when it comes to dining out. There are nearly 18,000 restaurants to choose from. At one end are the classics, such as Union Square Café, that seem to transcend fashion and continually turn out delicious cuisine to cross the Atlantic for; at the other end of the spectrum are eateries that are so hip they're practically going out of fashion before they've even served up their first plate of fusion food.

The *Brit's Guide* aims to help you to experience the must-eat-at places that have been around for years and those achingly hip joints that are as much about who you're going to spot air kissing as the food. We also include a smattering of restaurants that sit between the established and the new that are just plain good value – or unusual.

◀ BRITTIP

New Yorkers swear by the *Zagat Survey* as the best guide for foodies. It lists hundreds of top restaurants reviewed by members of the public, and you can buy it in most UK bookshops, or visit www.zagat.com.

One of the great things about New York restaurants is that they're usually excellent value for money when compared with eating out in the UK, particularly London.

You can get a first-class breakfast for under $10 and a slap-up dinner for less than $40. It's well worth heading off the beaten track to find some of your own delectable diners in the city's coolest neighbourhoods, but we have plenty of suggestions for you if you don't fancy chancing it. The chapter starts with a selection of our favourite restaurants for fine dining, romance and views, categories that cover the majority of enquiries we receive from Brits keen to sample the culinary delights of Manhattan in a wonderful environment.

DINING PRICE GUIDE

It's clear from the outset what price categories many Big Apple eateries fall into. Crisp white tablecloths, wine glasses the size of goldfish bowls and waiters in designer garb indicate a blow-the-budget $100-plus bill. Dark, dingy diners with Formica tabletops and a waitress with a nametag suggest that you're going to be paying cash, and not much of it. However, there are some restaurants where the tariff doesn't match the decor or the standard of food the façade, so we have compiled a price guide to help you make your dining decisions with confidence.

$	Cheap and cheerful
$$	Good value
$$$	Posh meal out
$$$$	Blow the budget

Tavern on the Green

BRITTIP

If you're a foodie, visit New York during Winter Restaurant Week 23–27 Jan and 30 Jan–3 Feb, when more than 100 of the city's best restaurants offer three-course prix fixe meals for a bargain $24 for lunch and $35 for dinner. (Tel 212-484 1222, www.nycvisit.com.)

A–Z AREA-BY-AREA GUIDE TO RESTAURANTS

BATTERY PARK AND BATTERY PARK CITY

2 WEST $–$$$
American fusion
- ✉ 2 West Street between Battery Place and West End
- ☎ 212-344 0800
- ⌂ www.ritzcarlton.com
- 🚗 Subway 1, 9 to Rector Street

The lobby-level restaurant of the Ritz-Carlton has fabulous views of the Hudson River and Statue of Liberty, plus outdoor seating for al fresco dining in the warmer months. A French-American steakhouse, the menu offers a choice of American classics plus some global fusions such as duo of ahi tuna carpaccio and tuna tartare and, of course, numerous dishes involving certified prime Angus beef. The lunch menu also offers quick and easy Bento Boxes with Italian and Spanish themes.

BATTERY GARDENS $$$$
Gourmet American
- ✉ South-west corner of Battery Park (State Street) by the river
- ☎ 212-809 5508
- ⌂ www.batterygardens.com
- 🚗 Subway 1, 9 to South Ferry

A superb American restaurant in an elegant, glass building that shows off the spectacular views of the Hudson and East Rivers and the

Battery Gardens

Statue of Liberty from every table. In good weather you can eat outside on the terrace. Sumptuous American dishes with an Asian inflection may include miso-glazed Chilean sea bass with jasmine rice, shitake mushrooms and haricots verts or Amish chicken breast with roasted chestnuts, broccoli flan and sherry mushroom sauce.

GIGINO AT WAGNER PARK $
Italian
- ✉ 20 Battery Place at Hudson River
- ☎ 212-528 2228
- ⌂ www.gigino-wagnerpark.com
- 🚗 Subway 1, 9 to South Ferry

Great little café/diner with outside dining near the Museum of Jewish Heritage in the relatively new Robert Wagner Junior Park. Great views of the harbour and Statue of Liberty while you tuck into delicious dishes like bruschetta ($9), caprese ($11) or prosciutto & mozzarella ($13).

BRITTIP

If you want an even cheaper pit stop than Gigino while in Battery Park City, opt for items from the snack cart in Wagner Park.

BROOKLYN

GRIMALDI'S $
Italian
- ✉ 19 Old Fulton Street between Front and Water Streets
- ☎ 718-858 4300
- ⌂ www.grimaldis.com
- 🚗 Subway A, C to High Street/Brooklyn Bridge

Their pizza has been rated number one in the city in the *Zagat Survey* and it truly is considered the best place in New York to get a delicious pizza at a great price.

NOODLE PUDDING $$
Italian
- ✉ 38 Henry Street between Cranberry and Middagh Streets
- ☎ 218-625 3737
- 🚗 Subway A, C to High Street/ Brooklyn Bridge

Despite its name, this is a dedicated Italian rather than an Asian eatery, and it's very good. Traditional dishes such as osso buco (veal knuckle) and penne arrabiata ensure that it attracts an Italian-American crowd and is constantly packed. It is also praised for its fine pizza.

RIVER CAFE $$$
Gourmet American

- ✉ 1 Water Street under the Brooklyn Bridge
- ☎ 718-522 5200
  Fax 212-875 0037
- 🖰 www.rivercafe.com
- 🚇 Subway A, C to High Street/Brooklyn Bridge

If a panoramic view of the Manhattan skyline makes you feel romantic, and it does the majority of us, then the River Café on Brooklyn's waterfront is for you. Even better, the food matches up to the location – in fact it's worth leaving Manhattan for. Superb dishes such as wild rock lobster, River Café oysters, yellowfin tuna and sautéed Hudson Valley foie gras.

CENTRAL PARK

PARK VIEW AT THE BOATHOUSE $$–$$$
American–seafood

- ✉ Central Park Lake, Park Drive North at East 72nd Street
- ☎ 212-517 2233
  Fax 212-744 3949
- 🖰 www.thecentralparkboathouse.com
- 🚇 Subway 6 to 68th Street/Hunter College

This picture-book restaurant boasts one of the most wonderfully romantic locations in New York. Set right by a lake dotted with blue rowing boats in the heart of Central Park, circled by the famous high-rise skyline, the outside terrace provides a particularly gorgeous place to bag a seat at sunset. After dark, the restaurant's sparkling lights add to the romantic atmosphere. The mainly seafood menu isn't what you'd call adventurous, but it's delicious and well cooked and *Zagat* recommends the tasting menu. There is also a roaring open fireplace in the bar for those wintry days, when you can almost feel as if you really were deep in the countryside. Be sure to book well in advance in the summer.

TAVERN ON THE GREEN $$$
Gourmet American

- ✉ Central Park at West 67th Street
- ☎ 212-873 3200
  Fax 212-580 4265
- 🖰 www.tavernonthegreen.com
- 🚇 Subway B, C to 72nd Street

Looking at the glitzy razzmatazz that is the Tavern, it's hard to imagine this building started life in 1870 as a house for the sheep

TOP FIVE NEW OPENINGS

The last 12 months has proved an exciting time for the dining capital of the world, with openings of new eateries adding around 5,000 more restaurant seats to a city that already boasts over a million. Here are the five that have been creating the most buzz in the gourmet world.

Chelsea
Buddakan, Pan-Asian (page 150)

Flatiron
A Voce, modern Italian (page 159)

Meatpacking District
Del Posto, Italian (page 160)

Midtown
Gordon Ramsay at London NYC Hotel, British fusion (page 162)
L'Atelier de Joël Robuchon, French (page 162)

that roamed Central Park. By the early 1930s, Parks Commissioner Robert Moses had spotted its potential as a restaurant. He banished the sheep to Brooklyn's Prospect Park and, in 1934, opened what was known as The Restaurant with a coachman in full regalia at the door and the blessing of Mayor Fiorello LaGuardia.

🇬🇧 BRITTIP
You don't have to eat at the Tavern to enjoy its fabulous garden. From May to October you can sip a cocktail in the garden bar.

In the 1970s, famous restaurateur Warner LeRoy spent $10 million turning it into a spectacle in its own right, creating the Crystal and Terrace Rooms with his lavish use of brass, stained glass, etched mirrors, antique paintings and prints and chandeliers – including genuine Baccarat crystal and stained-glass Tiffanys. The Tavern on the Green took the city by storm when it opened in 1976. Celebrities, politicians and anyone who was anyone flocked to see and to be seen here.

Now the Tavern pulls in out-of-towners, who've all been told by their friends to visit this unique site, and the restaurant has a staggering turnover of around $34 million a year! And what a riot of colours and textures its clients are greeted with. The food is classic gourmet American with typical main courses including cedar-planked salmon, herb-roasted chicken and prime rib.

CHELSEA

202 $$
British–Mediterranean
✉ 75 9th Avenue at 16th Street
☎ 646 638 1173
🚇 Subway A, C, E to 14th Street

The line between fashionable food and, well, fashion blurs here as this is a hot little restaurant tucked away in the Nicole Farhi store. It makes the perfect place for a spot of lunch or dinner, where you can watch the waistline by tucking into dishes such as warm goat's cheese salad and smoked salmon with blini-thin scallion pancakes, or add to the waistline with good old fish and chips.

BONGO $$$–$$$$
Seafood
✉ 299 10th Avenue between 27th and 28th streets
☎ 212-947 3654
🚇 Subway C, E to 23rd Street; 1, 9 to 28th Street

A swish oyster bar where Chelsea gallery types sip champagne and slip down oysters for $3 a pop. If you're not a fan, there are other delicacies, including smoked trout salad, lobster roll and cod cakes.

BOTTINO $$
Italian
✉ 246 10th Avenue between 24th and 25th Streets
☎ 212-206 6766
🖰 www.bottinonyc.com
🚇 Subway C, E to 23rd Street

This is the place to go if you want to see the chic art dealers in recreational mode. You can tuck into the delicious Tuscan cuisine, such as roast rack of lamb with rosemary, in either the minimalist dining room or the back garden. If you don't have time to stop and eat, grab a sarnie to take away from the next-door Bottino to Go.

NYC cab

BRIGHT FOOD SHOP $
Asian–Mexican
✉ 216 8th Avenue at West 21st Street
☎ 212-243 4433
🖰 www.kitchenmarket.com
🚇 Subway C, E to 23rd Street

A classic neighbourhood diner with a twist – it serves south-western and Asian versions of American classics like five-spice roast pork loin with pineapple salsa.

BUDDAKAN $$$–$$$$
Pan-Asian
✉ 75 9th Avenue at 16th Street
☎ 212-989 6699
🖰 www.buddakan.com
🚇 Subway 1, 2, 3, 9 to 14th Street

A Pan-Asian import from the successful restaurant of the same name in Philadelphia. It was introduced to New York by Stephen Starr and is watched over by consultant Angelo Sosa, formerly of Yumcha. The awe factor isn't just the food (delicacies like Cantonese spring rolls and steamed pork buns in bamboo containers), but the great hall, which has oak-covered walls two storeys high, huge chandeliers and a banquet table to seat 30. Expect seriously beautiful people and food.

CAFETERIA $$
American diner
✉ 119 7th Avenue at 17th Street
☎ 212-414 1717
🚇 Subway 1, 9 to 18th Street

Another diner comfort-food experience, only this time filled with the beautiful people who use the 24-hour joint before and after hitting the local clubs.

BRITTIP
Bottles of water can cost $10 at some of the pricier restaurants. Save your money! New York has access to the finest and cleanest tap water, direct from the Catskill Mountains upstate.

THE PARK $$$
Mediterranean
✉ 118 10th Avenue at 18th Street
☎ 212-352 3313
   Fax 212-352 9139
🖰 www.theparknyc.com
🚇 Subway C, E to 23rd Street

Once a mechanic's garage, this is one of the 'in' spots for film-industry executives. It's a huge industrial bar-cum-restaurant space

TOP FIVE FOR FINE DINING

Considering how many thousands of eating establishments there are in New York and how many of them serve up wonderful food in delightful environments, it's difficult to narrow them down to a top five. Yet all the restaurants listed below have earned their stripes for getting all the elements of fine dining and hospitality right: consistently excellent and innovative cuisine, attentive service and an enjoyable ambience in a wonderful setting. They obviously have prices to match, but for a once-in-a-holiday treat they won't disappoint.

Le Cirque: French–American, Midtown East (page 166)

Union Square Café: Gourmet American, Midtown East (page 167)

Le Barnardin: Seafood, Midtown West (page 168)

Babbo: Italian, Greenwich (page 155)

Nobu: Japanese, TriBeCa (page 175)

with a kind of African safari camp interior serving Mediterranean food. There's a huge garden at the back full of Japanese maple trees and wisteria vines that seats 400 and is a great place to dine in the summer.

THE RED CAT $$

Mediterranean–American
✉ 227 10th Avenue between 23rd and 24th Streets
☎ 212-242 1122
🖰 www.theredcat.com
🚇 Subway C, E to 23rd Street
One of the earlier arrivals in Chelsea, along with the original galleries, this is a real staple with the art pack. It serves up Mediterranean-influenced American food, but you can just go for a cocktail.

CHINATOWN

Hundreds of tiny restaurants line the Chinatown streets, mostly serving good-value food from various regions in China.

BRITTIP

Well-priced steaming hot food is the trademark of the restaurants in Chinatown. But don't expect elegance in the decor or any politeness from the waiters – it simply isn't available!

Here is our Top Five to get you started.

BIG WONG KING $

Cantonese
✉ 67 Mott Street between Bayard and Canal Streets
☎ 212-964 0540
🚇 Subway J, M, N, Q, R, W, A, Z, 6 to Canal Street
Cheap, tasty food – particularly the duck, shrimp and chicken noodles, and congee. Don't expect much of the decor but the service is good and lots of Chinese eat here, which is always a good sign. The wonton noodle soup, full of fun noodles, is a bargain.

DIM SUM GO GO $

Chinese–vegetarian
✉ 5 East Broadway between Catherine Street and Chatham Square
☎ 212-732 0797
🚇 Subway J, M, Z, 6 to Canal Street; F to East Broadway
One of the more popular restaurants in the area, thanks to its delicious dim sum, and fantastically priced: dim sum platter, $10.95 for ten pieces; roast chicken with fried garlic stems, $13.95; hamburger in a steamed bun with ginger sauce, $9.95.

JOE'S SHANGHAI $$

Chinese–Shanghai
✉ 9 Pell St between Bowery and Mott Street
☎ 212-233 8888
🖰 www.joesshanghairestaurants.com
🚇 Subway J, M, N, R, Z, 6 to Canal Street
A Chinese restaurant known for creating the most fabulous soup dumplings in New York. 'Lots of food for little money' according to the *Zagat Survey*.

Dim Sum Go Go

RESTAURANTS

City Hall

NEW GREEN BO $-$$
Chinese–Shanghai
- ✉ 66 Bayard Street between Elizabeth and Mott Streets
- ☎ 212-625 2359
- 🚇 Subway J, M, Z, N, Q, R, W, 6 to Canal Street

Up until recently Joe's Shanghai had little in the way of competition for delicious dim sum and dumplings at great prices, then along came this place, giving New Yorkers another place to rave about. There is a famous teahouse of the same name in Shanghai, and it feels like you could be there. The dumplings are extremely fresh, hot and succulent and their fish fillet in wine sauce is excellent.

NEW YORK NOODLE TOWN $
Hong Kong-style noodle house
- ✉ 281/2 Bowery at Bayard Street
- ☎ 212-349 0923
- 🚇 Subway J, M, Z, N, Q, R, W, 6 to Canal Street

GARDEN DINING

Aureole: French, Upper East Side, $$$$ (page 177)

Barbetta: Northern Italian, Midtown West, $$$$ (page 168)

Bottino: Italian, Chelsea, $$$ (page 150)

Provence: French, SoHo, $$ (page 171)

Remi: Italian, Midtown, $$$$ (page 163)

Tavern on the Green: Gourmet American, Central Park West, $$$ (page 149)

The Park: Mediterranean, Chelsea $$$ (page 150)

Noodles, of course, are a speciality here and come in fragrant broths with dumplings or stir-fried with vegetables, meat or seafood. According to the New York Metro, it's the city's best spot for delicious, succulent Chinese barbecue.

EAST VILLAGE

There are dozens of great places to dine in the East Village. It's a very safe part of town so, if you have the time, it's well worth taking a wander around at night and having a look at all of the various options before you make your choice.

ANGELICA KITCHEN $
Vegetarian–vegan
- ✉ 300 East 12th Street between 1st and 2nd Avenues
- ☎ 212-228 2909
- 🖰 www.angelicakitchen.com
- 🚇 Subway L, N, Q, R, W, 4, 5, 6 to 14th Street/Union Square

A surprise for anyone who thinks veggie food is boring. This cool spot serves up very tasty soups, chilli and noodle dishes like butternut squash and tempeh made from soya beans. Macrobiotic heaven? No alcohol.

FRANK $
Italian
- ✉ 88 2nd Avenue between 5th and 6th Streets
- ☎ 212-420 0202
- 🖰 www.frankrestaurant.com
- 🚇 Subway 6 to Astor Place

A tiny Italian restaurant with a real parlour feel. No matter the hour, Frank is full of hungry hipsters looking to fill up on Grandma Carmela's slow-cooked ragu.

🇬🇧 BRITTIP
There are more restaurants for the Village and Chelsea in Chapter 10 Gay New York, plus many of the bars referred to in Chapter 8 serve meals, too.

GNOCCO CUCINA & TRADIZIONE $$
Italian
- ✉ 337 East 10th Street between Avenues A and B
- ☎ 212-677 1913
- 🖰 www.gnocco.com
- 🚇 Subway 6 to Astor Place

Named after an Italian snack of crispy, puffy fried dough, you just know you're in for some good Italian fodder at this eatery owned by Pierluigi Palazzo. Lovely dishes such as pork tenderloin sprinkled with Parmigiano shavings.

LA PALAPA $$
Mexican
✉ 77 St Mark's Place between 1st and 2nd Avenues
☎ 212-777 2537
Fax 212-777 9730
🖰 www.lapalapa.com
🚇 Subway E, V to Lexington Avenue/ 53rd Street

Superb Mexican cuisine with shrimp dishes and barbecued cod with Chile guajillo and achiote rub. Rices are flavoured with tomato, saffron and tomatillo; sauces concocted from sesame seeds, pumpkin seeds and guajillo chillies. The restaurant is dark and sultry and serves refreshing fresh fruit margaritas. Check out the calendar on the website to find out about events such as a cocktail and small bites master class.

THE ELEPHANT $$
French–Thai fusion
✉ 58 East 1st Street between 1st and 2nd Avenues
☎ 212-505 7739
🖰 www.elephantrestaurant.com
🚇 Subway F, V to 2nd Avenue

The food is tasty Thai with a dash of French, but the interior is most definitely more of a French scene. A fun place to enjoy a cocktail or two; the cool crowd often end up spilling out on to the sidewalk.

BRITTIP
Sometimes the only way to get into a very popular restaurant is to go very early or very late in the evening. Ask what times are available when you book

YAFFA CAFÉ $
American diner
✉ 97 St Mark's Place between 1st and Avenue A
☎ 212-674 9302
🖰 www.yaffacafe.com
🚇 Subway 6 to Astor Place

A classic American diner with a grungy East Village twist. Open 24 hours.

TOP FIVE RESTAURANTS WITH A VIEW
Battery Gardens: Gourmet American, Battery Park (page 148)

Rainbow Room: Continental, Midtown (page 163)

The View: Continental, Theater District (page 174)

Water Club: Seafood, Midtown East (page 167)

World Yacht Dinner Cruises: Gourmet American, Midtown West (page 169)

FINANCIAL DISTRICT AND SOUTH STREET SEAPORT

ADRIENNE'S PIZZA BAR $-$$
Italian
✉ 54 Stone Street near Hanover Square
☎ 212-248 3838
🚇 Subway 2, 3 to Wall Street

If you're sightseeing Downtown and start to feel peckish, pop into this stylish place for some truly delicious thin-crust square, the restaurant's latest take on the pizza. There's also salads, antipasti and pastas to enjoy.

KOODO SUSHI $$
Japanese
✉ 129 Front Street on the lower level of Seaport Suites Hotel between Pine and Wall Streets
☎ 212-425 2890
🖰 www.koodoosushi.com
🚇 Subway 1, 2, 4, 5 to Wall Street

This place doesn't look like much, but it has one of the best sushi chefs in town. The fish is impeccable, but the chef really shines in his daily specials – take hostess Michelle's advice on this.

MARKJOSEPH STEAKHOUSE $$
Steakhouse
✉ 261 Water Street between Peck Slip and Dover Street
☎ 212-277 0020
Fax 212-277 0033
🖰 www.markjosephsteakhouse.com
🚇 Subway 1, 2, 4, 5, A, C, J, M, Z to Fulton Street/Broadway Nassau

This restaurant has made its mark as one of the best steakhouses in the city. The porterhouse steak is so tender some people have said it 'could be eaten through a straw'. Team it with the delicious hash browns. Wearing a jacket is advisable.

RESTAURANTS

GRAMERCY PARK

ELEVEN MADISON PARK　$$$$
French–American

- ✉ 11 Madison Avenue (the corner) at 24th Street
- ☎ 212-889 0905
- ⌂ www.elevenmadisonpark.com
- 🚇 Subway 6, N, R to 23rd Street

With a soaring ceiling, marble floors and French-influenced dishes, this is one of New York's hottest restaurants. It's expensive but not snooty and the service is attentive, as seen in *Sex And The City*.

GRAMERCY TAVERN　$$$
Gourmet American

- ✉ 42 East 20th Street between Broadway and Park Avenue South
- ☎ 212-477 0777
- ⌂ www.gramercytavern.com
- 🚇 Subway N, R to 23rd Street

Another real winner and again always highly ranked by the *Zagat Survey* – an excellent American restaurant.

PORCAO CHURRASCARIA　$$$
Brazilian

- ✉ 360 Park Avenue at 26th Street
- ☎ 212-252 7080
- ⌂ www.porcaous.com
- 🚇 Subway 6 to 28th Street

Hot from Rio de Janeiro is this new South American churrascaria where dozens of styles of meat are served up tableside in the 1,020sq m (11,000sq ft) space. There's also an ample salad bar with a bewildering array of options.

TAMARIND　$$
Indian

- ✉ 41–43 East 22nd Street between Broadway and Park Avenue South
- ☎ 212-674 7400
- ⌂ www.tamarinde22.com
- 🚇 Subway N, R to 23rd Street

Lovely modern decor that defies the normal Indian dining room cliché of flock wallpaper. The cuisine is equally contemporary, with lots of fruit-infused dishes such as fritters with spinach, banana and home-made cheese. If you want a cheaper, lighter snack try their tea room next door.

VERITAS　$$$$
Gourmet American

- ✉ 43 East 20th Street between Broadway and Park Avenue South
- ☎ 212-353 3700
- ⌂ www.veritas-nyc.com
- 🚇 Subway N, R to 23rd Street

The city's largest wine list can be found here – an impressive 2,700-plus bottles to choose from. The cuisine is as impressive, think tender braised ribs with parsnip purée and porcini mushrooms or scallops with a black truffle vinaigrette. The prix fixe dinner is $76.

◀▮▶ BRITTIP

If you're a true wine connoisseur you can download the most up-to-date list of Veritas' wine cellar before you go from www.veritas-nyc.com.

Eleven Madison Park

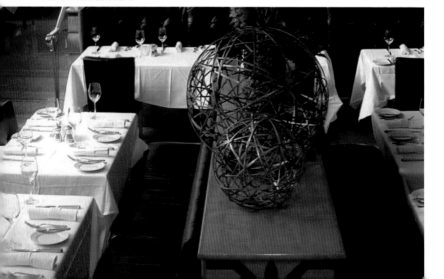

TOP FIVE RESTAURANTS TO BRING A BOTTLE TO

If you're on a budget, you can save a fortune on your NY dining experiences by picking restaurants that allow you to bring your own bottle of vino or beer to the table. There are liquor stores all over the city, giving you the opportunity to select a really good wine without the hefty price tag to accompany your meal. Be warned, however, that some restaurants will charge you for corkage (opening the wine on their premises), which can vary from under $10 to $25 plus. Here's our top five:

Angelica Kitchen: Great organic vegetarian and vegan cuisine. No corkage fee (page 152).

Cafe Himalaya: (78 East 1st Street at 1st Avenue, tel 212 358 0160). Global cuisine, cash only. No corkage fee.

Lamarca: (161 East 22nd Street at corner of 3rd Avenue; tel 212-674 6363). Filling Italian fodder. No corkage fee.

Les Sans Culottes: (329 West 51st Street; tel 212-581 1283). Hearty bistro food. Corkage $8.

Ottomanelli's Cafe 86: (1626 York Avenue at 86th Street; tel 212-772 7722). Italian specialities. No corkage fee.

GREENWICH & WEST VILLAGE

BABBO $$$$
Italian
⊠ 110 Waverly Place between MacDougal and 6th Avenues
☎ 212-777 0303
🖰 www.babbonyc.com
🚇 Subway A, B, C, D, E, F, Q to Washington Square

The crown jewel of Greenwich Village restaurants is unmatched for the quality and quantity of its Italian dishes; forewarned is forearmed so make sure you wear a skirt or trousers with an elasticated waist, because we're talking large, rich portions here. Everything in Mario Batali's restaurant is delightful, from the simple split-level dining room that seats 90 to the stunning bar area. However, it's the imaginative food that pushes this restaurant into the top five fine dining experiences. How about black tagliatelle with peas and pecorino? Or chocolate polenta cake with espresso gelato? Yum!

🇬🇧 BRITTIP

Order one of the fabulous tasting menus at Babbo for a really great choice of dishes. The pasta tasting menu is particularly mouth-watering, including black tagliatelle with parsnips and pancetta, garganelli with funghi trifolatia and pappardelle Bolognese. It's also a cheaper option than choosing individual dishes, as the menus ring in at around $69 per person.

CAFE DE BRUXELLES $$
Belgian
⊠ 118 Greenwich Avenue at West 13th Street
☎ 212-206 1830
🚇 Subway A, C east to 14th Street

Another friendly Belgian bistro serving great grub, like moules for $16.95 and waterzooi de poulet, a creamy chicken dish, for $17.95. There's also a great selection of Belgian beers to wash it all down with.

CORNELIA STREET CAFE $$
Eclectic
⊠ 29 Cornelia Street between Bleecker and West 4th Streets
☎ 212-989 9319
   Fax 212-243 4207
🖰 www.corneliastreetcafe.com

A fabulous neighbourhood restaurant with good service that serves lunch and dinner seven days a week. Specials include butternut squash risotto, sesame-crusted salmon, lobster ravioli and Thai bouillabaisse. Local artists' work hangs on the walls, and a small downstairs performance space for readings and acoustic performances, in particular its jazz club, which begins at 9pm and costs from $6 for the whole evening plus a house drink (page 198).

Cornelia Street Café

RESTAURANTS

GARAGE RESTAURANT & CAFÉ $
American
- ⊠ 99 7th Avenue South between Barrow and Grove Streets
- ☎ 212-645 0600
- ⌂ www.garagerest.com
- 🚗 Subway 1, 2, 3, 9 to Christopher Street

A friendly spot for contemporary American food in a great location; it also has live jazz and some cool people-watching.

GOTHAM BAR AND GRILL $$$
Gourmet American
- ⊠ 12 East 12th Street between 5th Avenue and University Place
- ☎ 212-620 4020
- ⌂ www.gothambarandgrill.com
- 🚗 Subway L, N, R, 4, 5, 6 to Union Square/ 14th Street

Always highly rated by *Zagat*, the excellent American cuisine is served up in a superb environment to a stylish crowd. It costs $27 for the lunch prix fixe.

JOHN'S PIZZERIA $
Italian
- ⊠ 278 Bleecker Street between 6th and 7th Avenues
- ☎ 212-243 1680
- ⌂ www.johnspizzerianyc.com
- 🚗 Subway A, B, C, D, E, F, V to West 4th Street

A great place for brick-oven pizzas.

PHILIP MARIE $$-$$$
American
- ⊠ 569 Hudson Street at West 11th Street
- ☎ 212-242 6200
  Fax 212-242 1278
- ⌂ www.philipmarie.com
- 🚗 Subway 1, 9 to Christopher Street

Hearty American fare. Try the newcomer's parsley salad with country ham, dried tomatoes and Wisconsin cheese.

SOTO $$$-$$$$
Japanese
- ⊠ 357 6th Avenue at Washington Place
- ☎ 212-4143088
- ⌂ www.soto.com
- 🚗 Subway A, B, C, E, F, V to West 4th Street/Washington Square

Opened in May 2007 by third generation sushi chef Sotohiro Kosugi, this is a very sleek restaurant where you can savour Eastern delights such as sea urchin wrapped in squid, sweet shrimp tartare with yuzu tobiko and soy foam. There's an $80, 15-course tasting menu.

TOMOE SUSHI $$
Japanese
- ⊠ 172 Thompson Street between Bleecker and West Houston Streets
- ☎ 212-777 9346
- 🚗 Subway 6 to Bleecker Street

This place looks pretty grotty but there is usually an incredible queue outside and not without reason. You can get the best sushi in New York here for about a tenth of the price it would cost you at Nobu.

HARLEM

AMY RUTH'S HOME STYLE SOUTHERN CUISINE $$
Southern soul food
- ⊠ 113 West 116th street at Lenox Avenue
- ☎ 212-280 8779
- 🚗 Subway 2, 3 to 116th Street

Absolutely delicious southern-style food, BBQ spare ribs, chicken and waffles, catfish and ham hocks.

GEORGE & GINA'S RESTAURANT $$
Puerto Rican
- ⊠ 169 East 106th Street between Lexington and 3rd Avenues
- ☎ 212-410 7292
- 🚗 Subway 6 to 103rd Street

A Puerto Rican restaurant with a casual ambiance, deep in the heart of Spanish Harlem.

RAO'S $
Italian
- ⊠ 455 East 114th Street at Pleasant Avenue
- ☎ 212-722 6709
- ⌂ www.raos.com
- 🚗 Subway 6 to 116th Street

An institution that you'll get into only if you come across the handful of people who actually have access to this eight-table Italian restaurant! Famous for its sauces, which Sinatra used to have flown to him around the world. Now the jukebox plays all the crooner's favourites.

BRITTIP
If you can't get in to Rao's, you can still taste their fabulous sauces, by buying them either direct from the restaurant or from Faicco's Sausage Store in Bleecker Street, Greenwich Village (page 142).

SYLVIA'S $

Southern soul food

✉ 328 Lenox Avenue between 126th and 127th Streets

☎ 212-996 0660

🖰 www.sylviassoulfood.com

🚇 Subway 2, 3 to 125th Street

Southern home-style cooking – aka soul food. Sylvia's place is a New York institution and famous for its Sunday gospel brunch, but you need to book a few weeks ahead as it's always very busy.

◀▥▶ BRITTIP

If you need a break around 110th Street, drop in for a cuppa and a delicious cake at Make My Cake, 103 West 110th Street at Lenox Avenue/Malcom X Boulevard. Tel 212-932 0833, www.makemy cake.com.

LITTLE ITALY

Mulberry Street from Hester to Kenmare Street and along Grand Street to Mott Street is all that remains of a once thriving Italian community. Thankfully, though – especially for anyone who feels relieved to have escaped the madness and mayhem of Chinatown – the tiny area is incredibly vibrant and filled with ambient pizzerias and trattorias, many with pavement tables and some even having gardens at the back.

Of course, the area gets packed with tourists, but locals also eat here so the food is 100 per cent authentic. The restaurants all have plenty in common – fading decor, if any, large portions of piping hot Italian

Mulberry Street

BEST OF LITTLE ITALY

It's hard to go wrong with any of the restaurants in Little Italy, but here is a round-up of five of the best, moving northwards along Mulberry from Hester to Grand Street: **Il Fornaio** (132a Mulberry, tel 212-226 8306); **Pellegrino's** (138 Mulberry, tel 212-226 3177); **Angelo's** (146 Mulberry, tel 212-966 1277, www.angelomulberry.com); **Taormina** (147 Mulberry, tel 212-219 1007); **Il Palazzo** (151 Mulberry, tel 212-343 7000). By the way, Taormina was once the local hangout of former Mafia boss 'Teflon Don' John Gotti (page 38).

To get to Little Italy, take subway 6 to Spring or Bleecker Streets.

classics, friendly service and great value for money. If you're really on a budget, stick to the excellent fixed-price menus, then just sit back and watch the world go by.

BAR MARTIGNETTI $$-$$$

Italian

✉ 406 Broome Street at Centre Street

☎ 212-680 5600

🖰 www.barmartignetti.com

🚇 Subway 6 to Spring Street

The Martignetti brothers have opened up this bustling bar and restaurant that has proved a real hit with locals. They've hired a top brasserie chef and you can order food all day and into the small hours.

BREAD $$

Italian

✉ 20 Spring Street between Elizabeth and Mott Streets

☎ 212-334 1015

🚇 Subway 6 to Spring Street

A lovely little café serving up delicious panini, soup and various salads and great fresh bread. There's also a good choice of wine, many of which are sold by the glass. There's an equally good Bread in TriBeCa (www.breadtribeca.com).

CAFE GITANE $$

French–North African

✉ 242 Mott Street at Prince Street

☎ 212-334 9552

🚇 Subway 6 to Spring Street

Great value Moroccan-style dining; think couscous and tajines. Tables and chairs are put out on the sidewalk in the summer, but they are in a hot spot so you're more likely to end up in the noisy but nice dining room.

RESTAURANTS

FERRARA $
Italian café

✉ 195 Grand Street between Mulberry and Mott Streets
☎ 212-226 6150
🖰 www.ferraracafe.com
🚗 Subway S to Grand Street

This is the oldest surviving pastry joint (it opened in 1892) in an area that was once teeming with cannoli caverns. A spacious area, it serves up delicious drinks and cakes and provides plenty of entertaining people-watching.

🇬🇧 BRITTIP
If you've been wandering around Chinatown for a while and don't want a meal but do need a WC, Ferrara's has a lovely clean one on the first floor (up the stairs at the back). Keep the owners happy, though, by at least buying something to take away.

SAL ANTHONY'S SPQR $$–$$$
Italian

✉ 133 Mulberry Street between Hern and Grand Streets
☎ 212-925 3120
🖰 www.salanthonys.com
🚗 Subway 6 to Spring Street

An authentic Italian that's big on fresh ingredients – the mozzarella is made twice a day on the premises to ensure it's perfect. There are lots of regional dishes such as trout with garlic and rosemary and fusilli pasta with prosciutto and tomato, all served in elegant, wood-panelled surroundings at prices far below what you'd expect to pay uptown for similar fare. There's also a three-course fixed-price menu served 4pm–6.30pm for $29.50.

Katz's Delicatessen

LOWER EAST SIDE

ALIAS $$
American

✉ 76 Clinton Street at Rivington Street
☎ 212-505 5011
🖰 www.aliasrestaurant.com
🚗 Subway F to Lower East Side/2nd Avenue

This cool bodega has lower lighting, tablecloths and a small but serious wine list, yet remains funky with laid-back clients and staff. Chef Scott Ehrlich turns out some pretty big tastes from his mini kitchen but at far less than Midtown pricing.

BEREKET $
Turkish

✉ 187 East Houston Street at Orchard Street
☎ 212-475 7700
🖰 www.bereketrestaurant.com
🚗 Subway F to 2nd Avenue

A good place to pop into if you've got the munchies after a big night out as it's open 24/7 and the food is filling but fresh. The hummus, stuffed vine leaves and lamb shawarma sandwich are recommended.

BONDI ROAD $$
Seafood

✉ 153 Rivington Street at Suffolk Street
☎ 212-253 5311
🖰 www.bereketrestaurant.com
🚗 Subway J, M, Z to Suffolk Street

Photomontages of Australia's Bondi Beach run down both sides of this laid-back eatery. The menu's simple: pick a fish, such as sea bass, barramunda or grouper, and then select a cooking method – grilled, breaded or fried.

KATZ'S DELICATESSEN $
American–Jewish

✉ 205 East Houston Street at Ludlow Street
☎ 212-254 2246
    Fax 212-674 3270
🖰 www.katzdeli.com
🚗 Subway F to 2nd Avenue

A real institution, this deli has been here since 1888. The sandwiches may sound pricey at around $9, but I defy you to finish one. Luckily, there are plenty of brown paper bags around to take your leftovers away with you (as everybody else does). Stick to the sandwiches though – the soups are a bit disappointing. You take a ticket on the way in, order your food at the counter and have your ticket filled out, then you pay for it all as you leave.

BRITTIP

If the canteen-style seating at Katz's seems familiar to you, it's because that fake orgasm scene with Meg Ryan and Billy Crystal in *When Harry Met Sally* was filmed here.

MADISON SQUARE/FLATIRON

AREZZO $$-$$$
Italian
- ✉ 46 West 22nd street at 6th Avenue
- ☎ 212-206 0555
- 🚇 Subway 6 to 23rd Street

Spartan room but excellent plates of Italian cuisine, such as cavatelli in hot sweet sausage ragu. Three-course lunch menu from $24.

A VOCE $$$-$$$$
Italian
- ✉ 41 Madison Avenue near 26th Street
- ☎ 212-545 8555
- 🚇 Subway 6 to 26th Street

A hot new opening by Andrew Carmellini who served under Daniel Boulud, one of the city's most legendary chefs. It's a great Italian menu, think chicken cacciatora, lamb shanks, veal chops and even tripe and the modern decor is very calming and sophisticated. The huge, Cathedral-size windows with views of the world passing by outside are a bonus.

TABLA $$$$
American Indian
- ✉ 11 Madison Avenue at 25th Street
- ☎ 212-889 0667
- 🖱 www.tablany.com
- 🚇 Subway N, R to 23rd Street

Danny Meyer's bi-level restaurant serving American Indian cuisine is a big hit and attracts a trendy crowd. Downstairs is cheaper, you'll be pleased to know.

MEATPACKING DISTRICT

Manhattan's Meatpacking District, between Chelsea and the West Village on the lower west side of Manhattan, used to be a no-go area for diners. Now it has become a style magnet for the kind of restaurants that you want to brag to your friends about. If you don't want to splash out in the chic venues, however, there are some groovy little coffee and cake shops that will take the weight off your feet but not your wallet.

5 NINTH $$$
American nouveau
- ✉ 5 9th Avenue at Gansevoort Street
- ☎ 212-929 9460
- 🖱 www.5ninth.com
- 🚇 Subway A, C, E to 14th Street; L to 8th Avenue

Discreet setting but buzzing on the inside, serving up expensive but delicious dishes such as pork belly, that are infused with ingredients from far-off destinations, particularly the East.

RESTAURANTS

Flatiron District

DEL POSTO $$$
Italian
- ✉ 85 10th Avenue at 16th Street
- ☎ 212-497 8090
- 🚇 Subway A, C, E to 14th Street

This new restaurant from Mario Batali and the Bastianich family is posh Italian nosh that has left the New York restaurant critics split. The surroundings are super-plush – think old-style gentleman's club – with a live pianist, and the food fancy; lobster risotto for two at $60.

FLORENT $
French
- ✉ 69 Gansevoort Street between Greenwich and Washington Streets
- ☎ 212-989 5779
- 🖰 www.restaurantflorent.com
- 🚇 Subway A, C, East to 14th Street

This is the Meatpacking District's original 24-hour hangout, with fine coffee at the Formica counter or steak frîtes served by a transsexual waitress.

MARKT $$
Belgian
- ✉ 401 West 14th Street at 9th Avenue
- ☎ 212-727 3314
- 🖰 www.marktrestaurant.com
- 🚇 Subway L to 8th Avenue; A, C east to 14th Street

A stylish Belgian brasserie with a popular bar. Great mussels and good beer selection.

OLD HOMESTEAD $$
American
- ✉ 56 9th Avenue between 14th and 15th Streets
- ☎ 212-242 9040
- 🖰 www.theoldhomesteadsteakhouse.com
- 🚇 Subway L, A, C, E to 14th Street/8th Avenue

An original chophouse joint, complete with tacky cow sculpture outside, that opened in 1868 and is still serving massive portions of good ol' steak and chips today.

Pastis

PASTIS $$$
French
- ✉ 9 9th Avenue at Little West 12th Street
- ☎ 212-929 4844
- 🖰 www.pastis.com
- 🚇 Subway A, C, E to 14th Street; L to 8th Avenue

One of the names that made the Meatpacking neighbourhood hip was Keith McNally, who set up this Parisian-style brasserie. It's always full and the atmosphere's buzzy, the food is good, not great, such as steak frîtes and sautéed prawns.

MIDTOWN

21 CLUB $–$$$
Gourmet American
- ✉ 21 West 52nd Street between 5th and 6th Avenues
- ☎ 212-582 7200
- 🖰 www.21club.com
- 🚇 Subway F to 5th Avenue

Despite its name, this landmark restaurant has never been a club, but during Prohibition it was a speakeasy, starting life in Greenwich Village before moving to its Midtown location in 1929. West 52nd Street between 5th and 6th Avenues was known then as the 'wettest block in Manhattan' because there were at least 38 speakeasies.

One of the most discreet was the 21 Club, which purposefully remained a tiny, clandestine retreat behind the iron gate of its townhouse façade, to avoid both the gangsters and police raids. Its success depended on an employee who was assigned to spot gangsters, policemen and revenue agents through the peephole – and who was so skilful that 21 escaped most raids and troubles except for one in 1930. After that the owners had a new security system designed to create false stairways and walls to hide its 2,000 cases of fine wines. It involved the building of a 2-tonne door to the secret cellar, made out of the original bricks to look like a wall. The cellar is still going strong and now houses $1.5 millions-worth of wine, much of which is owned by the celebrities and power brokers who call the 21 Club their own. Actress Liz Taylor and former President Gerald Ford still keep their bottles here.

Once Prohibition ended in 1932, many of the former speakeasies went out of business,

Lobby at the Royalton

but the 21 turned itself into a fine dining establishment that has been attracting celebrities and movers and shakers ever since. Patrons have included Joe DiMaggio, Aristotle Onassis, Franklin D Roosevelt, Humphrey Bogart, Ernest Hemingway and Jackie Gleason. The night before *Brit Guide* enjoyed lunch here, Margaret Thatcher had been at a private function and Joan Collins had dined in the main restaurant.

44 RESTAURANT $$$
Gourmet American
⊠ Royalton Hotel, 44 West 44th Street between 5th and 6th Avenues
☎ 212-944 8844
🖰 www.royaltonhotel.com
🚇 Subway B, D, F, Q to 42nd Street
A très trendy joint in the Philippe Starck-designed Royalton Hotel, serving new American cuisine. A favourite with posh magazine editors.

AJ MAXWELL'S $$-$$$
American
⊠ 57 West 58th Street, Rockefeller Centre
☎ 212-262 6200
🖰 www.ajmaxwells.com
🚇 Subway B, D, F, V to Rockefeller Centre
Recently opened steak house that hits the spot if you're looking to satisfy hunger pangs with big portions in pleasant surroundings. Good wine list and there's also an excellent range of seafood dishes if you don't want the filet mignon et al.

AQUAVIT $$$$
Scandinavian
⊠ 65 East 55th Street between Madison and Park Avenues
☎ 212-307 7311
🖰 www.aquavit.org
🚇 Subway E, V to 53rd Street/5th Avenue
Swedish chef Marcus Samuelsson won the Best Chef in New York City award four years ago, but the menu is still as varied and imaginative today. Seafood stew and brioche-wrapped salmon are mouth-watering, while the tasting menus, including a vegetarian one, are a great idea and comprise seven-course Aqua Bite meals.

BG $$$-$$$$
American nouveau
⊠ 754 5th Avenue at 58th Street
☎ 212-872 8977
🖰 www.bergdorfgoodman.com
🚇 Subway N, R, W to 5th Avenue/59th Street
The new restaurant at Bergdorf Goodman department store makes a posh place to stop for a long lunch during a shopping spree. Or head here for an early dinner, as the restaurant shuts at 8pm. You can also go for the afternoon tea option – which is fabulous, darling.

CHINA GRILL $$
Chinese
⊠ CBS Building, 60 West 53rd Street between 5th and 6th Avenues
☎ 212-333 7788
🖰 www.chinagrillmgt.com
🚇 Subway B, D, F, V to 47th–50th Streets/Rockefeller Center
Classy establishment serving eclectic food in a fairly noisy setting. Has a bar that gets pretty crowded.

Aquavit

dB BISTRO MODERNE $$$-$$$$
French–American
- ✉ City Club Hotel, 55 West 44th Street between 5th and 6th Avenues
- ☎ 212-391 2400
  Fax 212-391 1188
- 🖱 www.danielnyc.com/dbbistro
- 🚗 Subway B, D, F, V, S, 4, 5, 6, 7 to 42nd Street

The latest showcase for one of New York's superstar chefs, Daniel Boulud. It got lots of press for the $29 hamburger, and became an instant scene. Located in the very star-chic City Club Hotel, this is one of the few really good places to eat close to the Theater District.

DIWAN $$
Indian
- ✉ Helmsley Middletowne, 148 East 48th Street between Lexington and 3rd Avenues
- ☎ 212-593 5425
- 🖱 www.diwanrestaurant.com
- 🚗 Subway 6 to 51st Street

An upmarket Indian with more unusual dishes than your average vindaloo or tandoori – papad stuffed lamb crabmeat, for example.

GORDON RAMSAY AT LONDON NYC HOTEL $$$$
British fusion
- ✉ 151 West 54th Street at 7th Avenue
- ☎ 212-307 5000
- 🖱 www.thelondonnyc.com
- 🚗 Subway B, D, E to 7th Avenue

London's most notorious Michelin three-star chef hit the Big Apple in style early 2007 at

Diwan

the former Righa Royal Hotel, which, after a $50 million refurbishment and name change, is now the new darling of the dining and bar scene. His food didn't go down too well with NY food ciritcs, but we love it.

HARD ROCK CAFE $
American
- ✉ 1501 Broadway at 43rd Street
- ☎ 212-343 3355
- 🖱 www.hardrock.com
- 🚗 Subway N, Q, R, S, W, 1, 2, 3, 7, 9 to Times Square/42nd Street

Classic burger and chips 'cuisine' in a noisy, rock 'n' roll environment.

HARLEY DAVIDSON CAFE $
American
- ✉ 1370 6th Avenue at 56th Street
- ☎ 212-245 6000
- 🚗 Subway B, Q to 57th Street

Home-style American comfort food like meatloaf and chicken pot pie. Memorabilia includes a huge floor map of Route 66.

L'ATELIER DE JOEL RUCHON $$$$
French
- ✉ 57 East 57th Street
- ☎ 212-758 5700
- 🖱 www.fourseasons.com
- 🚗 Subway 4, 5, 6 to 59th Street

With famous restaurants in Paris, Tokyo and Las Vegas, this super chef has finally opened a place in New York at the Four Seasons Hotel. It's a very sophisticated and elegant dining experience, from the open kitchen in the centre of the restaurant so you can see the team in action to the red lacquer and light wood finishes on the furnishings. The best seats are the ones at the pearwood counter so you can see the kitchen, but there are only 20 so you are best to book well in advance. There are 26 other tables. Specialities include truffled mash potatoes and free-range quail stuffed with foie gras.

NOBU 57 $$$$
Japanese–Peruvian
- ✉ 40th West 57 Street between 5th and 6th Avenues
- ☎ 212-757 3000
- 🖱 www.noburestaurants.com
- 🚗 Subway F to 57th Street

Opened in 2005, the newest Nobu to hit the scene serves the same food in must-be-seen-to-be-believed surroundings according to *Zagat*, who describe it as a 'triumph of theatrical feng shui'. It is tipped to be as hot for people-watching as the original.

Rockefeller Center

NORMA'S $-$$
American
- ✉ Le Parker Meridien Hotel, 118 West 57th Street between 6th and 7th Avenues
- ☎ 212-708 7460
- 🖰 www.parkermeridien.com
- 🚇 Subway B, D, E to 7th Avenue

This award-winning all-day breakfast joint is très chi-chi, beautifully decorated and serves some of the most inventive 'breakfast' food going! Specialities include molten chocolate French toast with pineapple chutney, caramelised onion corned beef hash with poached eggs, and a serious stack of strawberry and rhubarb pancakes. Also desserts and fruit smoothies.

OPIA $$
French
- ✉ 130 East 57th Street at Lexington Avenue
- ☎ 212-688 3939
- 🖰 www.opiarestaurant.com
- 🚇 Subway 4, 5, 6, N, R, W to 59th Street/ Lexington Avenue

Antoine Blech, formerly of the great neighbourhood bistro Orienta, is the very welcoming host at this nifty and trendy hideaway for beautiful people in the Habitat Hotel. The French-inspired cuisine is absolutely delicious.

RAINBOW ROOM $$$-$$$$
Continental
- ✉ 65th Floor, 30 Rockefeller Plaza – entrance on 49th Street between 5th and 6th Avenues
- ☎ 212-632 5100
   Fax 212-632 5105
- 🖰 www.rainbowroom.com
- 🚇 Subway B, D, F, V to 47th–50th Streets/ Rockefeller Plaza

This legendary Art Deco landmark makes a fantastic location for dinner – complete with delicious Continental food. The opulent interior is matched only by the views and – get this – you can experience it all at a reasonable price if you opt for the fixed-price theatre menu served from 5.30pm. For a slice of real Hollywood glamour, find out when the ballroom is open to the public for dinner dances.

REMI $$$
Italian
- ✉ 145 West 53rd Street between 6th and 7th Avenues
- ☎ 212-581 4242
- 🚇 Subway N, R to 49th Street; B, D east to 7th Avenue

To New Yorkers, this special restaurant is like a taste of Venice with its enchanting Atrium Garden that offers foreign films and live music to accompany dinner al fresco. It also has rotating art exhibitions all year long in the Rialto Room. The food is delicious and you can even get Remi takeaways.

ROCK CENTER CAFE $$
American
- ✉ Rockefeller Center, 20 West 50th Street between 5th and 6th Avenues
- ☎ 212-332 7620
- 🖰 www.restaurantassociates.com
- 🚇 Subway B, D, F, Q to 47th–50th Streets/ Rockefeller Plaza

A Mecca for tourists, thanks to the scenic setting, though the American dishes are a little disappointing.

DB Bistro Moderne

SEAGRILL $$$$
Seafood

✉ Rockefeller Center, 19 West 49th Street
between 5th and 6th Avenues
☎ 212-332 7610
🖱 www.theseagrillnyc.com
🚗 Subway B, D, F, Q to 47th–50th Streets/
Rockefeller Centre

Surrounded by lush greenery, the outdoor tables topped with striped umbrellas in summer are replaced in winter by the famous skating rink. The seafood specialities include Australian barramundi with wilted arugala, poached lobster with truffled potato and herb-crusted skate. Note that the refurbished restaurant's dress code has changed to exclude jeans, shorts and trainers.

SEPPI'S $$
French–Italian–Turkish

✉ 123 West 56th Street between 6th and
7th Avenues
☎ 212-708 7444
🖱 www.parkermeridien.com
🚗 Subway B, D, E to 7th Street

Perfect for Carnegie Hall-goers and open until 2am. A French bistro, eclectic dishes range from escargots in garlic butter to beef carpaccio with baby arugula and Parmesan and crawfish ravioli with lobster bisque, which are served in an informal, laid-back environment.

THE RUSSIAN TEA ROOM $$$$
Russian

✉ 150 West 57th Street at 7th Avenue
☎ 212-581 7100
🖱 www.russiantearoomnyc.com
🚗 Subway B, D, E to 7th Avenue

You're in luck! The legendary tea room has been shut for some time and only just reopened after a group of investors stepped in to resurrect this New York institution. Opened in the 1920s, it was bought by Warner LeRoy in 1995 and poured $30 million into it and reopened in 1999. However, the starry clientele that adored the tea room weren't so impressed with LeRoy's theatrical furnishings and it sadly closed its doors. Thankfully, the public can now be let loose again in this over-the-top playground, which has swooping eagles on the walls, red leather banquettes and fake Picassos on the walls. As for the dining, it's caviare all the way here, the most expensive being the Iranian special reserve that costs $300 for 30g, brought to the table on silver trays. Lots of other dishes too, but not as memorable.

The Four Seasons

TOWN $$$
Gourmet American

✉ Chambers Hotel, 15 West 56th Street
between 5th and 6th Avenues
☎ 212-582 4445
🖱 www.townnyc.com
🚗 Subway F to 5th Avenue

A fashionista's favourite that's attached to an über trendy hotel. The menu changes each season but some recurring favourites include softshell crab in summer and white asparagus in spring.

UPSTAIRS AT 21 $$
Gourmet American

✉ 21 West 52nd Street between 5th and
6th Avenues
☎ 212-582 7200
🖱 www.21club.com
🚗 Subway F to 5th Avenue

Here you can get many of the 21 Club's classic dishes in a less formal but equally well-serviced restaurant – and see out of windows into the bargain! It has quickly become a favourite with the trendy jet set.

MIDTOWN EAST

ASIA DE CUBA $$$–$$$$
Asian–Cuban

✉ Morgan's Hotel, 237 Madison Avenue
between 37th and 38th Streets
☎ 212-726 7755
🖱 www.chinagrillmanagement.com
🚗 Subway 6 to 33rd Street; 4, 5, 6, 7 to
Grand Central/42nd Street

The Philippe Starck interior guarantees a trendy crowd for the fusion Asian and Cuban food.

TOP FIVE ROMANTIC RESTAURANTS

There are many restaurants in New York that can deliver on the food front, but don't quite get it right with the ambience. The venues listed below are the top places in town if you really want to inject a bit of romance into your dining experience, from tactile furnishings and soft lighting to sensuous food, they're a must-visit for lovers who are also food lovers.

Aureole: French, Upper East Side (page 177)

Daniel: French, Upper East Side (page 178)

Jean Georges: French, Midtown West (page 168)

Park View At The Boathouse: American–seafood, Central Park (page 149)

River Café: Gourmet American, Brooklyn (page 149)

BULL & BEAR $$$–$$$$
Steakhouse

✉ The Waldorf Hotel entrance on Lexington Avenue at 49th Street
☎ 212-872 4900
🖥 www.waldorfastoria.com
🚇 Subway 6 to 51st Street

A landmark restaurant renowned for its excellent hospitality and unashamedly masculine decor that pays homage to the stock market bull and bear symbols. This is the number one restaurant in New York for delicious, melt-in-the-mouth, prime, aged Black Angus beef dishes, yet has plenty to offer the less carnivorously inclined.

Chef Eric Kaplan has introduced a range of eclectic, mouth-watering dishes that include yellowfin tuna mignon and shrimp Creole with andouille sausage and rice. For something lighter opt for one of the salads, such as lobster salad with mango, avocado and corn.

CAVIAR RUSSE $$$$
Caviare

✉ 2nd floor, 538 Madison Avenue, between 54th and 55th Streets
☎ 212-980 5908
🖥 www.caviarerusse.com
🚇 Subway F to 5th Avenue

Posh caviare and cigar lounge where you can see how the other half lives.

CHIN CHIN $$
Chinese

✉ 216 East 49th Street between 2nd and 3rd Avenues
☎ 212-888 4555
🖥 www.chinchinny.com
🚇 Subway 6 to 51st Street

One of New York's finest Chinese restaurants, it frequently plays host to the city's power crowd.

DOCKS OYSTER BAR $$$
Seafood

✉ 633 3rd Avenue at 40th Street
☎ 212-986 8080
🖥 www.docksoysterbar.com
🚇 Subway 4, 5, 6, 7 to Grand Central/ 42nd Street

This raw fish and seafood speciality restaurant also has a popular bar. Main dishes, such as Atlantic salmon, from $23.

EUROPA GRILL $$
Mediterranean

✉ 599 Lexington Avenue at 53rd Street
☎ 212-755 6622
  Fax 212-755 1044
🚇 Subway E, F to Lexington/3rd Avenue

A welcoming restaurant that has been designed in natural elements of wood, stone and earth tones to create a soothing and tranquil environment. Lincoln Engstrom, formerly of the River Café (page 149), is the chef and he has created delicious and stylish Mediterranean dishes. They include poussin stuffed with ricotta salata and courgette, peppers and sage, pomegranate-marinated lamb with crispy panisse and fresh mint, and lemon-cured pork loin served with soft polenta.

FOUR SEASONS $$$$
Continental

✉ 99 East 52nd Street between Lexington and Park Avenues
☎ 212-754 9494
🖥 www.fourseasonsrestaurant.com
🚇 Subway 6 to 51st Street; E, F to Lexington/3rd Avenue

You have a choice between the Grill Room or the Pool Room at this landmark restaurant, and whichever you opt for will make you feel like one of New York's movers and shakers – this is where they come for their power lunches. The Continental dishes are exquisite, the setting elegant and the service impeccable. Pricey? You bet.

ISTANA $$

Mediterranean

✉ NY Palace Hotel, 455 Madison Avenue at 51st Street

☎ 212-303 6032

🖱 www.newyorkpalace.com

🚇 Subway 6 to 51st Street

A little-known but excellent restaurant serving Mediterranean cuisine in the incredibly beautiful environs of the former Villard Houses that are also home to Le Cirque (below).

LA GRENOUILLE $$$

French

✉ 3 East 52nd Street between 5th and Madison Avenues

☎ 212-752 1495

🖱 www.la-grenouille.com

🚇 Subway 6 to 51st Street

A sophisticated temple for Francophiles, the exquisite French food is well worth its price. If money's no object, go for dinner: otherwise go for a more economical lunch.

LE CIRQUE $$$–$$$$

French–American

✉ One Beacon Court, The Bloomberg Building, 151 58th Street at Lexington Avenue

☎ 212-759 5000

🖱 www.lecirque.com

Sirio Maccioni's family-run restaurant has been the toast of the city for 30 years. After shutting the doors on Le Cirque 2000 at the New York Palace Hotel, it has taken over a year for the master restaurateur to find a suitable place to reopen. He now has, in the shape of the shining new Bloomberg Tower, or One Beacon Court as it's officially known, which will also house luxury condominiums. Le Cirque, which has regular patrons from the political, financial, music and film

worlds, including Robert De Niro, Oprah Winfrey, Bill Clinton and The Rolling Stones, reopened to a glittering party in May 2006. The 1,486sq m (16,000sq ft) restaurant features a main dining room, separate bar area and private mezzanine for those who want to see but not be seen. Expect lots of jaw-dropping sights such as a soaring wine tower that connects the mezzanine to the first floor, an all-glass bar and giant abstract Big Top light shade. Foodies will salivate at the prospect of sampling the menu of executive chef Pierre Schaedelin, who began his career with Le Cirque in 1999 and mentored top chef Alain Ducasse.

MAMA MEXICO $$

Mexican

✉ 214 East 49th Street between 2nd and 3rd Avenues

☎ 212-935 1316

🖱 www.mamamexico.com

🚇 Subway 6 to 51st Street

A proper Mexican restaurant with bright colours, pulsating mariachi music and a festive crowd enjoying the extensive menu, which includes 20-plus appetisers and great main courses like grilled rack of lamb with chilli and pineapple sauce. The margaritas and over 40 types of tequila will help put you in the party mood.

OYSTER BAR $$

Seafood

✉ Grand Central Station, lower level, between 42nd Street and Vanderbilt Avenue

☎ 212-490 6650

🖱 www.oysterbarny.com

🚇 Subway 4, 5, 6, 7 to Grand Central/42nd Street

It seems only appropriate to have a landmark restaurant like this in the landmark that is Grand Central Station. Its fame stems from the generations of connoisseurs who have consumed 1,000 dozen oysters every day at the counters of this atmospheric saloon.

PALM $$

Seafood–steakhouse

✉ 837 2nd Avenue between 44th and 45th Streets

☎ 212-687 2953

🖱 www.thepalm.com

🚇 Subway 4, 5, 6, 7 to Grand Central/42nd Street

A family-run business and now the heart of a multi-million pound empire of Palm

Le Cirque

restaurants the length and breadth of North America, this establishment celebrated its 80th anniversary in 2006. Thanks to the double steak speciality, it had earned its reputation as one of New York's greatest steakhouses by the 1930s. In the 1940s, lobster was introduced, setting the seal on the surf-and-turf trend.

Palm continues to be a Mecca for celebrities and the wheelers and dealers of Manhattan, who come not only for the giant steaks and jumbo Maine lobsters but also for the Italian classics and wide choice of dishes. Palm Two across the road (840 2nd Avenue, tel 212-697 5198) was opened to take the overspill and now has its own loyal customers.

UNION SQUARE CAFE $$–$$$
American–Italian
- ✉ 21 East 16 Street between 5th Avenue and Union Square
- ☎ 212-243 4020
- 🖰 www.unionsquarecafe.com
- 🚇 Subway 4, 5, 6, L, N, R to Union Square.

One of America's most popular restaurants, Danny Meyer's Union Square Cafe serves robustly flavoured, seasonal American cuisine in a relaxed setting of casual elegance. It's worth noting that, despite the proliferation of fashionable eateries that regularly open in New York, it's this restaurant that the city's movers and shakers still flock to, to flex the company credit card. There are three dining areas: balcony seating and a cluster of tables on the lower level, both offshoots of the long mahogany bar, and an adjacent main dining room. The decor is simple but effective – think polished cherrywood floors, oversized pussy willows and colourful artwork on the walls. There's a full lunch and dinner menu with daily specials in the dining room and the bar.

◀▶ BRITTIP
Restaurant mogul Danny Meyer, the brains behind the Union Square Cafe, has opened a swish new restaurant: The Modern at the Museum of Modern Art (tel 212-333 1220, www.themodernnyc.com).

Union Square Cafe is as famous for its impeccable, friendly service as it is for its unusual but fabulous food. Top Chef Michael Romano's Tuscan-influenced menu includes delicacies such as grilled lamb chops with potato-Gruyère gratin and sautéed insalata tricolore, pan-roasted salmon with plum tomatoes, almonds, olives and bottarga, wild striped bass Barigoule, with a savoury artichoke-spring onion broth. Weekly specials include a lobster shepherd's pie and roast suckling pig. And don't forget to order the famous home-made garlic potato chips.

VONG $$$–$$$$
Thai–French
- ✉ 200 East 54th Street at 3rd Avenue
- ☎ 212-486 9592
- 🖰 www.jean-georges.com
- 🚇 Subway E, F to Lexington/3rd Avenue

Another of Jean-Georges Vongerichten's masterpieces, this Thai–French restaurant has sunken tables and deep booths that keep the trendy crowd happy.

WATER CLUB $–$$$
Seafood
- ✉ 500 East 30th Street at East River – entrance on East 23rd Street
- ☎ 212-683 3333
- 🖰 www.thewaterclub.com
- 🚇 Subway 6 to 28th Street, near Madison Square

Another delightful and special venue from the owner of the River Café (page 149), this nautical restaurant, set on an East River barge, also specialises in seafood. The Crow's Nest, a seasonal outdoor patio, sits atop the main dining room and features a moderately priced menu and fun drinks mid-May–late September and offers fab views of the East River. Although on the pricey side, it's well worth splashing out for the fine cuisine and, if you're counting the pennies, the weekend brunch option at a prix fixe is an excellent way to sample some delicious dishes while gazing at that view.

Union Square Café

MIDTOWN WEST

BARBETTA $$$
Italian

✉ 321 West 46th Street between 8th and 9th Avenues
☎ 212-246 9171
🖱 www.barbettarestaurant.com
🚇 Subway A, C east to 42nd Street

During the summer, the rather special Barbetta garden is one of the city's most sought-after sites for dining, with its century-old trees and the scented blooms of magnolia, wisteria, jasmine and gardenia. Having celebrated its 100th birthday in 2006, Barbetta is the oldest Italian restaurant in New York and features cuisine from Piedmont in the north-west region of Italy. Inside it's incredibly ornate and luxurious, with drapes, candles and chandeliers.

BOMBAY PALACE $$
Indian

✉ 30 West 52nd Street between 5th and 6th Avenues
☎ 212-541 7777
🖱 www.bombay-palace.com
🚇 Subway B, D, F, V, to 47th Street.

This upmarket Indian has a regal air, thanks to the dark wood panelling and crystal chandelier. It opened in 1979 and has been feeding the city masses every since with very good dishes, primarily Punjabi, which include seekh kebab, chicken tikka and tandoori shrimp and achar gosht, a chilli lamb stew.

JEAN GEORGES $$$$
French

✉ Trump International Hotel, 1 Central Park West between 60th and 61st Streets
☎ 212-299 3900
🖱 www.jean-georges.com

🚇 Subway A, B, C, D, 1, 9 to 59th Street/ Columbus Circle

Celebrity chef Jean-Georges Vongerichten's exquisite French dishes are served in an elegant and visually stunning landmark restaurant that is both romantic and relaxed. 'Prepare to sit open mouthed – when you're not eating, that is' declares a *New York Metro* review of this Adam Tihany-designed contemporary Art Deco-style restaurant. The upscale crowd that frequents it also gets to enjoy superb views of Central Park, while in good weather it's possible to sit outside. An advantage of this is the bargain $28 prix fixe lunches on the terrace, also served in the Nougatine Room. Dish highlights on a continually changing menu have included asparagus with rich morel mushrooms, Arctic char baked with wood sorrel, and Muscovy duck steaks with sweet and sour jus. It's an unbeatable combination, so plan ahead, book your table and get your partner to treat you!

🇬🇧 BRITTIP
If you want to experience Le Bernardin but aren't keen on seafood, you can put in a request with a waiter for pasta or lamb dishes.

LE BERNARDIN $$$$
Seafood

✉ 155 West 51st Street between 6th and 7th Avenues
☎ 212-554 1515
   Fax 212-554 1100
🚇 Subway V, F, B, D to Rockefeller Center

This is a truly marvellous restaurant. It's very pricey, the prix fixe lunch alone is $59, with dinner from $107 per person, but it's more than worth it as the mouth-watering dishes are sublime. Chef Eric Ripert's cuisine is regarded by NY gourmets as very inventive. He provides an almost raw menu, which has featured delicacies such as lemon-splashed scallops with olive oil and chives. From the cooked menu, tasty treats include celeriac open ravioli with lobster and shrimp with fois gras truffle sauce, or baked snapper in spicy sour broth. The dining room itself is also a pleasure to experience, featuring crisp white linen, rich furnishings and a wood-panelled bar with smart blue-and-gold striped chairs for lounging in pre and post-dinner.

Barbetta

RESTAURANTS

Café Habana

WORLD YACHT DINNER CRUISES $$$
Gourmet American

✉ Pier 81, West 41st Street at Hudson River
☎ 212-630 8100
🖰 www.worldyacht.com
🚇 Subway A, C, East to 42nd Street

If there's one thing that you do before you leave the city, it's to book a four-course dining experience with World Yacht. This seasonal cruise down the river and around the bay offers, without a doubt, the best views of Midtown and Lower Manhattan plus the Statue of Liberty. You can chow down on delicacies like steak and lobster skewer, filet mignon, sevruga caviare and mustard-marinated organic chicken cooked while gazing at the city spread out before you. The chefs are some of the finest in New York, yet the prix fixe meals are pretty reasonable – including a three-hour cruise and live music for dancing – $89.88 Sun–Thurs, $93.94 Fri and Sat.

NOHO

FIVE POINTS $$
American

✉ 31 Great Jones Street between Lafayette Street and Bowery
☎ 212-253 5700
🖰 www.fivepointsrestaurant.com
🚇 Subway B, V, S to Broadway/Lafayette; 6 to Bleecker Street

Named after the once infamous gangland area, this is a popular neighbourhood restaurant with a friendly bar, so now there's no need to worry. For a good, tasty meal, try out the Maine scallop with apple cider sauce or the home-made sweet potato ravioli.

INDOCHINE $$$
Vietnamese–French

✉ 430 Lafayette Street between Astor Place and East 4th Street
☎ 212-505 5111
🖰 www.indochinenyc.com
🚇 Subway 6 to Astor Place

This celebrity haunt serves delicious Vietnamese–French dishes, such as spring rolls and sole fish wrapped in banana leaf, in tiny portions.

NOLITA

CAFE HABANA $
Cuban

✉ 17 Prince Street at Elizabeth Street
☎ 212-625 2001
🚇 Subway N, R to Prince Street; 6 to Spring Street

A hot little restaurant filled with beautiful people eating spicy Cuban food – think chicken tacos with coriander and tomato salsa. Delish!

BRITTIP
Weird but true: some of the smaller restaurants don't take credit cards. Check in advance.

EIGHT MILE CREEK $$
Australian

✉ 240 Mulberry Street between Prince and Spring Streets
☎ 212-431 4635
🖰 www.eightmilecreek.com
🚇 Subway N, R to Prince Street; 6 to Spring Street

Just a few steps north of Little Italy, the laid-back Aussies have arrived serving up cuisine from Down Under. Good Aussie food is both deliciously exotic and pricey – and this tiny restaurant is no exception.

HOOMOOS ASLI $-$$
Middle Eastern

✉ 100 Kenmare Street between Mulberry and Center Streets
☎ 212-966 0022
🚇 Subway 6 to Spring Street

This is a great find if you're on a budget, small but not a dive and offering tasty Israeli cuisine – falafel, pittas, pan-fried chicken in bread crumb and spices, beef with caramelised onions and rice, with prices starting at around $8.

RESTAURANTS

BRITTIP

If you want a refreshment but are too busy shopping or sightseeing for a lengthy stop at a restaurant, then pop into the fantastically named Mud Spot (www.themudtruck.com), permanently parked by 307 East 9th Street, where you can buy a warming espresso to perk you up.

SOHO

SoHo is a great place to head for when eating out, day or night. Its diverse range of restaurants, at all different price points, means that you're pretty much guaranteed to find something to appeal to even the most picky of dining partners.

BALTHAZAR $$
Bistro
✉ 80 Spring Street between Broadway and Crosby Streets
☎ 212-965 1414
⌂ www.balthazarny.com
🚇 Subway N, R to Prince Street
A classy French brasserie, with a genuinely French ambience, serving up good food to a trendy crowd. Great oysters.

BLUE RIBBON $$$
Seafood
✉ 97 Sullivan Street between Prince and Spring Streets
☎ 212-274 0404
⌂ www.blueribbonrestaurants.com
🚇 Subway C east to Spring Street
This restaurant gets packed at any time of the day or night so don't decide to come

here if you are on a tight schedule. If you're not, the eclectic seafood dishes, like sweet and spicy catfish, sushi and paella, are definitely worth the wait.

DANI $$-$$$
Mediterranean
✉ 333 Hudson Street at King Street
☎ 212-633 9333
⌂ www.danirestaurant.com
🚇 Subway N, R to Prince Street
Chef Don Pintabona, who worked for years at the Tribeca Grill, has gone out on his own with this new eatery on the edge of SoHo that takes inspiration from his Sicilian roots. Expect delicious dishes such as chick pea fried calamari or rabbit cacciatore, all served up in trendy warehouse surroundings with wood floor and concrete columns.

DOS CAMINOS SOHO $$-$$$
Mexican
✉ 475 West Broadway at Houston Street
☎ 212-277 4300
⌂ www.brguestrestaurants.com
🚇 Subway C, E to Spring Street
Excellent margaritas here while you're gazing at the fab menu that includes salad with calamari and chorizo, red snapper scallop with spicy mango and passion fruit and lime cilantro marinated gulf shrimp.

FANELLI CAFE $
American
✉ 94 Prince Street at Mercer Street
☎ 212-226 9412
🚇 Subway N, R to Prince Street
Contemporary crowds pack this former speakeasy, which is now an old saloon-style bar and dining room serving American food. It does an excellent selection of sandwiches for lunch.

Dining al fresco in SoHo

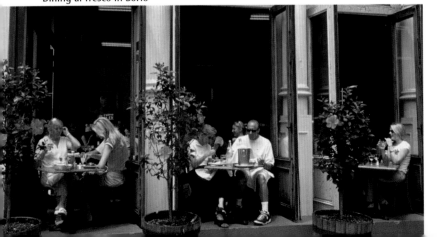

FIAMMA OSTERIA $$
Italian

✉ 206 Spring Street between 6th Avenue and Sullivan Street
☎ 212-653 0100
🖑 www.brguestrestaurants.com
🚆 Subway C, E to Spring Street

A bi-level restaurant that is very fancy, in a Hollywood type of way. The food is very good – think risotto with creamy arborio rice, wild mushrooms, seared scallops and shaved black truffles or sautéed red snapper, manila clam, Italian sausage and broccoli rabe.

KITTICHAI $$
American

✉ 60 Thompson Street between Spring and Broome Streets
☎ 212-219 2000
🖑 www.kittichairestaurant.com
🚆 Subway C, E to Spring Street

Based in trendy SoHo hotel 60 Thompson, this is a fashionable restaurant in its own right and serves up delicious American cuisine at reasonable prices.

L'ECOLE $$
French

✉ 462 Broadway
☎ 212-219 3300
🖑 www.frenchculinary.com/lecole
🚆 Subway 6, J, M, Z, N, Q, W to Canal Street; 6 to Spring Street.

This is the place to come if you want haute cuisine for café prices, as the chefs of this bright, airy restaurant are students of the French Culinary Institute who try out their cooking skills on willing customers. Just think, you could be eating poached sole with shrimp and mussels made by a star chef of the future.

LUCKY STRIKE $$
French

✉ 59 Grand Street between West Broadway and Wooster Street
☎ 212-941 0772
Fax 212-274 9365
🖑 www.luckystrikeny.com
🚆 Subway A, C, E, 1, 9, N, A, 6 to Canal Street

Restaurateur Keith McNally's hot spot has become a watering hole for models, celebrities and club kids, as well as SoHo's art crowd. Ask for the cocktail list and marvel at the many martinis, including chocolate and espresso.

MERCER KITCHEN $$$
French–eclectic

✉ Mercer Hotel, 99 Prince Street at Mercer Street
☎ 212-966 5454
🖑 www.jean-georges.com

Jean-Georges Vongerichten (he of Jean-Georges fame) oversees the eclectic French-inspired cuisine that is served to a trendy crowd in a chic environment.

PROVENCE $$
French

✉ 38 MacDougal Street at Prince Street
☎ 212-475 7500
Fax 212-602 9772
🖑 www.provence-soho.com
🚆 Subway 1, 9 to West Houston Street; C, E to Spring Street; A, C, E, B, D, Q, V, F to 4th Street

One of the hidden gems of SoHo, this is a beautifully rustic restaurant with a fountain in the garden. The food is country-style French cooking; order the pommes frites with everything as they're delicious. Try the prix fixe brunch for $19.50 or make a reservation for about 6.30pm to get a table in the garden.

ZOE $$$
Californian

✉ 90 Prince Street between Broadway and Mercer Street
☎ 212-966 6722
Fax 212-966 6718
🖑 www.zoerestaurant.com
🚆 Subway N, R to Prince Street; B. D, F, Q to Broadway–Lafayette; 6 to Spring Street.

Fabulous Californian-style American food in a beautiful environment. Dishes include seared arctic char with truffle-whipped potatoes, black trumpet mushrooms and caramelised shallots, or rotisserie Long Island duck breast with wheatberry salad with

Zoe

apricots and almonds and pomegranate vinaigrette. The amazing range of breads includes everything from soda to focaccia and comes with butter that includes sesame seeds, poppy seeds, salt and pepper and garlic, plus their own spread made with white beans. The award-winning all American wine list is pretty special, too.

THEATER DISTRICT (BROADWAY)

From 6th Avenue in the east to 9th Avenue in the west and from West 40th Street to West 53rd Street, the Theater District is as good a place as any to get a pre-theatre meal. As well as the many theatres, there are hundreds of restaurants and you'd be hard-pressed to go wrong.

BRITTIP
The main drag for eating in the Theater District is between 8th and 9th Avenues on West 46th Street and is known as Restaurant Row.

BLUE FIN $$
Seafood
- ✉ W Times Square Hotel, 1567 Broadway at 47th Street
- ☎ 212-918 1400
- ⌂ www.brguestrestaurants.com
- 🚗 Subway N, R, W to 49th Street

The Blue Fin made a big splash when it opened in 2000. It serves up fresh fish in theatrical surroundings. Sushi is available on the first floor.

Hudson Cafeteria

COLORS RESTAURANT $$–$$$
International
- ✉ 417 Lafayette Street at Astor Place
- ☎ 212-777 8443
- ⌂ www.colors-nyc.com
- 🚗 Subway 6 to Astor Place

Colors made the headlines in 2006 as the restaurant where dozens of surviving workers from Windows on the World, the restaurant that was atop the World Trade Center, have regrouped; and they not only work there, but also have a financial say and stake in it. It's a co-operative venture, owned and run by its waiters and waitresses, bus boys and cooks. The menu is as global as you can get, from Eastern spring rolls with shellfish to Caribbean goat stew, or American rib-eye steak and seared scallops.

FIREBIRD $$
Caviare–Russian
- ✉ 365 West 46th Street between 8th and 9th Avenues
- ☎ 212-586 0244
- ⌂ www.firebirdrestaurant.com
- 🚗 Subway A, C east to 42nd Street

The opulent Russian decor creates a fabulous setting for tucking into the caviare and blinis. The prix fixe pre-theatre dinner used to be good value, but prices have crept up.

BRITTIP
Due to the law that bans smoking in all indoor public spaces, it is no longer possible to smoke even at a restaurant's bar. Some restaurants with outdoor seating are able to set aside tables for smoking, though.

FRANKIE AND JOHNNIE'S STEAKHOUSE $$
Steakhouse
- ✉ 269 West 45th Street between Broadway and 8th Avenue
- ☎ 212-997 9494
- ⌂ www.frankieandjohnnies.com
- 🚗 Subway A, C, E, N, R to 42nd Street

This is considered to be one of the longest-running shows on Broadway, having first opened as a speakeasy in 1926. Now it still retains its intimate hideaway aura and archetypal New York reputation as a classic steakhouse that has become renowned for its generous portions.

Restaurant Row, 46th Street and 9th

HUDSON CAFETERIA $$
Asian
✉ The Hudson Hotel, 356 West 58th Street between 8th and 9th Avenues
☎ 212-554 6000
🖰 www.chinagrillmgt.com
🚇 Subway A, B, C, D, 1, 2 to 59th Street/ Columbus Circle

The restaurant at Ian Schrager's hotel is a haven for people- and celeb-watching and you'll enjoy the Asian cuisine.

BRITTIP
Don't be too put off by the prices of landmark restaurants – many offer fixed price menus and the cheapest is for lunch, when it's also easier to get a table. Go on, treat yourself!

MARS 2112 $
American
✉ 1633 Broadway at 51st Street
☎ 212-582 2112
🖰 www.mars2112.com
🚇 Subway 1, 9 to 51st Street

This theme restaurant offering will take you out of this world to Mars via the space shuttle. Fortunately, the food is pretty American Earthbound so you won't be eating little green men. Of course, it comes with the ubiquitous shop where you can buy your own Martian doll.

PALM NEW YORK
WEST SIDE $$-$$$
Seafood–steakhouse
✉ 250 West 50th Street between Broadway and 8th Avenue
☎ 212-333 7256
🖰 www.thepalm.com
🚇 Subway 1, 9 to 50th Street

A sister restaurant to the incredibly successful Palm restaurant (page 166), this has very quickly become a hot spot for celebrities, theatre-goers and tourists.

PETROSSIAN $$$
Caviare–Russian
✉ 182 West 58th Street at 7th Avenue
☎ 212-245 2214
🖰 www.petrossian.com
🚇 Subway N, R to 57th Street

Take advantage of the $42 prix fixe theatre menu to enjoy caviare, foie gras and smoked salmon.

PLANET HOLLYWOOD $
American
✉ 1540 Broadway at West 45th Street
☎ 212-333 7827
🖰 www.planethollywood.com
🚇 Subway N, Q, R, S, W, 1, 2, 3, 7 to Times Square

Brilliant Hollywood memorabilia with the standard American burger fare.

RESTAURANTS

TOP FIVE RESTAURANTS TO SPOT A CELEBRITY

Blue Water Grill: Union Square (page 176)

Lucky Strike: SoHo (page 171)

Mercer Kitchen: SoHo (page 171)

Nobu: TriBeCa (page 175)

Tribeca Grill: TriBeCa (page 175)

RENE PUJOL $$
Bistro
✉ 321 West 51st Street between 8th and 9th Avenues
☎ 212-246 3023
🖰 www.renepujol.com
🚗 Subway C east to 50th Street

A great French bistro serving delicious food in a delightful setting.

SUPPER CLUB $$$
Gourmet American
✉ 240 West 47th Street between Broadway and 8th Avenue
☎ 212-921 1940
🖰 www.thesupperclub.com
🚗 Subway 1, 9 to 50th Street

At this special place you'll find fine dining combined with swing dancing and a cabaret – the show is a mix of Cab Calloway, the Blues Brothers and other swing acts. The food is also delicious, particularly the lobster and steak, and I defy anyone not to like the New York cheesecake – so much lighter than European cheesecake, it just melts in your mouth. Stupendous!

Blue Water Grill

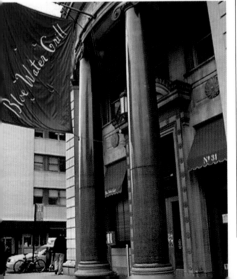

THE VIEW $$$-$$$$
Continental
✉ Top floor, Marriott Marquis Hotel, 1535 Broadway at 45th Street
☎ 212-704 8900
🖰 www.nymarriottmarquis.com
🚗 Subway N, R, S, 1, 2, 3, 7, 9 to Times Square/42nd Street

New York's recently spruced-up revolving restaurant attracts lovebirds and tourists in droves, and serves up a high standard of Continental cuisine. As expected, the views over Manhattan are spectacular, particularly at sunset.

TRIBECA

66 $$$-$$$$
Chinese
✉ 241 Church Street at Leonard Street
☎ 212-925 0202
🖰 www.jean-georges.com
🚗 Subway 1, 9 to Franklin Street

Expensive but worth it is the general consensus on this very chic Chinese restaurant. Its trendy interior – lots of minimalist metallic silver and sparkling white, plus some fish tanks – makes it a hit with the fashionable city crowd. Its dishes, such as steamed cod and Peking duck, are exceptionally good and the bar's cocktails are pleasant to sip while you wait for your table.

ACAPPELLA $$$-$$$$
Italian
✉ 1 Hudson Street at Chambers Street
☎ 212-240 0163
🖰 www.acappella-restaurant.com
🚗 Subway 1, 9 to Franklin Street

You can chow down on rabbit, wild boar, quail and venison at this lovely restaurant specialising in northern Italian cuisine. The decor is as impressive as the menu, with 5m (16ft) high beamed ceilings and Italian tapestries on the walls, plus huge windows offering views over TriBeCa.

CHANTERELLE $$$
French
✉ 2 Harrison Street at Hudson Street
☎ 212-966 6960
🖰 www.chanterellenyc.com
🚗 Subway 1, 9 to Franklin Street

'If this restaurant were any more romantic it would be illegal,' gushes one of the entries in New York's *Zagat Survey*. A 'first class trip' to 'heaven on earth' says another. It's true that it's a premier spot in the city for a romantic night out, and the great food matches the ambience. The $42 prix fixe lunch is one of the best bargains in NY and includes dishes such as striped bass sauté with red wine and sage.

HARRISON $$
Continental
✉ 355 Greenwich Street at Harrison Street
☎ 212-274 9310
🖰 www.theharrison.com
🚇 Subway 1, 2 to Franklin Street

Created by the owners of the hip Red Cat in Chelsea (page 151), this chic restaurant serves up delicious Continental cuisine in an elegant setting.

LE ZINC $
Bistro
✉ 139 Duane Street between West Broadway and Church Street
☎ 212-513 0001
🖰 www.lezincnyc.com
🚇 Subway A, C, 1, 2 to Chambers Street

A casual, well-priced bistro. Here you'll get French food infused with Asian and Hungarian influences. Delicious stuff.

NOBU $$$$
Japanese-Peruvian
✉ 105 Hudson Street at Franklin Street
☎ 212-219 0500
🖰 www.myriadrestaurantgroup.com
🚇 Subway 1, 9 to Hudson Street

It's been around for 13 years now (ancient for a fashionable New York restaurant), but this TriBeCa Mecca is still without a doubt the best Japanese restaurant in the US, serving excellent fresh cuisine that will find 'tastebuds you never knew you had' according to the restaurant researchers at *Zagat*. The decor, by architect David Rockwell, is East meets West, with birch trees, wood floors, seaweed mats and subdued lighting. The multi-award-winning menu includes lots of cooked and raw

🇬🇧 BRITTIP

If you can't get into the celeb-jammed Nobu, try Nobu Next Door (212-334 4445), which only takes walk-ins and is, unsurprisingly, located next door to the main restaurant. It is a more reasonably priced outlet for mere mortals who would rather wait for an hour than a month to sample some of the food everyone is raving about.

BEST FOR DINING AND DANCING

Cornelia Street Café: Greenwich Village (page 155)

Rainbow Room: Rockefeller Plaza (page 163)

Supper Club: Times Square (page 174)

Swing 46 Jazz & Supper Club: Times Square (page 198)

The View: Times Square (page 174)

World Yacht Dinner Cruises: from Midtown West (page 169)

---

delicacies, the black cod with miso continues to be a favourite and the new-style sashimi lightly cooked with garlic is also amazing.

ODEON $$
American–French
✉ 145 West Broadway between Duane and Thomas Streets
☎ 212-233 0507
🖰 www.theodeonrestaurant.com
🚇 Subway 1, 9 to Chambers Street

A très hip hangout that still attracts celebrities for its cool atmosphere and American–French cuisine. You'll need to book ahead. A great late night stop as it stays open until 2am.

TRIBECA GRILL $$$
American
✉ 375 Greenwich Street at Franklin Street
☎ 212-941 3900
🖰 www.tribecagrill.com
🚇 Subway 1, 9 to Franklin Street

Robert De Niro and Drew Nieporent's popular American restaurant opened in 1990 and is one of the main reasons why TriBeCa has become such a hip hangout in recent years. It's located on the first two floors of the TriBeCa Film Center where De Niro has his film production company, so it's a good place to try to spot a celeb or two. Dishes like braised short ribs with foie gras ravioli are rich and filling. The lunch menu attracts major crowds, with dishes like rare seared tuna and citrus marinated shrimp cocktail.

Manhattan Island skyline

NEW YORK FOODS AND FOOD TERMS

Arugula: The American name for rocket, used in salads.

Bagels: As opposed to bialys, these are the delicious Jewish creations, which are at their very best when filled with smoked salmon and cream cheese.

Bialy: A cousin of the bagel, it originates from Bialystock in Eastern Europe and is kosher Jewish food. The dough is not as chewy as a bagel and there is no hole in the middle, just a depression in which garlic and onions are put. Without any tasty extras such as cream cheese, this is truly boring food.

Cannoli: Tubular-shaped biscuit bells with fresh cream on the inside, these come from Italy and are truly delicious.

Cilantro: American name for the fresh leaves of coriander.

Cobbler: A fruit pie topped with a biscuit-style crust.

Grits: Corn kernels.

Halva: Sweetened, crushed sesame paste. It originates from the Mediterranean, Turkey and Arabia.

Konja: A Chinese dessert that you can buy in bags – they are individual mouth-size pots of lychee jelly.

Lox: Thinly sliced pieces of smoked salmon, generally sold with a 'schmear' of cream cheese. It tastes the same as a smoked salmon and cream cheese bagel but works out much cheaper.

Morels: Deliciously meaty mushrooms from Oregon.

Pie: Used to refer to an entire pizza. Most are much larger than the ones we eat in the UK, so people tend to buy by the slice or share a whole 'pie'.

Scallion: Spring onion.

Schmear: A spreading of cream cheese on a bagel.

Sub: An extra large, long roll, named for its submarine-like shape.

You can find a list of more general US foods and food terms on page 21.

UNION SQUARE

BLUE WATER GRILL $$$$
Seafood

✉ 31 Union Square West at 16th Street
☎ 212-675 9500
🖰 www.brguestrestaurants.com
🚇 Subway L, N, Q, R, W, 4, 5, 6 to Union Square

Rated highly by *Zagat*, this place is not only brilliant for people- and celeb-watching, it is also a Mecca for all those who love their seafood. Dishes include lobster-glazed mahi mahi with mango coulis, ginger-crusted big eye tuna with shiitake mushrooms, and blackened swordfish with sweet potato-crabmeat hash. It also has an oyster bar and a 150-seat jazz club for nightly entertainment and dining. Or you can go on Sundays for the wonderful jazz brunch, which is served from 10.30am.

CHAT 'N' CHEW $
American diner

✉ 10 East 16th Street between 5th Avenue and Union Square West
☎ 212-243 1616
   Fax 212-243 2895
🖰 www.chatnchewnyc.com
🚇 Subway L, N, R, 4, 5, 6 to Union Square/14th Street

Classic 1950s American diner with huge servings of meatloaf etc. Regulars know to order the crispy-topped macaroni and cheese, with chicken or bacon added.

BRITTIP

Wine is incredibly expensive in New York. Do as New Yorkers do – have a glass of wine or cocktail before you go out and drink beer with your meal or just stick to the one glass of wine.

MESA GRILL $$
South-western

✉ 102 5th Avenue between 15th and 16th Streets near Union Square

☎ 212-807 7400
Fax 212-989 0034

🖰 www.mesagrill.com

🚗 Subway L, N, R, 4, 5, 6 to Union Square/14th Street

Delicious and inventive south-western cuisine from chef Bobby Flay. A real winner, so give it a try if you are in the area.

REPUBLIC $
Asian

✉ 37 Union Square West between 16th and 17th Streets

☎ 212-627 7172

🖰 www.thinknoodles.com

🚗 Subway L, N, R, 4, 5, 6 to Union Square/14th Street

Specialists in excellent, quick, noodle-based pan-Asian dishes in a canteen-style environment that seats 150. There is also a branch in Upper West Side.

STRIP HOUSE $$
American

✉ 13 East 12th Street between 5th Avenue and University Place

☎ 212-328 0000

🖰 www.theglaziergroup.com

🚗 Subway L, N, Q, R, W, 4, 5, 6 to 14th Street/Union Square

You can eat succulent beef here, especially, of course, the New York 'strip'. Lots of other cuts are available as well as some fish, all served in the glorious surroundings of leather banquettes and velvet.

UPPER EAST SIDE

ATLANTIC GRILL $$-$$$
Seafood

✉ 1341 3rd Avenue between 76th and 77th Streets

☎ 212-988 9200

🖰 www.brguestrestaurants.com

🚗 Subway 77th Street

A long-standing popular restaurant with the fussy Upper East Side set. It's all very chic, from the polished wood floors and artwork to the well-prepared, very fresh fish. There's also an excellent wine list.

AUREOLE $$$$
French

✉ 34 East 61st Street between Madison and Park Avenues.

☎ 212-319 1660

🖰 www.charliepalmer.com

🚗 Subway 4, 5, 6 to 59th Street; N, R to Lexington Avenue

The courtyard garden of this superb restaurant is what makes it so especially romantic. One of New York's best-kept secrets is tucked behind the brownstone that houses Aureole, and makes an idyllic spot for outdoor dining and is always incredibly romantic in candlelight. Inside is a curvaceous balcony, elegant decor and hot-house flower arrangements. Celebrity chef Charlie Palmer – considered the king of New York chefs – frequently changes the menu, but delicious concoctions have included sesame-seared Atlantic salmon with orange-miso vinaigrette and sticky rice croquettes, and foie gras with port-glazed Bing cherries and young onions. Expensive, but worth it to

RESTAURANTS

Mesa Grill

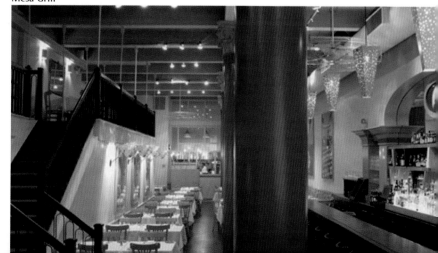

experience dining in one of the best restaurants in town. Closed on Sundays.

BLUE GROTTO $
Mediterranean

⊠ 1576 3rd Avenue between 88th and 89th Streets

☎ 212-426 3200

🚇 Subway 4, 5, 6 to 86th Street

This is more Yorkville than 'silk stocking' Upper East Side, which is reflected in the reasonable prices. It's popular with the locals and serves Italian and Mediterranean-style cuisine in a lounge-like space.

CAFE SABARSKY $$
Bistro

⊠ 1048 5th Avenue at 86th Street

☎ 212-288 0665
Fax 212-645 7127

🖰 www.wallse.com

🚇 Subway 4, 5, 6 to 86th Street

This is not just in a fabulous location – all but opposite the Metropolitan Museum of Art, yet quietly tucked away in the new Neue Galerie Museum for German and Austrian Art (page 105) – but is a wonderful pit stop for light breakfasts, lunches and afternoon tea; crêpes with smoked trout, $15, scallops with asparagus, $20. You'll also

love its elegant decor to match the Austrian-German art theme of the museum itself.

CANDLE 79 $–$$
Vegetarian

⊠ 154 East 79th Street near Lexington Avenue

☎ 212-537 7179

🖰 www.candlecafe.com

🚇 Subway 6 to 77th Street

An unusual place in this swish neighbourhood as it's veggie – though undoubtedly upscale. The menu is well thought out and attracts plenty of meat-eaters because it's so tasty. There's organic wine on offer, along with fresh juices and smoothies.

CARLYLE $$$
French

⊠ Carlyle Hotel, 35 East 76th Street at Madison Avenue

☎ 212-744 1600
Fax 212-717 4682

🖰 www.thecarlyle.com

🚇 Subway 6 to 77th Street

An old establishment that attracts an older 'silk stocking' clientele, but if you want to see how the other half lives try the divine French cuisine for breakfast or brunch.

DANIEL $$$$
French

⊠ 60 East 65th Street between Park and Madison Avenues

☎ 212-288 0033

🖰 www.danielnyc.com

🚇 Subway 6 to 68th Street; F to Lexington Avenue/63rd Street

This is the place to 'dazzle a date' according to hip website www.gonyc.about.com. It's a grand, elegant place with soaring ceilings, gilded columns, plush wall hangings and upholstery, plus fine art and mosaics. Daniel Boulud's sumptuous haute cuisine best of which are the amazing, award-winning desserts; the chocolate bombe is indeed the bomb. It's fine dining with excellent service that will transport you as close to heaven as a mortal can get! A jacket is required to start the journey.

Daniel

BRITTIP
Café Boulud at 20 East 76th Street (212-772 2600) also offers the Daniel's creativity at more accessible prices in a casual setting.

Serafina Fabulous Grill

ITHAKA $$
Greek
- ✉ 308 East 86th Street between 1st and 2nd Avenues
- ☎ 212-628 9100
- 🖱 www.ithakarestaurant.com
- 🚇 Subway 4, 5, 6 to 86th Street

A superb Greek restaurant with exposed brick walls painted white, stone floor and recessed lighting filtered through white fabric. It's known for its large portions, a real locals' favourite with the added benefit of a guitar player Wed–Sat.

MARK'S $$$
French–American
- ✉ The Mark, 25 East 77th Street at Madison Avenue
- ☎ 212-879 1864
- 🖱 www.mandarinoriental.com/themark
- 🚇 Subway 6 to 77th Street

Excellent French–American cuisine. The prix fixe lunch and pre-theatre deals are great value – just make sure you give yourself time to soak up the ambience.

ROSA MEXICANO $$
Mexican
- ✉ 1063 1st Avenue at 58th Street
- ☎ 212-753 7407
- 🖱 www.rosamexicano.com
- 🚇 Subway 4, 5, 6 to 59th Street

Extremely popular Mexican eatery that is known as much for its margaritas as for its delicious food. Its signature dish is its guacamole mashed right beside your table.

SERAFINA FABULOUS GRILL $$$
Italian
- ✉ 393 Lafayette Street at 4th Street or 2nd floor, 1022 Madison Avenue at 79th Street
- ☎ 212-702 9595/212-734 2676
- 🖱 www.serafinarestaurant.com
- 🚇 Subway 4, 5, 6 to 59th Street

Famous for thin-crust pizzas that have been voted the best in the world by gourmets, this is a haunt of both Prince Albert of Monaco and Ivana Trump. Toppings include Al Porcini with porcini mushrooms, fontina cheese, and mozzarella and Al Caviare with salmon caviare, potatoes and crème fraîche. The signature focaccias – two layers of stuffed dough with delicious fillings – range from a delicious Scottish smoked salmon, asparagus and Italian robiola cheese, to truffle oil and robiola.

UPPER WEST SIDE

ALOUETTE $$$
Bistro
- ✉ 2588 Broadway between 97th and 98th Streets
- ☎ 212-222 6808
- 🖱 www.alouettenyc.com
- 🚇 Subway 1, 2, 3, 9 to 96th Street

This French bistro attracts the crowds despite having a very simple menu.

CAFE DES ARTISTES $$
French
- ✉ 1 West 67th Street between Columbus Avenue and Central Park West
- ☎ 212-877 3500
- 🖱 www.cafenyc.com
- 🚇 Subway 1, 9 to 66th Street

A reasonably priced, fine dining establishment that serves up wonderful French cuisine in a romantic setting.

Ithaka

THE AMERICAN DINER

We don't have a real equivalent of an American diner in the UK but the closest is probably a cross between a transport café and a Garfunkels. In a nutshell, diners are relatively cheap, have a homey feel to them but are a lot smarter than your average café. They specialise in American comfort food – pancakes, waffles, crispy bacon, eggs, grill foods, meatloaf – the kind of things that we would choose for a brunch. Go to just about any American city or town and you'll find a good smattering of diners. The one exception is Manhattan, where they are very thin on the ground. Some of the few diners in New York include:

Chelsea
Empire Diner: 210 10th Avenue at 22nd Street. Tel 212-243 2736 www.empire-diner.com. A real New York institution and a great pitstop for clubbers as it's open 24 hours a day. The interior is fabulous with its Art Deco style and the people are pretty gorgeous, too.

Garment District
Cheyenne Diner: 411 9th Avenue at 33rd Street. Tel 212-465 8750. In the heart of the Garment District and just around the corner from Penn Street Station, this is a great place to fill up.

Harlem
M&G Soul Food Diner: 383 West 125th Street at Morningside Avenue. Tel 212-864 7326. This is the southern soul food version of a diner and a great venue for a meal in Harlem. You'll also enjoy the background soul music.

Midtown East
Comfort Diner: 214 East 45th Street between 2nd and 3rd Avenues. Tel 212-867 4555, www.comfortdiner.com. A classic retro diner known for its friendliness and also its wholesome staples of meatloaf and fried chicken.

Midtown West
Market Diner: 572 11th Avenue at West 43rd Street. Tel 212-695 0415. One of the most famous diners in Manhattan, this is where clubbers go to get breakfast or to fill up before the evening run.

Morningside Heights
Tom's Restaurant: 2880 Broadway at 112th Street. Tel 212-864 6137. The exterior was made famous by its use in Seinfeld. If you come here you'll be sharing the space with Columbia University students, who enjoy the cheap comfort food.

NoLiTa
Jones Diner: 371 Lafayette Street at Great Jones Street. Tel 212-673 3577. Pretty dingy-looking from the outside, this is one of the cheapest and best places in the area to get very basic grills and sarnies.

SoHo
Moondance: 80 6th Avenue between Grand and Canal Streets. Tel 212-226 1191. A cracking spot for a cheap meal, it gets packed at the weekends when it's open all night.

Theater District
Ellen's Stardust Diner: 1650 Broadway at 51st Street. Tel 212-956 5151, www.ellensstardustdiner.com. Tourists and children love this 1950s-style diner thanks to its kitsch-retro decor and the singing waitresses. It's great fun, but you wouldn't want to eat here too often – think burgers, chips and anything else that's greasy!

Upper East Side
Comfort Diner: 142 East 86th Street at Lexington Avenue. Tel 212-369 8628. The Upper East Side/Yorkville branch of the friendly diner.

Upper West Side
EJ's Luncheonette: 447 Amsterdam Avenue between 81st and 82nd streets. Tel 212-873 3444. A traditional American diner that serves a mean cup of coffee.

EL MALECON II $

Dominican Caribbean

✉ 764 Amsterdam Avenue between 97th
and 98th Streets

☎ 212-864 5648

🖰 www.maleconrestaurants.com

🚇 Subway 1, 9 to 66th Street

Great value for money. Locals pop in for the
fried chicken, plantain, rice, peas and steak.
The dining room is pretty mediocre, but who
cares when the food is this tasty and $6 for
the best roasted chicken outside the
Caribbean. You can eat in or take out.

OUEST $$-$$$

French–American

✉ 2315 Broadway between 83rd and 84th
Streets

☎ 212-580 8700

🖰 www.ouestny.com

🚇 Subway 1, 2 to 86th Street

Once you can get your tongue around the
restaurant's name – it's simply pronounced
'West'! – you'll be ready to enjoy the French–
American cuisine created by Valenti.

PASHA $$

Turkish

✉ 70 West 71st Street between Columbus
Avenue and Central Park West

☎ 212-579 8751

🖰 www.pashanewyork.com

🚇 Subway 1, 2 to 86th Street

A delightfully sumptuous restaurant that
looks like part of a palace; think deep reds
and yellows, luxurious fabrics and tapestries
hanging on the walls. You can order Turkish
delights, from stuffed vine leaves to kebabs.

PICHOLINE $$$

Mediterranean

✉ 35 West 64th Street between Broadway
and Central Park West

☎ 212-724 8585

🚇 Subway 1, 9 to 66th Street/Lincoln
Center

A beautiful restaurant serving exquisite
Mediterranean dishes in a refined and
elegant setting. Opt to make it one of your
'special' treats while in the city so you can
sample the amazing cheese trolley – yes
trolley, not board. Each day more than 50
different cheeses, out of a total of 70
varieties, are on offer and, if you don't know
which to choose, all the waiters are well
versed in what cheeses go well with what
wines and for what kind of palates. Take
advantage of their considerable knowledge.
A tradition to be savoured.

PIZZERIA UNO $

Italian

✉ Columbus Avenue at 81st Street

☎ 212-595 4700

🖰 www.unos.com

🚇 Subway B, C to 81st Street

OK, so this is a chain restaurant, but it
actually provides good-quality food for
those wanting a simple, but tasty, meal at a
very good price. This one is a great little
neighbourhood joint offering an excellent
range of family-friendly dishes just around
the corner from the American Museum of
Natural History (page 88). There is an
excellently priced children's menu, plus
crayons. What more could you ask after
tramping round dinosaur exhibits?

RUBY FOO'S $$

Asian

✉ 2182 Broadway at 77th Street

☎ 212-724 6700

🖰 www.brguestrestaurants.com

🚇 Subway 1, 9 to 79th Street

Beautiful Asian decor combined with
delicious Asian food. Dim sum is a speciality
of the house.

SPAZZIA $$

Mediterranean

✉ 366 Columbus Avenue at West 77th
Street

☎ 212-799 0150

🚇 Subway 1, 9 to 79th Street

This restaurant serves delicious
Mediterranean food just a stone's throw
away from the American Museum of Natural
History (page 88).

Ruby Foo's

Restaurant reference guide

Name	Area	Style	Price range	Page
2 West	Battery Park	American fusion	$-$$$	148
5 Ninth	Meatpacking District	American nouveau	$$$	159
21 Club	Midtown	Gourmet American	$-$$$	160
44	Midtown	Gourmet American	$$$	161
66	TriBeCa	Chinese	$$$-$$$$	174
202	Chelsea	British–Mediterranean	$$	150
A Voce	Madison Square/Flatiron	Italian	$$$-$$$$	159
Acappella	TriBeCa	Italian	$$$-$$$$	174
Adrienne's Pizza Bar	Financial District	Italian	$-$$	153
Alias	Lower East Side	American	$$	158
AJ Maxwell's	Midtown	American	$$-$$$	161
Alouette	Upper West Side	Bistro	$$$	179
Amy Ruth's Home Style Southern Cuisine	Southern Soul Food	Harlem	$$	156
Angelica Kitchen	East Village	Vegetarian–vegan	$	152
Angelo's	Little Italy	Italian	$	157
Aquavit	Midtown	Scandinavian	$$$$	161
Arezzo	Madison Square/Flatiron	Italian	$$-$$$	159
Asia de Cuba	Midtown East	Asian–Cuban	$$$	164
Atlantic Grill	Upper East Side	Seafood	$$-$$$	177
Aureole	Upper East Side	French	$$$$	177
Babbo	Greenwich Village	Italian	$$$$	155
Balthazar	SoHo	Bistro	$$	170
Bar Martignetti	Little Italy	Italian	$$-$$$	157
Barbetta	Midtown West	Italian	$$$	168
Battery Gardens	Battery Park	Gourmet American	$$$$	148
Bereket	Lower East Side	Turkish	$	158
BG	Midtown	American nouveau	$$$-$$$$	161
Big Wong King	Chinatown	Cantonese	$	151
Blue Fin	Theater District	Seafood	$$	172
Blue Grotto	Upper East Side	Mediterranean	$	178
Blue Ribbon	SoHo	Seafood	$$$	170
Blue Water Grill	Union Square	Seafood	$$$$	176
Bombay Palace	Midtown West	Indian	$$	168
Bondi Road	Lower East Side	Seafood	$$	158
Bongo	Chelsea	Seafood	$$$-$$$$	150
Bottino	Chelsea	Italian	$$	150
Bread	Little Italy	Italian	$$	157
Bright Food Shop	Chelsea	Asian–Mexican	$	150
Buddakan	Chelsea	Pan–Asian	$$$-$$$$	150
Bull & Bear	Midtown East	Steakhouse	$$$-$$$$	165
Café de Bruxelles	West Village	Belgian	$$	155
Café des Artistes	Upper West Side	French	$$	179
Café Gitane	Little Italy	French–North African	$$	157
Café Habana	NoLiTa	Cuban	$	169
Café Sabarsky	Upper East Side	Bistro	$$	178
Cafeteria	Chelsea	American diner	$$	150
Candle 79	Upper East Side	Vegetarian	$-$$	178
Carlyle	Upper East Side	French	$$$	178
Caviar Russe	Midtown East	Caviare	$$$$	165
Chanterelle	TriBeCa	French	$$$	174
Chat 'n' Chew	Union Square	American diner	$	176
Cheyenne Diner	Garment District	Diner	$	180
Chin Chin	Midtown East	Chinese	$$	165
China Grill	Midtown	Chinese	$$	161
Colors	Theater District	International	$$-$$$	172
Comfort Diner	Midtown East	Diner	$	180
Comfort Diner	Upper East Side	Diner	$	180
Cornelia Street Café	Greenwich Village	Eclectic	$$	155
Dani	SoHo	Mediterranean	$$-$$$	170
Daniel	Upper East Side	French	$$$$	178
db Bistro Moderne	Midtown	French–American	$$$$	162
Del Posto	Meatpacking District	Italian	$$$	160
Dim Sum Go Go	Chinatown	Chinese–vegetarian	$	151
Diwan	Midtown	Indian	$$	162

Name	Area	Style	Price range	Page
Dock's Oyster Bar	Midtown East	Seafood	$$$	165
Dos Caminos Soho	SoHo	Mexican	$$–$$$	170
Eight Mile Creek	NoLiTa	Australian	$$	169
EJ's Luncheonette	Upper West Side	Diner	$	180
El Malecon II	Upper West Side	Dominican Caribbean	$	181
Eleven Madison Park	Gramercy Park	French–American	$$$$	154
Ellen's Stardust Diner	Theater District	Diner	$	180
Empire Diner	Chelsea	Diner	$	180
Europa Grill	Midtown East	Mediterranean	$$	165
Fanelli Café	SoHo	American	$	170
Ferrara	Little Italy	Italian café	$	158
Fiamma Osteria	SoHo	Italian	$$	171
Firebird	Theater District	Caviare–Russian	$$	172
Five Points	NoHo	American	$$	169
Florent	Meatpacking District	French	$	160
Four Seasons	Midtown East	Continental	$$$$	165
Frank	East Village	Italian	$	152
Frankie & Johnnie's	Theater District	Steakhouse	$$	172
Garage Restaurant & Café	West Village	American	$	156
George & Gina's Restaurant	Harlem	Puerto Rican	$$	156
Gigino at Wagner Park	Battery Park	Italian	$	148
Gnocco Cucina & Tradizione	East Village	Italian	$$	152
Gotham Bar and Grill	Greenwich Village	Gourmet American	$$$	156
Gordon Ramsay	Midtown	British fusion	$$$$	162
Gramercy Tavern	Gramercy Park	Gourmet American	$$$	154
Grimaldi's	Brooklyn	Italian	$	148
Hard Rock Café	Midtown	American	$	162
Harley Davidson Café	Midtown	American	$	162
Harrison	TriBeCa	Continental	$$	175
Hoomoos Asli	NoLiTa	Middle eastern	$–$$	169
Hudson Cafeteria	Theater District	Asian	$$	173
Il Fornaio	Little Italy	Italian	$	157
Il Palazzo	Little Italy	Italian	$	157
Indochine	NoHo	Vietnamese–French	$$$	169
Istana	Midtown East	Mediterranean	$$	166
Ithaka	Upper East Side	Greek	$$	179
Jean Georges	Midtown West	French	$$$$	168
Joe's Shanghai	Chinatown	Chinese–shanghai	$$	151
John's Pizzeria	Greenwich Village	Italian	$	156
Jones Diner	NoLiTa	Diner	$	180
Katz's Delicatessen	Lower East Side	American–Jewish	$	158
Kittichai	SoHo	American	$$	171
Koodo Sushi	Financial District	Japanese	$$	153
La Grenouille	Midtown East	French	$$$	166
La Palapa	East Village	Mexican	$$	153
L'atelier De Joel Ruchon	Midtown	French	$$$$	162
Le Bernardin	Midtown West	Seafood	$$$$	168
L'Ecole	SoHo	French	$$	171
Le Cirque	Midtown East	French–American	$$$–$$$$	166
Le Zinc	TriBeCa	Bistro	$	175
Lucky Strike	SoHo	French	$$	171
M&G Soul Food Diner	Harlem	Diner	$	180
Mama Mexico	Midtown East	Mexican	$$	166
Market Diner	Midtown West	Diner	$	180
MarkJoseph Steakhouse	South Street Seaport	Steakhouse	$$	153
Mark's	Upper East Side	French–American	$$$	179
Markt	Meatpacking District	Belgian	$$	160
Mars 2112	Theater District	American	$	173
Mercer Kitchen	SoHo	French–eclectic	$$$	171
Mesa Grill	Union Square	South-western	$$	177
Moondance	SoHo	Diner	$	180
New Green Bo	Chinatown	Chinese–shanghai	$–$$	152
New York Noodle Town	Chinatown	Hong Kong-style noodle house	$	152
Nobu	TriBeCa	Japanese–Peruvian	$$$$	175
Nobu 57	Midtown	Japanese–Peruvian	$$$$	162
Nobu Next Door	TriBeCa	Japanese	$$	175
Noodle Pudding	Brooklyn	Italian	$$	148
Norma's	Midtown	American	$–$$	163

RESTAURANTS

Name	Area	Style	Price range	Page
Odeon	TriBeCa	American–French	$$	175
Old Homestead	Meatpacking District	American	$$	160
Opia	Midtown	French	$$	163
Ouest	Upper West Side	French–American	$$$	181
Oyster Bar	Midtown East	Seafood	$$	166
Palm	Midtown East	Seafood–steakhouse	$$	166
Palm New York West Side	Theater District	Seafood–steakhouse	$$–$$$	173
Park View at the Boathouse	Central Park	American–seafood	$$–$$$	149
Pasha	Upper West Side	Turkish	$$	181
Pastis	Meatpacking District	French	$$$	160
Pellegrino's	Little Italy	Italian	$	157
Petrossian	Theater District	Caviare–Russian	$$$	173
Philip Marie	West Village	American	$$–$$$	156
Picholine	Upper West Side	Mediterranean	$$$	181
Pizzeria Uno	Upper West Side	Italian	$	181
Planet Hollywood	Theater District	American	$	173
Porcao Churrascaria	Gramercy Park	Brazilian	$$$	154
Provence	SoHo	French	$$	171
Rainbow Room	Midtown	Continental	$$$–$$$$	163
Rao's	Harlem	Italian	$	156
Remi	Midtown	Italian	$$$	163
René Pujol	Theater District	Bistro	$$	174
Republic	Union Square	Asian	$	177
River Café	Brooklyn	Gourmet American	$$$	149
Rock Center Café	Midtown	American	$$	163
Rosa Mexicana	Upper East Side	Mexican	$$	179
Ruby Foo's	Upper West Side	Asian	$$	181
Sal Anthony's SPQR	Little Italy	Italian	$$–$$$	158
Seagrill	Midtown	Seafood	$$$$	164
Seppi's	Midtown	French–Italian–Turkish	$$	164
Serafina Fabulous Grill	Upper East Side	Italian	$$$	179
Soto	Greenwich & West Village	Japanese	$$$–$$$$	156
Spazzia	Upper West Side	Mediterranean	$$	181
Strip House	Union Square	American	$$	177
Supper Club	Theater District	Gourmet American	$$$	174
Sylvia's	Harlem	Southern soul food	$	157
Tabla	Madison Square	American Indian	$$$$	159
Tamarind	Gramercy Park	Indian	$$	154
Taormina	Little Italy	Italian	$	157
Tavern on the Green	Central Park	Gourmet American	$$$	149
The Elephant	East Village	French–Thai fusion	$$	153
The Park	Chelsea	Mediterranean	$$$	150
The Red Cat	Chelsea	Mediterranean–American	$$	151
The Russian Tea Room	Midtown	Russian	$$$$	164
The View	Theater District	Continental	$$$–$$$$	174
Tomoe Sushi	Greenwich Village	Japanese	$$	156
Tom's Restaurant	Morningside Heights	Diner	$	180
Town	Midtown	Gourmet American	$$$	164
TriBeCa Grill	TriBeCa	American	$$$	175
Union Square Cafe	Midtown East	American–Italian	$$–$$$	167
Upstairs at 21	Midtown	Gourmet American	$$	164
Veritas	Gramercy Park	Gourmet American	$$$$	154
Vong	Midtown East	Thai–French	$$$–$$$$	167
Water Club	Midtown East	Seafood	$–$$$	167
World Yacht Dinner Cruises	Midtown West	Gourmet American	$$$	169
Yaffa Café	East Village	American diner	$	153
Zoe	SoHo	Californian	$$$	171

CHAPTER 8

Nightlife

New York is known for its shopping and exciting nightlife. After a hard day hitting the shops and sightseeing, it's time to take to the streets at night to discover exactly what makes the Big Apple one of the top cities in the world for partying.

A glance at any of the listings pages in the press will confirm that there is an amazing amount of evening entertainment to choose from. Any night of the week you'll find comedy shows with stand-up routines from some of the best in the business and live music from the hottest bands. The bar scene in NYC is particularly exciting: whether it's soaking up some cool jazz in the West Village, partying into the small hours in the hip Meatpacking District or sipping apple martinis in a sophisticated Upper East Side joint, there's a bar or lounge to suit every type of person.

BARS, LOUNGES AND PUBS

Here's a selection of bars to drop into while you are out and about in the city, including some that are super swish, some more grungy and some lounges that stay open into the early hours. Lounges are very much an integral part of the New York nightlife scene. Placed somewhere between a plush bar and a club, they're somewhere for you to stay late, listen to DJs and sip cocktails, but most don't have dance floors. Pubs may not be quite the same as the Brit equivalent, but

> **BRITTIP**
>
> Get yourself in the Manhattan mood before you even arrive by whipping up one of Bungalow 8's most popular cocktails, The Valentini. Mix 30ml (1oz) of passion fruit purée, 30ml (1oz) Stoli strawberry vodka, 15ml (½oz) grenadine and a dash of sugar. Pour into a champagne flute, top with Moet & Chandon and garnish with a strawberry – good enough for Lindsey Lohan.

there are some great neighbourhood joints where you can get a pint of Guinness or beer.

BROOKLYN

Bar Below: 209 Smith Street at Baltic Street. Tel 718-694 2277.
A funky basement bar that stays open until 4am where you'll find hip-hop kids at the extremely long bar. Head to the back for chilled-out sounds from the DJ. Chocolate-lovers should definitely try the delicious Snickers martini.

CHELSEA

Bungalow 8: 515 West 27th Street at 10th Avenue. Tel 212-629 3333, www.bungalow8.com
One of the snobbiest door policies in Manhattan may prevent you from actually getting into this notorious lounge and blowing all your money on mega-priced drinks, such as $350 for a $25 bottle of Absolut Mandrin. If you do manage to wheedle your way in, you may well spot a celeb or three, not to mention lots of Park Avenue princesses. If you don't have a car waiting for you outside, the concierge can arrange a helicopter!

Chelsea Brewing Company: West Side Highway at 20th Street. Tel 212-336 6440, www.chelseabrewingcompany.com
A venue that caters for all types of night time needs, it's a micro-brewery, with more than 30 brews on tap. Downstairs there's a sports bar atmosphere, while upstairs in the mezzanine lounge it's more romantic, with a fireplace and two-storey glass windows

7th Avenue

overlooking the river. Outside a rowdy crowd gathers post-work. From all angles, the view of New Jersey at sunset is worth a visit alone. The fact that you can also eat here – light bites like salads and pizzas – makes it even more appealing.

Kanvas: 219 9th Avenue between 23rd and 24th Streets. Tel 212-727 2616, www.kanvasnyc.com.
This popular Chelsea hang-out is owned by two fire-fighters, who have furnished a couple of giant loft rooms with comfy banquettes, subtle lighting and a chilled line in music. There's also gallery space on both floors so you can snap up some art while you're sipping your sour apple Martini, the bar's speciality.

EAST VILLAGE

11th Street Bar: 510 East 11th Street at Avenue A. Tel 212-982 3929, www.11thstbar.com.
Marked only by an illuminated Guinness sign, this Irish pub is somewhere you know you can sit and enjoy a decent pint without having to look like you walked out of the pages of a lifestyle magazine. Sometimes has live music.

Angel's Share: 8 Stuyvesant Street between East 9th and East 10th Streets. Tel 212-777 5415.
Dedicated to the art of mixology, this little gem of a bar will rustle up any cocktail you desire. Part of its charm is the fact that it's so hard to find, you'll feel as if you've stumbled across a city secret. Take the stairs to the second floor and veer left past the restaurant to the door at the rear. Inside you'll find a dark, intimate bar where classy city dwellers take their first dates.

Bar on A: 170 Avenue A near 11th Street. Tel 212-353 8231.
This bar's been popular with villagers for more than a decade and it's easy to understand why. It's got a lovely laid-back vibe, snakeskin bar stools, lots of cooling ceiling fans and an excellent selection of beers.

Korova Milk Bar

Beauty Bar: 231 East 14th Street between 2nd and 3rd Avenues. Tel 212-539 1389, www.beautybar.com.
Deb Parker's theme bar is equipped with 1960s-style hairdryers and chairs, real manicurists, great drinks and a heavy dose of the hip and beautiful.

Buddha Lounge: 29 East 3rd Street between 2nd Avenue and Bowery. Tel 212-505 7344.
Exposed brick walls, pricey cocktails and popular mid-week and at weekends. Some say it's pretentious, others love it; you decide.

KGB: 85 East 4th Street between 2nd and 3rd Avenues. Tel 212-505 3360, www.kgbbar.com.
Decorated with deep-red walls, portraits of Lenin and Brezhnev, propaganda posters and an oak bar from when it was a front for the Communist party. The crowd is a mix of actors, writers and drunks who love the private-parlour feel. Up-and-coming writers and successful authors often do free readings, so call to see who's on.

Korova Milk Bar: 200 Avenue A between 12th and 13th Streets. Tel 212-254 8838, www.korovamilkbar.com.
Wacky retro-futuristic style that pays homage to Stanley Kubrick's *A Clockwork Orange*. It attracts a sci-fi crowd who love its surreal quality and the ice-cream drinks.

Sutra: 16 1st Avenue at East 1st Street. Tel 212-677 9477.
Red velvet and lots and lots of candles create an intimate atmosphere in this sumptuous new lounge bar.

GARMENT DISTRICT

Stitch: 247 West 37th Street between 7th and 8th Avenues. Tel 212-852 4826, www.stitchnyc.com.
A good name for a new bar in the heart of the clothing district. Cocktails, such as the Stiletto, are just as well named.

GREENWICH VILLAGE

Madame X: 94 West Houston Street between Thompson Street and La Guardia Place. Tel 212-539 0808, www.madam exnyc.com.
There's a real London Soho den-of-iniquity feel to this joint, bathed as it is in red and lit by the glow of lanterns. Known for serving pretty potent cocktails and rare imported beers. In summer, head for the black door at the rear and you'll find the new outdoor

TOP FIVE BARS FOR ALFRESCO DRINKING

Brooklyn
Gowanus Yacht Club: 323 Smith Street, tel 718-246 1321. You'll feel you've really got off the tourist trail at this small outdoor beer garden close to the lovely Carroll Gardens. It attracts a chilled crowd of locals who sip beer and wine beneath the fairylight-bedecked trees before and after sunset. Bar food is also available.

Chelsea
Glass: 287 10th Avenue, tel 212-904 1580. 'Cool' is usually the reaction staff get when people see the bamboo-filled patio in this hip bar for the first time. It's a place to see and be seen in, so if you don't mind rubber-necking alongside models and aspiring actors, you'll fit right in.

Lower East Side
Barramundi: 67 Clinton Street between Rivington and Stanton Streets, tel 212-529 6900. A gorgeous walled garden covered with twinkling fairylights is très romantic or cool depending on whether you're with a partner or friends. Attracts a mixed crowd of internationals.

Upper East Side
Rooftop at the Met: 1000 5th Avenue at 82nd Street, tel 212-535 7710, www.moma.org. The terrace (open in the summer) at the Metropolitan Museum of Art (see page 98) offers stunning views of the city, particularly at sunset. It's also known as a great singles pick-up joint.

West Village
B-Bar & Grill: 40 East 4th Street, tel 212-475 2220, www.bbarandgrill.com. The large outside patio here, with bar, chic furniture and trees, is a magnet for fashionable West and East Villagers.

alcove, where red lights above the benches bring the boudoir theme outside. Best of all, you'll probably be able to find a free corner.

◄► BRITTIP

If you're looking for a romantic bar go to Rise (14th floor, 2 West Street, Battery Park City, tel 917 790 2626) where sweeping views of the New York Harbor and the outside balcony is the perfect spot to sip a drink together at sunset.

LITTLE ITALY
GoldBar: 389 Broome Street at Mulberry Street. Tel 212-274 1568.
This hot new bar from the owners of Cain and former GM of Lotus is lavished in gold, from the skulls in the wall to the chains separating the rooms and even the ceiling. There are also golden love bracelets for drinks tables engraved with Latin sayings and the theme of the cocktails is golden honey.

LOWER EAST SIDE
205 Club: 205 Chrystie Street at Stanton Street. Tel 212-477 6688.

The reinvention of this former rock dive into a spacey club has proved popular. Graffiti artists decorated the outside of the building, while inside the upstairs takes its inspiration from Andy Warhol's Factory, with tinfoil brick and gunmetal filing cabinets under the bar. There's also a low-ceilinged, candle-lit basement with dark electronica.

BLVD: 199 Bowery near Rivington Street. Tel 212-982 7767.
An expensive club where you have to buy a bottle to secure a table and mix with the B- and C-listers. It is worth trying to get in, though, if you are looking for a big night out in a big NY club, as there are several rooms to wander around and a large dance floor where you can join good-looking NY scenesters dancing to hip-hop and rock.

Boss Tweed's: 115 Essex Street between Rivington and Delancey Streets. Tel 212-475 9997, www.bosstweeds.com.
Previously on the site of Smithfields bar, this is the closest you'll get to a local in Manhattan. The glass-bricked bar offers everything from pints of Guinness to vodka shots, each served up with a great story by bartender and co-owner Stuart Delves. Very entertaining.

TOP FIVE BARS TO ENJOY A CIGARETTE

We're not encouraging you to smoke, but the reality is there are lots of Brits who like to. New York was well ahead of the UK with its smoking ban in public places, so don't expect to be able to light up anywhere here. Just to keep all readers happy, we've tracked down five places where you won't be chucked out for smoking.

Circa Tabac: 32 Watts Street at Thompson Street

Hudson Bar & Books: 626 Hudson Street between Horatio and Jane Streets, www.barandbooks.net

Karma: 51 First Avenue between 3rd and 4th Streets

Lexington Bar & Books: 1020 Lexington Avenue between 72nd and 73rd Streets, www.barandbooks.net

Shebeen: 202 Mott Street between Princes and Spring Street

Dark Room: 165 Ludlow Street between Stanton and Houston Streets. Tel 212-353 0536.
A bar that draws a rock-loving clientele and named by www.nymag.com as one of the best places in the city to pick up a musician. It occupies a bunker-like basement, with low ceilings and dim lighting, and a horseshoe-shaped bar serves a great selection of beers to a decidedly unposey crowd.

Good World: 3 Orchard Street between Canal and Hester Streets. Tel 212-925 9975, www.goodworldbar.com
A mellow bar with a semi-regular DJ and an attractive young crowd. Stars that have been spotted here include Keanu Reeves, Bjork, Courtney Love and Matt Dillon. Best time to go is Sun–Thurs and order the Scandinavian-style Good World, an elderberry-infused caipirinha.

Inoteca: 98 Rivington Street at Ludlow Street. Tel 212 614-0473, www.inotecanyc.com
The staff at this wine bar are ingratiating and knowledgeable. The crowd is a mixture of neighbourhood denizens and drop-ins from uptown, creating a good atmosphere. Serves food too.

Kush: 191 Chrystie Street between Rivington and Stanton Streets. Tel 212-677 7328, www.kushlounge.com.
Get a taste of paradise by sipping a few cocktails and nibbling on tasty bar snacks like mixed olives and salted almonds in this Moroccan oasis. The decor is fab, with wonderful tiling and whitewashed walls lit by candles. Open until 4am Tues–Sat.

Orchard Bar: 200 Orchard Street between Houston and Stanton Streets. Tel 212-673 5350.
One of the best lounges on the Lower East Side, the decor at the Orchard Bar is very different (think rocks for seats and bamboo shoots hanging from the walls). Cutting-edge DJs, cheapish drinks and a trendy crowd of artists and musicians mean it gets packed at the weekends, so if you want to try it out, you'll need to plan ahead.

Punch & Judy: 26 Clinton Street between Houston and Stanton Streets. Tel 212-982 1116.
Loud and buzzy wine bar with comfy deep red sofas – not that you'll be able to get on them – that's got a really varied menu, from cheapish wines by the glass through to vintages that are going to cost you much more. You can get food here, too.

SX 137: Essex Street between Stanton and Rivington Streets. Tel 212-674 6931.
It's hard not to have a fun night here. There's a black leather bar, shiny flip-up tables and killer cocktails. The art on the walls is for sale if you want to return with a souvenir.

 BRITTIP

Many of the hip bars get packed out on Friday and Saturday nights with the people who live outside Manhattan. If you want to experience the scene without tourists, choose another night.

MEATPACKING DISTRICT

AER Lounge: 409 West 13th Street near 9th Avenue, tel 646-989 0100, www.aerlounge.com
A very slick two-level lounge is a mix of dazzling neon and dark corners, with no discernable dance floor. Instead clientele end up grooving on the ottomans, cocktail tables, banquettes and carpeted platform. If you want something more intimate, there are a couple of tiny rooms with throne chairs and movies playing on the walls. There's a heated veranda glassed off from the main bar where you can smoke.

TOP FIVE BARS TO SPOT STARS

Alphabet City – East Village
2A: 25 Avenue A. Tel 212-505 2466. A real musos hangout. Band of the moment The Strokes is just one of the combos that you may find enjoying the New Wave and punk 1970s music in this supercool bar and lounge.

Meatpacking District
Lotus: 409 West 14th Street between 9th and 10th Avenues. Tel 212-243 4420, www.lotusnewyork.com. Three storeys devoted to nightlife, including a bar, restaurant and club. Jennifer Lopez, Bruce Willis and Britney Spears have been seen here, but the celeb scene has cooled off since it opened in 2000. There are still star DJs, though, plus B-listers and their model girlfriends to gaze at. Avoid the weekend crush by going midweek. Try their Tartini – a Cosmo with Chambord.

Midtown East
Wet Bar at W New York, The Court Hotel: 130 East 39th Street between 5th and Madison Avenues. Tel 212-592 8844, www.starwoodhotels.com. George Clooney, Whoopi Goldberg and D'Angelo Marc Anthony have all been spotted in this sleek and uncluttered setting, which plays host to professionals and hotel guests. Try their apple martini.

NoHo
Joe's Pub: 425 Lafayette Street between 4th Street and Astor Place. Tel 212-539 8770, www.web.joespub.com/web_joes. This newish cabaret continues to be a real hot spot. An extension of the Public Theater, Joe's brings you live music, spoken-word performances and a crowd jam-packed with trendy types. Stars spotted here include Ethan Hawke, Minnie Driver, Janeane Garofalo and Camryn Manheim. The drink to order is the Lady Macbeth – 115ml (4 fl oz) of champagne and 115ml (4 fl oz) of ruby port. Strong stuff!

The Bowery
Kos: 264 Bowery near Houston Street.
This new lounge owned by Denzel Washington and Lenny Kravitz is incredibly hard to get in to, but if you do manage entry be prepared to have to further blag your way in to meet the stars hanging out in the shag-carpeted Kitty Box VIP room.

APT: 419 West 13th Street at 10th Avenue. Tel 212-414 4245, www.aptwebsite.com. A real hit with trendy New Yorkers since the day it opened, this intimate bar/club makes you feel you are somewhere extra special. The dark, candlelit first floor is furnished like an apartment, complete with bed, dining table and chairs and sofas, offering comfortable lounging. Charming staff serve up tasty cocktails, such as Moscow Mules and Appletinis, for around $10. The wood-walled room downstairs has a more modern vibe, and punters propping up the long bar often end up strutting their stuff to the DJ's hip tunes. Book in advance for the weekend.

◀🇬🇧▶ BRITTIP

If you're after a quality cigar bar, take a trip to Florio's Grill & Cigar Bar, 192 Grand Street near Mulberry Street in Little Italy (tel 212-226 7610), where the large humidor is filled with cigars from around the world.

Earth NYC: 116A 10th Avenue at 17th Street. Tel 212-337 0016, www.earth-nyc.com.
Two floors with plush red sofas and a wall lined with 130 candles makes for a romantic, laid-back setting in this Karma Sutra-inspired lounge. Great Indian tapas.

Hogs & Heifers: 859 Washington Street at West 13th Street. Tel 212-929 0655, www.hogsandheifers.com.
The hogs are the motorcyclists and the heifers are the dames, who are known for hanging their bras on the ceiling. There's no longer bar dancing here though!

MIDTOWN
Campbell Apartment Bar: Gallery Level, Grand Central Station. Tel 212-953 0409. This apartment used to be the office/salon of the 1920s tycoon John W Campbell. The beamed ceiling, huge leaded-glass window and the massive stone fireplace make a unique, almost castle-like space. But the dark wood, couches and club armchairs create an intimate place for a drink.

D'Or: 204 West 55th Street at Broadway. Tel 212-245 7715.

Just opened new lounge in the basement of the Amalia restaurant, where you reach the bar via an illuminated stained-glass staircase. Once down there it's hard not to gawp at the crystal chandeliers, gilded mirrors, and clientele sprawled on leather banquettes.

Langans: 150 West 47th Street near 7th Avenue. Tel 212-869 5482.

This Irish pub is a hangout for journalists from the newspaper world, in particular the *New York Post*. Good place to pick up some brunch or an early-evening pint and listen to the gossip. Rupert Murdoch has been known to pop in from time to time.

Russian Vodka Room: 265 West 52nd Street between Broadway and 8th Avenue. Tel 212-307 5835, www.russianvodka room.com.

A brilliant vodka bar that doesn't require you to take out a second mortgage. There are 53 different vodkas, plus cheap smoked fish platters, delicious cocktails and marvellous vodka infusions. It tends to attract the publishing crowd.

SOHO AND TRIBECA

Antarctica: 287 Hudson Street at Spring Street. Tel 212-352 1666, www.antarctica bar.com

This is one of the best places in the city to enjoy a beer and a game of pool, as it's rarely packed so you can actually get a table. There's also a good jukebox and a friendly crowd once you've finished your game.

Blind Tiger: 281 Bleecker Street at Jones Street. Tel 212-462 4682.

Hogs & Heifers

Recently opened micro-brewery offering more than 30 beers, with great names like Sly Fox Irish stout. It's got a garden for summer, a fireplace for winter and is popular with the locals.

Botanica: 47 East Houston Street between Mott and Mulberry Streets. Tel 212-343 7251.

Serving drinks at decent prices in très chic SoHo, this dark and rather grungy basement bar is a watering hole for artists and college students.

Brandy Library: 25 North Moore Street at Varwick Street. Tel 212-226 5545, www.brandylibrary.com.

As its name suggests, this new bar is dedicated to the finest brandies, plus there are more than 100 cocktails on the menu. Waitresses climb ladders to pick out your chosen tipple from the brandy-lined shelves. A lovely place to end a sophisticated evening, as it stays open until 4am.

Café Noir: 32 Grand Street at Thompson Street. Tel 212-431 7910.

An extensive wine list at this cute urban oasis that also serves Moroccan comfort food meets Spanish tapas. Think tagines, stews and pitchers of sangria. There's also the occasional live jazz session.

Dekk: 134 Reade Street between Hudson and Greenwich Streets. Tel 212-941 9401, www.thedekk.com.

A new TriBeCa haunt, which has modelled itself on a traditional Parisian wine bar. It also has a cool restaurant and screening room that shows old movies.

Merc Bar: 151 Mercer Street between Prince and Houston Streets. Tel 212-966 2727, www.mercbar.com.

A long-time fixture on the SoHo scene, this cool bar draws an attractive crowd to its luxuriously deep sofas. It's at its best in summer when worn leather chairs get an airing on the sidewalk – a great place to sit and people-watch. Be warned: the drinks are pricey at $10-plus.

Milady's: 160 Prince Street at Thompson Street. Tel 212-226 9340.

If you want a beer and not a ridiculously priced cocktail, and a down-to-earth atmosphere then pop in here. It's tiny, plays rock music during later hours and the people-watching is great, from pensioners who have lived in SoHo for decades to young city slickers.

Caroline's Comedy Club

UPPER WEST SIDE

Kama: 380 Columbus Avenue at 78th Street. Tel 212-724 2363.

An exotic place for a romantic evening. This new lounge has sari drapes, beds, private tents and a rose-petal wading pool to get you in the mood for love; if the furnishings don't, the orgy cocktails might!

NorthWest: 392 Columbus Avenue at 79th Street. Tel 212-799 4530.

A very tasteful upstairs lounge – there's a restaurant below – with white walls and wooden furniture that make the perfect setting for the wine aficionados that gather here. There's a 50-bottle list and you can have three or four glass tastings.

WEST VILLAGE

Chumley's: 86 Bedford Street between Grove and Barrow Streets. Tel 212-675 4449.

A former literary speakeasy, it's still a great place to drink and have a spot of shepherd's pie while you look over the book jackets that line the wall. Yes, they were all donated by the authors who used to frequent the establishment such as Jack Kerouac and F Scott Fitzgerald. You'll find their signatures imprinted on some of the older tables. There's even a roaring fire giving a cosy atmosphere in winter.

Peculiar Pub: 145 Bleecker Street between Laguarida Place and Thompson Street. Tel 212-353 1327.

A truly impressive selection of beers, with two separate menus – one listing domestic brews, the other international. It's a bit like a museum to beer once you're inside, from the art of brewing to the evolution of the aluminium can on the walls. It gets packed with students during peak times, so it's best to visit early on week nights so you can chat to the bartender about the various brews.

COMEDY CLUBS

While comedy clubs have started to spring up in cities all over the UK, they've been firmly cemented in New York nightlife since the 1970s. It's a real experience and always worth the money to visit one of these Manhattan institutions, which have produced some of the world's top comedians.

CHELSEA

Comix: 353 West 14th Street between 8th and 9th Avenues. Tel 212-524 2500, www.comixny.com.

Large 320-seat club in a renovated supermarket attracting big names. Don't expect a dive – there are marble floors, plasma TVs and a $25 cover charge.

FLATIRON DISTRICT

Gotham Comedy Club: 34 West 22nd Street between 5th and 6th Avenues. Tel 212-367 9000, www.gothamcomedy club.com.

This club opened in 1996 and was an instant success. It's elegant and sophisticated, with a solid oak bar and a chandelier. The line-ups are equally dazzling, from surprise guests to comedians who have appeared on *Saturday Night Live* and *The Tonight Show*.

MIDTOWN

Caroline's Comedy Club: 1626 Broadway between 49th and 50th Streets. Tel 212-757 4100, www.carolines.com.

It opened in 1981 as a small club in Chelsea but proved such a hit it moved uptown, where it offers live comedy every night of the year, including big names such as Jerry Seinfeld and Rosie O'Donnell.

TIMES SQUARE

The Laugh Factory: 303 West 42nd Street at 8th Avenue. Tel 212-586 7829, www.laughfactory.com

A firm favourite on the West Coast, The Laugh Factory is also going down well in New York though it hasn't yet attracted the likes of Steve Martin and Chris Rock who appeared in the LA branch. The main room seats 280 with four smaller rooms for special events and spoken word and improv night.

UPPER EAST SIDE

Comic Strip Live: 1568 Second Avenue at 81st Street. Tel 212-861 9386, www.comicstriplive.com
Founded in 1975, this is still one of the best comedy clubs in the city with some of the biggest names in the business appearing, such as Chris Rock and Adam Sandler. If you can't get in for one of the big nights or you fancy yourself as a bit of a comedian, then go to Monday's Talent Spotlight where up-and-coming comics get a chance to shine.

Dangerfield's: 118 First Avenue at 61st Street. Tel 212-593 1650, www.danger fields.com.
Allegedly the oldest comedy club in the country, it was established in 1969 by actor and comedian Roger Dangerfield. It's a magnet for tourists because of its reputation, but locals still frequent it too, drawn by the decent line-ups both new and regulars.

UPPER WEST SIDE

Stand-Up NYC: 236 West 78th Street near Broadway. Tel 212-595 0850.
This club has been hosting huge names in comedy – Robin Williams, Roseanne Barr, Jerry Seinfeld – since it opened in 1986. It's not a flashy venue and there's seating for just 175 punters, but it really pulls in the best on the circuit. From $15 cover charge.

WEST VILLAGE

The Comedy Cellar: 117 MacDougal Street between West 3rd Street and Minetta Lane. Tel 212-254 3480, www.comedycellar.com.
This club has been a starting ground for many famous faces for more than 20 years. It's basic, with brick walls and cramped seating, and in a basement so it's not a glam night out in New York, but it will certainly be a funny one. The cover charge is $10 Sun–Thurs, $15 Fri and Sat.

North Square

Hotel bars have always been a popular place to meet for New Yorkers. From sinking into leather sofas in legendary hangouts, propping up the bars in some of Midtown's trendy hotels where the fashionable crowds gather, they make an ideal place to start or end a big night out.

BATTERY PARK

Rise at the Ritz–Carlton Hotel: 2 West Street between Battery Place and West End. Tel 212-344 0800, www.ritzcarlton.com. Subway 1, 9 to Rector Street; 4, 5 to Bowling Green.
A big hit with both visitors and the Wall Street crowd is this 14th floor bar. They go for the comfy, plush chairs with fabulous views of the harbour, Statue of Liberty and amazing sunsets. The bar specialises in a series of colourful martinis served in gorgeous corkscrew-stemmed glassware and 710ml (25 fl oz) margaritas, sangrias and mojitos, which are a perfect size for sharing. If you fancy a nibble, either go for the dim sum or signature 'tiers' – platters of food for up to four people. They include the Pacific Union with sesame chicken, cured salmon and seared beef with dipping sauces. You can sit inside or outside and, best of all, the service is excellent.

◀▶ BRITTIP

If you can, visit Plunge (see box on page 193) on a Monday night when it's much quieter so you are guaranteed a space and you'll be able to hear what the person next to you is saying.

GREENWICH VILLAGE

North Square at the Washington Square Hotel: 103 Waverly Place at MacDougal Street. Tel 212-254 1200, www.wshotel.com. Subway A, B, C, D, E, F, V to West 4th Street/Washington Square.
The small, cosy basement space's classic bar and luxurious leather chairs are a reminder of another era, while beautifully stencilled windows offer a glimpse of the current street scene. It attracts a large European crowd, who find it the perfect spot to pore over a map and a martini, but locals – as well as the occasional celeb – can also be found enjoying the laid-back atmosphere.

MIDTOWN

Cellar Bar at the Bryant Park Hotel: 40 West 40th Street between 5th and 6th Avenues. Tel 212-869 0100, www.bryant parkhotel.com. Subway B, D, F, V, 7 to 42nd Street/Bryant Park.

A must-do for any fashionista, because this new boutique hotel on the block has been adopted by the fashion pack. Expect to see models, designers and magazine editors propping up the bar, but don't even think about dropping in during fashion week – you won't be able to move for the wafer-thin clientele.

The Bar at the Four Seasons Hotel: 57 East 57th Street between 5th and Park Avenues. Tel 212-758 5700, www.fourseasons.com/newyork. Subway N, R, Q, W to 5th Avenue.

The Four Seasons is dynamic in early evening when celebs rub shoulders with power-broking businessmen and hip hotel guests, while a pianist provides the background music. Be sure to sample some of the 15 types of martini on offer.

Sky Bar at La Quinta Manhattan: 17 West 32nd Street between Broadway and 5th Avenue. Tel 212-736 1600, www.applecorehotels.com. Subway N, R, W to 28th Street.

A cross between a backyard deck and a funky beach bar, this partially enclosed rooftop watering hole is packed year-round with international visitors who appreciate the casual atmosphere and towering views of the Empire State Building.

MIDTOWN EAST

Gilt at the New York Palace Hotel: 455 Madison Avenue between 50th and 51st Streets. Tel 212-888 7000, www.newyorkpalace.com. Subway E, V to 5th Avenue; 6 to 51st Street.

TOP FIVE HIPPEST HOTEL BARS

Chelsea

Cabana at the Maritime Hotel: 88 9th Avenue between 16th and 17th Streets. Tel 212-242 4300, www.themaritimehotel.com. Subway A, C, E to 14th Street.

So hot it's practically on fire, this plant-filled rooftop retreat is the perfect place to sip a martini in winter as it has patio heaters. Sean Penn and Paris Hilton are recent celeb visitors.

Plunge at Hotel Gansevoort: 18 9th Avenue at 13th Street. Tel 877-426 7386/212-206 6700, www.hotelgansevoort.com. Subway A, C, E to 14th Street.

Take the lift to the penthouse on the 15th floor and you'll arrive at one of NYC's most happening bars of the moment. On a dry day it's open-air; if it's rainy or cold there's a glass cover, so you still get the views. The only downside of Plunge is that, despite its name, you're not allowed in the rooftop swimming pool unless you're a guest and it's absolutely packed for most of the week.

Lower East Side

Thor Bar & Restaurant at Hotel On Rivington: 107 Rivington Street. Tel 212-475 2600, www.hotelonrivington.com. Subway F to Delancey Street.

One of New York's trendiest hotels has an equally hip bar. Thor is housed in a lofty glass atrium designed by Marcel Wanders and closes at 3am.

Midtown

Morgans Bar at the Morgans Hotel: 237 Madison Avenue between 37th and 38th Streets. Tel 212-726 7755, www.morganshotel.com. Subway 4, 5, 6, 7 to 42nd Street/Grand Central.

Heaving with an attitude-heavy Upper East crowd, it's a sleeker, more sophisticated version of the bar that opened in London's St Martin's Lane Hotel and should be at the top of your must-go-there list. If you like your drinks deliciously expensive and served in punchbowl-size glasses, you'll love it.

Thom's Bar at the 60 Thompson Hotel: 60 Thompson Street between Broome and Spring Streets. Tel 212-219 2000, www.60thompson.com. Subway 6, C, E to Spring Street.

A sophisticated decor of dark wood, soft violet seats, brown leather club chairs and white Venetian plaster walls make for pleasant surroundings. The entertainment is provided by the chic crowd who know that this boutique hotel is the only place to be seen in midweek. Drinks are surprisingly cheap, like flavoured vodka for $7.50.

Located inside the Madison Avenue courtyard gates of the Palace Hotel's historic Villard Mansion, this new restaurant and bar has been pulling in the city's most glamorous movers and shakers since it opened. You'll be wowed by the gilded walls, cathedral ceilings, funky lighting and amazing food whipped up by super chef Paul Liebrandt (that's if you can get a table).

Oasis at W New York: 541 Lexington Avenue at 49th Street. Tel 212-755 1200, www.starwoodhotels.com. Subway 6 to 51st Street.
An oasis of tranquillity, the bar heats up when the fashion, art and music crowd descends for cocktails before dinner at the hotel's Heartbeat restaurant. The ambience is Californian and casual with clever touches that include a waterfall and backgammon tables disguised as tree stumps. Also at the hotel is the Whiskey Blue, overseen by Randy Gerber, otherwise known as Cindy Crawford's husband. The hip clientele enjoy cosy sofas that are great for people-watching and a top-notch sound system that plays until the wee small hours.

MIDTOWN WEST

Hotel Metro Rooftop Bar: 45 West 35th Street between 5th and 6th Avenues. Tel 212-279 3535, www.hotelmetronyc.com. Subway B, D, F, N, Q, R, V, W to 34th Street.
The views of the Empire State Building from this compact rooftop retreat are one reason why this is well worth a visit. The cheap beer and laid-back vibe created by the DJ are two others.

Hudson Hotel Bar at the Hudson Hotel: 356 West 58th Street between 8th and 9th Avenues. Tel 212-554 6000, www.hudsonhotel.com. Subway A, B, C, D, 1, 9 to 59th Street/Columbus Circle.
This Ian Schrager and Philippe Starck-designed Mecca for the in crowd provides wonderful theatre. There's a glowing glass floor, flashy DJ and dark and enticing Games Room. In the summer, the after-work crowd heads to the Private Park – the hotel garden – and sip cocktails next to giant watering cans. Pure, surreal magic.

Mobar

King Cole Bar at the St Regis Hotel: 2 East 55th Street. Tel 212-339 6721, www.starwoodhotels.com/stregis. Subway E, V to 5th Avenue at 53rd Street.
The specialities of the (very upscale) house are the Bloody Mary and the mural behind the bar, by noted American illustrator Maxfield Parrish.

Living Room at the W Times Square Hotel: 1567 Broadway at 47th Street. Tel 212-930 7444, www.starwoodhotels.com. Subway 4, 5, 6, L, N, Q, R, W to 14th Street.
Another of the cool W Hotel bar scenes, a magnet for fashion models (many agencies are in the area) and other pretty people.

Mobar at the Mandarin Oriental: 59th Street at Columbus Circle. Tel 212-805 8800, www.mandarinoriental.com. Subway A, B, C, D, 1, 9 to Columbus Circle.
In the dazzling new AOL Time Warner Center, the sleek lobby lounge is drawing the crowds. The cocktails are $15 but the spectacular view of Central Park from the 35th floor (not to mention celebrity sightings) is free.

Pen-Top Bar at the Peninsula Hotel: 700 5th Avenue, 23rd Floor. Tel 212-956 2888, www.newyork.peninsula.com. Subway E, V to 5th Avenue/53rd Street; N, R, W to 5th Avenue/59th Street.
The view is breathtaking and the prices can be, too, but in beautiful weather you'll feel you're at the centre of the universe – like the power brokers who surround you.

Round Bar at the Royalton: 44 West 44th Street between 5th and 6th Avenues. Tel 212-869 4400, www.royaltonhotel.com. Subway B, D, F, V to 42nd Street; 7 to 5th Avenue.
The first of the Philippe Starck-designed hotels is still holding its own against all newcomers. The Round Bar is inspired by Hemingway's favourite bar at the Ritz in Paris and is secretly tucked away in a quiet part of the lobby. It boasts curved, tufted leather walls, built-in leather banquettes and a chequerboard floor and seats just 20. It's a real treat before a night out.

The Oak Room at the Algonquin: 59 West 44th Street between 5th and 6th Avenues. Tel 212-840 6800, www.algonquinhotel.com. Subway B, D, F, V to 42nd Street; 7 to 5th Avenue.
Once world-famous as the New York literary set's salon of choice, this handsome room provides an intimate and civilised setting for

Madison Square Garden

some of the country's leading jazz and cabaret artists, who are usually booked for extended runs. The clientele is clubby and patrician, but anyone can buy dinner or drinks here.

Town at the Chambers Hotel: 15 West 56th Street between 5th and 6th Avenues. Tel 212-974 5656, www.chambershotel.com. Subway F to 57th Street.
A very sophisticated place to drink or dine (page 164), with lush leather sofas, one of the city's largest cocktail menus and wonderful, attentive staff.

TRIBECA
Church Lounge at TriBeCa Grand Hotel: 2 6th Avenue at White Street. Tel 212-519 6600, www.tribecagrand.com. Subway A, C, E to Canal Street.
The Wall Street crowd has made this upscale bar an after-work hangout. It's meant to look like a living room – if your living room was full of beautiful people. Sanctum Lounge with DJs, open Thurs–Sun only, is the even more exclusive adjunct.

LIVE MUSIC
There are some fantastic live music venues in the city, from dingy rock clubs to vast stadiums where legends have played. As many of the venues get booked up quickly, do check websites for listings well before you visit the city so that you'll be able to book tickets in advance.

34TH STREET
Madison Square Garden: 4 Pennsylvania Plaza at 33rd Street and 7th Avenue. Tel 212-465 MSG1 info, www.thegarden.com. Subway A, C, E, 1, 2, 3, 9, B, D, F, N, Q, R, V, W to 34th Street/Penn Street Station
New York's biggest and most famous rock venue, which doubles up as a sports stadium. Also the Theater at Madison Square Garden, which is underneath, plays host to big-name stars who want to share some intimacy with their audience.

GARMENT DISTRICT
Hammerstein Ballroom: 311 West 34th Street between 8th and 9th Avenues. Tel 212-279 7740, www.livenation.com. Elegant pre-war ballroom that holds up to 2,500 people for events, from rock music gigs from the likes of the Arctic Monkeys to top DJs.

GREENWICH
Cafe Wha?: 115 MacDougal Street between West 3rd and Bleecker Streets. Tel 212-254 3706, www.cafewha.com.
Village hangout since the beginning of time. There is something fun and exciting on every night of the week here, including live Brazilian dance parties with the Brazooka band on Mondays and the Cafe Wha? disFUNKtion night on Tuesdays, which is, as the name suggests, live funk from the likes of Inaya Day and Mike Davis.

Sweet Rhythm: 88 7th Avenue South between Bleecker and Grove Streets. Tel 212-255-3626, www.sweetrhythmny.com
Housed in the space once occupied by the legendary jazz club Sweet Basil, this club features live music from all over the world including jazz, samba, merengue, flamenco, salsa and reggae. Call in for the weekly Monday night shows from talented students at the Jazz and Contemporary music programme at the New School University.

HARLEM
Apollo Theater: 253 West 125th Street between Adam Clayton Powell Jr and Frederick Douglas Boulevards. Tel 212-531 5300 info; 212-531 5301 events hotline, www.apollotheater.com. Subway A, B, C, D, 2, 3 to 125th Street
This venue started life as a burlesque house for whites only when Harlem was actually a white neighbourhood, but it very quickly changed and became a theatre for blacks with live entertainment. The Amateur Night has been a launching-pad for Stevie Wonder and James Brown. When Ella Fitzgerald came here she planned to dance, but at the last moment she decided to sing and, as the saying goes, a star was born. Wednesday's Amateur Night is still going strong and is shown on NBC at 1am on Saturday night/Sunday morning.

NIGHTLIFE

LOWER EAST SIDE

Bowery Ballroom: 6 Delancey Street near Bowery. Tel 212-533 2111, www.boweryballroom.com
Consistently voted one of New York's best live rock venues, it's been packing in the punters since it opened its doors in 1998. Great acoustics, a well-stocked bar and lots of great acts. Log on to the website to see who's playing and for advance tickets.

CBGB: 315 Bowery between 1st and 2nd Streets. Tel 212-982 4052, www.cbgb.com. Subway 6, F to Bleecker Street.
Legendary underground club that's been the toast of the hip New York rock scene for more than 27 years. The likes of Guns 'n Roses and The Ramones have graced the stage and you're sure to catch an exciting new band if you drop by.

MIDTOWN

B B King Blues Club & Grill: 237 West 42nd Street near 7th Avenue. Tel 212-997 4144. Subway 1, 2, 3, 7, N, Q, R, S Times Square/42nd Street.
An intimate supper club that's played host to some of the greats – James Brown, Peter Frampton and Chic. There's a souvenir stall upstairs so you can wear the T-shirt.

Carnegie Hall: 154 West 57th Street at 7th Avenue. Tel 212-247 7800, www.carnegie hall.org. Subway B, D, E, N, R, Q, W to 57th Street
Built in the Beaux Arts style under the patronage of Andrew Carnegie, this is perhaps one of the most famous classical concert venues in New York and a real landmark. Check the listings sections of newspapers or *Time Out* for details of visiting artists or take a guided tour Mon–Fri 11.30am, 2pm and 3pm.

Radio City Music Hall: 1260 6th Avenue at 50th Street. Tel 212-247 4777, www.radiocity.com. Subway B, D, F, V to 47th–50th Street/ Rockefeller Centre.
Recently renovated, this home to the Rockettes in its Art Deco splendour also plays host to some big-name stars.

TRIBECA

Knitting Factory: 74 Leonard Street between Broadway and Church Street. Tel 212-219 3132, www.knittingfactory.com. Subway 2, 3, 9 to Franklin Street.
A funky performance venue run by The Knitting Factory Record Label that's well known for avant-garde live bands spanning all types of music, from heavy rock to a choir. There are three spaces, Main Space, Tap Bar and Old Office, the latter being the most intimate and where there are sometimes poetry readings and film screenings as well as music. Check out the website to see who'll be playing when you're in town. Open until 4am.

UPPER EAST SIDE

Café Carlyle at the Carlyle Hotel: 35 East 76th Street at Madison and Park Avenues. Tel 212-744 1600, www.rosewood hotels.com/www.thecarlyle.com. Subway 6 to 77th Street.
A highly glamorous bar and restaurant that

> ### ◄► BRITTIP
> If want to go to a Cabaret Club, visit Don't Tell Mama (343 West 46th Street near 9th Avenue, Hell's Kitchen, tel 212-757 0788). There's a piano bar and two side rooms for excellent shows, with up to three performances nightly.

Carnegie Hall

specialises in cabaret. Woody Allen still plays clarinet with The Eddie Davis New Orleans Jazz Band on Monday nights and Bobby Short, a New York favourite, plays piano during spring and autumn. $75 per person cover charge.

UPPER WEST SIDE

Lincoln Center: 65th Street at Columbus Avenue. Tel 212-875 5400, www.lincolncenter.org. Subway 1, 9 to 66th Street/Lincoln Center

The major venue for classical music in New York, the Lincoln Center, a collection of buildings that includes the home of the Metropolitan Opera, was built on slums that were featured in the film *West Side Story*. The Alice Tully Hall (tel 212-875 5050) houses the Chamber Music Society of Lincoln Center; the Avery Fisher Hall (tel 212-875 5030) is home to the New York Philharmonic; the Metropolitan Opera House (tel 212-362 6000); the New York State Theater (tel 212-870 5570) is the base of New York City Opera; and the Walter Reade Theater (tel 212-875 5600) is home to the Film Society of Lincoln Center. Jazz at Lincoln Center is at the AOL Time Warner Center (page 198).

You can take a behind-the-scenes tour of the Lincoln Center, which is really the only way to see beyond the ornate lobbies of the buildings, unless you're paying big bucks for a performance. The tours are fabulous and give a really good insight into the workings of the various venues. Options include a one-hour Lincoln Center tour, Tours with a Bite – at Café Vienna, the Piano Forte tour, which takes you to Klavierhouse, a piano restoration museum, and Starry Nights, the full treatment including a performance and, if in a group, meeting the artists. The tours are very popular so it's best to book in advance on 212-875 5350.

BRITTIP

Standing room tickets to the Met go on sale on the day of the performance for $20.

In addition to the tours, you can enjoy the Lincoln Center environment with a series of jazz and folk bands that entertain the crowds for free during the summer. The Autumn Crafts Fair is held in the first week of September.

BRITTIP

If you're on a budget, get down to the new Crocodile Lounge (325 East 14th Street between 2nd and 3rd Avenues, tel 212-477 7747), a funky bar covered in, you've guessed it, crocodiles – even the door handles are crocs – that gives out free pizza from its ovens for every beer you buy.

NIGHTCLUBS

The club scene in New York literally changes by the week. Venues are constantly opening, closing and relaunching so we've picked out the best of the well-established clubs, plus a scattering of new or smaller places that are currently creating a stir. By the way, while many of the clubs stay open until 4am, hours do vary so check out the listings in the *Village Voice, Paper, New York Press* and *New Yorker* and on websites such as www.nymag.com and www.nyclubs.com.

CHELSEA

Bungalow 8: (page 185).

Crobar: 530 West 28th Street between 10th and 11th Avenues. Tel 212-629 9000, www.crobar.com. Subway C, E to 23rd Street. A New York import from Chicago and Miami, it's a paradox: a wild and crazy spot that's very well run, and a venue that evokes the huge clubs of the past.

Home: 532 West 27th Street near 10th Avenue. Tel 212-273 3700. Subway, C, E to 23rd Street.

Taking on the might of Bungalow 8 as the hippest place in town, Home has kicked up a bit of a storm, attracting the likes of Lindsay Lohan and Sting. The second floor has chandeliers and a leather ceiling and a very swish party crowd dancing the night away. There are black day beds to lounge on and DJs such as Stretch Armstrong spin hip-hop, rock and pop.

Marquee: 289 10th Avenue at 26th Street. Tel 645-473 0202, www.marqueeny.com. Subway C, E to 23rd Street.

One of the coolest clubs in the city, or so the hype would have you believe, so there's always a massive queue. We can confirm that once inside it's worth the wait; intimate banquettes around the edge of the room with chandeliers overhead and models making some moves on the dance floor.

ALL THAT JAZZ

A visit to New York City wouldn't be complete without an evening at one of the various jazz venues, but it can get very expensive, so it's good to know your way around. At all the main venues it'll cost you around $25 to hear one set which lasts only 1–1½ hours. It's worth it if you're happy with the music, but the idea of having to move on after only one set is a bit strange to us Brits, so be warned!

The most important new venue is **Jazz at Lincoln Center**'s recent $128-million home at the AOL Time Warner Centre at Columbus Circle, with three performance spaces – two large and one intimate. Visit www.jalc.org to find out about events or call the JazzTix hotline, 212-258 9800.

THE MAIN CLUBS

One of the best jazz clubs is the **Iridium** (1650 Broadway at 51st Street, tel 212-582 2121, www.iridiumjazzclub.com). It's not too touristy, is smaller than many clubs and has a nice intimate feel. Try it for Sunday brunch! The entrance fee varies but there's a $10 minimum. **The Village Vanguard** (178 7th Avenue South at Perry Street, tel 212-255 4037, www.villagevanguard.com), probably the most famous club of all, always hosts great talent and sets last the full 1½ hours. Another famous Greenwich Village venue is the **Blue Note** (131 West 3rd Street between MacDougal and 6th Avenue, tel 212-475 8592, www.bluenote.net), but this is more touristy, very expensive and has a Las Vegas-style interior. **Swing 46 Jazz and Supper Club** (349 West 46th Street between 8th and 9th Avenues, tel 212-262 9554, www.swing46.com) offers big bands and small combos to suit hip downtown loungers and traditional uptown swingers – it's rapidly becoming an institution.

Other good venues include **Birdland** (315 West 44th Street between 8th and 9th Avenues, tel 212-581 3080, www.birdlandjazz.com) in Midtown West; the **Jazz Standard** (116 East 27th Street between Park and Lexington Avenues, tel 212-576 2232, www.jazzstandard.com) near Madison Square; **Bubble Lounge** (228 West Broadway at White Street, tel 212-431 3433, www.bubblelounge.com) in TriBeCa, which has live music Mon and Tues, closed Sunday. **55 Bar** (55 Christopher Street, tel 212-929 9883, www.55bar.com) has been a West Village institution since 1919 and has shows all week from 6/7pm and late shows 9.30/10pm; open until 4am. **Smoke** (2751 Broadway, tel 212-864 6662, www.smokejazz.com) is an intimate club with low-hanging chandeliers, red velvet curtains and seating for 70. Open until 4am. Finally, book early for Monday nights at Hotel Carlyle (page 224) where Woody Allen and friends play a set.

CHEAP AND CHEERFUL

One of the best off-the-beaten-track jazz venues is in the heart of Greenwich Village at the **Cornelia Street Café** (29 Cornelia Street, tel 212-989 9319, http://corneliastreetcafe.com). You'll get to see some great musicians play and feel like you're part of the village scene. **Zinc Bar** (90 West Houston Street between Thompson Street and LaGuardia Place, tel 212-477 8337, www.zincbar.com) is one of the most intimate places in town to enjoy live jazz, open until 4am weekends and it's only $5 to get in. **Arthur's Tavern** (57 Grove Street near 7th Avenue, tel 212-675 6879) is a West Village jazz joint that's been going since the 1930s. Some say it's lost its sparkle, but most still love it's scruffy, old-world charm and enjoy a night free of pricey cover charges listening to great jazz.

The cheapest jazz clubs tend to be in Harlem, Queens and Brooklyn, but because they can't afford to advertise you really don't hear about them. Furthermore, most don't even have names on the door. Good places to look for venues are the *New York Times* weekend edition and the *Village Voice*. The latter is a lot better and it's free, visit www.village voice.com.

NIGHTLIFE

BRITTIP

For the lowdown on what's happening on the jazz scene in New York, from shopping to tours to clubs, click on to www.bigapplejazz.com.

Ruby Falls: 609 West 29th Street between 11th and 12th Avenues. Tel 212-643 6464. Subway A, C, E to 34th Penn Station. You can buy the art on the walls of this Chelsea club, which is appropriate as the vast warehouse space it is housed in is a bit like a gallery. The music veers between hip-hop and techno and it's attracting a fashionable crowd.

CHINATOWN

Happy Endings: 302 Broome Street at Forsyth Street. Tel 212-334 9676, Subway 6, N, R to Canal Street.
A brothel-turned-bar with a DJ in the basement dance room and a mixed lounge scene that attracts hip young things.

EAST VILLAGE

Lit: 93 2nd Avenue between 5th and 6th Streets. Tel 212-777 7987. Subway 6 to Astor Place; F, V to Lower East Side/2nd Avenue. If you've always wanted to see a hot bartender in action, this art-meets-celebs joint is the place to come. A haven for indie filmsters, it has an art gallery – The Fuse – and a cellar-like dance room downstairs.

Webster Hall: 125 East 11th Street between 3rd and 4th Avenues. Tel 212-353 1600, www.webster-hall.com. Subway L, N,Q, R, W, 4, 5, 6 to 14th Street/Union Square. There are lots of different rooms with different sounds, so you're bound to find something you enjoy. The best area is the main dance floor in the huge, ornate ballroom. It attracts a fairly straight crowd from the suburbs, but is a fun night out.

FLATIRON

40/40 Club: 6 West 25th Street between Broadway and 6th Avenue. Tel 212-832 4040, www.the4040club.com.
If you want some serious bling, and a possible celebrity sighting, then look no further than rapper Jay-Z's lavish two-level club. It's like being on an MTV set; seven cream-coloured leather swing chairs are suspended from the ceiling; sleek Italian marble shines on the floor, and a collection of LCD flat-screen televisions (including

TOP FIVE CLUBBING TIPS

- On Friday and Saturday nights, the clubs are packed with crowds from boroughs outside Manhattan. For a quieter night, go on Thursday. Sunday is the big night for Manhattanites, so you'll get the real vibe then, along with the crowds.

- Call ahead early in the evening to find out if there's a cover charge, when to arrive and how to dress. Also find out if there's a party theme on the night that you plan to go. Clubs can change nightly – for example, catering for straights one night, gays the next.

- The real nightlife doesn't get going until after midnight, so get some zeds in before you go out.

- Carry some ID with you just in case – it would be terrible if you couldn't get a drink when you're over 21.

- Large groups of men don't stand much hope of getting into straight clubs – they'll have more chance if they are with a woman.

three 60-inch plasmas) display ESPN. There's also a cigar lounge and two VIP rooms are tucked away on the second level. After you've watched the game on the screens, the DJ blasts R&B and hip-hop. The club stays open until 4am.

Avalon: 47 West 20th Street near 6th Avenue. Tel 212-807 7780.
Housed in a former church, it's a really impressive venue for a dance club. A pod-like DJ booth hovers between the two balconies overlooking the dance floor and upstairs there's the tree-filled Spider Club. Go-go dancers sometimes appear.

There's a vibrant jazz scene in New York

NIGHTLIFE

NIGHTLIFE

BRITTIP

As clubs and club nights change so frequently, log on to websites www.papermag.com and www.clubnyc.com to find out what's on where.

GARMENT DISTRICT

Arena: 135 West 41st Street near Broadway. Tel 212-278 0988.
New club that's proving to be a hit with New Yorkers. Matt silver walls and a cool dome ceiling above the dance floor make it visually pleasing, while the four bars, giant digital screens and excellent nights, such as Susanne Bartsch's Thursday Freakfest, keep clubbers happy until 4am. Cover charge $20.

GREENWICH VILLAGE

Roxy: 515 West 18th Street between 10th and 11th Avenues. Tel 212-645 5156, www.roxynyc.com. Subway A, C, E to 14th Street; L to 8th Avenue.
A huge venue with plenty of different themes such as roller disco, blading and disco.

SOBs: 204 Varick Street at Houston Street. Tel 212-243 4940, www.sobs.com. Subway 1, 9 to Houston Street.
The name stands for Sounds Of Brazil, which says it all. It's the place to come for the last word in Latin music from salsa to samba and even reggae. DJ Rekha's new monthly Bhangra Basement party has got New Yorkers in a spin.

One Little West 12th

LOWER EAST SIDE

Pianos: 158 Ludlow Street between Rivington and Stanton Streets. Tel 212-505 3733, www.pianosnyc.com. Subway F, J, M, Z to Delancey Street/Essex Street.
A former piano shop turned clean, whitewashed bar space that attracts trendy fashionistas plus the NYU students from the area. Local and national up-and-coming rock bands play in the somewhat dingy back room, while there's also a more intimate lounge upstairs.

Sapphire Lounge: 249 Eldridge Street between Houston and Stanton Streets. Tel 212-777 5153, www.sapphirenyc.com. Subway F to 2nd Avenue.
Pretension and attitude are left at the door in this tiny dance club that plays a great mix of hip-hop, reggae, acid jazz, R&B and disco classics. Opens at 7pm.

Slipper Room: 167 Orchard Street between Rivington and Stanton Streets. Tel 212-253 7246, www.slipperroom.com. Subway F, M, J, Z to Delancey Street/Essex Street.
Adding some real showbiz panache to the Lower East Side, this glitzy retro lounge is the venue for genuinely good cabaret as well as some far out, gender-bending burlesque. A great evening out.

MADISON SQUARE

Cheetah: 12 West 21st Street between 5th and 6th Avenues. Tel 212-206 7770. Subway F, N, R to 23rd Street.
An intimate venue with attractive animal-print decor and snuggly booths. Attracts a great mix, ranging from ghetto fabulous to the supercool.

MEATPACKING DISTRICT

Cielo: 18 Little West 12th Street between 9th Avenue and Washington Street. Tel 212-645 5700, www.cieloclub.com. Subway A, C, E to 14th Street; L to 8th Avenue.
The dance floor is sunken but the fabulous sound system hits the heights. This is one of the hottest spots in the city, and the good news (and bad news) is that it draws the big crowds.

One: 1 Little West 12th Street at 9th Avenue. Tel 212-255 9717. Subway A, C to 14th Street; L to 8th Avenue.
It's big (465 sq m/5,000 sq ft), it's bi-level and there's lots of action on the dance floor. A popular spot with the college crowd – though it helps if they're on big allowances!

TOP FIVE HOT CLUBS

Chelsea

Cain: 544 West 27th Street between 10th and 11th Avenues. Tel 212-947 8000, www.cainnyc.com. Based around a safari theme– elephant-trunk door handles, zebra-hide bar and game lodge style wood pillars – it's caught the imagination of young Manhattanites, including film star Lindsay Lohan who's been spotted here.

Lower East Side

Libation: 137 Ludlow Street between Stanton and Rivington Streets. Tel 212-529 2153, www.libationnyc.com. Subway F to Delancey Street. DJs play Wed–Sat at this sleek club that attracts a good mix of people. It also boasts a seasonal cocktail and tapas menu to help keep you going through the night.

Meatpacking District

Glo: 431 West 16th Street between 9th and 10th Avenues. Tel 212-229 9119. Subway A, C, E to 14th Street; L to 8th Avenue. Divided into three levels, this chic, white, modern club has more than enough room for dancers, divas, people-watchers and any other trendy types who want to enjoy the district's latest place to be. The main bar is lit by neon tubing and the dance floor has white speakers hovering above it.

Murray Hill

Vapor: 143 Madison Avenue between 31st and 32nd Streets. Tel 212-686 6999, www.vapornyc.com. Subway 5 to 23rd Street. Drinkers get misted with air-purifying vapour in the back room of this new two-storey cocktail bar. DJs provide the sounds to the eager just-out-of-work crowd.

Union Square

Aura: 5 East 19th Street at 5th Avenue. Tel 212-671 1981. Subway 4, 5, 6, I, N, Q, R to West 14th Street/Union Square. Newly opened club with posh cocktails, light box bar that glows, small hardwood dance floor to move to thumping house and a VIP balcony that combined equal a fun night out.

Passerby: 436 West 15th Street at Washington Street. Tel 212-206 7321. Subway A, C, E, 1, 2 3, 9 to 14th Street; L to 8th Avenue.
Hurry before everyone else discovers this place: plenty already have. Tiny but with an awesome dance floor.

PM: 50 Gansevoort Street. Tel 212-255 6676, http://pmloungenyc.com. Subway A, C to 14th Street; L to 8th Avenue.
Half-a-dozen doormen enforce the beautiful-person policy that's considered the most brutal in the area. But if you get in, you'll experience Hawaiian island decor with big booths, big signs prohibiting dancing, and a big tab. The bottle service doesn't come cheap, but the attitude is laid back and the place gets really hot well past midnight.

MIDTOWN EAST

Light: 125 East 54th Street between Park and Lexington Avenues. Tel 212-583 1333, www.lightnyc.com. Subway 6 to 51st Street; E, V to Lexington Avenue/53rd Street.
This has had a good run with young professionals and glamorous *Sex And The City* types. Sip a Cosmo and tuck into the Asian-inspired appetisers while DJs spin a wide range of lounge music Wed–Sat.

Vue: 151 East 59th Street between Lexington and 3rd Avenues. Tel 212-753 1144. Subway 6 to 51st Street; E, V to Lexington Avenue.
Is it the visuals projected on a planetarium-type dome or is it the great sound and big club feeling? Whatever... this is still one of the most popular clubs in the city.

MIDTOWN WEST

Copacabana: 617 West 57th Street between 11th and 12th Avenues. Tel 212-582 2672, www.copacabanany.com. Subway A, C, B, D, 1, 9 to Columbus Circle/59th Street.
A mostly Latin clientele who go for the live bands playing salsa and merengue. Everyone is fairly well dressed – not casual but not overdone. It's great but it does get packed.

Nest: 215 West 28th Street between 7th and 8th Avenues. Tel 212-760 6378. Subway 1 to 28th Street.
A four-storey club that's pure minimalism – think hardwood floors, plain orange walls and cream banquettes. It occasionally pulls

in some famous faces, particularly on a Tuesday night when the door policy is extra heavy. There are seats on the mezzanine level, but head downstairs for the best part, which is the low-ceilinged basement that only those-in-the-know frequent, and dance into the small hours.

SOHO

Culture Club: 179 Varick Street at Charlton Street. Tel 212-243 1999. Subway 1 to Houston Street.
If you love all things 1980s, and we mean really love the '80s, this is your Mecca. There are giant murals of Debbie Gibson and Prince on the walls, Smurf curacao drinks served in commemorative cups, a neon *ET* moon and a Rubic cube above the dance floor. If this proves too much, head upstairs for a more '90s vibe and treat yourself to a speciality drink such as liquid Prozac. An experience.

Don Hill's: 511 Greenwich Street at Spring Street. Tel 212-219 2850, www.donhills.com. Subway 6, C, E to Spring Street; N, R to Prince Street. Open nightly 9pm–4am.
One of the top rock venues in the city, Don Hill's is a live venue, club and bar all rolled into one, with great effect. It used to attract lots of celebs and the in-crowd; now it's not so showy, there's very little attitude and it's a fun place for a top night out.

◀▶ BRITTIP

Do make an effort to get dressed up if you are going clubbing. If it's got a entrance fee on the website, don't wear trainers or jeans – you won't get in.

NoCa: 323 West Broadway between Grand and Canal Streets. Tel 212-334 2232, www.nocalounge.com. Subway 6, C, E to Spring Street; N, R to Prince Street.
Very sophisticated lounge and club, with an elevated DJ booth, a lower floor popular

NoCa

with locals and an upper floor which is intimate yet big enough for a dance.

THEATER DISTRICT

Show: 135 West 41st Street between 6th Street and Broadway. Tel 212-278 0988. Subway N, Q, R, S, W, 1, 2, 3, 7, 9 to 42nd Street/Times Square.
A Moulin Rouge-inspired hot spot with scantily-clad burlesque dancers, swinging trapeze artists, go-go girls aplenty and a gilded stage for dancing to the mainstream music. Edgier hip-hop is played in the small upstairs lounge.

UNION SQUARE

Underbar at the W Hotel Union Square: 201 Park Avenue South at 17th Street. Tel 212-253 9119, www.starwoodhotels.com/ whotels. Subway 4, 5, 6, L, N, Q, R, W to 14th Street/Union Square.
The plush velvet couches, the insistent throb of the music and the curtained-off private nooks all help send a seductive message in a way that some find amusing, others find a touch unsubtle. Still, the crowds – especially Europeans – keep coming.

UPPER WEST SIDE

Shalel Lounge: 65 West 70th Street between Central Park West and Columbus Avenues. Tel 212-799 9030. Subway B, C to 72nd Street.
Dark and dangerous – in the nicest kind of way. The exotic North African atmosphere transports aficionados directly to Morocco or a similar locale.

WEST VILLAGE

Love: 179 Macdougal Street at 8th Street. Tel 212-477 5683. Subway A, B, C, D, E, F, V to West 4th Street/Washington Square
If you like your clubbing to have an underground vibe, then go to this below-the-radar set up. It takes place in an unmarked basement beneath a barber shop. You'll start in the cave-like bar, complete with faux stone walls, then move into the main room where they play house and electronic. Sometimes goes on until 8am, so ideal if you want an all-nighter.

Sullivan Room: 218 Sullivan Street between Bleecker and West 3rd Streets. Tel 212-252 2151, www.sullivanroom.com. Subway A, B, C, D, E, F, V to West 4th Street.
An absolutely brilliant, intimate club with no attitude, which is rare in New York. You can dance to soulful house with other friendly types, or just lounge around and chat.

CHAPTER 9

Theatre and Film

Think about theatre in New York and just one word comes to mind: Broadway, and all the glamour and clamour that goes with it. One of the first things you discover about Broadway, as we Brits think of it, is that it is just one tiny stretch of almost the longest thoroughfare on Manhattan. The Theater District, as it is known, is a congregation of theatres between Broadway and 8th Avenue from about 44th to 52nd Streets (take the N, R, Q, W, 1, 2, 3, 7, 9, S lines to 42nd Street/Times Square). This is Broadway. You'll also see and hear the terms 'Off Broadway' and 'Off-Off Broadway' (yes, really), which refer to uptown and downtown theatres, particularly in Greenwich Village, East Village and SoHo. These theatres are well worth a visit, as they may be offering rarely seen revivals, the innovative work of new playwrights, or productions featuring hilarious, off-the-wall humour. But they do change frequently, so we have included only a sample selection.

Of course, Broadway productions are changing all the time, but many of the big shows – the ones that many Brits want to see – do stay around a little longer. We have included reviews of those shows we believe will be available for the next couple of years, but for a completely up-to-date guide to what's on at the theatre, look in *The New York Times*, which has comprehensive listings of dance, classical music, opera, Broadway, Off Broadway and Off-Off Broadway every day. Other papers and magazines that you can check out include the *New Yorker*, *Village Voice*, *New York Metro* and *New York Press*. If you want to find out what's on before you go, visit the Keith Prowse or Theatre Direct websites given below.

BOOKING YOUR TICKETS

You can book tickets in advance in the UK through either your travel agent or Keith Prowse (tel UK 0870 840 1111 or US 800-669 8687 toll free, www.keithprowse.com). An alternative is to use TicketMaster (tel 212-307 7171, www.ticketmaster.com).

If booking in New York, try Theater Mania (tel 212-352 3101, or 866-811 4111 toll free, www.theatermania.com); Prime Tickets and Tours (tel 305-661 8646, www.primetickets.com); Continental Guest Services (tel 800-BWY-TKTS/299 8587, www.continentalguestservices.com), Telecharge.com (tel 212-239 6200, www.telecharge.com) and All Tickets Inc. (tel 800-922 0716, www.allticketsinc.com).

For cheaper tickets, go to one of the **Theater Development Fund's TKTS** two booths (tel 212-221 0013, www.tdf.org). The less crowded (but less convenient) downtown booth is in South Street Seaport at 199 Water Street at the corner of Front Street and John Street, open Mon–Fri 11am–6pm, Sat 11am–7pm, Sun 11am–3pm; matinee tickets bought here are for the following day's performance. A temporary booth just outside the Marriott Marquis Hotel in the middle of Times Square at West 46th Street between Broadway and 8th Avenue will move to Father Duffy Square after renovations. It's open Mon–Sat 3pm–8pm, Wed and Sat 10am–2pm for matinee

Times Square TKTS stand

BRITTIP

Look for discount coupons for Broadway shows at neighbourhood information stands and barrows throughout Manhattan as well as picking up coupons from NYC's Visitor Information Centre at 810 Seventh Avenue at 53rd Street (tel 212-484 1222).

tickets, Sun 11am–3pm for matinees, 3–7pm for evening performances. It gets very busy so arrive early for the best selection, then spend the day in Midtown (see Chapter 2 New York Neighbourhoods, page 41).

Discounts range from 25–50 per cent for same-day tickets to Broadway, Off-Broadway shows and other arts events, but bear in mind that the booths only accept cash or travellers' cheque and have plenty of options. If you are flexible about what you would like to see, you can decide to go to a show at the very last minute, since TKTS Midtown is open right until show time. For Off-Broadway shows, the Alliance of Resident Theatres (www.offbroadway online.com) has dozens of performances for all budgets daily across New York.

Bookings for all the shows and performances below can be made with Theater Direct International (tel 800-BROADWAY, www.broadway.com) or for the best seats in the house, via the official information and ticket resource, the Broadway Ticket Center, in the Times Square Information Center at 1560 Broadway, bang in the heart of Times Square (next to the Palace Theatre at 226 West 47th Street between 46th and 47th Street).

BRITTIP
Watch out for ticket touts. An increasing number of the tickets they sell are fakes.

MUSICALS

All the Broadway and Off Broadway shows listed here have one interval (unless stated). The suggested ages are for guidance only.

AVENUE Q
✉ John Golden Theater, 252 West 45th Street between Broadway and 8th Avenue
⌁ www.avenueq.com
⏱ Mon–Sat 8pm, Sun 7pm, Sat and Sun 2pm

A bright and entertaining show with people and puppets about the struggles with life when you're straight out of college. Funny and urbane. Has been called a mix of *Sesame Street*, *The Simpsons* and *Sex And The City*. Now playing in London, too.
Awards: Several Tony Awards in 2004, including Best Musical
Length of show: 2 hours 15 minutes
Age: 18 and over (even with puppets!)

BRITTIP
The Hit Show Club (630 9th Avenue at 45th Street, 8th Floor, tel 212-581 4211, www.hitshow club.com) and Broadway Bucks (226 West 47th Street between Broadway and 8th Avenue, l0th floor, tel 212-398 8383, 800-233 7565 toll free, www.bestofbroadway.com) distribute coupons that can be redeemed at the box office for one-third or more off regular ticket prices. If you don't see them in your hotel, pick them up from the offices.

THE COLOR PURPLE
✉ Broadway Theater, 1681 Broadway between West 52nd and 53rd Streets
⌁ www.colorpurple.com
⏱ Tues 7pm, Thurs, Fri, Sat 8pm, Sun 7.30pm; matinees Wed, Sat, Sun 2pm

This family saga of hope, inspiration and triumph from Pulitzer-prize wining novelist Alice Walker, Oprah Winfrey's favourite musical tells the story of a woman who overcomes adversity through love to discover her unique voice in the world, vividly brought to life through blues, gospel, jazz, swing and ragtime music.
Length of show: 2 hours 40 minutes
Age: 10 years and over

BRITTIP
Many theatres have started scheduling Tuesday performances at 7pm, an hour earlier than customary, to accommodate those who have to travel far or want to dine afterwards.

CHICAGO
✉ Ambassador Theater, 219 West 49th Street between Broadway and 8th Avenue
⌁ www.chicagothemusical.com
⏱ Mon, Thurs, Fri, Sat 8pm, Tues, Sun 7pm; matinees Sat, Sun 2pm

This great musical with wonderful dancing is the winner of six Tony Awards and has other productions throughout the world, but many still consider this one to be the best. In fact, on 14 November 2007, it celebrates its 10th Anniversary. *Chicago* tells the story of a chorus girl who kills her lover and then escapes the noose and prison with the help

Chicago

of a conniving lawyer. If greed, corruption, murder and treachery are your bag, then this is the musical for you.
Awards: 6 Tony Awards in 1997
Length of show: 2 hours 30 minutes
Age: 12 and over (parental guidance)

THE DROWSY CHAPERONE

⊠ Marquis Theatre, 1535 Broadway
⏀ www.drowsychaperone.com
☉ Tues 7pm, Thurs, Fri, Sat 8pm, Sun 7.30pm; matinees Wed, Sat, Sun 2pm

Heralded as 'the funniest musical on Broadway' this original comedy is a hilarious tale of a glamorous bride and her uproarious wedding day.
Awards: 2 Tonys in 2006, Drama Critic's Circle 2006 Best Musical
Length of show: 1 hours 50 minutes (no interval)
Age: 12 and over

HAIRSPRAY

⊠ Neil Simon Theater, 250 West 52nd Street between Broadway and 8th Avenue
⏀ www.hairspraythemusical.com
☉ Tues 7pm, Wed, Thurs, Fri, Sat 8pm, Tues 7pm; matinees Tues, Sat 2pm, Sun 3pm

A fabulous production based on John Waters' cult 1988 movie, it tells the story of how a bumbling Baltimore teenager is turned from social outcast to star when she gets the chance to dance on the popular Corny Collins Show (well, it is set in 1962!). But then her troubles really start. Hilarious – and the girls have hair that Marge Simpson would be proud of! The movie version is due to hit cinemas in 2007.
Awards: 8 Tony Awards in 2003
Length of show: 2 hours 40 minutes
Age: 12 and over

JERSEY BOYS

⊠ August Wilson theatre, 245 West 52nd Street
⏀ www.jerseyboysbroadway.com
☉ Wed-Sat 8pm, Tues 7pm; matinees Wed, Sat 2pm, Sun 3pm

This musical chronicles the rags to riches story of a group of Frankie Valli and The Four Seasons, four blue-collar boys who became one of the biggest American pop music sensations of all time. Sing along to classics such as 'Sherry', 'Big Girls Don't Cry' and 'Can't Take My Eyes off You'.
Awards: Tony for Best Musical in 2006
Length of show: 2 hours 30 minutes
Age: 12 and over

THE LION KING

⊠ Minskoff Theater, 200 West 45th Street between Broadway and 8th Avenue
⏀ www.disneyonbroadway.com
☉ Tues–Sat 8pm, Sun 6.30pm; matinees Wed, Sat, 2pm, Sun 1pm

With the original music from Elton John and Tim Rice (which won them Oscar and Grammy awards) combined with new music from Hans Zimmer and Lebo M, Disney tells the story of Simba, a lion cub who struggles to accept the responsibilities of adulthood and his destined role as king.
Awards: 6 Tony Awards in 1998
Length of show: 2 hours 45 minutes
Age: From the very young to the very old

✠ BRITTIP
Visit www.disneyon broadway.com for details of *Mary Poppins* and *Tarzan*, both showing on Broadway.

The Lion King

MAMMA MIA!

- ✉ Cadillac Winter Garden Theater, 1634 Broadway at 50th Street
- 🖰 www.mamma-mia.com
- 🕐 Wed–Sat 8pm, Sun 7pm; matinees Wed, Sat, Sun 2pm

If you haven't had a chance to see this fabulously uplifting musical in London, then why not try it in New York? Set on a mythical Greek island, it tells the story of a single mum and her daughter on the eve of her daughter's wedding – and comes with 22 cracking ABBA songs.

Length of show: 2 hours 30 minutes
Age: 5 and over

MARY POPPINS

- ✉ New Amsterdam Theater, 214 West 42nd Street
- 🖰 http://disney.go.com/theatre/marypoppins
- 🕐 Tues–Sat 8pm; matinees Wed, Sat 2pm, Sun 3pm

Mary Poppins flew into Broadway with her carpetbag packed and her umbrella unfurled in November 2006 high on the success of her hit debut in the West End of London. Based on the Oscar-winning 1964 Walt Disney film, the world's most famous nanny is bringing 'Supercalifragilisticexpialidocious' to a new generation of children under the directorship of legendary producer Cameron Mackintosh.

Length of show: 2 hours 45 minutes
Age: 6 and over

Times Square

MONTY PYTHON'S SPAMALOT

- ✉ Shubert Theater, 225 West 44th Street between Broadway and 8th Avenue
- 🖰 www.montypythonsspamalot.com
- 🕐 Tues–Sat 8pm, Sun 7pm; matinees Sat, Sun 2pm

Eric Idle, co-founder of Monty Python, is behind this musical adaptation of *Monty Python and the Holy Grail*, which tells the legendary tale of King Arthur and the Knights of the Round Table.

Awards: Tony Award for Best Musical 2005
Length of show: 2 hours 20 minutes
Age: 12 and over

THE PHANTOM OF THE OPERA

- ✉ Majestic Theater, 247 West 44th Street between Broadway and 8th Avenue
- 🖰 www.thephantomoftheopera.com
- 🕐 Tues 7pm, Mon, Wed–Sat 8pm; matinees Wed, Sat 2pm

The longest running show in Broadway history, Andrew Lloyd Webber's famous musical of Gaston Leroux's novel set in 19th-century Paris tells the timeless story of a mysterious spectre who haunts the Paris opera house, spooking the owners and falling in love with a beautiful singer.

Awards: 7 Tony Awards in 1998, including Best Musical
Length of show: 2 hours 30 minutes
Age: 5 and over, depending on whether your child may be scared of the mask.

🇬🇧 BRITTIP

For fantastic views of Times Square, treat yourself to a drink at the Broadway Lounge on the 8th floor lobby level of the Marriott Marquis Hotel at 1535 Broadway (www.nymarriottmarquis.com).

RENT

- ✉ Nederlander Theater, 208 West 41st Street between 7th and 8th Avenues
- 🖰 www.siteforrent.com
- 🕐 Mon–Sat (except Wed) 8pm, Sun 7pm; matinees Sat, Sun 2pm

The Tony Award and Pulitzer Prize-winning musical is based on Puccini's opera *La Bohème*, but is set in New York's East Village. It tells the story of struggling young artists who are living on the edge in the search for glory, and is now in its 11th year.

Awards: 4 Tony Awards in 1996
Length of show: 2 hours 45 minutes
Age: 16 and over due to adult themes

Wicked

TARZAN

✉ Richard Rodgers Theater, 226 West 46th Street at Broadway

🖰 http://disney.go.com/theatre/tarzan

🕐 Wed–Sat 8pm, Sun 6.30pm; matinees Wed 2pm, Sun 1pm

Disney has brought the classic story of a shipwrecked boy raised by gorillas in West Africa to the Broadway stage. When the grown boy meets 'Jane', his life is transformed forever. Based on the film of the same name, expect great songs, high jinks and lots of fun as well as fabulous music and lyrics by Oscar and six-time Grammy Award winner Phil Collins. Opened May 2006.

Length of show: 2 hours 20 minutes
Age: From the very young to the very old

WICKED

✉ Gershwin Theatre, 222 West 51st Street

🖰 www.wickedthemusical.com

🕐 Wed–Sat 8pm, Sun 6.30pm; matinees Wed 2pm, Sun 1pm

Long before Dorothy drops in, two other girls meet in the Land of Oz. One, born with emerald-green skin, is smart, fiery and misunderstood. The other is beautiful, ambitious and very popular. Based on the 1995 novel by Gregory Maguire, this musical tells the story of their remarkable odyssey, how these two unlikely friends grow to become the Wicked Witch of the West and Glinda the Good Witch.

Awards: 3 Tonys in 2004
Length of show: 2 hours 45 minutes
Age: From the young to the very old

RECENTLY OPENED MUSICALS

SPRING AWAKENING

✉ Eugene O'Neill Theatre, 230 West 49th Street

🖰 www.springawakening.com

🕐 Mon, Wed–Sat 8pm, Sun 7pm; matinees Sat, Sun 2pm

This rock musical has arrived after a sold-out run on Off-Broadway. Based on Franz Wedekind's controversial and once banned 19th-century German play about teenagers grappling with their emerging sexuality and with an acclaimed musical score by Duncan Sheik and Steven Sater. Expect passion and lasting regrets.

Length of show: 2 hours 15 minutes
Age: 13 years and over

COMPANY

✉ Ethel Barrymore Theatre, 243 West 47th Street between Broadway and 8th Avenue

🖰 www.companyonbroadway.com

🕐 Wed–Sat 8pm, Tues 7pm; matinees Wed, Sat 20m, Sun 3pm

From the Tony-winning director of the memorable 2005 revival of *Sweeney Todd* comes the revival of another Sondheim classic. This musical takes an unconventional peek at love and commitment in a complex modern world as married life is weighed up through the eyes of Bobby, a single, 30-something bachelor.

Length of show: 2 hours 15 minutes
Age: 8 years and over

GREY GARDENS

✉ Walter Kerr Theatre, 219 West 48th Street between Broadway and 8th Avenue.

🖰 www.greygardensthemusical.com

🕐 Wed–Sat 8pm, Tues 7pm; matinees Wed, Sat 2pm, Sun 3pm

Last spring's much-heralded Off Broadway hit is based on a 1975 documentary film

Pedicab

about Jacqueline Kennedy Onassis's deliciously eccentric aunt and cousin who, once shining socialites, became the Hampton's most famous recluses.
Length of show: 2 hours 30 minutes
Age: 13 and over

LES MISERABLES

✉ Broadhurst Theatre, 235 West 44th Street between 7th and 8th Avenue
⌂ www.lesmisnewyork.com
🕐 Wed-Sat 8pm, Tues 7pm; matinees Wed, Sat 2pm, Sun 3pm

One of the longest productions in Broadway history, for 16 years and one of the great mega-musicals of the last few decades, Les Mis came back to Broadway in 2006 and is a tear-jerker of a story about an ill-fated revolution on the streets of 19th-century Paris.
Awards: Tony Award in 1987
Length of show: 3 hours
Age: 5 and over

◄◼► BRITTIP

Entertainment Link has detailed info on Broadway and other theatre as well as sports and family events, the performing arts and music as well as discounts on www.entertainment-link.com.

TOP JUST-OPENED BROADWAY MUSICALS

CURTAINS

✉ Al Hirschfield Theatre, 302 West 45th Street
⌂ www.curtainsthemusical.com
🕐 Wed-Sat 8pm, Sun 7pm; matinees Wed, Sat , Sun 2pm

A tribute to the big, brassy musical comedies of the 1950s, set in the theatre, an

Times Square at night

unexpected backstage romance for a detective investigating the death of the leading lady, results in trying to make the musical a smash hit. The score is from the Tony Award-winning songwriters Kander & Ebb, best known for 'New York, New York' .
Length of show: 2 hours 40 minutes
Age: 12 and over

LEGALLY BLONDE

✉ Palace Theatre, 1564 Broadway
⌂ www.legallyblondethemusical.com
🕐 Wed-Sat 8pm, Sun 7pm; matinees Wed, Sat , Sun 2pm

A hot new comedy by Tony-award winning choreographer Jerry Mitchell about sorority girl Elle Woods, a girl who doesn't take 'no' for an answer. When her boyfriend dumps her for someone more 'serious', she puts down the credit card, hits the books and goes to Harvard Law. Along the way, it proves that being true to yourself never goes out of style.
Length of show: 2 hours 30 minutes
Age: 12 and over

PIRATE QUEEN

✉ Hilton Theatre, 214 West 43rd Street
⌂ www.thepiratequeen.com
🕐 Tues-Sat 8pm; matinees Wed, Sat 2pm, Sun 3pm

From the creators of *Les Misérables* and the producers of *Riverdance*, this exciting new musical is an extraordinary romantic epic of a legendary Irish chieftain in the 16th century who fights for her country and one true love. Based on a true story.
Length of show: 2 hours 30 minutes
Age: 12 and over

BROADWAY PLAYS

THE COAST OF UTOPIA

✉ Vivian Beaumont Theatre, 150 West 65th Street
⌂ www.coastofutopia.com
🕐 Schedule varies

If you're up for an epic, look no further than Tom Stoppard's trilogy of young Russian romantics and revolutionaries coming of age under Czar Nicholas I in 19th-century Russia with an all-star cast. Part I *Voyage*, Part II *Shipwreck* and Part III *Salvage* can be watched separately or as a marathon on certain dates.
Length of show: 3 hours (one interval)
Age: Adults

CINEMAS

Catch some great blockbuster movies! For complete listings of movies and cinemas near your hotel, check *Time Out* or the free *Village Voice* and *New York Press*.

AMC Empire 25: 234 West 42nd Street between 7th and 8th Avenues, tel 212-398 3939, www.amctheatres.com. This has 25 screens on five levels and has devoted seven screens on the top floor, known as the Top of the Empire, to repertory classics and independent films. You can catch a pre-show snack – pizza to ribs – in the 42nd Street Food Court.

Film Forum: 209 West Houston Street between 6th and 7th Avenues, tel 212-727 8110, www.filmforum.org. A three-theatre venue showing independent and vintage films. There are seasons, such as a run of films dedicated to Audrey Hepburn, and talks given by directors plus film merchandise on sale.

Regal E-Walk Stadium 13: 247 West 42nd Street between 7th and 8th Avenues, tel 212-840-7761, www.regalcinemas.com. This mega-plex cinema with 13 screens and all-stadium seating is a modern-day movie palace. A one-storey high, hand-painted mural honours the local landmarks of Broadway and Times Square.

The Angelika Film Center: 18 West Houston Street, tel 212-995 2000, http://angelikafilmcenter.com. A good selection of the latest art films is shown here, as well as at the **Lincoln Plaza Cinemas**, 1886 Broadway at 62nd Street, tel 212-757 2280, http://lincolnplaza.moviefone.com. The Angelika has a café and the Lincoln Plaza Cinemas sell sandwiches and pastries.

DEUCE

✉ Music Box Theatre, 239 West 45th Street between Broadway and 8th Avenue

🎫 www.deuceonbroadway.com

🕐 Tues–Sat 8pm; matinees Wed, Sat 2pm, Sun 3pm

A play by four-time Tony award winner Terence McNally, who wrote *Kiss of the Spider Woman*, this is the story of two former female doubles stars who reunite at a tennis match and dig up past successes, old rivalries and astonishing secrets.

Length of show: 1 hour 40 minutes (no interval)

Age: 14 and over

OFF BROADWAY

BLUE MAN GROUP: TUBES

✉ Astor Place Theater, 434 Lafayette Street at Astor Place

🎫 www.blueman.com

🕐 Mon–Thurs, Sun 8pm, Fri, Sat 7pm, 10pm; matinees Sat 4pm, Sun 2pm, 5pm

One of the most successful Off-Broadway shows. Take a trio of post-modern clowns, cover them in blue rubber and allow them to be outrageous with sound and art and you have this wonderful avant-garde extravaganza that is both hilarious and challenging to watch.

Length of show: 2 hours

Age: 15 and over

THE FANTASTICKS

✉ Snapple Theatre Center, 210 West 50th Street

🎫 www.thefantasticks.com

🕐 Tues, Sun 7pm, Fri, Sat 8pm; matinees Wed, Sat, Sun 2.00pm

The world's longest musical returned to New York in 2006. A young couple fall in love in the hands of their meddling fathers, but soon grow restless and stray. Can they return to the love they once shared?

Length of show: 2 hours and 10 minutes

Age: Adult

Dakota Building where John Lennon lived

LOVE YOU, YOU'RE PERFECT, NOW CHANGE

✉ Westside Theater Upstairs, 407 West 43rd Street between 8th and 9th Avenues

🖰 www.loveperfectchange.com

🕒 Mon, Tues, Sun 7pm, Fri, Sat 8pm; matinees Wed 2.30pm, Sat 4pm, Sun 3pm

For a thoroughly modern take on the whole notion of dating and romance, you can't go wrong with this comedy. It's a kind of *Seinfeld* set to music. It's also the most 'proposal-friendly' musical in town!

Length of show: 2 hours
Age: Adult

BRITTIP

Queues for the Times Square TKTS booth start long before it opens, so arrive early to get a good choice. But even if you arrive at the last minute, you may catch a show, because the booth stays open right until show time.

JEWTOPIA

✉ Westside Theater, 407 West 43rd Street between 8th and 9th Avenues

🖰 www.jewtopiaplay.com

🕒 Tues–Sat 8pm; matinees Wed, Sat 2pm, Sun 3pm

The story of two 30-year-old single men, Chris O'Connell and Adam Lipschitz who take on the Jewish dating world. Chris, a gentile, wants to marry a nice Jewish girl so he'll never have to make another decision. After forming a secret pact, Adam promises to help Chris shed his gentile-ness and bring

Broadway billboards

COOL SCREENINGS

Cool screenings in New York City can be found at the **American Museum of the Moving Image** Astoria, Queens (see page 275) and where early each year the **Annual New York Film Critics: Great Documentaries** series featuring more than 20 of the nation's top film critics introducing their favourite documentaries. Also check out the **BAMcinématek** programme at the **Brooklyn Academy of Music** (718-636 4100, www.bam.org), which holds The African Diaspora Film Festival in February. Perhaps one of the coolest film festivals of them all is **The Tribeca Film Festival** (www.tribecafilmfestival.org) in different locations around the city in Spring, which has a great line-up of actors and filmmakers for Q&A sessions with the audiences.

BRITTIP

Phone 212-777-FILM or visit www.moviefone.com for accurate movie show times and, to make sure you don't miss out, buy tickets in advance. You can also book online at www.movietickets.com.

him undercover into the Jewish world.
Length of show: 2 hours
Age: 11 and over

STOMP

✉ Orpheum Theater, 126 2nd Avenue at 8th Street

🖰 http://stomponline.com

🕒 Tues–Fri 8pm, Sat 7pm, 10.30pm, Sun 7pm; matinees Sun 3pm

A very unusual show now in its 13th year. Dancers make their own music by using everyday objects such as dustbin lids, brooms and sticks. The rhythmic beats are infectious and the performers' stamina amazing.

Length of show: 1 hour 45 minutes
Age: All ages (although tots might not like the noise)

BRITTIP

AMCinema is AMC Theatres offers its cheapest deal on all shows before noon Friday, Saturday, Sunday and holidays. Check show times for prices and availability at www.amctheatres.com.

CHAPTER 10

Gay New York

The West Village is traditionally the spiritual home of gays and lesbians in New York, but in today's cosmopolitan city a person's sexual persuasion rarely raises an eyebrow. Gay bars, clubs and restaurants have sprung up all over Manhattan, and Chelsea has become the new 'gaybourhood'. In fact, most restaurants and bars across the Big Apple are open to everyone – whether you're gay or straight.

If you'd like to get to know more about the gay and lesbian culture in New York, Big Onion's tour **A Gay and Lesbian History Tour** gives a good insight into the historical side, tracing the development of Greenwich Village as a community Mecca (see Big Onion Walking Tours, page 83). For a tour of the modern-day Gay New York, try Limotour's **VIP Gay Tour of New York City**, which looks at everything from the importance of rent parties to what led to camp culture. It can be arranged online (www.limotours.com) and costs $85 per hour for the whole limo. Check out year-round gay art tours around the Chelsea Galleries led by Rafael Risemberg PhD gay studies professor and art critic for gay newspaper the *New York Blade* (tel 212-946 1548, www.nygallerytours.com). They run Sat 1pm and cost $20.

INFORMATION

THE LESBIAN, GAY, BISEXUAL & TRANSGENDER COMMUNITY CENTER

- ✉ 208 West 13th Street between 7th and 8th Avenues
- ☎ 212-620 7310
- 🖰 www.gaycenter.org
- 🚇 Subway A, C, E, 1, 2, 3 to 14th Street; L to 8th Avenue

By far the best organisation in New York for information, you'll find millions of leaflets and notices about gay life in the city, as well as information on events online. There are now around 400 groups that meet here and it also houses the National Museum and Archive of Lesbian and Gay History.

PUBLICATIONS

The main gay weeklies are *HX* (Homo Xtra), *HX for Her* (www.hx.com) and *Next* (www.nextmagazine.net), which are available in gay bars, clubs, hotels and cafés. They include listings of bars, dance clubs, sex clubs, restaurants and cultural events. Good newspapers are the *LGNY* (Lesbian and Gay New York), though it's a lot more serious and covers political issues, and the *New York Blade* (www.hx.com).

BRITTIP

Download a free gay map to Manhattan from www.funmaps. com to find everything from hot nude yoga to gay-friendly shops.

ACCOMMODATION

Turn to pages 221–222 for some hotel tips and booking info. Prices are per room.

CHELSEA PINES INN
Chelsea
- ✉ 317 West 14th Street between 8th and 9th Avenues
- ☎ 212-929 1023
- 🖰 www.chelseapinesinn.com
- 🚇 Subway A, C East to 14th Street; L to 8th Avenue
- $ Rooms $125–275 including breakfast

In an excellent location in Chelsea on the border with the Village, this hotel, which is one of the best gay hotels in the city, has recently been given a facelift, and now each

Time Warner Building

Chelsea Savoy

room is named after a film star (yes, there is a Judy Garland). In the morning, guests wake to the aroma of homemade bread and doughnuts. Open to both men and women. You need to book at least six to eight weeks in advance.

CHELSEA SAVOY HOTEL
Chelsea
- ✉ 204 West 23rd Street
- ☎ 212-929 9353/866-929 9353 toll free
- 🖱 www.chelseasavoynyc.com
- 🚇 Subway 1, 9, 3 to 23rd Street
- $ Rooms $145–325

This hotel is in a superb location, being close to the Theater District, Financial District, great restaurants, museums and galleries, and SoHo just down the road. The rooms are a good size for NY with all essential amenities such as bathroom and television. Great value, too.

COLONIAL HOUSE INN
Chelsea
- ✉ 318 West 22nd Street between 8th and 9th Avenues
- ☎ 212-243 9669
- 🖱 www.colonialhouseinn.com
- 🚇 Subway C east to 23rd Street
- $ Rooms $95–145

A beautiful place to stay and also spotlessly clean. The economy rooms are tiny, but all have cable TV, air con, phone and daily maid service, and smoking is allowed in rooms.

◀🇬🇧▶ **BRITTIP**

Chelsea is the top 'gaybourhood' in New York City, although Hell's Kitchen is creeping into style. The headquarters for *HX*, Chelsea is one of the best places for gay people to base themselves.

The price includes breakfast, which is eaten in the Life Gallery where there are works by gay and lesbian artists. Book as early as you can because this place gets packed with groups coming into town for drag conventions and so on. It's especially popular in the summer months because of its roof deck with a clothing-optional area. The hotel has a 24-hour doorman. Mostly for gay men.

EDISON HOTEL
Theater District
- ✉ 228 West 47th Street between Broadway and 8th Avenue
- ☎ 212-840 5000
- 🖱 www.edisonhotelnyc.com
- 🚇 Subway N, R to 49th Street
- $ Rooms $190, suites from $220

One of New York's great hotel bargains. The Art Deco Edison's 700 rooms have been totally refurbished, and it has a new coffee shop, the Café Edison, considered to be the best place to spot lunching theatre luminaries. Note: in 2007, it became a smoke-free zone. Book well in advance.

HOTEL WOLCOTT
Midtown
- ✉ 4 West 31st Street between 5th Avenue and Broadway
- ☎ 212-268 2900
- 🖱 www.wolcott.com
- 🚇 Subway N, R to 28th Street
- $ Rooms $200; suites from $210

Well, darling, it's location, location, location, for this 300-room hotel. Just three blocks down from 5th Avenue and the Empire State Building, this is a favourite with the serious tourist and budget-minded business traveller. Complimentary coffee, tea and muffins served in the lobby each morning. Call in advance to find out the bargain seasonal, weekend and holiday rates on offer.

INCENTRA VILLAGE HOUSE
West Village
- ✉ 32 8th Avenue between West 12th and Jane Streets
- ☎ 212-206 0007
- 🖱 www.incentravillage.com
- 🚇 Subway A, C east to 14th Street; L to 8th Avenue
- $ Rooms $179; suite $209

A moderately priced guesthouse in two redbrick townhouses from the 1840s (that's old by American standards!). The 12 suites all have kitchens, phones and private bathrooms and some can even accommodate groups of four or five. All the rooms are well decorated with different themes. The Bishop Suite is a lovely split-level apartment, the Garden Room has a private garden filled with flowers and the Maine Room has a four-poster bed. All rooms are smoker-friendly. A 1939 Steinway piano stands in the parlour and anyone is allowed to play.

THE INN AT IRVING PLACE
Gramercy Park

✉ 56 Irving Place between 17th and 18th Streets
☎ 212-533 4600/ 800-685 1447
🖥 www.innatirving.com
🚗 Subway L, N, R, 4, 5, 6 to 14th Street/ Union Square
$ Rooms $484–631

The building is filled with exquisite antique furniture and elegant decor, if you feel like splashing out. All 12 rooms have queen-size beds and come with private facilities; some even have study areas. There is a 24-hour concierge, plus laptops and fax on request, laundry and dry-cleaning, video rentals, a gym within walking distance and 24-hour massage.

🇬🇧 BRITTIP

The main event of the gay year is the Heritage of Pride Parade (formerly Gay Pride) in June (page 251), where half a million people turn up to parade the streets and party all week. If you're coming then, also catch the NewFest gay film festival in mid-June.

THE ROYALTON
Theater District

✉ 44 West 44th Street between 5th and 6th Avenues
☎ 212-869 4400/ 800 697 1791
🖥 www.royaltonhotel.com
🚗 Subway 4, 5, 6 to 42nd Street; 7 to 5th Avenue
$ Rooms from $500

Ian Schrager's beautiful hotel, designed by Philippe Starck, is now considered to be the

TOP HOTELS

Best location: Hotel Wolcott, Midtown

Best economy: Colonial House Inn, Chelsea

Best luxury: The Inn At Irving Place, Gramercy Park

best address for gays and lesbians into the power thing. A chic tone is set by the lively fashion and publishing crowd that frequents the lobby bar and restaurant. The modern rooms all have CD players, VCR, mini bar and two phone lines.

CLUBS AND LOUNGES FOR HIM

CHELSEA

Barracuda: 275 West 22nd Street between 7th and 8th Avenues. Tel 212-645 8613. Subway C, E to 23rd Street.
This club attracts a mellow mix of people. Head to the rear lounge, which has a better atmosphere than the dingy front bar and a decent pool table. Monday night is the hilarious Star Search, where drag queens battle it out between each other to reign supreme. Open 4pm–4am every day and a popular two-for-one Happy Hour 4pm–9pm during the week. Cash only.

XES Lounge: 157 West 24th Street between 6th and 7th Avenues. Tel 212-604 0212, www.xesnyc.com. Subway F, V, 1 to 23rd Street.
Queer folk will love the Starck furniture in here, which goes with the exposed brick walls and patio sporting Japanese maple trees. Drag shows and parties every weekend and smoking allowed, this was voted the Best Gay Bar in 2006 by Citysearch. Open daily 4pm–4am.

Eagle: 554 West 28th Street between 10th and 11th Avenues. Tel 646-473 1866, www.eaglenyc.com. Subway C, E to 23rd Street.
No-expense-spared renovation of the original Eagle, the new incarnation is a spacious two-storey watering hole filled with congenial leather-clad S&M New Yorkers. No surprise then that it was voted Best Leather Bar by *New York Magazine*. Open Mon–Sat 10pm–4am, Sun 5pm–4am.

Wolcott Hotel

TOP FIVE CLUBS AND LOUNGES FOR HIM

B Bar & Grill: East Village (page 214)

The Cock: East Village (page 215)

g Lounge: Chelsea (page 214)

Manhattan Monster Inc: Greenwich Village (page 215)

Vlada Lounge: Hell's Kitchen (page 215)

Gym Sports Bar: 167 Eighth Avenue between 18th and 19th Avenues. Tel 212-337 2439, www.gymsportsbar.com. Subway 1, 9 to 18th Street.
This first and only gay sports bar was among the city's top gay picks in 2007. It serves big drinks at low prices and offers after-work billiards, as well as parties around gay sports leagues and nightly sports events shown on big screens. 2-4-1 Happy Hour Mon–Fri 4pm–9pm and all night Mon.

g Lounge: 225 West 19th Street between 7th and 8th Avenues. Tel 212-929 1085, www.glounge.com. Subway C, E to 23rd Street; 1 to 18th Street.
A super-popular, sophisticated nightspot for gorgeous hunks to see and be seen. Its centrepiece is its oval bar, which the sexy clientele prop up when they're not shimmying to house music. It gets packed later on when the queues build up outside. Open nightly 4pm–4am; DJ 6pm–1am, Happy Hour Mon–Fri 4pm–9pm. Cash only, but a handy ATM on site.

Kurfew: Tel 212-533 1222, www.kurfew.com. Subway A, C, E, F to 34th Street.
America's youngest all-gay party, with big nights out at different gay clubs around town. Sunday night is college fest at the Avalon. Also holds events at SBNY (see opposite). Eight beers for $10, anyone?

B Bar & Grill

Rawhide: 212 8th Avenue at 20th Street. Tel 212-242 9332, www.rawhide-nyc.com. Subway C, E to 23rd Street.
A darkly lit, leather and Levi's bar in the heart of Chelsea. A great place to start a New York visit, where you can meet friendly down-to-earth locals who will let you in on all the news of what is going on that week in the Big Apple. Famous for its pool tables and beer specials. Closes 4am.

SBNY: 50 West 17th Street between 5th and 6th Avenues. Tel 212-691 0073, www.splashbar.com. Subway L, N, R, W, 4, 5, 6 to 14th Street/Union Square.
Formerly known as Splash, this a popular place to hang out on any night of the week, and not just because the handsome bartenders are shirtless. It's done out South Beach style, with a huge dance floor emporium, a downstairs bar for cruising and an adult store in the basement. It's popular with preppy men and those who enjoy attention. Open daily 4pm–5am with a cover charge of $5-20. Happy Hour Mon–Sat 5-9pm, but Sun is the big night with $8 Budweiser drafts from 4pm–5am.

View Bar: 232 Eighth Avenue at 22nd Street. Tel. 212-929 2243, http://viewbar nyc.com. Subway 1, C, E at 23rd Street.
This trendy new spot delivers what it suggests: a view of the Chelsea boys parading down 8th Avenue through floor to ceiling windows. Martinis and jazz on Wed. Open every night. Daily Happy Hour and *Six Feet Under* and *Queer as Folk* reruns.

◀▮▶ BRITTIP
Check out Travel Gayzette's New York City guide for stores, gyms, accommodation and nightlife at www.travelgayzette.com/newyork.htm.

EAST VILLAGE

B Bar & Grill: 40 East 4th Street between Lafayette Street and the Bowery. Tel 212-475 2220, www.bbarandgrill.com. Subway B, D, F, V to Broadway/Lafayette Street; 6 to Bleecker Street.
This is a super-trendy lounge filled with models and gorgeous people. Madonna has been known to drop in. Beige, the weekly A-list gay party, is the place to be on Tuesday night, and it's free. Open Mon 11.30am–2am, Tues, Thurs and Fri 11.30am–4am, Wed 11.30am–3am, Sat and Sun 10.30am–3am.

The Cock: 29 2nd Avenue at 2nd Street. Tel 212-777 6254. Subway F, V to Second/Lower East Side.
'Rock out with your cock out' – their mantra says it all really. The Cock has one of the wildest crowds in the city and has a penchant for irony-laced depravity. The club attracts pretty boys, drag queens, gay celebrities and their friends, and then mixes in lots of alcohol and some serious cruising. Drinks are cheap though there is a cover charge of $5–10. Cash only. Open nightly 9pm–4am.

Dick's Bar: 192 2nd Avenue at 12th Street. Tel 212-475 2071. Subway L to 3rd Avenue.
No-frills, theme-free East Village gay bar without the usual cruise-or-die desperation. Dick's is a friendly place that features nightly drink specials and a jukebox playing alternative rock and 1970s music, as well as a disco ball and the occasional pornographic movie. Musical Mondays is Dick's casual show tune party. Cash only. Open daily 2pm–4am.

Eastern Bloc: 505 East 6th Street. Tel 212-777 2555.
The old gay haunt, The Wonderbar has been given a Russian refit, with its walls painted a tongue-in-cheek red and black. Surprisingly attitude-free, it was *New York Magazine*'s Best Gay Bar 2007. This is the place to ditch the vodka-sodas and have a beer with the locals.

GREENWICH VILLAGE

Stonewall: 53 Christopher Street between 6th and 7th Avenues. Tel 212-463 0950. Subway 1 at Christopher Street/Sheridan Square.
Restored and reopened, Stonewall is the historic spot where gay activism began and therefore a centre point for the gay community, with multicoloured lights, disco balls and cheesy tunes. Mostly male, there are nightly drag impresarios upstairs. Open daily 3pm–4am; Happy Hour 3pm–9pm. Cash only.

Manhattan Monster, Inc: 80 Grove Street at Sheridan Square. Tel 212-924 3558, www.manhattan-monster.com. Subway 1 to Christopher Street/Sheridan Square.
Probably the most popular bar in Greenwich Village. Right on Sheridan Square across from the infamous Stonewall. Happy piano bar draws older crowd: downstairs dance floor draws younger hotties; Monday night has a drag show. There is a cover charge of $5-7 after 10pm and after 8pm Sundays, probably the only club with cover charge in the Village. Happy Hour weekdays 4pm–9pm and Sat 2pm–9pm, draws the crowds for its free hors d'oeuvres. Open 4pm–4am, party starts at 10pm. Cash only.

MIDTOWN EAST

OW Bar: 221 East 58th Street at 2nd Avenue. Tel. 212-355 3395, http://owbar. com. Subway 4, 5, 6 at 59th Street, N, R, W at 5th Avenue/59th Street.
OW are Oscar Wilde's initials, but this gay bar is lively, too, with drag and cabaret and nightly parties spilling on to an outdoor patio. Open daily 4pm–4am. Happy Hour 4pm–8pm.

 BRITTIP
Visit www.gayorbit.com for a list of upcoming parties.

Vlada Lounge: 331 West 51st Street. Tel 212-974 8030, www.vladabar.com. Subway C, E to 50th Street.
Winner of *City Guide Magazine*'s Best Gay Bar 2007, its worth checking out this sleek

Therapy

Hell's Kitchen bar where the vodka flows, the escargot rolls and drag queens drift. There's no cover charge for the nightly shows. Open Tues–Sun 4pm–4am.

Therapy: 348 West 52nd Street between 8th and 9th Avenues. Tel 212-397 1700, www.therapy-nyc.com. Subway C, E at 50th Street.

A chic and sceney lounge with stylish wood-panelled walls under a vaulted skylight in the heart of 'New Chelsea' district Hell's Kitchen. Try one of the appropriately named house cocktails such as Pavlov's Dog or The Freudian Slip. Nightly entertainment, open Sun–Wed 5pm–2am, Thurs–Sat 5pm–4am. Happy Hour 5pm–8pm daily.

MIDTOWN WEST

Chase: 255 West 55th Street between 7th and 8th Avenues. Tel 212-333 3400. Subway B, D, E to 7th Avenue; N, R, Q to 57th Street.

Chase is a sleek, chic, multi-level gay bar in a neighbourhood with a growing gay population. Located 30 blocks north of Chelsea, it manages to avoid much of that area's attitude. Yet, it still provides everything one has come to expect from a gay bar, including attractive bartenders who are clearly not hired for their drinks-making skills. Friday night date crowd. Looking for love? The crowd is diverse enough for there to be someone for almost everyone.

La Nueva Escuelita: 301 West 39th Street at 8th Avenue. Tel 212-631 0588, www.escuelita.com. Subway A, C east to 42nd Street.

A fantastic Latino club famed for its fabulous shows and nights of salsa, merengue and Latin-style drag shows. Shows Fri 2.30am ($8), Sat 2am ($20), Sun 9.30pm and 1.30am ($10). No shows Thurs.

Tenth Avenue Lounge: 642 10th Avenue at 45th Street. Tel 212-245 9088. Subway A, C east to 42nd Street.

Open daily with Happy Hour 4pm–8pm. There is a light menu in the back room, and frozen drinks. Not exclusively for gays.

UPPER EAST SIDE

Pegasus Bar: 119 East 60th Street between Park and Lexington Avenues. Tel 212-888 4702. Subway 4, 5, 6 to 59th Street; N, R to Lexington Avenue.

Gentlemen's piano bar featuring karaoke and cabaret shows on various rotating nights of the week. Friday and Saturday focus on entertainment for Asian gays. It's also the

time of the week when the groovy back room opens up to reveal plastic-wrapped, leopard-print benches and intimate lighting. Happy Hour 4pm–8pm every day and a complimentary brunch is served Sun 1pm.

WEST VILLAGE

The Dugout: 185 Christopher Street between Washington and West Streets. Tel 212-242 9113, www.thedugoutny.net. Subway 1 to Christopher Street/Sheridan Square.

A great neighbourhood bar and club especially popular for its Sunday afternoon beer blast where 20oz drafts cost just $3. The foremost Chelsea Bear bar, it attracts African-American guys and an older crowd. Open Mon–Sat 4pm–4am, Sun from 3pm. Happy Hour Mon–Fri 4pm–9pm. Cash only.

Lips: 2 Bank Street at Greenwich Avenue. Tel 212-675 7710, http://lipsnyc.com. Subway 1 to Christopher Street, 1, 2, 3 to 14th Street.

This buzzy place is the Hard Rock Café of drag, with supper and shows from 6.30pm until midnight weeknights, Fri and Sat until 1am. The Bitchy Bingo Show on Wednesdays – free, open from 8pm – sees Sherry Vine and Yvon Lame preside over the bitchiest bingo game in the world. On Tuesday you can take part in some drag karaoke, and on Sundays a riotous brunch.

CLUBS AND LOUNGES FOR HER

BROOKLYN

Cattyshack: 249 Fourth Avenue between Carroll and President Streets, Park Slope. Tel 718-230 5740. http://cattyshackbklyn.com. Subway M, R at Union Street.

A two-storey industrial chic oasis in the heart of Brooklyn's hottest district advertising cheap drinks, heated smoking deck, go-go pole and hot bar staff. Wednesday night Meow Mix favourites Don and Isabel host a sing-along and shows at midnight and Fridays go-go dancers grind around the pole to hip hop favourites on the dancefloor. Open Mon–Fri 2pm–4am, Sat and Sun noon–4am. Daily Happy Hour 4pm–8pm.

Ginger's Bar: 363 Fifth Avenue between 6th and 7th Streets, Park Slope. Tel 718-788 0924. Subway M, R to Union Street.

The drinks are generous, the pool table at the back is always full of sexy dykes, and this dark wooden bar is a friendly, neighbourhood place to hang out. Open Mon–Fri 6pm–4am, Sat and Sun 2pm–4am.

TOP FIVE CLUBS AND LOUNGES FOR HER

Bluestockings: Lower East Side (page 217)

Cattyshack: Brooklyn (page 216)

Chueca: Queens (page 217)

Cubby Hole: West Village (page 217)

Starlight: East Village (page 217)

EAST VILLAGE

Starlight: 167 Avenue A between 10th and 11th Streets. Tel 212-475 2172. Subway L to 1st Avenue.

A fabulous bar and lounge that has been voted the best gay bar in New York by *Zagats*. Starlette, ladies' night on Sunday evening, is a popular party with a cool vibe that reflects its trendy East Village location. Open Sun–Thurs 6pm–3am, Fri and Sat 6pm–4am.

LOWER EAST SIDE

Bluestockings: 172 Allen Street between Rivington and Stanton Streets. Tel 212-777 6028, www.bluestockings.com. Subway F, V to Lower East Side/2nd Avenue.

A great neighbourhood joint that gives women the opportunity to showcase their talents at open-mike sessions. Open daily 11am–11pm.

MIDTOWN WEST

La Nueva Escuelita: 301 West 39th Street at 8th Avenue. Tel 212-631 0588, www.escuelita.com. Subway A, C east to 42nd Street

Fever on Friday night is a classic venue for a hot night out. Mostly filled with Latin women from the über-feminine to the ultra-butch, there are go-go dancers galore on which to feast the eyes, a drag show at 2am and a lap-dancing lounge.

Bedford and Grove, West Village

QUEENS

Chueca: 69-04 Woodside Avenue, Woodside. Tel 718-424 1171, www.chueca bar.com.

A great Latin girl bar and restaurant, famous for gorgeous shot girls. Happy Hour Wed-Sun 6pm–8pm. Join their group on myspace to find out what the next month has in store. $10 cover charge on Sat.

WEST VILLAGE

Cubby Hole: 281 West 12th Street between West 4th and West 12th Streets. Tel 212-243 9041. Subway 1, 2, 3 to 14th Street.

It looks as though the owners of this lesbian bar have raided a New Orleans thrift store a few days after Mardi Gras: hundreds of illuminated plastic blowfish, goldfish and Chinese lanterns dangle from the ceiling. Old-timers straggle in long before sunset for half-price drinks (Mon–Sat 4pm–7pm); after 9pm, younger gals (and a fair number of guys) take centre stage. There's no karaoke here anymore, but it almost doesn't matter. Like a pianoless piano bar, Cubby Hole is packed full of regulars who like to belt out tunes along with the jukebox. It was voted Best Lesbian Bar by *New York Magazine* in 2007. Open Mon–Fri 4pm–4am, Sat and Sun 2pm–4am. Cash only.

Henrietta Hudson's: 438 Hudson Street at Morton Street. Tel 212-924 3347, www.henriettahudson.com. Subway 1, 9 to Christopher Street.

A no-nonsense party bar for rocker girls and brainy dykes looking to kick back without pretence. Even when there's no specific party, gals come from far and wide to hang out at this great watering hole. Lush on Sunday is a popular night, with Latin sounds from DJ Culi attracting an exotic crowd. Mamacita is a popular Thursday night dance with R&B, hip-hop and Latin music. If you're into go-go girls, the Back Room Booty Friday night extravaganza is the party for you – and hordes of others, too! Open Mon–Fri 4pm–4am and Sat–Sun 2pm–4am.

RESTAURANTS

BROOKLYN

Superfine: 126 Front Street between Jay and Pearl Streets, Dumbo. Tel 718-243 9005. Cool is moving out of Manhattan, and this hip place proves it. Serves mainly Mediterranean fare but is best known for its themed brunches.

TOP RESTAURANTS FOR GAY PEOPLE

Florent: West Village (page 220)

Lips: West Village (page 220)

Primitivo Osteria: Chelsea (page 218)

Townhouse Restaurant: Midtown East (page 219)

CHELSEA

Better Burger NYC: 178 8th Avenue at 19th Street. Tel 212-989 6688, www.betterburgernyc.com. Subway C, E to 23rd Street.
Low-fat, health-conscience, 100 per cent organic, antibiotic-free and hormone-free fare – ostrich, turkey, chicken, soy and vegetarian burgers (and the classic beef) plus other options. Open 11am–11pm.

Empire Diner: 210 10th Avenue at 22nd Street. Tel 212-924 0011.
This humble diner has made appearances in countless commercials and movies. It's very low key and a great pit stop for a burger at the end of a heavy night. You'll be rubbing shoulders with all sorts of people, from drag queens to artists in need of a late night snack (page 000).

Foodbar: 149 Eighth Avenue between 17th and 18th Streets. Tel 212-243 2020.
Tiny and super-cool. This is Chelsea's gayest restaurant, with a generous window to ogle the passers-by. Try the big brunch omelette or some of the more international fare.

Daily News Building featured in *Superman*

Java Boy/View Bar: 232 Eighth Avenue at 22nd Street. Tel. 212-929 2243, http://viewbarnyc.com. Subway 1, C, E at 23rd Street.
This fills the space left by The Big Cup with, as the name promises, a great view of the passing talent. Famous for its American cuisine with Caribbean and Asian influences, it's packed on Sunday for gospel brunches.

Pad Thai: 114 8th Avenue at 16th Street. Tel 212-691 6226.
Elegant, mellow and seductive noodle lounge with above-average Thai fare.

Primitivo Osteria: 202 West 14th Street. Tel 212-255 2060, www.primitivo restaurant.com.
Modern authentic Italian fare with the best home-made pasta around, plus seafood, salad and steak. Open 11.30am–11pm daily.

Sapa: 43 West 24th Street between Broadway and 6th Avenue.
Tel 212-929 1800, www.sapanyc.com.
Gorgeous French-Vietnamese restaurant with a gay lounge night and complimentary cocktails (and perhaps some celebrity-spotting) Sun 6pm–7pm.

EAST VILLAGE

Manahatta: 316 Bowery at Bleecker Street. Tel 212-253 8644.
This Moroccan-style lounge plays host to a gay party on Wednesdays, as well as a French/Mediterranean restaurant.

B Bar & Grill: 40 East 4th Street between Lafayette Street and Bowery. Tel 212-475 2220, www.bbarandgrill.com.
Home to Beige on a Tuesday night, this gorgeous bistro serves excellent food.

Benny's Burritos: 93 Avenue, near 6th Street. Tel 212-254 3286, www.harrysburritos.com.
This establishment looks as though it has survived from the 1960s: lava lamps, pink walls and Formica tables make up the decor. Serves super-filling burritos and enchiladas, but watch out for the lethal margaritas. (You'll find a larger and more crowded Benny's at 113 Greenwich Ave in the West Village.)

Lucien: 14 1st Avenue at 1st Street. Tel 212-260 6481, www.luciennyc.com.
Always packed, this tiny French bistro serves delicious food and is particularly known for its Sunday brunch. Also open until 2am for late night munchies. It's sister restaurant is Pink Pony (page 219).

Marion's Continental: 354 Bowery between 4th and Great Jones Streets. Tel 212-475 7621, www.marionsnyc.com.
Great, eclectic cuisine and fun, boisterous atmosphere. Now with an XXX Cocktail menu, including concoctions called the Hard Nuts and the Busted Cherry.

Pangea: 178 2nd Avenue between 11th and 12th Streets. Tel 212-995 0900, www.pangeanyc.com.
Known for its wonderful home-made pastas and Mediterranean cuisine.

Yaffa Café: 97 St Marks Place at 1st Avenue. Tel. 212-674 9302, www.yaffacafe.com
This 24-hour hipster hangout serves up hummus, sandwiches, pasta and chicken entrées (page 153). Very inexpensive and with a large garden – and they hand out free condoms to the clientele!

MIDTOWN EAST
Arriba Arriba!: 762 9th Avenue at 51st Street. Tel 212 489 0810.
Neighbourhood queens flock to this Mexican-style joint.

Comfort Diner: 214 East 45th Street between 2nd and 3rd Avenues. Tel 212-867 4555, www.comfortdiner.com.
Authentic and delicious American cuisine served in a 1950s-style diner setting with a friendly atmosphere that has been going strong for 11 years (page 180).

Juice Generation: 644 9th Avenue at 45th Street. Tel. 212-541 5600, www.juicegeneration.com.
Delicious fresh juices, smoothies, protein shakes and bakery products served seven days a week.

Maracas: 317 East 53rd Street at 2nd Avenue. Tel 212-593 6600, www.maracasnyc.com.
Fiesta time at this new Mexican bar and grill from the creators of Lips. Frozen margaritas, explosive visuals, electric ambience. Champagne brunch on Sunday.

Spanky's BBQ: 127 West 43rd Street. Tel 212-302 9507, www.spankysnyc.com.
As Spanky's so succinctly puts it: 'Get porked before the show!'

Townhouse Restaurant: 206 East 58th Street between 2nd and 3rd Avenues. Tel 212-826 6241, www.townhouseny.com.
This is owned by the same people as The Townhouse Bar, one of the oldest, most upscale and gay-safe haunts, especially

among the more mature crowd. It serves delicious food at reasonable prices.

NOLITA, SOHO AND TRIBECA
Amici Miei: 475 West Broadway at Houston Street. Tel 212-533 1933.
A chic Italian restaurant open for lunch and dinner with outdoor seating.

Basset Café: 123 West Broadway at Duane Street. Tel 212-349 1827.
Tuck into a delicious salad or sandwich, or treat yourself to the home-made cakes at this light and airy haven. Smoking permitted here.

Lola Restaurant and Rhythm & Blues Lounge: 15 Watts Street, SoHo. Tel 212-675 6700, www.lolaissoul.com.
Tenement: 157 Ludlow Street at Rivington Street. Tel 212-598 2130.
Refurbished from a brothel to a parlour, Tenement pays homage to old New York with fine eclectic American fare.

The Pink Pony: 178 Ludow Street at Stanton Street. Tel 212-253 1922.
Young, laid-back, unpretentious crowd enjoying inexpensive comfort food.

THEATER DISTRICT
Coffee Pot: 350 West 49th Street at 9th Avenue. Tel 212-265 3566.
Nice little coffee bar with live music and tarot card readings. Open seven days a week until 11pm.

44 & X Hell's Kitchen: 622 Tenth Avenue at 44th Street. Tel 212-977 1170.
Great post-theatre sleek spot, packed with queens and serving tasty American fare.

Comfort Diner

Mangia East Bevi: 800 9th Avenue at 53rd Street. Tel 212-956 3976.
An excellent, popular Italian in the middle of Midtown's gay district.

Revolution: 611 9th Avenue between 43rd and 44th Streets. Tel 212-489 8451.
A club-like restaurant with great food and music videos. It has a DJ every night, a youngish crowd and American menus.

Vintage: 753 9th Avenue at 51st Street. Tel 212-581 4655.
A hip bar/restaurant that serves dinner until midnight and cocktails until 4am.

WEST VILLAGE

Caffe Dell'Artista: 46 Greenwich Avenue between 6th and 7th Avenues. Tel 212-645 4431.
A European-style café serving simple, light meals and desserts.

Cowgirl: 519 Hudson Street at West 10th Street. Tel 212-633 1133, www.cowgirl nyc.com.
This isn't just great for men and women who feel at home surrounded by cowgirl memorabilia, but is also frequented by families. It serves cheap American food – fried onion loaf, huge spare ribs and chicken-fried steak – and is also known for its margaritas. It has a big lesbian following and the people-watching outside the restaurant in summer is a treat.

Florent: 69 Gansevoort Street at Washington Street. Tel 212-989 5779, www.restaurantflorent.com.
Good French food served 24 hours a day at weekends and until 5am weekdays. Busy after the clubs close (page 160).

Garage Restaurant: 99 7th Avenue South at Christopher Street. Tel 212-645 0600, www.garagerest.com.
Serves American cuisine including steaks

and a raw bar, with live jazz nightly and a friendly crowd (page 156).

La Ripaille: 605 Hudson Street at West 12th Street. Tel 212-255 4406.
Authentic French country dining since 1980. A small, cosy and romantic restaurant with excellent bistro food. Proudly serving the gay community for more than 20 years.

Lips: 2 Bank Street at Greenwich Avenue. Tel 212-675 7710, www.lipsnyc.com.
Italian menu with dishes named after popular queens; all the waitresses are in drag and plenty of entertainment is provided (page 216).

Nadine's: 99 Bank Street at Greenwich Street. Tel 212-924 3165.
Eclectic and good-value food in a funky but glamorous setting.

Rubyfruit Bar and Grill: 531 Hudson Street at Charles Street. Tel 212-929 3343.
Dedicated lesbian restaurant and bar. Serves good eclectic food both downstairs and in the fun bar upstairs. Live music nightly.

Sacred Chow: 227 Sullivan Street between Bleecker and West 3rd Streets. Tel 212-337 0863, www.sacredchow.com.
Healthy bohemian vegan food shop and café.

Stonewall Bistro: 113 7th Avenue at Christopher Street. Tel 917 661 1335.
An elegant and cosy dining experience from the creators of the famous Stonewall; continental cuisine with a French flair. Cabaret every night; dinner and drink specials all week. Thurs networking night.

Sushi Samba 7: 87 7th Avenue at Barrow Street. Tel 212-691 7885, www.sushisamba.com.
This establishment serves up excellent sushi, ceviches, tiraditos and pratos.

Lips

CHAPTER 11

Where to Stay

The beauty of a city as diverse and cosmopolitan as New York is that you can find pretty much any kind of accommodation that you desire. From über-romantic suites in super swish hotels to quirky little downtown boutique retreats, you're guaranteed to find something that meets your taste and budget.

By the end of 2007, there will be more than 75,000 hotel rooms in Manhattan, with nearly 13,000 new or renovated rooms expected by 2010. Less than half of these hotels belong to national or international chains, so the Big Apple is bursting with hotels of character and charm that you're unlikely to find anywhere else.

You may be surprised at the size of some of the rooms in the city, which are on the small side, but remember that Manhattan is a small island where space is at a premium. What rooms lack in size they usually make up for in decor and views; many of the high-rise hotels such as the Four Seasons offer breathtaking panoramic vistas.

If you're visiting the city for the first time, be sure to do some research before you book so that you can decide which area you would like to be based in. This will save you much time and money on getting around. For example, if your prime reason for visiting the city is for theatres and shopping, you're going to want to be staying in Midtown where everything is on your doorstep. It may be that if you intend to stay for a week it would work out best to stay at two hotels – one in Lower Manhattan and one in Midtown, helping you save on travelling time and expensive cab fares.

The most upmarket hotels have always been clustered on the east side of Manhattan from Midtown up to 96th Street. However, in recent years first-class hotels have been popping up all over the place and there are now several in SoHo, Greenwich Village and the Financial District. The best deals tend to be around Herald Square and on the Upper West Side, but if you go for these options check you won't be spending more than you need to on transport. The average rate for a room that can accommodate two people is around $225 a night – so if you get something for less (and there are plenty of ways to do this), you will be doing well.

> **BRITTIP**
>
> If you are planning to take in the sights of Lower Manhattan, Chinatown, Lower East Side, SoHo and the Village, choose a downtown hotel. It'll save you loads of time on travel and money on cab fares.

HOTEL TIPS

➡ Demand for hotel rooms at peak times of the year is high, so your best bet for both ensuring a bed and getting the best price is to go in the off-peak times of January to March and July and August.

➡ Most hotels reduce their rates at weekends – including some of the poshest. If you're staying for more than a weekend, negotiate the best rate you can for the rest of your time or switch to a cheaper hotel.

➡ If noise is a particular problem for you, bear in mind that hotels downtown and uptown tend to be quieter than those in Midtown. Also, hotels on streets tend to be quieter than those on avenues, except those nearer the river.

SoHo Grand

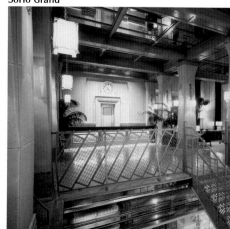

➡ For longer stays, try to choose a hotel room with a kitchenette, then you won't have to eat out all the time.

➡ Smaller hotels tend not to book large groups, so they often have rooms available even during peak periods.

➡ When booking your room, check there isn't going to be a major convention on at the same time. If there is, ask to be put on a different floor.

➡ Ask for a corner room – they are usually bigger and have more windows and, therefore, more light than other rooms and don't always cost more.

➡ Renovation work is often going on in New York hotels so, when making a reservation, ask if any is being done there and, if it is, ask for a room as far away as possible from the work.

Below is the *Brit's Guide* pick of the best hotels in Manhattan, priced by room per night, covering all price brackets. They range from romantic hideaways to the latest hip openings to grand hotels that have been on the map for nearly a century.

$	Less than $100
$$	$100–200
$$$	$200–300
$$$$	$300–400
$$$$$	$400 and over

LANDMARK HOTELS

These hotels aren't simply hotels, they are institutions. Brimming with history, which most hotel staff will be only too willing to tell you about, these grand dames of the New York hotel scene are in a class of their own, and we're not just talking about the high prices.

Waldorf Astoria

MIDTOWN

THE PLAZA $$$$$

✉ 768 5th Avenue at 59th Street
☎ NA
🖰 www.fairmont.com
🚇 Subway 6 to 51st Street

A true New York landmark built in the style of a French Renaissance chateau. Built by Henry Janeway Hardenbergh and opened to the public in 1 October 1907, its position next to Central Park and 5th Avenue is unbeatable as a base in NYC. The hotel has actually been closed for two years, but NYC & Co confirms that it is due to open its doors again late 2007/early 2008, after a major refurbishment by the Elad group, which bought the property for $675 million in 2005. It has also previously been owned by Donald Trump who bought it for $407.5 million in 1988, an immense figure at the time, and he was quoted as saying, 'I haven't purchased a building, I've purchased a masterpiece.' It's certainly worth checking out, even if you can't afford to stay in what are rumoured to be 282 refurbished hotel rooms plus 152 condo hotel units for sale. You're likely to recognise the building from the string of films that have been shot in and around it, such as *North by Northwest*, *Funny Girl*, *The Way We Were*, *Cotton Club*, *Crocodile Dundee*, *Home Alone 2* and *The Sopranos*, as well pictures from celebrity events, such as Catherine Zeta-Jones and Michael Douglas's wedding.

MIDTOWN EAST

WALDORF ASTORIA $$$–$$$$$

✉ 301 Park Avenue at 50th Street
☎ 212-355 3000
   Fax 212-872 7272
🖰 www.waldorfastoria.com/
   www.hilton.com
🚇 Subway 6 to 51st Street

A colossus of a hotel in more than one sense, it's an Art Deco marvel with a wonderful history and has been designated a New York City landmark since 1993. Now is a great time to visit as it's just had a $50 million makeover, which includes a $5.5 million revamp of Peacock Alley, the hotel's top restaurant headed by chef Cedric Tovar.

It all started in 1893 when millionaire William Waldorf Astor opened the 13-storey Waldorf Hotel at 33rd Street. It was the embodiment of Astor's vision of a grand hotel and came with two innovations –

electricity throughout and private bathrooms in every guest chamber – and immediately became the place to go for the upper classes. Four years later the Waldorf was joined by the 17-storey Astoria Hotel, built next door by Waldorf Astor's cousin, John Jacob Astor IV. The corridor between the two became an enduring symbol of the combined Waldorf and Astoria Hotels.

In 1929 it closed, and on its original site now stands another icon of the New York skyline, the Empire State Building. In the meantime, the Waldorf Astoria was rebuilt in Midtown, opening its doors in 1931 and immediately dubbed New York's first skyscraper hotel. It rose 42 storeys high, stretched from Park Avenue to Lexington and contained an astonishing 2,200 rooms. It was such an amazing event, opening as it did in the middle of the Depression, that President Herbert Hoover broadcast a message of congratulations. Ever since, the Waldorf Astoria has had a long association with presidents of countries and corporations.

The Art Deco aspects of the hotel were brought back into view during a restoration in the 1980s when architects found a huge cache of long-lost treasures, including a magnificent 148,000-piece mosaic depicting the Wheel of Life, by French artist Louis Regal, in the Park Avenue lobby, 13 allegorical murals by the same artist and ornate mouldings on the ceilings. The legendary Starlight Roof nightclub with its retractable roof, which had epitomised glamour and sophistication in the 1930s and 1940s, was restored during the same period.

BRITTIP

If you're not happy with the quality of your room, change it. Americans wouldn't tolerate anything but the best, so why should you?

Another $60-million upgrade in 1998 saw the Park Avenue Cocktail Terrace and Sir Harry's Bar being restored to their full Art Deco glory. Oscar's, named after the Waldorf Astoria's famous style-setting maître d' Oscar Tschirky, was redesigned by Adam Tihany, the hottest restaurant designer in town.

Of course, you'll want to know about the service – excellent – and the standard of the rooms – huge, beautifully decorated and with marble-encased en-suite bathrooms. What more could you ask for?

WALDORF TOWERS $$$$$

✉ 100 East 50th Street
☎ 212-355 3100
   Fax 212-872 7272
🖥 www.waldorf-towers.com/
   www.hilton.com
🚗 Subway 6 to 51st Street

A boutique hotel occupying the 28th to the 42nd floors of the Waldorf Astoria, this is one of the most exclusive addresses in New York, filled as it is with presidents of countries and global corporations. Thanks to the hotel's security arrangements (it has its own private car parking facilities underground), this is the place where treaties and mergers have been negotiated and signed, momentous peace initiatives have begun and unforgettable music has been made.

The hotel has its own dedicated entrance, lobby, concierge desk, reception and private lifts operated by 'white-gloved' attendants. Guests have included the Duke and Duchess of Windsor, who maintained their New York residence here, Jack and Jackie Kennedy, Frank Sinatra and Cole Porter, who wrote many of his most famous compositions in a room here.

The rooms are not so much rooms or suites, but rather more like apartments. Many come with dining rooms, full kitchens and maids' quarters. Some even have televisions in their bathrooms! Four-footed guests are greeted with a biscuit.

The Night Hotel

UPPER EAST SIDE

HOTEL CARLYLE $$$$–$$$$$

✉ 35 East 76th Street between Madison
and Park Avenues

☎ 212-744 1600
Fax 212-717 4682

🖰 www.rosewoodhotels.com,
www.thecarlyle.com

🚇 Subway 6 to 77th Street

Established in the 1930s, the Carlyle is a
timeless classic, patronised by a wide range
of people from world leaders and top
businessmen to It girls and leading lights in
entertainment and the arts. Brilliantly
positioned on Madison Avenue, it is a true
New York landmark. The 180 apartment-
style rooms and suites are elegant and very
plush – some even have grand pianos and all
have whirlpools in the bathrooms. In fact it
feels as though you're staying in your
elegant Upper East Side pied-à-terre rather
than renting a hotel room. If you really want
to push the boat out, there's a new,
breathtaking Royal Suite on the 22nd floor.
It's famous for its impeccable and discreet
service but also for its live music in Cafe
Carlyle where Woody Allen still plays jazz on
Monday nights (page 000).

🇬🇧 BRITTIP

It looks like Brooklyn is set to
be the new hotel hot spot in
town. The 93-room Smith Hotel has
just opened its doors to much
approval, and there are aloft and
Sheraton hotels planned to open in
mid-2008.

COMING SOON

If you're the type of person that likes all
things new and fashionable and to be the
first to try something before all your friends
then check out this list of hip hotels
scheduled to be opening in the Big Apple in
the next 12 months. Be warned, however,
that New York hoteliers are notorious for
going way over their scheduled opening
time, so do check ahead to find out the
latest developments on www.nycvisit.com
before turning up with your suitcase.

ALLEN STREET HOTEL

✉ Allen Street between Houston and
Stanton Streets, Lower East Side

Following on from the success of his 60
Thompson Hotel (page 230), Jason Pomeranc

Ritz–Carlton

is developing a 112-room property in the
extremely trendy Lower East Side. There will
also be 32 luxury condominiums, plus a spa
and swimming pool, when it's finished,
which those in the know say is likely to be
Autumn 2007.

THE DOWNTOWN HOTEL

✉ 377-383 Greenwich Street at
Northmoore Street, Tribeca

Actor Robert DeNiro, with his partner Ian
Drukier, has plans to add a $43 million, six-
storey luxury hotel to his portfolio, which
already includes the TriBeCa Film Institute.
It's taking shape in a terracotta brick
building at the corner of Northmoore and
Greenwich Streets in Tribeca and will have
83 rooms with features such as skylights and
angled windows. Don't hold your breath
though, as this was scheduled to open late
2006 and as yet it's still unfinished.

THE LAMBS CLUB HOTEL

✉ 130 West 44th Street, Midtown

Cool hotelier Vikram Chatwal, also owner of
Time and Dream hotels (pages 230 and 231)
is now converting the landmark 1904
Sandford White-designed Lamb's Club, a
private member's club for the theatrical
world, into a luxury hotel. With Thierry
Despont in charge of design, it's said to have
72 rooms and due to open late 2007.

SANCTUARY HOTEL NEW YORK

✉ 132 West 47th Street, Midtown

The Times Square property was previously
the worn-out Portland Square Hotel. It's
been snapped up by hotelier Keith Menin
and is being transformed, with the help of

$7.5 million, into a slick, cutting-edge 115-room deluxe hotel. The Sanctuary brand is already popular with Americans in Miami and Arizona, and this one, which is due to open in winter 2007, is set to be as popular.

THE STANDARD

✉ West 13th Street between Washington and West Streets, Meatpacking District
Andre Balazs' third foray into New York City hospitality is this super-cool 344-room new build in the Meatpacking District. Scheduled to open late 2007, enticements include a rooftop swimming pool.

MODERN LUXURY

A rash of large, new super-stylish hotels have opened in Manhattan in the last couple of years, which have set new standards worldwide for architecture and interiors. We also include a couple of hotels that have been around for a decade that were so ahead of their time they're still attracting a modern crowd. These are the places to check into if you want contemporary rooms with all the trimmings; think fluffy white bathrobes, designer toiletries in the bathroom, plasma screen TVs and a hip cocktail bar or restaurant to spend some time in.

BATTERY PARK CITY

RITZ-CARLTON NEW YORK $$$$$

✉ 2 West Street between Battery Place and West End
☎ 212-344 0800
   Fax 212-344 3804
⌂ www.ritzcarlton.com
🚇 Subway 4, 5 to Bowling Green
A world-class, award-winning hotel with Art Deco-inspired interiors, incredible views of the Hudson River and Statue of Liberty, state-of-the-art business support services and unparalleled service. A 39-storey glass-and-brick edifice in Lower Manhattan, it has 298 sumptuous guest rooms, an outdoor waterfront deck and even the Skyscraper Museum (page 107).

   The rooms come with the very finest Frette linens, feather beds and goose-down pillows, cotton bathrobes, Ritz-Carlton pyjamas, marble bathtubs and separate marble shower stalls, silk curtains, in-room safe, working desk with two chairs, dual-line cordless phones with voicemail and high-speed internet access. The extensive guest services include a fully equipped health club

and spa, massage treatments, limo, complimentary shuttle service in Lower Manhattan and a bath butler! Sheer luxury!

GRAMERCY PARK

GRAMERCY PARK HOTEL $$$–$$$$

✉ 2 Lexington Avenue at Gramercy Park North
☎ 212-201 2161
⌂ www.gramercyparkhotel.com
🚇 Subway L, N, R, 4, 5, 6 to 14th Street/ Union Square
Once a famous hotel where the likes of JFK and Humphrey Bogart liked to spend time. Now it's back on the style radar once again thanks to a multi-million dollar refurb by über hotelier Ian Schrager. It's got all the flair that you usually find in a Schrager creation; think jaw-dropping reception area, quirky bar and super-sexy bedrooms. The penthouse is incredible, too, with wonderful views of Gramercy Park and a massive bedroom, dining room, multi-media centre and kitchen.

MIDTOWN

FLATOTEL $$$–$$$$

✉ 135 West 52nd Street
☎ 212-887 9400
⌂ www.flatotel.com
🚇 Subway B, D, F, Q to 42nd Street
A towering glass complex just around the corner from Radio City Music Hall (page 64) that's home-from-home for rock stars thanks to the large, light rooms that have fab marble bathrooms, flatscreen TVs, CD players and huge beds. The view from the floor-to-ceiling windows is awesome.

Ritz-Carlton Park View room

THE LONDON NYC $$$$

⊠ 151 West 54th Street
☎ 212-307 5000
⌐ www.thelondon-nyc.com

The former Rihga Royal New York Hotel has been transformed into an über hip destination; out with the tired furnishings and in with deluxe rooms with high-speed internet access. London chef Gordon Ramsey's first restaurant in the city is here (though it didn't go down well with New York food critics) and a concierge service by Camilla Parker Bowles's son Tom's upper crust do-it-all company. This is the hot hotel for grown-ups. Introductory rates from $399 per night.

ROYALTON $$$–$$$$

⊠ 44 West 44th Street between 5th and 6th Avenues
☎ 212-869 4400
  Fax 212-869 8965
⌐ www.royaltonhotel.com
🚇 Subway B, D, F, Q to 42nd Street

Still an in place with the magazine and showbiz crowd despite the fact that this hotel, designed by Philippe Starck, first opened in the 1980s. Its theatre-style lobby, which runs the length of an entire block, is worth a visit alone. Each room has a futon, slate fireplace and round bathtub.

The Royalton

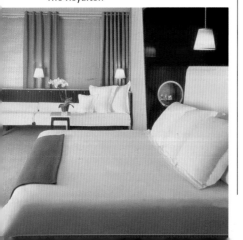

MIDTOWN EAST

FOUR SEASONS $$$$–$$$$$

⊠ 57 East 57th Street between Madison and Park Avenues
☎ 212-758 5700
  Fax 212-758 5711
⌐ www.fourseasons.com
🚇 Subway 4, 5, 6 to 59th Street

Put on your best power suits to rub shoulders with New York's movers and shakers. The Art Deco-style rooms come with electronically controlled curtains and marble-clad bathrooms.

SOHO

SOHO GRAND $$$$

⊠ 310 West Broadway between Grand and Canal Streets
☎ 212-965 3000
  Fax 212-965 3200
⌐ www.sohogrand.com
🚇 Subway C east to Canal Street

Famous for its style, this was the first real top-notch hotel to open in the SoHo area. Cocktails and light meals are served in the Grand Bar, an intimate, wood-panelled club room, as well as the fashionable Salon, a lively lounge that is excellent for people-watching and pet-friendly, so perhaps dog-watching, too.

TRIBECA

TRIBECA GRAND $$$$–$$$$$

⊠ 2 Avenue of the Americas (6th Avenue) at Church Street
☎ 212-519 6600
  UK freephone 0800-028 9874
  Fax 212-519 6700
⌐ www.tribecagrand.com
🚇 Subway 1, 9 to Franklin Street

Sister property to the extremely stylish Soho Grand, this is the first major hotel to open in the TriBeCa area. It's popular with the film crowd, thanks to its 98-seat private screening room and the annual TriBeCa Film Festival that it hosts. Amenities in the 203 rooms, including studio 'digital lifestyle' rooms and a Grand Suite with rooftop terrace, include iPods, complimentary local phone calls and faxes, digital cable TV with movies-on-demand, Bose sound dock, and radio/CD player with library, wireless internet access, and complimentary pet goldfish on request.

UPPER WEST SIDE

MANDARIN ORIENTAL $$$$–$$$$$
- ✉ 80 Columbus Circle at 60th Street
- ☎ 212-805 8800
  Fax 212-805 8888
- 🖰 www.mandarinoriental.com
- 🚇 Subway A, B, C, D, 9 to 59th Street/
  Columbus Circle

Set in the top floors of the AOL Time Warner Center on the north-west arc of the Columbus Circle, it sits steps away from Central Park and just a stroll from 5th Avenue. Inside, the luxurious rooms are simply breathtaking, with floor-to-ceiling windows offering spectacular views of the Manhattan skyline. Have fun hanging out at the trendy MO bar, or flex your credit card and enjoy dinner in Asiate on the 35th floor, which offers a fusion of French and Japanese cuisine. If you're tired after your journey, behave like a celeb and book yourself a massage at the hotel spa.

TRADITIONAL LUXURY

The following hotels are all about plush furnishings, impeccable service and the right location. They are often very discreet, which is why celebrities love them, and most have the added advantage of extremely good gourmet restaurants.

GRAMERCY PARK

INN AT IRVING PLACE $$$$–$$$$$
- ✉ 56 Irving Place between East 17th and
  East 18th Streets
- ☎ 212-533 4600
  Fax 212-533 4611
- 🖰 www.innatirving.com
- 🚇 Subway L, N, R, 4, 5, 6 to 14th Street/
  Union Square

Delightful, tiny Victorian boutique hotel. Each room has a romantic fireplace and four-poster bed.

TOP FIVE HOTEL SPAS

The Cowshed Spa at SoHo House (page 230)

The Peninsula Spa at The Peninsula New York (page 233)

Plus One Spa at Trump International Hotel & Tower (page 233)

Spa at Four Seasons Hotel (page 226)

Spa at Mandarin Oriental (page 227)

MIDTOWN EAST

ELYSEE $$$$–$$$$$
- ✉ 60 East 54th Street between Park and
  Madison Avenues
- ☎ 212-753 1066,
  Fax 212-980 9278
- 🖰 www.elyseehotel.com
- 🚇 Subway 6 to 51st Street

A small hotel dating from the 1920s whose decor includes antique furnishings and Italian marble bathrooms. Home from home to movie stars, guests have use of a nearby sports club.

NEW YORK PALACE $$$$–$$$$$
- ✉ 455 Madison Avenue between 50th and
  51st Streets
- ☎ 212-888 7000
  Fax 212-303 6000
- 🖰 www.newyorkpalace.com
- 🚇 Subway 6 to 51st Street

Built in 1882, the Palace rises 55 floors from its prime spot in Midtown Manhattan and is a favourite stopover for celebs visiting New York. The main hotel is in the atmospheric Villard Houses, but the adjacent Towers has the advantage of more luxurious rooms. Its new restaurant, Gilt, serves modern European cuisine and the Villard Bar and Lounge is perfect for a cocktail.

UPPER EAST SIDE

HOTEL PLAZA-ATHENEE
$$$$–$$$$$
- ✉ 37 East 64th Street between Madison
  and Park Avenues
- ☎ 212-734 9100
  Fax 212-722 0958
- 🖰 www.plaza-athenee.com
- 🚇 Subway 6 to 68th Street

What the rooms lack in size they make up for in elegant antique French furnishings. The hotel has introduced a great range of packages for tourists, including a shopping package with discounts at lots of stores including Bloomingdales and private car pick-up. The Arabelle Restaurant is also the place to have brunch in the city.

🇬🇧 BRITTIP
If you're a smoker, make sure you ask for a smoking room as most hotels are now predominantly non-smoking.

THE LOWELL $$$$$

✉ 28 East 63rd Street at Madison Avenue
☎ 212-838 1400
🖰 www.lowellhotel.com
🚗 Subway N, R, W to Lexington Avenue/
59th Street

Classic Upper East Side retreat, far from the hustle and bustle of Midtown. Everything here looks and feels very expensive, from the marble floors to the mahogany desk lobby. The guest rooms are decorated like the interiors of an ageing Park Lane princess; think rich fabrics and plush sofas. Some even have a working fireplace, although there are hi-tech touches, too, such as a flat-screen TV at the foot of the bathtub.

THE MARK $$$$-$$$$$

✉ 25 East 77th Street between 5th and
Madison Avenues
☎ 212-744 4300
Fax 212-744 2749
🖰 www.mandarinoriental.com/themark
🚗 Subway 6 to 77th Street

In terms of luxury, it vies with the Carlyle – only this hotel is infused with Italian Neo-Classicism compared with the Carlyle's English gentility. It is currently closed but was due to open again in June 2007, after a major refurbishment. Mark fans need not worry though; the city's first really beautiful upmarket boutique hotel will still enjoy the most discreet service in town, which has been enjoyed by a long list of celebrity clients. Unfortunately, some of them have tended to get a bit out of hand. Johnny Depp and Kate Moss had their notorious lovers' tiff here, which took its toll on the furniture before Depp was finally arrested at 5am. Fellow celebrity guests George Michael and Ali McGraw were apparently deeply disturbed by Depp's tantrum. On a happier note, such an event is a rarity, which explains why many celebs make the hotel their home-from-home when they're in New York. There will still be a complimentary car service to Wall Street and the Theater District for all guests, a small health club and a top-notch restaurant.

◀🇬🇧▶ BRITTIP

The posh Mark hotel does such good weekend and summer rates that you could afford to stay here and enjoy all that fabulous luxury. It's family-friendly too.

The Inn at Irving Place

SHERRY-NETHERLAND $$$$-$$$$$

✉ 781 5th Avenue at East 59th Street
☎ 212-355 2800
Fax 212-319 4306
🖰 www.sherrynetherland.com
🚗 Subway 4, 5, 6 to 59th Street

A true New York secret, this is one of the grand hotels with real charm and is also the permanent home of many a celebrity. It's just undergone a multi-million dollar renovation of all its suites, with internet access in all rooms now included. It also boasts the Cipriani Restaurant, popular with ladies who like to lunch.

◀🇬🇧▶ BRITTIP

When making a booking directly with a hotel, make sure they send you confirmation of your reservation (by fax or email is simplest).

BOUTIQUE CHIC

These hotels are stylish and small (100 rooms or less). If you love modern design and crave the latest looks, then check them out. If you can't stay, most have great bars where you can soak up the ambience for an evening.

LOWER EAST SIDE

BLUE MOON $$$

✉ 100 Orchard Street, Lower East Side
☎ 212-533 9080
🖰 www.bluemoon-nyc.com
🚗 Subway F to East Broadway

Recently opened 22-room boutique retreat in the trendy Lower East Side that gets its inspiration from another era, with each room individually styled and named after screen celebrities. Situated down a quaint cobbled street, it's a little gem if you don't want to break the bank. The complimentary continental breakfast served in the lobby includes delicious bagels.

HOTEL ON RIVINGTON $$$$–$$$$$

✉ 107 Rivington Street between Ludlow and Essex Streets.
☎ 212-475 2600
🖳 www.hotelonrivington.com
🚇 F to Delancey Street

Another hip hotel to open up in the Lower East Side, this glass and aluminium 20-storey building is very slick. The entrance of deep red carpet and velvet curtains isn't the same tone as the rest of the hotel. On the ground floor is hip restaurant Thor; above this is the sleek concierge desk with low-lying sofas and tables with arty books; and above this lie the rooms, all very minimalist and tasteful with cloud-like duvets, boxy armchairs in slate grey and flat-screen TVs. If you can afford it, go for one of the upper level rooms with great views of the East River from floor-to-ceiling windows.

MEATPACKING DISTRICT

HOTEL GANSEVOORT $$$–$$$$$

✉ 18 9th Avenue at 13th Street
☎ 212-206 6700
Fax 212-660 6744
🖳 www.hotelgansevoort.com
🚇 Subway N, R to 5th Avenue

In the trendy Meatpacking District, the Gansevoort is a 187-room hang-out that's just a stroll away from Stella McCartney and some good restaurants. The feature that really makes it a place to head for is the 14m (45ft) long rooftop pool with underwater music. The new spa is great, too.

MIDTOWN

BRYANT PARK $$$$–$$$$$

✉ 40 West 40th Street
☎ 212-869 0100
🖳 www.bryantparkhotel.com
🚇 Subway D, B, V, F to 42nd Street

This hide-out for the fashion pack overlooks the park that gives the hotel its name. It's just off 5th Avenue, so ideal if you are on a shopping trip and convenient for visiting all of the major sights. Inside, the rooms resemble New York lofts; think white walls, sleek Italian furniture in warm orange and ochre and cool bathrooms with giant porcelain sinks and stainless steel shelves.

CHAMBERS $$$–$$$$$

✉ 15 West 56th Street between 5th and 6th Avenues
☎ 212-974 5656
Fax 212-974 5657
🖳 www.chambershotel.com
🚇 Subway B, Q to 57th Street

Owned by the same team behind the Mercer Hotel in SoHo, it attracts the likes of Jennifer Love Hewitt and Kid Rock to its gorgeous rooms. The ultra-modern decor is comfortable and luxurious and the hotel displays over 500 pieces of original art. The bath tubs are deep, cashmere throws adorn the beds and flat-screen TVs with DVD and CD players grace every room. Its restaurant, Town (page 000), is still a hip place to dine.

 BRITTIP

If you hire a car, bear in mind that most hotels charge a parking fee of around $30 a night.

CITY CLUB HOTEL $$$–$$$$

✉ 55 West 44th Street between 5th and 6th Avenues
☎ 212-921 5500
Fax 212-944 5544
🖳 www.cityclubhotel.com
🚇 Subway 7 to 5th Avenue; B, D, F, V to 42nd Street

The owner-manager Jeffrey Klein is one of the most socially visible hoteliers in the city and some of his very famous friends cocoon themselves in his hotel. Based in an old gentlemen's club building, it is one of the smartest but least showy boutique hotels in New York. There's no queuing in the lobby as check-in happens in your room, which has a big TV hidden in the wall, a day bed and possibly even the latest Jackie Kennedy Onassis biography. These rooms are designed to spend time in!

Hotel Gansevoort pool

MORGANS $$$–$$$$

- ✉ 237 Madison Avenue
- ☎ 212-686 0300
  Fax 212-779 8352
- 🖰 www.morganshotel.com
- 🚗 Subway 4, 5, 6 to 6th Avenue and 34th Street

This Ian Schrager hotel started the boutique phenomenon and is still going strong today thanks to its unique sense of style and effortless cool. The bedrooms are apartment-style havens, all ivory, camel and taupe soft furnishings plus it has one of Manhattan's most popular restaurants, Asia de Cuba (page 164), and Morgans Bar (page 193) is certainly the hot spot to sip a cocktail.

MIDTOWN EAST

DYLAN $$$–$$$$

- ✉ 52 East 41st Street between Madison and Park Avenues
- ☎ 212-338 0500
  Fax 212-338 0569
- 🖰 www.dylanhotel.com
- 🚗 Subway S, 4, 5, 6, 7 to Grand Central/42nd Street

Located in the former Chemist's Club building, this small hotel was developed to preserve the 1903 Beaux Arts structure. A mezzanine lounge and bar overlooks the dramatic, high-ceilinged restaurant, The Chemist Club. In-room amenities include a state-of-the-art digital entertainment system with large cable TV, DVD and CD players that can access a library of thousands of video and CD titles, two-line telephones with voicemail and data port, complimentary high-speed and wireless internet, large safes and complimentary newspaper.

Loft at the 60 Thompson

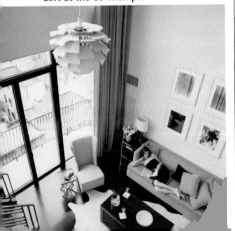

SOHO

6 COLUMBUS CIRCLE $$$

- ✉ 6 Columbus Circle between West 58th and 60th Streets
- ☎ 212-431 0400
  Fax 212-204 5005
- 🖰 www.60thompson.com

Overlooking Columbus Circle and Central Park, this 90-room and suite inspired urban retreat with a 1960s modernist feel opened in summer 2006. The renovation was masterminded by Jason Pomerac, who opened 60 Thompson three years ago.

60 THOMPSON $$$–$$$$$

- ✉ 60 Thompson Street between Broome and Spring Streets
- ☎ 877-431 0400
  Fax 212-431 0200
- 🖰 www.60thompson.com
- 🚗 Subway C, E to Spring Street

A sleek, 14-storey, 100-bedroom hotel that is a great retreat from the bustling streets of SoHo. Rooms are designed for relaxing in – the best are on the top floor and have breathtaking panoramic views of landmarks such as the Empire State Building. The front patio, sheltered by stands of black bamboo, is a wonderful place to just sit and people-watch. Outstanding!

MERCER $$$–$$$$

- ✉ 147 Mercer Street at Prince Street
- ☎ 212-966 6060
  Fax 212-965 3838
- 🖰 www.mercerhotel.com
- 🚗 Subway N, R to Prince Street

A bijou 75-room boutique hotel in a Romanesque revival building slap-bang in the middle of SoHo. Offering a taste of New York loft living, it quickly gets packed with the fashionable and young corporate sets. Rooms even provide condoms in the bathroom and video games to play on the TV, and The Kitchen re-creates the casual feeling of a meal at home.

SOHO HOUSE NEW YORK $$$$–$$$$$

- ✉ 29–35 9th Avenue between West 13th and 14th Streets
- ☎ 212-627 9800
  Fax 212-627 4766
- 🖰 www.sohohouseny.com
- 🚗 Subway 1, 9 to 14th Street

Soho House is the baby sister of London's Soho House and has already proved a similar magnet for celebrities and media bigwigs with its chandeliers-meets-Corbusier decor, 24 bedrooms, Cowshed Spa and cinema. It's actually a private members' club, but if you're lucky enough to book one of the rooms you can use the members' facilities, which includes the fabulous rooftop pool that has already gained iconic status as the set for one of the classic *Sex And The City* episodes.

BRITTIP

For sleek New York style without the hefty price tag, check into one of the W New York hotels, a small chain of five designer hotels that have sprung up around the city. *W New York The Court* (tel 212-685 1100), *W New York The Tuscany* (tel 212-686 1600), *W New York Union Square* (tel 212-253 9119), *W New York Times Square* (tel 212-930 7400) and *W New York on Lexington Avenue* (tel 212-755 1200) each offer exceptional standards of minimalist-style accommodation. View them all at www.whotels.com.

THEME HOTELS

CHELSEA

MARITIME HOTEL $$-$$$$
✉ 363 West 16th Street at 9th Avenue
☎ 212-242 4300
   Fax 212-242 1188
🖰 www.themaritimehotel.com
🚗 Subway 1, 9 to 14th Street

A fun, stylish hotel where all rooms have a maritime theme; think porthole windows overlooking the Hudson River, teak panelling

SoHo House

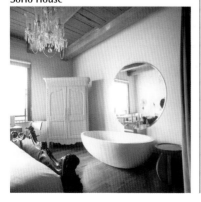

and blue and white nautical stripes. The 24-hour room service can be enjoyed with the latest on-demand movies plus computer games. There's a sizeable roof terrace and it's in a great location for exploring Chelsea and the trendy Meatpacking District.

MIDTOWN

THE LIBRARY $$$$-$$$$$
✉ 299 Madison Avenue at 41st Street
☎ 212-983 4500
   Fax 212-499 9099
🖰 www.libraryhotel.com
🚗 Subway 4, 5, 6, 7, S to 41st Street/Grand Central

A fabulous new hotel that, you've guessed it, has the theme of a city library. It has the feel of a cosy gentlemen's club when you first walk in, all mahogany panelling, fancy artwork and bookcases. The rooms are a revelation. Each of the 10 floors is dedicated to a category that you'd find in a real library, such as Philosophy or Art & Literature, and there are books and artworks in rooms to match the theme of each level. Original and luxurious, but pricey.

MIDTOWN WEST

DREAM $$-$$$
✉ 210 West 55th Street
☎ 212-247 2000
   Fax 212-974 0595
🖰 www.dreamny.com
🚗 Subway N, R to 5th Avenue

If you're seeking peace, tranquillity and possibly even a spiritual experience, then this new hotel promises to deliver. It's the unique

TOP FIVE CELEBRITY HOTELS

Check out where the stars check in...

60 Thompson: Jessica Simpson, Christina Aguilera, Matt Damon (page 230)

Flatotel: Coldplay, Jane's Addiction, Joan Collins, David Navarro, Stephen Gately (page 225)

Soho Grand: Heidi Klum, Kevin Spacey, Gwyneth Paltrow, Uma Thurman (page 226)

W New York: Cindy Crawford, Leonardo DiCaprio, Gwyneth Paltrow (see Brit Tip above)

Waldorf Astoria: Winona Ryder, Richard Gere, Ewan McGregor, Kid Rock, Alicia Keys, Paris and Nicki Hilton (page 222)

WHERE TO STAY

BOOKING IT YOURSELF

Of course, you can use a travel agent to make room reservations for you, but you can also do it yourself through companies that specialise in offering excellent rates at off-peak and low-peak times or can even just guarantee finding you a room during busy periods. These include:

Hotel America Ltd: Tel 08700 464010, www.hotelanywhere.co.uk/america. A British company providing hotel discounts anywhere in the world.

Hotel Conxions: Tel 212-840 8686, fax 212-221 8686, www.hotelconxions.com. You can find out about availability and price and book a room on their website.

Quikbook: Tel 212-779 7666, fax 212-779 6120, www.quikbook.com. A service providing discounts on hotels all over America. They promise there are no hidden cancellation or change penalties, and pre-payment is not required.

A great internet discount reservation service can be found at www.hotres.com and www.hoteldiscount.com, or you can look for cheaper rates through the hotel discount service on www.usacitylink.com.

When discussing room rates with any of these organisations, always check that the prices you are quoted include the New York City hotel tax of 13.25 per cent and the $2 per night occupancy tax or 4 per cent for a one-bedroom suite.

vision of hotelier Vikram Chatwal and is all about promoting spiritual well-being, from the mind-enhancing lobby with its Subconscious Lounge to the Ayurvedic healing centre created by spiritualist Deepak Chopra. But you needn't forego the hi tech; its modern, eclectic-style rooms have 37-inch plasma TVs and iPod digital audio players.

THE NIGHT HOTEL $$$–$$$$$
- ✉ 132 West 45th Street between 6th and 7th Avenues
- ☎ 212-835-9600
  Fax 212-835 9610
- 🖱 www.nighthotelny.com

This stylish, petite 72-room hotel is Vikram Chatwal's latest offering, inspired by the

Kitano

pulse and passion of the city. It offers a sense of seclusion in what feels like a private home.

THEATER DISTRICT

TIME $$–$$$
- ✉ 224 West 49th Street between Broadway and 8th Avenue
- ☎ 212-246 5252
  Fax 212-245 2305
- 🖱 www.thetimeny.com
- 🚇 Subway C, E, 1, 9 to 50th Street

Themed around Alexander Theroux's book *The Primary Colours* (not Times Square as you might think), this brightly coloured bolthole is the perfect place if you want to stay in a touristy area in style. Primary colours are used throughout, of course: red rooms are for lovers, blue if you're feeling sad and yellow if you're a bit lacklustre. The colours continue through to the finishing touches, such as bowls of jellybeans in matching shades. There's a buzzing bar downstairs, where guests have included the likes of Liza Minnelli.

◀🇬🇧 BRITTIP

If you're driving in New York there aren't many hotels with car parks. Our tip is the Ramada Inn Eastside (212-545 1800, www.the.ramada.com), which is a clean, pleasant hotel on 30th Street at Lexington Avenue where rates start from $110.

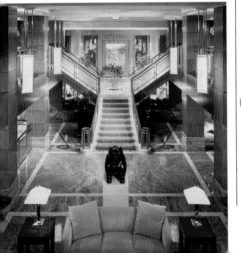

UPMARKET

If you want your hotel to be smart and sophisticated rather than ultra-trendy or traditional, these are for you.

CENTRAL PARK

TRUMP INTERNATIONAL HOTEL & TOWER $$$$–$$$$$

- ✉ 1 Central Park West between 60th and 61st Streets
- ☎ 212-299 1000
  Fax 212-299 1150
- ⌂ www.trumpintl.com
- 🚇 Subway N, R to 5th Avenue

Billionaire Donald Trump's foray into hotels is a shimmering tower that houses 167 rooms and suites, as well as various shops and restaurants. The best thing about the hotel is the views of Central Park and 5th Avenue through floor-to-ceiling windows – simply spectacular. The spa is a must-visit for those in need of pampering. The staff are charming and helpful, from booking theatre tickets to handing you an umbrella if it's raining.

MIDTOWN

LE PARKER MERIDIEN $$$$–$$$$$

- ✉ 118 West 57th Street between 6th and 7th Avenues
- ☎ 212-245 5000
  Fax 212-307 1776
- ⌂ www.parkermeridien.com
- 🚇 Subway B, D, E to 7th Avenue

A classic New York hotel in the design sense, yet with a traditional French feel, this hotel is not only in an excellent location just minutes from Central Park and Carnegie Hall, but also offers great service and amenities. The recently refurbished rooms have a Zen-like calmness, thanks to the minimalist and cherrywood decor. Great touches include a revolving unit that allows you to watch the massive TV screen either in the sitting area or in the bedroom. It also has a useful desk unit, CD and DVD players.

◀▮▶ BRITTIP

Make sure you look upwards when you enter the lifts of Le Parker Meridien – all three have a TV screen offering classic film clips of *Abbott and Costello* or *Tom and Jerry*.

Even if you don't plan to use the swimming pool, you must visit its penthouse

Trump International Hotel & Tower

location to see the fab views of Central Park. Down in the basement is the massive Gravity gymnasium, which covers everything from Cybex training to aerobics, sauna, massage rooms, spa services and squash courts.

Other facilities include the much-raved-about Norma's restaurant in the lobby, which serves creative breakfast dishes throughout the day (page 163). Its other restaurant is Seppi's (page 164).

THE PENINSULA $$$$$

- ✉ 700 5th Avenue at 55th Street
- ☎ 212-956 2888
  Fax 212-903 3949
- ⌂ www.newyork.peninsula.com
- 🚇 Subway F to 53rd Street; 6 to 51st Street

A beautiful hotel that has undergone a massive $45-million renovation in the public areas, restaurants and 239 guestrooms and suites. These are of classic contemporary style with touches of art nouveau, and oversized marble bathrooms where you can watch TV from the bath. The state-of-the-art technology allows you to control your environment with the touch of a button, and a water bar is on hand for hangover recovery.

MIDTOWN EAST

KITANO HOTEL $$$$–$$$$$

- ✉ 66 Park Avenue at East 38th Street
- ☎ 212-885 7000
  Fax 212-447 5918
- ⌂ www.kitano.com
- 🚇 Subway S, 4, 5, 6, 7 to Grand Central/42nd Street

A first-class, Japanese-run hotel with top-notch service and a deliciously decadent, deep-soaking tub in each room. In the Murray Hill area, it has Manhattan's only authentic Japanese tatami suite.

Rick's Café at the Casablanca

MIDTOWN WEST

HILTON NEW YORK $$$$$
✉ 1335 6th Avenue at 53rd Street
☎ 212-586 7000
🖰 www.hilton.com
🚗 Subway B, D, F, Q to 47th–50th Streets/
   Rockefeller Center
After a recent $100-million renovation, the
city's largest hotel now has a beautiful new
façade and entrance lobby, plus two new
restaurants and lounges.

JUMEIRAH ESSEX HOUSE
$$$$–$$$$$
✉ 160 Central Parade at 7th Avenue
☎ 212-247 0300
🖰 www.jumeirah.com
🚗 Subway 1, A, B, C, D at 59th Street/
   Columbus Circle
An Art Deco hotel formerly known as the
Westin Essex House & St Regis Club is now a
plush hotel loved by well-heeled travellers.
As well as the usual upmarket hotel touches,
such as heated towel rails and cosy white
fluffy robes, there are some cool extras, such
as tub phones in the bathroom and an on-
site health spa. The rooms are also
fabulously quiet, so make a welcome retreat
from the noisy city.

SOFITEL $$$$
✉ 45 West 44th Street at 5th Avenue
☎ 212-354 8844
🖰 www.sofitel.com
🚗 Subway 7 to 5th Avenue/Bryant Park
French-run outfit that soars 29 storeys in a
curved limestone tower. The 398 rooms are
tightly packed and on the small side, but the
decor is tasteful. The top floors, added in
2000, have private balconies and wonderful
views.

MEDIUM-PRICED GEMS

FINANCIAL DISTRICT

MILLENIUM HILTON $$–$$$$$
✉ 55 Church Street between Fulton and
   Dey Streets
☎ 212-693 2001
   Fax 212-571 2316
🖰 www.newyorkmillenium.hilton.com
A black skyscraper geared to business, with a
fitness centre and pool. For a stunning view
of the harbour, ask for a room on one of the
higher floors.

◀🇬🇧 BRITTIP
Hotels in the Financial District
can be especially good value at
weekends when many business
people leave the city.

WALL STREET INN $$$
✉ 9 South William Street opposite 85
   Broad Street
☎ 212-747 1500
   Fax 212-747 1900
🖰 www.thewallstreetinn.com
🚗 Subway 2, 3 to Wall Street; J, M, Z to
   Broad Street
An elegant boutique hotel in an old office
building in the heart of the financial and
historic district. Original features include
mahogany panels on the walls and granite
floors.

◀🇬🇧 BRITTIP
Confusingly, American hotel lifts
use the letter 'L' or the number
'1' to indicate the ground floor. The
L stands for lobby, by the way.

GRAMERCY PARK

THE MARCEL HOTEL $$–$$$
✉ 201 East 24th Street at 3rd Avenue
☎ 212-696 3800
🖰 www.nychotels.com
🚗 Subway 6 to 23rd Street
Catering to a clientele of international
crowds from the arts, film and fashion
worlds, you'd expect this hotel to be pricier
than it is. You can get a standard room from
around $160 upwards, which are average
size for New York and pleasantly decorated.
Its great location for Midtown and
Downtown makes it a winner.

WHERE TO STAY

MIDTOWN

CASABLANCA $$$–$$$$
- ✉ 147 West 43rd Street off Times Square
- ☎ 212-869 1212,
  Fax 212-391 7585
- 🖰 www.casablancahotel.com
- 🚇 Subway 1, 2, 3, 7, 9, N, R, S to Times Square/42nd Street

Calling itself 'an oasis in the heart of Times Square', its elegant Moroccan theme includes ceiling fans, palm trees and mosaic tiles. Small, with just 48 newly renovated luxury rooms, the service is good and it also offers complimentary use of the New York Sports Club, with pool, just steps away.

MANSFIELD $$$–$$$$$
- ✉ 12 West 44th Street between 5th and 6th Avenues
- ☎ 212-944 6050
  Fax 212-764 4477
- 🖰 www.mansfieldhotel.com
- 🚇 Subway B, D, F, Q to 47th–50th Street/ Rockefeller Centre

A beautiful lobby with vaulted ceiling and white marble marks the Mansfield out as an elegant hotel for those also wanting the charm of a boutique establishment. The rooms have plush robes and Aveda toiletries and its M Bar, with its domed skylight and mahogany bookshelves, has been described by *Zagat*'s as 'an off the beaten path, classy, romantic sweet spot'.

ALL WIRED UP!
America has different plugs and works on 115 volts, not 240, so you'll need a travel appliance that works on both voltages, or bring an adaptor with you.

SHOREHAM $$$–$$$$$
- ✉ 33 West 55th Street at 5th Avenue
- ☎ 212-247 6700
  Fax 212-765 9741
- 🖰 www.shorehamhotel.com
- 🚇 Subway F to 5th Avenue

This hotel has won awards for its ultra-modern decor following its renovation. It now has a new bar, restaurant, fitness centre and some more good-sized rooms.

WARWICK $$$–$$$$
- ✉ 65 West 54th Street at 6th Avenue
- ☎ 212-247 2700
  Fax 212-247 2725
- 🖰 warwickhotelny.com
- 🚇 Subway B, D, F, Q to 47th–50th Streets/ Rockefeller Center

A medium-sized hotel built in 1927 with good-quality rooms and excellent service in an excellent location. In its heyday many a Hollywood celeb stayed here, including Cary Grant. Randolph's Bar remains a favoured meeting place and a great spot for lunch or a light dinner in its recently opened restaurant, Murals on 54, which offers innovative Continental cuisine.

The Mansfield

The Roosevelt

MIDTOWN EAST

70 PARK AVENUE $$$–$$$$
- ✉ 70 Park Avenue at 38th Street
- ☎ 212-973 2400
   Fax 212-973 2497
- ⌂ www.70parkave.com
- 🚇 Subway 4, 5, 6 to 42nd Street

A beautiful, four-star boutique hotel with a home-from-home atmosphere whose motto is 'Live Life Well'. It has a bar, restaurant and excellent room facilities as well as services such as the Mind, Body & Spa programme with in-room yoga and a nightly complimentary living room reception.

FITZPATRICK $$$–$$$$
- ✉ 687 Lexington Avenue between East 56th and East 57th Streets
- ☎ 212-355 0100
   Fax 212-355 1371
- ⌂ www.fitzpatrickhotels.com/manhattan
- 🚇 Subway 4, 5, 6 to 59th Street

The rooms are equipped with everything from trouser presses to towelling robes, useful after indulging in the whirlpool bath you'll find in many of the rooms.

FITZPATRICK GRAND CENTRAL $$$
- ✉ 141 East 44th Street between Lexington and 3rd Avenues
- ☎ 212-351 6800
   Fax 212-818 1747
- ⌂ www.fitzpatrickhotels.com/grandcentral
- 🚇 Subway S, 4, 5, 6, 7 to Grand Central/ 42nd Street

The Fitzpatrick Family Group of hotels continues its Irish theme at this hotel just across from Grand Central Station. It includes an Irish pub and you can order a traditional Irish breakfast here.

ROOSEVELT $$–$$$$
- ✉ East 45th Street at Madison Avenue
- ☎ 212-661 9600
   Fax 212-885 6161
- ⌂ www.theroosevelthotel.com
- 🚇 Subway S, 4, 5, 6, 7 to Grand Central/42nd Street

Built in 1924, this classy hotel completed a $70-million renovation in 1998 when the lobby was restored to its original grandeur with crystal chandeliers hanging from the ceiling, columns and lots of marble.

MIDTOWN WEST

HUDSON $$–$$$$$
- ✉ 356 West 58th Street between 8th and 9th Avenues
- ☎ 212-554 6000
   Fax 212-554 6001
- ⌂ www.hudsonhotel.com
- 🚇 Subway A, B, C, D, 1, 9 to 59th Street/ Columbus Circle

Built on the site of the former *Sesame Street* studios, this Ian Schrager and Philippe Starck collaboration is heaving with chic guests. It's loud and proud, so don't check in if you are looking for peace and quiet in the city. From the neon entrance escalator to the glowing glass floor of the Hudson Bar, you'll be in the limelight. The rooms are stylish but very small. In a great location for Central Park, the Lincoln Center and Theater District, but definitely on the west side of town so keep this in mind when considering your sightseeing plans.

MODERNE $$$–$$$$
- ✉ 243 West 55th Street between Broadway and 8th Avenue
- ☎ 212-397 6767
   Fax 212-397 8787
- 🚇 Subway C, E, 1, 9 to 50th Street

Opened in 1998, this bijou hotel was converted from a five-storey dance studio. It's in a good location close to Carnegie Hall, though it has had mixed reviews.

WELLINGTON $$$–$$$$
- ✉ 871 7th Avenue at 55th Street
- ☎ 212-247 3900
   Fax 212-581 1350
- ⌂ www.wellingtonhotel.com
- 🚇 Subway N, R to 57th Street

Recent renovations, which include a swish new marquee, have moved the Wellington from bargain stay category. The rooms are comfortably furnished, with a mix of king, twin and double rooms plus a scattering of

WHERE TO STAY

THE PERFECT APPLE

A major hotel chain, Apple Core, runs five hotels in excellent Midtown locations with extremely reasonable rates of $89–199 a night. They are: **Red Roof Inn Manhattan** on 32nd Street, west of 5th Avenue; the smoke-free **Comfort Inn Midtown** on 46th Street west of 6th Avenue; **Super 8 Hotel Times Square** on 46th Street between 5th and 6th Avenues near the Rockefeller Center (page 63); **La Quinta Manhattan** on 32nd Street between Broadway and 5th Avenue; and **Ramada Inn Eastside** at 30th Street and Lexington Avenue.

All the hotels offer complimentary Continental breakfast, well-equipped fitness centres and business centres. In-room facilities include cable television and pay-per-view movies, free wireless internet, telephones with data port and voicemail, coffee makers, irons and ironing boards. The modern bathrooms all come with marble units and hairdryers.

Occupancy rates are above 90 per cent – so book early through Apple Core's central reservations: tel 212-790 2710, www.applecorehotels.com.

one-bedroom suites. All have high-speed wireless internet access. The best thing about this hotel is still its location – deep in the heart of Midtown within striking distance of Carnegie Hall, 5th Avenue, the Rockefeller Center and Times Square. If you can get a corner room with a view of 7th Avenue, you'll understand the big deal about the bright lights associated with the Theater District – they're absolutely stunning viewed from this position.

THEATER DISTRICT

NEW YORK MARRIOTT MARQUIS $$–$$$$

✉ 1535 Broadway at 45th Street
☎ 212-398 1900
    Fax 212-704 8930
🚇 Subway N, R, S, 1, 2, 3, 7, 9 to Times Square/42nd Street

In 1998 this hotel completed a $25-million upgrade of all its rooms, so each one now includes console desks, ergonomic chairs, two phone lines and voicemail. A sushi bar, Katen, is in the atrium lobby and it's also home of The View, New York's only revolving restaurant.

ON THE AVE $$–$$$$

✉ 2178 77th Street at Broadway
☎ 212-362 1100
    Fax 212-787 9521
🖰 www.ontheave-nyc.com
🚇 Subway 1, 9 to 79th Avenue

This hotel is a breath of fresh air to the rather jaded Upper West Side hotel scene. It has 16 floors, 266 rooms of gorgeous minimalism, lots of white, floating beds that appear to hover and industrial sinks with walk-in showers big enough for two. Its location, close to Central Park, is superb. It's also very pet-friendly, so the ideal place to

bring your pooch. You can have food treats, water/food bowl, a list of local dog runs and parks and a list of pet stores in the area for an extra $25.

PARAMOUNT $$–$$$$$

✉ 235 West 46th Street between Broadway and 8th Avenue
☎ 212-764 5500
    Fax 212-354 5237
🖰 www.paramountnewyork.solmelia.com
🚇 Subway C, E, 1, 9 to 50th Street

A hip hotel with a glorious sweeping staircase in the lobby. The 610 rooms are small but well-equipped. The mezzanine restaurant is good for people-watching.

PREMIER $$$–$$$$

✉ 133 West 44th Street between 6th Avenue and Broadway
☎ 212-768 4400
    Fax 212-768 0847
🖰 www.milleniumhotels.com
🚇 Subway N, R, S, 1, 2, 3, 7, 9 to Times Square/42nd Street

The Millennium Broadway in Times Square built this 22-storey tower in 1999 to increase its total room count to 752. The

Paramount Hotel

New York Marriott Marquis

WHERE TO STAY

Premier has its own private entrance on 44th Street and elegant, modern guest rooms with large bathrooms, two phone lines, voicemail and a separate modem and fax machine.

WESTIN NEW YORK AT TIMES SQUARE $$$$

- ✉ 270 West 43rd Street at 8th Avenue
- ☎ 212-201 2700
  Fax 212-201 2701
- 🖰 www.westinny.com
- 🚇 Subway A, C, E, N, R, S, 1, 2, 3, 7, 9 to 42nd Street/Times Square

A fab hotel for all types. Sophisticated sleek rooms with 'heavenly beds and baths'. It is particularly family-friendly; families will love the Kids Club, which gives children a sports bottle, toys, colouring books and even a bedtime story! Toddlers get a Molton Brown designer amenities box with baby wash, nappy hamper, potty seat and step stool.

🏴 BRITTIP

If you've fallen in love with the Big Apple and keep returning, Hilton Grand Vacations, part of the Hilton Group (www.hilton.com), is developing a 28-storey timeshare property on West 57th Street. So you get the luxury of a hotel when you visit but make money by letting it out during the rest of the year.

UPPER EAST SIDE

FRANKLIN $$$

- ✉ 164 East 87th Street between 3rd and Lexington Avenues
- ☎ 212-369 1000
  Fax 212-369 8000
- 🖰 www.franklinhotel.com
- 🚇 Subway 4, 5, 6 to 86th Street

Known for its good service, this pleasant Art Deco boutique hotel has lovely touches in its rooms that include canopies over the beds, fresh flowers and cedar closets.

EXCELLENT VALUE

BROOKLYN

NEW YORK MARRIOTT AT THE BROOKLYN BRIDGE $$-$$$

- ✉ 333 Adams Street at Tillary Street
- ☎ 718-246 7000
  Fax 718-246 0563
- 🖰 www.brooklynmarriott.com
- 🚇 Subway A, C, F to Jay Street/Borough Hall; N, R to Court Street; 2, 3, 4, 5 to Borough Hall just 5 minutes' walk away

This is the only full-service hotel in Brooklyn and 282 more rooms were added in late 2006. Although over the water from Manhattan, you get excellent facilities at very good prices.

Chelsea Hotel

CHELSEA

CHELSEA HOTEL $$
✉ 222 West 23rd Street between 7th and 8th Avenues
☎ 212-243 3700
🖱 www.chelseahotel.com
🚇 Subway A, C, E, 1, 2, 3, 9 to 23rd Street
A true icon of New York City, this hotel has been associated with artistic and literary types since it opened in 1912. Residents have included Dylan Thomas, Jack Kerouac, Mark Twain and Thomas Wolfe and it still pulls in the celebs. On the darker side, Sex Pistols singer Sid Vicious is alleged to have killed his girlfriend Nancy Spungen here. Besides that, Andy Warhol filmed *Chelsea Girls*, the stairwell has starred in Bon Jovi and Mariah Carey videos, and room 822 was used to shoot Madonna's book *Sex*.

Downstairs in the basement is Serena's, a Moroccan den lounge bar that has been attracting a new round of celebs, such as Leonardo DiCaprio and Brazilian supermodel Giselle, and is popular with the trendy Brit-pack crowd.

CHINATOWN/ LOWER EAST SIDE

HOLIDAY INN DOWNTOWN $$
✉ 138 Lafayette Street at Canal Street
☎ 212-966 8898
   Fax 212-966 3933
🚇 Subway N, R to Canal Street
Well-equipped, spotless rooms available at excellent prices.

FINANCIAL DISTRICT

HOLIDAY INN WALL STREET
$$–$$$$
✉ 15 Gold Street at Platt Street
☎ 212-232 7700
   Fax 212-425 0330
🖱 www.holidayinnwsd.com
🚇 Subway J, M, Z, 2, 3, 4, 5 to Fulton Street
Opened in 1999, billing itself as the most high-tech hotel in New York, complete with high-speed internet connectivity.

FLATIRON DISTRICT

CARLTON $$–$$$
✉ 22 East 29th Street between 5th and Madison Avenues
☎ 212-532 4100
🖱 www.carltonhotelny.com
🚇 Subway 4, 5, 6 to 28th Street
A tourist-class hotel with a view of the Empire State Building and in an excellent location for 5th Avenue and Garment District shopping. Restaurant, lounge and business services.

GIRAFFE $$–$$$
✉ 365 Park Avenue South between 26th and 27th Streets
☎ 212-685 7700
   Fax 212-685 7771
🖱 www.hotelgiraffe.com
🚇 Subway 6 to 23rd Street
Small boutique hotel, in lavish colours and textures. Each floor has seven rooms, many with their own balconies adorned with fresh flowers. There's also an on-premises restaurant and access to a nearby health club for guests.

Times Square

WHERE TO STAY

WHERE TO STAY

TOP FIVE HOTEL POOLS WITH VIEWS

If you like a swim while you're away, check into one of these establishments whose penthouse pools offer some of the best views in Manhattan.

Le Parker Meridien: The penthouse pool provides a perfect retreat for relaxation and a sun deck offers scenic views of Central Park. It's available to hotel guests for free, or you can pay $50 for a day-pass to use it as well as the gym (page 233).

Mandarin Oriental: Floor-to-ceiling windows light up an inviting 23m (75ft) indoor lap pool on the 35th floor, with amazing views of the New York skyline (page 227).

Hotel Gansevoort: This trendy hotel has a suitably cool pool. Take the elevator straight to the top floor and you'll be rewarded with a 14m (45ft) heated outdoor pool that also has underwater music. There are plenty of people to watch while you have your dip page 229).

Crowne Plaza Times Square Manhattan: (1605 Broadway, between 48th and 49th Streets, tel 212-9777 4000, www.manhattan.crowneplaza.com). The 15th floor of this plush hotel houses a 15m (50ft) indoor pool, which costs $10 for hotel guests or $25 for non-residents. It has a glass roof through which you can see the skyscrapers.

Millennium UN Plaza Hotel New York: (1 United Nations Plaza, 44th Street and 1st Avenue. Tel 212-758 1234, www.millenniumhotels.com). Take a trip up to the 27th floor and you'll be wowed by the wonderful panoramic views through the floor-to-ceiling windows of this 13m (44ft) city oasis.

GREENWICH VILLAGE

WASHINGTON SQUARE HOTEL $$

✉ 103 Waverly Place between 5th and 6th Avenues
☎ 212-777 9515
Fax 212-979 8373
🖰 www.wshotel.com
🚇 Subway A, B, C, D, E, F, Q to West 4th Street/Washington Square

A family-run hotel with a bohemian air that overlooks Washington Square. The rooms are small but the rates very reasonable and include breakfast. Bob Dylan was known to stay here in the 1960s.

MIDTOWN

ALGONQUIN $$–$$$

✉ 59 West 44th Street between 5th and 6th Avenues
☎ 212-840 6800
Fax 212-944 1618
🖰 www.algonquinhotel.com
🚇 Subway B, D, F, Q to 47th–50th Streets/Rockefeller Center

Famous for the literary meetings held here by Dorothy Parker and her cohorts, the Algonquin underwent a $45 million refurbishment in 2004 and is listed in the *Michelin Guide 2006* as one of New York's top hotels.

METRO $$–$$$

✉ 45 West 35th Street between 5th and 6th Avenues
☎ 212-947 2500
Fax 212-279 1310
🖰 www.hotelmetrony.com
🚇 Subway B, D, F, N, Q, R to 34th Street

Well located near the Empire State Building, which can be seen from its rooftop garden terrace, this hotel is great value for money, offering plenty of Art Deco style.

Metro

SUPER 8 $$

- ✉ 59 West 46th Street between 5th and 6th Avenues
- ☎ 212-719 2300
  Fax 212-790 2760
- 🖰 www.applecorehotels.com
- 🚇 Subway B, D, F, Q to 47th–50th Streets/ Rockefeller Center

A well-priced hotel with excellent amenities that include a fitness centre, coffee makers and irons in the rooms, free local phone calls, wireless internet and Continental breakfast. (See The Perfect Apple, page 237.)

MIDTOWN EAST

CLARION HOTEL 5TH AVENUE
$$-$$$

- ✉ 3 East 40th Street just off 5th Avenue
- ☎ 212-532 4860
  Fax 212-545 9727
- 🖰 www.choicehotels.com
- 🚇 Subway 7 to 5th Avenue; S, 4, 5, 6, 7 to Grand Central/42nd Street

In an excellent location near Grand Central Station. The rooms have all the latest business equipment.

MIDTOWN WEST

AMERITANIA $$

- ✉ 230 Broadway at West 54th Street
- ☎ 212-247 5000
  Fax 212-247 3316
- 🖰 www.nychotels.com/ameritania.html
- 🚇 Subway 1, 9 to 50th Street; B, D east to 7th Avenue

Located just outside the Theater District and near Restaurant Row. Well-appointed with modern, comfortable rooms.

THEATER DISTRICT

COURTYARD BY MARRIOTT TIMES SQUARE SOUTH $$-$$$

- ✉ 114 West 40th Street between 6th Avenue and Broadway
- ☎ 212-391 0088
  Fax 212-391 6023
- 🖰 www.courtyardtimessquare.com
- 🚇 Subway B, D, F, Q to 42nd Street

This hotel, which opened in 1998, is part of the massive redevelopment of Times Square. The spacious rooms all have a sitting area, large work desk, two phones and in-room coffee facilities.

HOLIDAY INN MARTINIQUE ON BROADWAY $$-$$$$$

- ✉ 49 West 32nd Street at Broadway
- ☎ 212-736 3800
  Fax 212-277 2703
- 🖰 www.holidayinnbroadway.com
- 🚇 Subway B, D, F, N, Q, R to 34th Street

Opened in 1998 on the site of the former Hotel Martinique, this hotel is decorated in a French Renaissance style.

MILFORD PLAZA $$-$$$

- ✉ 270 West 45th Street at 8th Avenue.
- ☎ 212-869 3600
- 🖰 www.milfordplaza.com
- 🚇 Subway A, C, E to 42nd Street

Although the rates, which were always rock bottom, have risen slightly, it's still a total bargain of a place, with rooms from $110 per night. You'll have to put up with decor that hasn't changed much since the 1980s and not much space in the 1,300 rooms, but there's also a concierge and fitness centre and you're slap bang in the middle of the action.

TRIBECA

COSMOPOLITAN HOTEL $$-$$$

- ✉ 95 West Broadway at Chambers Street
- ☎ 212-566 1900
- 🖰 www.cosmohotel.com
- 🚇 Subway 1, 2, 3 to Chambers Street

Finding a pleasant, comfortable Downtown hotel that's not going to cost you hundreds of dollars a night can be tricky. That's where this hotel steps in. It's not exactly the Tribeca Grand, but most of the 20 and 30-somethings who stay here are happy with the neutral decor and grateful for added extras like hairdryers and satellite TV.

Martinique on Broadway

UPPER EAST SIDE

BENTLEY $$–$$$
✉ 500 East 62nd Street at York Avenue
☎ 212-644 6000
   Fax 212-207 4800
🖱 www.nychotels.com
🚇 Subway 4, 5, 6, N, R to Lexington Avenue/59th Street

A recently renovated hotel within walking distance of Bloomingdale's. Rates include breakfast.

UPPER WEST SIDE

DAYS HOTEL BROADWAY $$–$$$
✉ 215 West 94th Street at Broadway
☎ 212-866 6400
🖱 www.dayshotelnyc.com
🚇 Subway 4, 5, 6, N, R to Lexington Avenue/59th Street

BRITTIP
If you're travelling in a group of ten or more, the Days Hotel Broadway offers discounts on rooms.

A 349-room hotel situated in a far from happening part of town, but it's a clean and inexpensive place to lay your head for the night.

HOTEL BEACON $$
✉ 2130 Broadway at 75th Street
☎ 212-787 1100
   Fax 212-724 0839
🖱 www.beaconhotel.com
🚇 Subway 1, 2, 3, 9 to 72nd Street

Good-sized rooms with kitchenettes, plus the 25-storey hotel is well located for the American Museum of Natural History, the Lincoln Center and Central Park.

Hotel Beacon

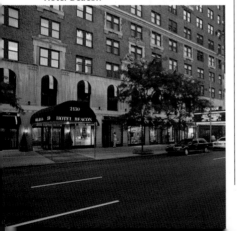

TOTAL BARGAINS

BROOKLYN

GLENWOOD HOSTEL $
✉ 339 Broadway between Rodney and Keap Streets
☎ 718-387 7858
🖱 www.glenwoodhotelny.com
🚇 Subway J, M, Z to Marcy Avenue

The choice of backpackers on a tight budget. The rooms are tiny, there's space for a bed and little else, and the walls are paper thin so you can hear every move your neighbour makes. On the plus side the staff are friendly and rates are from $30 for a single. Rentals are available on a nightly, weekly or monthly basis.

FLATIRON DISTRICT

GERSHWIN $–$$
✉ 7 East 27th Street between 5th and Madison Avenues
☎ 212-545 8000
   Fax 212-684 5546
🖱 www.gershwinhotel.com
🚇 Subway 6 to 28th Street

A character-crammed budget boutique with some of the best rates in the city. You can opt for plain doubles or dormitory-style rooms with 10 beds and the hotel has theatre, stand-up comedy, poetry and live music on site.

GRAMERCY PARK HOTEL 17 $–$$
✉ 45 225 East 17th Street at Union Square
☎ 212-475 2845
   Fax 212-677 8178
🖱 www.hotel17ny.com
🚇 Subway 6, A, C, E to 14th Street

An undiscovered chic hideaway well off the tourist radar. It's where Woody Allen filmed *Manhattan Murder Mystery* and Madonna used to stay and did many photo shoots.

HERALD SQUARE HOTEL $$
✉ 19 West 31st Street between 5th Avenue and Broadway
☎ 212-279 4017
   Fax 212-643 9208
🖱 www.heraldsquarehotel.com
🚇 Subway N, R to 28th Street

Once the headquarters of *Life* magazine, now a small, extremely well-priced hotel near the Empire State Building and Macy's.

FOR SOMETHING DIFFERENT...

Abode Ltd: PO Box 20022, New York, NY 10021. Tel 212-472 2000, www.abodenyc.com. **$–$$$**
Unhosted, good-quality studios and apartments all over the city, but you have to book for a minimum of four days.

Bed and Breakfast (and Books): 35 West 92nd Street, Apt. 2C, New York, NY 10025. Tel 212-865 8740. Fax 212-865 8740. **$–$$**
Hosted and unhosted apartments – and you may end up being the guest of a writer.

Bed and Breakfast in Manhattan: PO Box 533, New York, NY 10150. Tel 212-472 2528, fax 212-988 9818. **$–$$$**
From comfortable to smart and both hosted and unhosted.

Inn New York City: 266 West 71st Street between Broadway and West End Avenue. Tel 212-580 1900, Fax 212-580 4437, www.innnewyorkcity.com. **$$$–$$$$**
This romantic boutique retreat has just four suites, each with a kitchen, and is fantastically placed for shopping, theatres and restaurants.

Jazz on the Park Hostel: 36 West 106th Street at Central Park West. Tel 212-932 1600, www.jazzonthepark.com. **$**
Clean, comfortable rooms for the budget traveller. Double and 'dormitory' rooms, laundry room, rooftop terrace and garden. Price includes breakfast. Sister hostels include **Jazz on the Town** (307 East 14th Street in the midst of the bars, restaurants and clubs of East Village, tel 212-228 2780) and a new hostel, **Jazz on Harlem** (104 West 128th Street, tel 212-222 5773).

THIRTY THIRTY
NEW YORK CITY $–$$

- ✉ 30 East 30th Street between Park and Madison Avenues
- ☎ 212-689 1900
  Fax 212-689 0023
- 🖰 www.thirtythirty-nyc.com
- 🚇 Subway 6 to 29th Street

Formerly the Martha Washington Hotel, this was turned into a modern, sophisticated but affordable boutique hotel in 1999.

Thirty Thirty

GREENWICH VILLAGE

LARCHMONT $–$$

- ✉ 27 West 11th Street between 5th and 6th Avenues
- ☎ 212-989 9333
  Fax 212-989 9496
- 🖰 www.larchmonthotel.com
- 🚇 Subway F to 14th Street

Clean, well-sought-after Village boutique hotel. No private baths in any rooms.

LOWER EAST SIDE

HOWARD JOHNSON
EXPRESS INN $–$$

- ✉ 135 Houston Street between Forsyth and Eldridge Streets
- ☎ 212-358 8844
  Fax 212-473 3500
- 🖰 www.hojo.com

The Lower East Side can now celebrate the arrival of its first hotel – modern, without frills but incredibly well-priced. Right next door is the renovated landmark Sunshine Cinema, which was once a showplace for Yiddish vaudeville and films and is now a multiplex for art films.

WHERE TO STAY

OFF SOHO SUITES $-$$

✉ 11 Rivington Street between Chrystie
   Street and The Bowery
☎ 212-979 9808
   Fax 212-979 9801
🖰 www.offsoho.com
🚗 Subway F to Delancey Street

Good-sized, clean suites with fully equipped
kitchens. Well-positioned.

MADISON SQUARE GARDEN

CHELSEA STAR HOTEL $

✉ 300 West 30th Street at 8th Avenue
☎ 212-244 7827
   Fax 212-279 9018
🖰 www.starhotelny.com
🚗 Subway 1, 2, 3, 9 to 28th Street

Very low budget but bright and comfy and
in a great location. Corridors are bright
yellow with starbursts, the carpet is red and
there are dormitories or private rooms, some
of which can sleep up to four.

MURRAY HILL

HOTEL 31 $-$$$

✉ 120 East 31st Street at Lexington
   Avenue
☎ 212-685 3060
🖰 www.hotel31.com
🚗 Subway 6 to 33rd Street

Seventy-two newly renovated rooms, some
shared, some private, packed full of young
European tourists. Standard US essentials
such as air con and cable TV and even a 24-
concierge service.

MIDTOWN EAST

PICKWICK ARMS HOTEL $

✉ 230 East 51st Street between 2nd and
   3rd Avenues
☎ 212-355 0300
   Fax 212-755 5029
🖰 www.pickwickarms.com
🚗 Subway 6 to 51st Street

A cheap place to stay in a pricey
neighbourhood. The rooms are tiny but the
hotel does have a roof garden and cocktail
lounge.

Rockefeller Center

VANDERBILT YMCA $-$$

✉ 224 East 47th Street at 2nd Avenue
☎ 212-756 9600
🖰 www.ymcanyc.org
🚗 Subway 6 to 51st Street

One of the oldest buildings in Manhattan,
though not the plushest, is named after its
benefactor Cornelius Vanderbilt. The rooms
are tiny but will only set you back around
$83 for a single; if you want a double with a
private bathroom it rises to $110 per night.
It's part of a community centre, so you get
access to two swimming pools and a gym.

MIDTOWN WEST

PORTLAND SQUARE HOTEL $

✉ 132 West 47th Street between 6th and
   7th Avenues
☎ 212-382 0600
   Fax 212-382 0684
🖰 www.portlandsquarehotel.com
🚗 Subway B, D, F, Q to 47th–50th Streets/
   Rockefeller Center

This hotel is under new management and
they're making positive additions such as
queen-sized beds and free WiFi. The rooms
are small but the hotel is very near the
Theater District, so it's convenient if that
features on your itinerary.

FURTHER AFIELD

If you're planning on going on a huge
shopping spree at the 200-plus discount
stores at Woodbury Common Premium
Outlets (page 145) then you may want to
stay overnight to make the most of opening
hours.

THE THAYER HOTEL $$-$$$

✉ 674 Thayer Road, West Point, New York
☎ 845-446 4731 or freephone 800-247
   5047
   Fax 845-446 0338
🖰 www.thethayerhotel.com

A three-star hotel at West Point – the scene
of a decisive battle in the War of
Independence and now home to one of the
most famous officer training camps in
America, with fabulous views of the Hudson
River. The hotel has comfortable en-suite
rooms, which have been refurbished in the
last couple of years. There's a restaurant
open for breakfast, lunch and dinner and the
lounge, which overlooks the river, is open
until 1am Fri–Sat. Shop-and-stay packages
are available.

Accommodation reference guide

Hotel	Area	Style	Price range	page
6 Columbus Circle	SoHo	Boutique chic	$$$	230
60 Thompson	SoHo	Boutique chic	$$$–$$$$$	230
70 Park Avenue	Midtown East	Medium-priced gem	$$$–$$$$	236
Algonquin	Midtown	Excellent value	$$–$$$	240
Ameritania	Midtown West	Excellent value	$$	241
Bentley	Upper East Side	Excellent value	$$–$$$	242
Blue Moon	Lower East Side	Boutique chic	$$$	228
Bryant Park	Midtown	Boutique chic	$$$$–$$$$$	229
Carlton	Flatiron District	Excellent value	$$–$$$	239
Casablanca	Midtown	Medium-priced gem	$$$–$$$$	235
Chambers	Midtown	Boutique chic	$$$–$$$$$	229
Chelsea	Chelsea	Excellent value	$$	239
Chelsea Star	Madison Square Garden	Total bargain	$	244
City Club	Midtown	Boutique chic	$$$–$$$$	229
Clarion Hotel 5th Avenue	Midtown East	Excellent value	$$–$$$	241
Cosmopolitan	TriBeCa	Excellent value	$$–$$$	241
Courtyard by Marriott Times Square South	Theater District	Excellent value	$$–$$$	241
Days Hotel Broadway	Upper West Side	Excellent value	$$–$$$	242
Dream	Midtown West	Theme	$$–$$$	231
Dylan	Midtown East	Boutique chic	$$$–$$$$	230
Elysée	Midtown East	Traditional luxury	$$$$–$$$$$	227
Fitzpatrick	Midtown East	Medium-priced gem	$$$–$$$$	236
Fitzpatrick Grand Central	Midtown East	Medium-priced gem	$$$	236
Flatotel	Midtown	Modern luxury	$$$–$$$$	225
Four Seasons	Midtown East	Modern luxury	$$$$–$$$$$	226
Franklin	Upper East Side	Medium-priced gem	$$$	238
Gershwin	Flatiron District	Total bargain	$–$$	242
Giraffe	Flatiron District	Excellent value	$$–$$$	239
Glenwood	Brooklyn	Total bargain	$	242
Gramercy Park	Gramercy Park	Modern luxury	$$$–$$$$	225
Gramercy Park Hotel 17	Gramercy Park	Total bargain	$–$$	242
Herald Square	Flatiron District	Total bargain	$$	242
Hilton New York	Midtown West	Upmarket	$$$$$	234
Holiday Inn Downtown	Chinatown/Lower East Side	Excellent value	$$	239
Holiday Inn Martinique	Theater District	Excellent value	$$–$$$$$	241
Holiday Inn Wall Street	Financial District	Excellent value	$$–$$$$	239
Hotel 31	Murray Hill	Total bargain	$–$$$	244
Hotel Beacon	Upper West Side	Excellent value	$$	242
Hotel Carlyle	Upper East Side	Landmark	$$$$–$$$$$	224
Hotel Gansevoort	Meatpacking District	Boutique chic	$$$–$$$$$	229
Hotel on Rivington	Lower East Side	Boutique chic	$$$$–$$$$$	229
Hotel Plaza-Athenee	Upper East Side	Traditional luxury	$$$$–$$$$$	227
Howard Johnson Express Inn	Lower East Side	Total bargain	$–$$	243
Hudson	Midtown West	Medium-priced gem	$$–$$$$$	236
Inn at Irving Place	Gramercy Park	Traditional luxury	$$$$–$$$$$	227
Jumeirah Essex House	Midtown West	Upmarket	$$$$–$$$$$	234
Kitano	Midtown East	Upmarket	$$$$–$$$$$	233
Larchmont	Greenwich Village	Total bargain	$–$$	243
Le Parker Meridien	Midtown	Upmarket	$$$–$$$$$	233
Library	Midtown	Theme	$$$$–$$$$$	231
London NYC	Midtown	Modern luxury	$$$$	226
Lowell	Upper East Side	Traditional luxury	$$$$$	228
Mandarin Oriental	Upper West Side	Modern luxury	$$$$–$$$$$	227
Mansfield	Midtown	Medium-priced gem	$$$–$$$$$	235
Marcel	Gramercy Park	Medium-priced gem	$$–$$$	234
Maritime	Chelsea	Theme	$$–$$$$	231

WHERE TO STAY

Hotel	Area	Style	Price range	page
Mark	Upper East Side	Traditional luxury	$$$$–$$$$$	228
Mercer	SoHo	Boutique chic	$$$–$$$$	230
Metro	Midtown	Excellent value	$$–$$$	240
Milford Plaza	Theater District	Excellent value	$$–$$$	241
Millennium Hilton	Financial District	Medium-priced gem	$$–$$$$	234
Moderne	Midtown West	Medium-priced gem	$$$–$$$$	236
Morgans	Midtown	Boutique chic	$$$–$$$$	230
New York Marriott at the Brooklyn Bridge	Brooklyn	Excellent value	$$–$$$	238
New York Marriott Marquis	Theater District	Medium-priced gem	$$–$$$$	237
New York Palace	Midtown East	Traditional luxury	$$$$–$$$$$	227
Night	Midtown West	Theme hotel	$$$–$$$$	232
Off Soho Suites	Lower East Side	Total bargain	$–$$	244
On The Ave	Theater District	Medium-priced gem	$$–$$$$	237
Paramount	Theater District	Medium-priced gem	$$–$$$$	237
Peninsula	Midtown	Upmarket	$$$$$	233
Pickwick Arms	Midtown East	Total bargain	$	244
Plaza	Midtown	Landmark	$$$$$	222
Portland Square	Midtown West	Total bargain	$	244
Premier	Theater District	Medium-priced gem	$$$–$$$$	237
Ritz-Carlton New York	Battery Park City	Modern luxury	$$$$$	225
Roosevelt	Midtown East	Medium-priced gem	$$–$$$$	236
Royalton	Midtown	Modern luxury	$$$–$$$$	226
Sherry-Netherland	Upper East Side	Traditional luxury	$$$$–$$$$$	228
Shoreham	Midtown	Medium-priced gem	$$$–$$$$$	235
Sofitel	Midtown West	Upmarket	$$$$–$$$$$	234
Soho Grand	SoHo	Modern luxury	$$$$	226
Soho House New York	SoHo	Boutique chic	$$$$–$$$$$	230
Super 8	Midtown	Excellent value	$$	241
Thayer	West Point	Further afield	$$–$$$	244
Thirty Thirty New York City	Flatiron District	Total bargain	$–$$	243
Time	Theater District	Theme	$$–$$$	230
TriBeCa Grand	TriBeCa	Modern luxury	$$$$–$$$$$	226
Trump International Hotelr & Towe	Central Park	Upmarket	$$$$–$$$$$	233
Vanderbilt YMCA	Midtown East	Total bargain	$–$$	244
Waldorf Astoria	Midtown East	Landmark	$$$–$$$$$	222
Waldorf Towers	Midtown East	Landmark	$$$$$	223
Wall Street Inn	Financial District	Medium-priced gem	$$$	234
Warwick	Midtown	Medium-priced gem	$$$–$$$$	235
Washington Square	Greenwich Village	Excellent value	$$	240
Wellington	Midtown West	Medium-priced gem	$$$–$$$$	236
Westin New York at Times Square	Theater District	Medium-priced gem	$$$$	238

Dream

CHAPTER 12

Festivals and Parades

New Yorkers love an excuse to party, from celebrating the changing of the seasons to championing their cultural roots. In fact, judging by the number of parades, open-air concerts and festivals taking place every month, it's a wonder anyone gets any work done. The good news is that you can be sure that whatever time of year you decide to visit the Big Apple, there will be some truly spectacular entertainment going on, and what's more, most of it is free!

ANNUAL AND BIENNIAL EVENTS

JANUARY AND FEBRUARY

Paint the Town
Citywide. 2 Jan–throughout Feb. Tel 212-484 1222, www.nycvisit.com/paintthetown.
Offers and discounts on everything from restaurants and theatres to accommodation, shopping and tours.

Winter Restaurant Week
Citywide. Last two weeks in Jan. Tel 212-484 1222, www.nycvisit.com.
Dive out from the January sales to grab a lunch for $24.07 (to reflect the 24/7 New York lifestyle) or dinner for $35 with this great promotion.

Winter Antiques Show
18–27 Jan 2008. 7th Regiment Armory, Park Avenue at 67th Street. Tel 718-292 7392 or 718-665 5250, www.winterantiquesshow.com.
Admission $20 with catalogue. Open daily noon–8pm; Sun and Thurs noon–6pm.
The Winter Antiques Show kicks off New York's winter season with a glitzy Opening Night Party on 17 January, but as tickets for that event start at $1,000 each your best bet is to wait until the next day to see the treasures within. From the simplicity of arts and crafts to ornate baroque clocks, you can be sure there will be fine antiques to suit everyone's taste. Private collections from all over America are also on show.

Chinese New Year parade

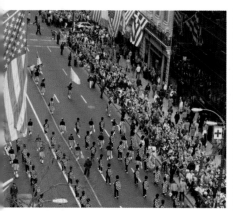

St Patrick's Day parade

Chinese New Year Parade/ Lunar New York
From the first day of the full moon between 21 Jan and 19 Feb. Chinatown around Mott Street. Tel 212-484 1216, www.explorechinatown.com.
New York City is known for having some of the most authentic celebrations of the Chinese New Year in the US, and the festivities range from a firecracker ceremony to the magnificent dragon parade in Chinatown to various other performances around the city. The party continues for 10 days.

Black History Month
Throughout Feb. A series of shows is put on to celebrate the African-American experience in New York. See the newspapers and guides for cultural events, concerts and lectures scheduled around the city, or visit http://nymag.com for detailed listings of events.

BRITTIP
A central number for New York events is 212-484 1222; and a website that reports many free events is www.newyorkled.com. A good events site for planning ahead is www.new.york.eventguide.com.

Grammy Awards
Late Feb. Madison Square Garden. Tel 212-465 6741, www.grammy.com.
The Grammy Awards are to music what the Oscars are to the movies. Over the years Los Angeles and New York have played tug-of-war with the Grammy Awards show and

New York has won. You may not get to attend the Awards, but you can go stargazing by the red carpet as celebs arrive in their limos.

MARCH AND APRIL
Whitney Biennial – 2008
March–June. Whitney Museum of American Art (page 110). Tel 212-570 3676 or 1-800 WHITNEY, www.whitney.org.
The exhibition's line-up of contemporary art is as controversial as Damien Hirst's cow. So for art from the apocalyptic to the ethereal and the fantastic to the political, this is a show that can't be missed. It's coming up in 2008; why wait another two years?

St Patrick's Day Parade
17 March. 5th Avenue between 44th and 86th Streets. www.st-patricks-day.com.
One of the bigger parades the city has to offer. If you're in town, you won't be able to miss the sea of green that goes with this annual Irish-American day. The parade starts at 11am up 5th Avenue from 44th to 86th Streets and the festivities go on late into the night. The 2008 parade will be the 246th!

BRITTIP
A good vantage point to watch the St Patrick's Day parade is the steps of St Patrick's Cathedral (page 74), where the Bishop of New York greets the marching bands.

Greek Independence Day Parade
The Sunday closest to 25 March (when Greek Independence Day falls in the Orthodox Lent, the parade is shifted to April or even May). Along 5th Avenue to 49th Street. Tel 718-204 6500, www.greekparade.org.
This one's a Zorba-style parade with lots of flag waving and national dress, as well as plenty of Greek food, music and dancing.

Rhythm in the Kitchen Music Festival
End of March. Metro Baptist Church, 410 West 40th Street. $15 per evening or $35 for a three-day pass. www.hkculturalcenter.org.
Only in its second year, this three-day concert series ranging from Latin music to electronica in Hells' Kitchen, once the centre of jazz in the city, looks set to be an annual event.

Easter Parade
Easter Sunday. 5th Avenue between 49th and 57th Streets.
This is not an official parade, just a chance to watch strollers flaunting Easter bonnets

St Patrick's Cathedral

from gorgeous to outrageous. The steps of St Patrick's Cathedral (page 74) are an advantageous viewing spot. Kick-off is at 10am, so arrive early to bag a space.

Upper West Fest
End April–May. Download the brochure and plan your visit at www.upperwestfest.com. From 60th Street to 120th Street, the doors of more than 20 world-class arts and cultural organisations open their doors and more than 50 performances and exhibitions are laid on. Highlights include Symphony Space's free 12-hour opera marathon, the NY Yiddish Film Festival and jazz at the Lincoln Center.

New York City Ballet Spring Season
Late April to June. New York State Theater, 20 Lincoln Center Plaza, 65th Street at Columbus Avenue. Tel 212-870 5570, www.nycballet.com. Student rush tickets (available on day of performance) cost $12. Tel 212-870-7766. Even ordinary tickets start from a bargain $15.
The New York City Ballet performs its spring season in New York before touring. Go to see the world-famous dancers, trained in the classic style of ballet masters Balanchine and Robbins.

MAY AND JUNE
See also New York City Ballet (above) and Whitney Biennial (page 248).

American Ballet Theater
May–July. Metropolitan Opera House at the Lincoln Center. Tel 212-362 6000, www.abt.org.
Going to see the ABT at the Met is exhilarating. The majesty of the Metropolitan Opera House combines with the passion, power and movement of one of the world's most innovative dance companies to create a magical experience. The Theater also runs an ABTKids programme (see page 197).

Cuban Day Parade
Early May. Free. Lively day-long Cuban carnival with salsa bands and partying into the night along 6th Avenue that ends at the Cuban Independence statue of José Marti on Central Park South.

TriBeCa Film Festival
Second week in May. TriBeCa area. Tel 212-941 2400, www.tribecafilmfestival.org.
The 12-day TriBeCa Film Festival was founded in 2002 by Robert DeNiro, Jane Rosenthal and Craig Hatkoff as a response to the attacks on the World Trade Center. The now prestigious festival showcases independent movies, runs workshops and has a children's film programme, as well as Q&A sessions with actors and filmmakers. During the week, local restaurants offer cut-price meals.

9th Avenue International Food Festival
Mid-May. 9th Avenue between 37th and 57th Streets. Tel 212-581 7029, www.hellskitchen.bz.
This festival is a gourmet's delight. Hell's Kitchen cooks up a feast of foods from around the world and hundreds of stalls line the streets selling every type of food imaginable. Go for lunch and then walk it all off by strolling on down to Chelsea's fabulous art galleries nearby.

New York City Ballet

FESTIVALS AND PARADES

TOP FIVE FESTIVALS & PARADES

Grammy Awards: January

St Patrick's Day Parade: March

Heritage of Pride Parade: June

Bryant Park Free Summer Season: June–August

Macy's Thanksgiving Day Parade: November

Fleet Week

Last week in May. www.fleetweek.navy.mil.
New York City Fleet Week brings thousands of sailors and marines from US naval vessels to the Big Apple and includes dozens of military demonstrations. Unless you're a boat nut, it's normally not worth visiting the huge armada of US Navy – free tours are offered daily – and other ships that visit New York, but this week they'll be very hard to miss.

Lower East Side Festival of the Arts

Last weekend in May. Along East 10th Street. Theater for the New City. Tel 212-254 1109, www.theaterforthenewcity.net/les.htm.
Deep in the heart of the neighbourhood that helped create the East Coast Beat Movement, method acting and pop art, is a free, three-day indoor and outdoor annual arts festival and carnival for everyone.

Washington Square Outdoor Art Exhibition

Late May–early June, then again in September. Washington Square. Tel 212-982 6255.
An old and revered tradition of arty Greenwich Village, this is a huge outdoor art show with easels and food trolleys set up in the streets all around the park.

Puerto Rican Day Parade

Second Sunday in June from 11am. 5th Avenue between 44th and 85th Streets. Tel 718-401 0404, www.nationalpuertorican dayparade.com.
This is a New York parade on a grand scale – expect more than 100,000 marchers and three million spectators. The largest of several Puerto Rican celebrations in the city, with three hours of colourful floats, music and dancing.

Museum Mile Festival

Second Tuesday in June. 5th Avenue between 82nd and 104th Streets. Tel 212-606 2296, www.museummilefestival.org.
Museum Mile is neither a museum nor a mile, but nine museums stretching along 5th Avenue and Central Park on the Upper East Side. All are worth a visit. During the festival you can get into all of them, including the fabulous Metropolitan, for free. An added perk is the fascinating street entertainment.

New York Jazz Festival

Mid to late June. Various clubs. www.festivalproductions.net.
See some of the biggest names in jazz at various venues throughout Manhattan. Even those of you who are not true aficionados of jazz can enjoy the festival atmosphere provided by the 300 acts taking part in this event.

Broadway Under The Stars

Third Monday in June. The Great Lawn, mid-park from 79th to 85th Street, Central Park. Tel 212-768 4242, www.centralpark.com or www.nycvisit.com.

Central Park

Central Park West

Broadway kicks off New York's summer outdoor concert season with a free showcase of its hottest talent performing major show songs at 8.30pm.

◀▶ BRITTIP

Check out the many street fairs from spring to autumn throughout the city with food, craft and other stalls. Visit www.nycstreet fairs.com and www.nyctourist.com.

Mermaid Parade

Last Saturday in June. 8th Street between Steeplechase Park and Broadway, Coney Island, Brooklyn. Tel 718-372 5159, www.coneyisland.com.
The Mermaid Parade celebrates the beginning of summer. Catch the B, D or F trains to Stillwell Avenue on the Saturday following the first official day of summer to sample a wild and boisterous scene of carnival floats and costumes. The parade is followed by the Mermaid Parade Ball.

Heritage of Pride Parade

Last Sunday in June. From Columbus Circle along 5th Avenue and 52nd Street to Christopher Street in Greenwich Village. Tel 212-807 7433, www.nycpride.org.
Formerly known as the Gay Pride Parade, this parade kicks off every year at 5th Avenue and ends with PrideFest, a street party and rally in the traditional heart of the gay community. There is a packed club schedule, fireworks and an open-air dance party on the West Side piers.

Central Park SummerStage

June–Aug. Rumsey Playfield, Central Park at 72nd Street and Central Park West. Tel 212-307 7171 for tickets to benefit concerts or 212-360 2756 for information, www.summerstage.org. Subway 1, 2, 3, 9, B, C to 72nd Street.
You can experience many kinds of entertainment for free in New York and some of the best are the free weekend afternoon concerts put on by the SummerStage, featuring over 33 performances from top international artists. On weeknights, dance and spoken-word events are also put on in Central Park.

New York Philharmonic/Metropolitan Opera Parks Concerts.

Various sites in summer, www.nycgovparks.org. Tel 212-875 5656, www.newyorkphilharmonic.org (Philharmonic)/212-362 6000, www.metopera.org (Met).
These free, open-air events in parks around the city are wildly popular so arrive early to stake out a site.

Shakespeare in the Park

Late June–late Aug. Delacorte Theater, Central Park at 81st Street. Tel 212-539 8500 info, 212-967 7555 to order tickets, www.publictheater.org.
Plays held in the open-air theatre every summer are free. There are two each year – one Shakespeare and one American, with performances almost nightly. Although free, you still have to get tickets to see them, which are available from 1pm on the day of the performance, and the queues are long.

Bryant Park

Bryant Park

FESTIVALS AND PARADES

Bryant Park Summer Film Festival
Every Monday June–Aug. 6th Avenue at 42nd Street. Tel 212-768 4242, www.bryantpark.org. Subway F, V, B, D to 42nd Street/Bryant Park.
Bryant Park is one of the few green spaces available in the Midtown area, and this is a summer-long series of free classical music, jazz, dance and film showings during the day and evening. Classic films shown in the park on Mondays are a great way to unwind after a hard day's shopping or sightseeing. The lawn opens at 5pm for blankets and picnicking. The films begin at dusk.

Midsummer Night Swing
Mid-June to mid-July. Lincoln Center for Performing Arts, Josie Robertson Plaza, Columbus Avenue at 63rd Street. Tel 212-875 5766, www.lincolncenter.org. Single tickets from $15, the swing passes that admit two start from $78 for six nights. Considered the city's hottest outdoor dance party, with dance-filled nights when energetic bands play everything from swing to salsa. Lots of dance instructors are on hand to give lessons in every type of dance, or you can just pop by to listen to the live music.

Celebrate Brooklyn! Performing Arts Festival
All summer. Prospect Park Bandshell, 9th Street at Prospect Park West, Park Slope, Brooklyn. Tel 718-855 7882, www.celebratebrooklyn.org.

Here's a very good reason to break out of Manhattan and visit one of the outer boroughs – for New York's longest running festival of free music, dance, theatre and film events lasting nine weeks.

JULY AND AUGUST
See also American Ballet Theater at the Met, Thursday Night Concert Series, Central Park SummerStage, New York Philharmonic/Met Opera Concerts, New York Shakespeare Festival, Bryant Park Free Summer Season, Midsummer Night Swing and Celebrate Brooklyn! Performing Arts Festival (above).

Fourth of July
The Americans still insist on celebrating achieving independence from their colonial masters – and they do it in style! Throughout New York there are various celebrations going on, but by far the biggest and most spectacular is Macy's Fireworks Spectacular, which is held on the East River between 14th and 51st Streets. Tel 212-494 4495, www.macys.com A good spot to see the $1 million, 30-minute firework extravaganza is from FDR Drive (Franklin D Roosevelt Drive) or from Pier 17 at South Street Seaport. Another popular event is the Travis Fourth of July Parade (tel 718-494 0378) where the town of Travis is decorated in red, white and blue and marching bands and costumed characters take to the streets.

Summer Restaurant Week
Mid-July. Tel 212-484 1222, www.nycvisit.com/restaurantweek. For two weeks, more than 150 of the city's finest restaurants offer three-course fixed-price lunches and dinners at prices that reflect the year.

The Stars and Stripes on Liberty Island

SUMMER IN THE CITY FOR FAMILIES

Puppet shows, free story-telling, films and workshops in libraries – these form just a part of what's on offer in the city throughout the summer, so you'll be hard pressed to find a moment's peace! To find out what's going on where and when, pick up a copy of *Events For Children* from any branch of the New York Public Library. Most are free or very good value for money.

Here is an outline of some of the many activities available for children in summer. More details can be found by month in this chapter or in Chapter 13 Sports & Leisure.

Central Park
The park is a year-round winner, but summer time is when it really comes into its own. Specific children's events abound, from canoeing to field days, all listed under the Kids to Do section on www.centralparknyc.org, while the whole family can enjoy offerings put on by the **Central Park SummerStage** (tel 212-360 2756, www.summerstage.org) and Shakespeare in the Park (tel 212-539 8500, www.publictheater.org).

Bryant Park Summer Film Festival (tel 212-768 4242, www.bryantpark.org)
Perfect for adults and children alike, head to Bryant Park on a Monday night and pull up a chair or lay out a rug to enjoy a free outdoor film on the massive screen. Remember to take some snacks and drinks. Children can let off steam before or after at the nearby carousel.

New York Philharmonic Young People's Concerts (Avery Fisher Hall, 10 Lincoln Center Plaza, tel 212-875 5656, www.newyorkphilharmonic.org)
A series of summer Saturday concerts where children aged 6–12 get to meet the musicians and try out their instruments for an hour before the concert. Book early, however, as they're very popular. You'll also be in the right spot for the Lincoln Center's free Out-of-Doors Festival, with events throughout August (see above). The Lincoln Center also offers a family programme of music and dance afternoons for children.

Puppet Theater (tel 212-680 1400, www.hensonfoundation.org)
Sign up on the website for puppet happenings that may time with your visit.

Lincoln Center Out-of-Doors (Lincoln Center plazas and Damrosch Park. Tel 212-LIN COLN, www.lincolncenter.org).
A free festival for all ages running throughout August with specific events for families and children. As well as storytelling and puppetry, there's the Iced Tea Dance where children get to dance with professionals, a Homemade Instrument Day in which children can make their own musical instruments and play them, and a Play Day.

Summer Garden Concerts
July–Aug. Flushing Town Hall, 137-35 Northern Boulevard, Queens. Tel 718-463 7700, www.flushingtownhall.com.
A diverse line-up with many musical styles including country, jazz, soul and oldies.

Concerts in the Abby Aldrich Rockefeller Sculpture Garden
July–Aug. Museum of Modern Art, 11 West 53rd Street between 5th and 6th Avenues. Tel 212-708 9400, www.moma.org. Subway E, V to 5th Avenue/53rd Street.

Lincoln Center Festival
Mid-late July. Lincoln Center for the Performing Arts, 140 West 65th Street, although venues vary. 212-875 5766, www.lincolncenter.org.

The Lincoln Center

Sakwa Matsui festival in Brooklyn Botanic Garden's Japanese Garden

A veritable feast of dance, drama, ballet, children's shows and multimedia and performance art, involving both repertory companies and special guests, at venues inside and outside at the Lincoln Center (page 197).

An added bonus to visiting the little gem that is MoMA (reopened in autumn 2004 after major renovation, page 101) is the series of free classical and jazz concerts that are presented in the museum's sculpture garden every summer.

Lincoln Center Out of Doors
Aug. Lincoln Center plazas and Damrosch Park. Tel 212-LIN COLN, www.lincolncenter.org.
Over 100 free outdoor performances including an exciting line-up of music, dance events, storytelling, puppetry and other family events.

Greenwich Village Halloween Parade

Harlem Week
Aug. Along 5th Avenue from West 125th to West 135th Streets. Tel 212-862 7200, www.harlemdiscover.com.
The largest black and Hispanic festival in the world, its highlight is the street party with R&B, gospel and All That Jazz. In addition to the music, there are films, dance, fashion, sports and exhibitions. What a great way to experience Harlem!

Sounds at Sunset
Aug. Hudson River Park (tel. 212-627 2020, www.hudsonriverpark.org). (tel 212-416 5328, www.batteryparkcity.org).
The Battery Park City Authority presents a free summer series of poetry readings, cabaret and classical music in this park.

SEPTEMBER AND OCTOBER
See also Washington Square Outdoor Art Exhibition (May and June); Concert Series in the Rockefeller Sculpture Garden (above).

West Indian-American Day Parade
First weekend Sept. 5th Avenue to Christopher Street in Brooklyn. Tel 718-467 1797, www.wiadca.org.
Fabulous festival celebrating Caribbean culture with food (all along Eastern Parkway) and entertainment from top Caribbean artists. Brightly costumed marchers put on a special children's parade on the Saturday, with an even bigger event on Labor Day (first Monday in September).

Feast of San Gennaro

Mid-Sept for 11 days. Mulberry Street to Worth Street in Little Italy. Tel 212-768 9320, www.sangennaro.org.

Held in honour of the Neapolitan saint, this is the best time to see what is left of the once-bustling Little Italy that is now reduced to just Mulberry Street. There are lots of fairground booths, plenty of food – look out for the cannoli-eating contest – and even more vino.

Broadway on Broadway

Sept (varies) at 11.30am Times Square. Tel. 212-768 1560, www.broadwayonbroadway.com.

Quintessentially New York – a free annual concert when numbers from Broadway shows are performed live on a giant outdoor stage by a galaxy of celebrities surrounded by TV cameras. It all ends in a big finale with loads of confetti.

◀▶ BRITTIP

Parades are great fun, but they also provide perfect opportunities for pickpockets, so keep your bags and wallets close to you – and never put your wallet in your back pocket.

Columbus Day Parade

Second Monday in Oct. 5th Avenue between 44th and 79th Streets. Tel 212-249 9923, www.columbuscitizensfd.org.

The traditional celebration of the first recorded sighting of America by Europeans is now somewhat controversial in some quarters but, despite its lack of political correctness, Columbus Day still gets the big 5th Avenue parade treatment, which is well worth a view. The parade has nearly one million participants plus celebrities – the likes of Frank Sinatra, Sophia Loren and Luciano Pavarotti have all paraded in the past.

New York City Marathon

Last Sunday in Oct/first Sunday in Nov. Staten Island to Central Park. Tel 212-423 2249, www.ingnycmarathon.org.

Starts at the Staten Island side of the Verrazano Narrows Bridge as a mad pack of 35,000 men and women run 42km (26.2 miles) around all five boroughs, to finish at the Tavern on the Green in Central Park at West 67th Street. If you would like to enter the marathon you need to fill out an application form, pay a small fee, and then wait to see if you get picked. You can do this through the website.

Halloween Parade

31 Oct at 6.30pm. 6th Avenue from Spring Street, Greenwich Village to 21st Street. Tel 212-475 3333, www.halloween-nyc.com.

A uniquely Village event, with the outlandishly over-the-top costumes (or lack of them!) on (or off!) many of its participants. The organisers decree a different theme each year and a lot of work goes into the amazing outfits that range from the exotic to the nearly non-existent. It attracts between 50,000 ghouls, ghosts and onlookers. So get creative and dress up to join in – only those in fancy dress can march.

NOVEMBER AND DECEMBER

See also New York City Marathon (above).

Macy's Thanksgiving Day Parade

Thanksgiving Day, 9am. From Central Park West at 77th Street to Macy's (page 113) on Broadway at 34th Street. Tel 212-494 4495, www.macysparade.com.

Definitely one for the family, this is the Big Mama of all New York's parades, with enormous inflated cartoon characters, fabulous floats and the gift-giving Santa Claus himself. New Yorkers in the know like to come by and watch it being set up the night before between 77th and 81st Streets off Central Park West. The parade is even

Macy's Thanksgiving Day Parade

televised for the rest of America. If you miss it, you can go to see Santa in Santaland in Macy's until Christmas.

Christmas Tree Lighting Ceremony
Late Nov or early Dec. The Rockefeller Center, from 5th-7th Avenue between 47th and 51st Streets. Tel 212-632 3975, www.rockefellercenter.com.

The Rockefeller Center (page 63) in front of the towering RCA building provides the magical setting for the annual switching on of nearly 8km (5 miles) of dazzling lights on a huge Christmas tree. The plaza leading up to the tree is decked with lights too!

New Year's Eve Ball Drop
31 Dec, midnight, Times Square. Tel 212-768 1560, www.timessquarenyc.org.

This event is a real New York classic, though you may prefer to watch safely on TV rather than be packed in with the freezing masses. Remember, Times Square is a misnomer – it's a junction, so there isn't really that much room and all the side streets get packed too. If you do manage to get a good spot, though, you'll see the giant glitterball of 180 bulbs and 12,000 rhinestones being dropped along with 1 tonne (yes, really) of confetti, to bring in the New Year. The revellers kick off at 5pm, so get there early.

AMERICAN HOLIDAYS
New Year's Day: 1 January
Martin Luther King Jr Day: Third Monday in January
President's Day: Third Monday in February
Memorial Day: Last Monday in May
Independence Day: 4 July
Labor Day: First Monday in September
Columbus Day: Second Monday in October
Election Day: First Tuesday after the first Monday in November
Veterans' Day: 11 November
Thanksgiving: Fourth Thursday in November
Christmas Day: 25 December

New Year's Eve Fireworks in Central Park
31 Dec, midnight. 5th Avenue and 90th Street or Bethsheda Fountain (Central Park at 72nd Street) are the best viewing spots. Tel 212-360 3456, www.nycgovparks.org. The hot apple cider and spirit of camaraderie begin at 11.30pm.

Fireworks above the Statue of Liberty

— CHAPTER 13 —

Sports and Leisure

New York is as famous for its parks as it is for the Statue of Liberty. Of course, Central Park is the one everyone knows about, but there are many others dotted throughout the city. The parks are very busy and remarkably safe, but be prudent about going into the less populated areas and especially cautious about visiting them at night if you are unfamiliar with the neighbourhood. A great website to keep you safe and in the know is www.nycgovparks.org – it has loads of information about every park in New York.

CENTRAL PARK

✉ From Central Park South at 59th Street to 110th Street in Harlem

☎ 212-310 6600

🖰 www.centralparknyc.org

🚗 Subway A, B, C, D run along the Upper West Side to 59th, 72nd, 81st, 86th, 96th and 103rd Streets; 1, 9 to 59th Street/Columbus Circle; 2, 3 to 110th Street in the North; N, R, W to 57th Street or Fifth Avenue on the South side

🕐 Daily 6am–1am; visit the website for weekly scheduled events and tours around the park

$ Free

This is the New Yorkers' playground and meeting place and attracts 25 million visitors every year. Covering 6% of Manhattan, its 341 hectares (843 acres) stretch 6 miles from Central Park South at 59th Street to Central Park North at 110th Street, with 5th Avenue and Central Park West forming its eastern and western boundaries. It was created over a 20-year period by architect Calvert Vaux and landscaper Frederick Law Olmsted,

🇬🇧 BRITTIP

To find out exactly what's going to be on in Central Park when you're visiting, log on to www.centralparknyc.org for a complete listing of year-round activities.

was completed in the 1860s and had its 150th Anniversary in 2003.

To enter from the south, cross the street from **Grand Army Plaza** at 5th Avenue and 59th Street. Immediately in front of you is the Pond, and then the **Wollman Memorial Rink** (62nd Street), which hosts a Victorian amusement park in the summer and ice-skating in the winter. Close by is the **Visitor Information Center**, where you can pick up free maps and schedules of events, including the series of free concerts and dramas performed at the **SummerStage** (page 235). Here also are the **Gotham Miniature Golf Course** (a gift from Donald Trump), **The Dairy**, a 19th century-style building with an interactive touch-screen information kiosk and an exhibition on the park's history and design and the antique carousel (65th Street). To the east is the **Central Park Wildlife Center** (63rd–66th Streets) and the **Children's Zoo and Wildlife Center** (page 259).

🇬🇧 BRITTIP

Put sturdy shoes on, as this park is big. To get an idea, if you walked all of the paths it would add up to 58 miles (93km)!

The **Sheep Meadow** (66th–69th Streets) to the north of the carousel is much used by New Yorkers for picnics and sunbathing. To

SPORTS AND LEISURE

Yankee Stadium

Strawberry Fields

its left is the **Tavern on the Green** restaurant (page 149) and to the right is the **Mall** (69th–72nd Streets), a tree-lined walkway where locals skate and run in summer. Follow the Mall to the top and you will find the **Central Park Bandshell** (70th Street), one of the park's concert venues. Further north is the **Loeb Boathouse** (74th and 75th Streets), which is home to the **Park View at the Boathouse** restaurant (page 149) and where you can hire bikes and boats (page 263). One of the Parks' most visited spots is **Strawberry Fields** (72nd Street). With a mosaic of the word 'Imagine' in the centre, it is a memorial to John Lennon who lived in the Dakota Building nearby.

Continuing north, you will come to the **Ramble** (71st Street), a heavily wooded area scattered with paths and streams and a great place for bird-watching, which leads (if you can find the way through) to the Gothic revival **Belvedere Castle** (74th Street) housing another information centre. Also here are the **Delacorte Theater**, where

BRITTIP

The Philharmonic/Met Concerts are thrilling, surprisingly tranquil summer experiences. Join tens of thousands of New Yorkers in laying down a blanket on the Great Lawn and setting up a picnic two or three hours ahead of concert time. The first concert of the season ends with fireworks.

summer productions are presented by Shakespeare in the Park (tel 212-539 8750, www.publictheater.org for tickets) and the **Great Lawn** (79th–86th Streets) where the **Philharmonic and Metropolitan Opera** concerts are held – the only time you can witness tens of thousands of New Yorkers all being quiet at the same time (page 269).

BRITTIP

A really great way to find out more about Central Park's history and modern-day uses is by taking the two-hour Big Onion walking tour (page 83) (tel 212-439 1090 www.bigonion.com), which costs $15 for adults, $12 seniors, $10 students.

Further north again is the huge **Jacqueline Kennedy Onassis Reservoir** (86th–96th Streets). A well-kept secret is the formal 2.4-hectare (6-acre), three-part **Conservatory Garden** (104th–106th Streets), where dozens of wedding parties come for photographs on summer weekends. It was bequeathed by the Vanderbilt family, and there are free tours and concerts in the summer.

BRITTIP

If short on time, a walk from 59th to 79th Streets takes in some of the best the Park has to offer, passing through The Ramble (71st Street) and to Bethseda Terrace, with its newly restored exquisite Minton tile ceiling roof.

CENTRAL PARK FOR FAMILIES

Top of the pile for all-round entertainment, Central Park has 21 playgrounds, a small but perfectly formed Wildlife Conservation Center and Children's Petting Zoo, the fun carousel, ice-skating at the Wollman Rink and the Discovery Center at Belvedere Castle, a children's theatre plus a whole host of fun activities. For the schedule of current events, exhibits and workshops visit www.centralparknyc.org and click on 'Bring the Kids' or on the following attractions.

Entering through the Grand Army Plaza at the southern end of the park at 59th Street, you will find the following family-friendly places to visit:

BELVEDERE CASTLE DISCOVERY CENTER

- ✉ Mid-park at 97th Street
- ☎ 212-722 0210
- ⇦ Subway B, C to 79th Street
- ◷ Tues–Sun 10am–5pm; 4pm in winter
- $ Free

Sitting on Vista Rock, this is the highest point in the park and gives great views in all directions. The Henry Luce Nature Observatory includes exhibits on flowers, trees and birds in the park. The kids can borrow Discovery Kits, a backpack with binoculars, guidebook, maps and sketching materials for bird-watching in the Ramble and other locations. For children aged 6 and up; those under 12 must be with an adult.

CAROUSEL

- ✉ Mid-park at 64th Street and 5th Avenue
- ☎ 212-879 0244
- 🚇 Subway N, R to 5th Avenue; 6 to 68th Street
- ◷ Apr–Oct Mon–Fri 10am–6pm, Sat–Sun 10am–7pm; Nov–Dec daily 10am–4.30pm; Jan–Mid-March weekends and holidays only 10am–4.30pm
- $ $1.25 a ride

A carousel has been on this site since 1870 when the original was powered by a blind mule and a horse that walked a treadmill in an underground pit. Fortunately, no animals have to be put through such torture any more as the current electrical ride was donated by the Michael Friedsam Foundation in 1951. It features some of the largest hand-carved horses in the US.

CHARLES A DANA DISCOVERY CENTER

- ✉ North East Corner at the Harlem Meer/110th Street between 5th and Lenox Avenues
- ☎ 212-860 1370
- 🚇 Subway 2, 3, 6 to 110th Street
- ◷ Tues–Sun 10am–5pm, closes 4pm in winter
- $ Free

This is the park's only environmental educational centre with children's workshops year-round. Free to all, the centre sponsors workshops, musical performances and park tours and also loans fishing poles for fishing in the well-stocked Meer. Its catch-and-release fishing programme is open to all ages and gives people the chance to fish for large-mouth bass, catfish, golden shiners and bluegills. Open April–Oct.

CENTRAL PARK ZOO AND TISCH CHILDREN'S ZOO

- ✉ Mid-park at 5th Avenue between 63rd Street and 66th Streets
- ☎ 212-439 6500
- 🚇 Subway N, R to 5th Avenue; 6 to 68th Street
- ◷ Apr–Oct Mon–Fri 10am–5pm, Sat and Sun 10am–5.30pm; Nov–end March daily 10am–4.30pm
- $ $8 adults, $4 seniors, $3 3–12, under 3s free

A small but perfectly formed zoo and conservation centre. Exhibits include a polar bear, tamarin monkeys and red pandas, plus other endangered species. Watch the sea lions being fed at 11.30am, 2pm and 4pm. Close Encounters of the Critter Kind is available for toddlers and a rainforest journey for older children. Call to register for programmes. The Leaping Frog Café is kid-friendly and healthy!

NORTH MEADOW RECREATION CENTER

Central Park

- ✉ Mid-park at 97th Street
- ☎ 212-348 4867
- 🚇 Subway B, C, 6 to 96th Street
- ◷ End May–Sept Tues–Fri 10am–8pm, Sat and Sun 10am–6pm; early Sept–mid-Oct Tues–Fri 10am–6pm, Sat and Sun 10am–6pm; mid-Oct–mid-Mar Tues–Fri 10am–6pm, Sat and Sun 10am–4.30pm
- $ Free

Open to all ages, the park's largest open space at 9.3 hectares (23 acres) provides free Field Day Kits that include everything you need to equip a family for a day of fun and games in the park, including a basketball,

Central Park Zoo

football, Frisbee, skipping rope and hula-hoops. Call in advance to register. The Center also has a 6m (20ft) climbing wall with adventure programmes for children and lends equipment for the basketball and handball courts.

SWEDISH COTTAGE MARIONETTE THEATER
Central Park West
✉ Mid-park West at 79th Street
☎ 212-988 9093
🚇 Subway B, C to 79th Street
🕐 Oct–Jun Tues–Fri 10.30am and noon, Sat 1pm
$ $6 adults, $5 children

Formerly a 19th-century Swedish schoolhouse, this cottage was moved to Central Park in 1876 and now holds various marionette plays for children throughout the year. Book in advance (note: credit cards are not accepted).

THE WOLLMAN RINK
Central Park
✉ Mid-park East between 62nd and 63rd Streets
☎ 212-439 6900
🖥 www.wollmanskatingrink.com
🚇 Subway N, R W to 5th Avenue/59th Street
🕐 Nov–Mar Mon and Tues 10am–2.30pm, Wed and Thurs 10am–10pm, Fri and Sat 10am–11pm, Sun 10am–9pm
$ $9.50–12 adults, $4.75–5 children; skate rental $5 extra

Skating for beginners and ice dancing are offered on this popular rink. An ideal and

✚ BRITTIP
The best way to beat a hot summer in New York City is with a cool lifeguard job earning $11.72 an hour at the city's pools and beaches. British students are encouraged to apply by April.

Brooklyn Botanic Garden

scenic place to take children and join in the traditional activity of a New York winter.

THE MAIN PARKS

Battery Park: With a decent yet distant view of the Statue of Liberty, this park is visited by thousands. Situated at the southern tip of Manhattan, it is a beautiful space overlooking New York Harbor (page 60) (tel 212-417 2000, www.batterypark city.org).

Brooklyn Botanic Garden: Across in the outer borough of Brooklyn, this botanic garden is famous for its cherry trees that bloom from mid-March to late May – you can watch their progress on the garden's website. More details are given in Chapter 14 Taste of the Outer Boroughs (page 266) (tel 718-623 7200, www.bbg.org).

Bryant Park: This small park is a great spot for a picnic lunch or you could dine at the fancy restaurant here. It even puts on free films and concerts on Monday nights during the summer (page 252). The Beaux Arts-style Le Carrousel – specially created to complement the park's French classical style – costs $2 a ride and is open 11am–7pm daily (tel 212-768 4242, www.bryantpark.org).

✚ BRITTIP
Go Fish! in the 500 miles of shoreline, inland lakes and rivers around New York City. Get the low-down from www.nycgovparks.org.

Carl Schurz Park: In the family-friendly Upper East Side, this park sits right next to Gracie Mansion (page 69), once the official residence of the mayor of New York, and has an esplanade along the river. It is a popular destination for families and fitness fanatics, especially at weekends (tel 212-459 4455, www.carlschurzparknyc.org).

TOP FIVE PARKS AND GARDENS
Battery Park (above)
Brooklyn Botanic Garden (above) in spring or **New York Botanical Garden** (page 261) for the rest of the year
Central Park (page 257)
Luna Park, Union Square (page 261)
Riverside Park (page 261)

City Hall Park: This space near the fabulous Woolworth Building and civic buildings (page 72) is charming. Given a major facelift in 1999, parts of the park have been restored to the way they were in the 18th and 19th centuries, in particular the beautiful lanterns surrounding the gorgeous Jacob Wrey Mould Fountain.

Gramercy Park: East 20th and 21st at Irving Place. One of the prettiest squares in the city, and New York's last private park: visitors can only peek through the railings. The townhouses here were designed by some of the cities best architects – think Stanford White and Calvert Vaux – and lived in by some of its most distinguished residents. The new brasserie opening in 2007 in the Gramercy Park Hotel (page 225) on the square following Ian Schrager's renovations is a hot new place for lunch.

BRITTIP

Get the low down on New York park events and activities by category from sports to arts from www.cityparksfoundation.org.

Luna Park, Union Square: This public park is the gateway to Downtown, a stone's throw from the East Village, SoHo and Greenwich Village, and as close as New York gets to a European piazza. It has an open-air restaurant of the same name and is right by the Union Square green market (www.union squarejournal.com/greenmarket.htm), one of the city's largest farmers' markets where regional purveyors sell their products at stalls in the middle of what is now one of the hippest areas of New York. The market operates year round on Monday, Wednesday, Friday and Saturday.

New York Botanical Garden: From antique treasures to family adventures, this extensive, wonderful garden in the Bronx is a must-see. In 2006, it launched the Nolen Greenhouses for Living Collections, considered the most sophisticated behind-the-scenes greenhouses in botanic gardens in America. Get there by train from Grand

BRITTIP

For an up-to-date map of green markets around the city, their locations and opening times, visit www.cenyc.org.

Central Station. More details are given in Chapter 14 Taste of the Outer Boroughs (page 273) (tel 718-817 8700, www.nybg.org).

Prospect Park: A 213-hectare (526-acre) urban oasis in the heart of Brooklyn, this is an incredible park that was landscaped by the same designers as Central Park. It has a wealth of open spaces, activities, events and museums. More details are given in Chapter 14 Taste of the Outer Boroughs (page 268) (tel 718-965 8951, www.prospectpark.org).

Riverside Park: Stretching over 6.5km (4 miles) along the Hudson River from 68th to 155th Streets, this is New York's narrowest park. It is also one of only five official scenic landmarks in the city, designed by Frederick Olmstead of Central Park fame. A combination of winding paths and rock outcrops and English country garden, it also has a buzzing marina at 79th Street where you can have a light meal and watch the pleasure craft and houseboats. Make sure you get a glimpse of Riverside Drive, which winds along it as its one of the most attractive streets in the city, with a canopy of American Elms hanging over late 19th-century townhouses. Open 6am–1am daily (tel 212-870 3070, www.riversidepark fund.org).

Washington Square Park: In the heart of Greenwich Village, the park is best known for its bohemian and rebellious character and is very popular. It is not so much a park as an area covered in tarmac and filled with a hotchpotch of individuals who flock here to snack and people-watch. The main park attraction is the marble Washington arch designed by Stanford White built in honour of George Washington's inauguration as the first US president. More details on the park are given in Chapter 2 New York Neighbourhoods (page 33) (tel 212-NEW YORK, www.washingtonsquarepark.org).

Bryant Park

BRITTIP

Be one of the first to peek at the newest, hippest park that will be opening on a disused railway bridge right in the heart of Chelsea, next to The Standard Hotel. You heard it here first!

SPECTATOR SPORTS

Ask any New Yorker and they'll tell you that they read their newspapers from back to front. That's just how important sports are to them, and they have plenty to choose from: two football teams and two baseball teams to support, plus basketball, hockey, tennis and racing. But it can be really tough to get in to watch some of the games, especially to see football's New York Giants and the Mets baseball team in action. Still, it's worth making the effort just to see another side of New York life. If you can't get tickets directly through the box offices listed below, then try TicketMaster on 212-307 7171, www.ticket master.com. They've got most games covered.

An incredibly expensive alternative is to try one of the companies that specialises in selling tickets at exorbitant prices – anything from $100 for a football game to $1,000 for a baseball game. They include Prestige Entertainment on 800-243 8849 or 800-2 GET TIX, www.prestigeentertainment.com; Ticket City on 1-800-SOLD-OUT or 800-765 3688, www.ticketcity.com.

A third alternative is to try a ticket tout – they're known as 'scalpers' in New York – outside Madison Square Garden. However, your best bet is probably to ask the concierge at your hotel. They have an amazing ability to come up with the goods.

MADISON SQUARE GARDEN

This venue on 7th Avenue at 32nd Street (subway A, C, E, 1, 2, 3, 9 to 34th Street/Penn Street) is home to all the following teams. Buy tickets from the Garden Box Office in person at 4 Pennsylvania Plaza, call TicketMaster on 212-307 7171 or visit www.thegarden.com.

NBA's New York Knicks basketball team: Nov–June

NHL's New York Rangers ice-hockey team: Oct–April

WNBA New York Liberty women's pro basketball team: May–Aug

Madison Square Garden is also famous for its boxing Fight Nights, and it hosts college/high school basketball matches. Since January 2007, the New York Titans of the National Lacrosse Team have also been playing here.

FOOTBALL

The two teams are the **New York Giants** (tel 201-935 8111, www.giants.com) and the **New York Jets** (tel 516-560 8200, www.newyorkjets.com). Both teams play at the Giants Stadium at Meadowlands (www.meadowlands.com) in New Jersey (get there on a bus from the Port Authority's 41st Street bus terminal at 42nd Street and 8th Avenue – 0800 772 2222). Meadowlands event information hotline is 201-935 3900 and the box office is 201-507 8900 or TicketMaster at 212-307 7171, www.ticketmaster.com. You'll have just as hard a time getting tickets for the Jets as for the Giants. The season runs Sept–Jan.

BASEBALL

Try the Yankee Stadium (page 274) in the Bronx at 161st Street (subway 4 (weekdays only), D to 161st Street/Yankee Stadium) to

Yankee Stadium

New England Patriots play the New York Jets

see the **New York Yankees** at play. The box office is 718-293 4300 or visit www.yankees.com.

The **New York Mets** play at Shea Stadium (page 278) in Flushing Meadows, Queens (subway 7 to Willetts Point/Shea Stadium). The box office is 718-507 8499/TI000 or visit http://newyork.mets. mlb.com. The season for both teams is April–Sept. Post-season games are played in Oct/Nov by the best teams for a gargantuan amount of money. It costs a fortune to get into one of these games, which is why the stands are usually filled with season ticket holders and celebs.

TENNIS
The **US Open** is held every year at the US Tennis Center in Flushing Meadows, Queens (subway 7 to Willetts Point/Shea Stadium), from late Aug–early Sept. For tickets call TicketMaster on 1-866-OPEN-TIX or the USTA Billie Jean King Tennis Center Ticket office on 718-760 6200 or visit www.usopen.org. Like Wimbledon, tickets for the finals are impossible to get, but it's worth seeing some of the earlier rounds to watch how it's done American style (page 278 in Chapter 14 Taste of the Outer Boroughs for details on Shea Stadium and Queens).

HORSE RACING
One of the four local tracks is **Aqueduct Stadium** in Queens (110-00 Rockaway Blvd, Jamaica) (subway A to Aqueduct Racetrack) Oct–May every Wed–Sun. Free admission 2 Jan–early March. Tel 718-641 4700, www.nyra.com/aqueduct.

The $1 million **Belmont Stakes** race, on a Saturday in early June, is the major event at the **Belmont Park Racetrack** (2150 Hempstead Turnpike, Elmont, Long Island) (take the Long Island Rail Road's 'Belmont Special' from Penn Station at 7th Avenue and 34th Street) May– July. Tel 516-488 6000, www.nyra.com/belmont. Admission to the clubhouse costs $5, the grandstand $2.

GET STUCK IN
If you want to take part in some kind of sporting activity while in New York, your best bet is to go to Central Park. Probably the most popular sports here are boating, biking, skating and running.

BIKING
You can rent bikes from the Loeb Boathouse, Central Park, East 72nd Street and Park Drive North (tel 212-517 2233, www.thecentralparkboathouse.com) for $15/$6 (kids) per hour, including helmet, or a tandem for $20 per hour, leaving a credit card deposit; 10am–dusk. Try tackling the 11km (6-mile) road loop closed to traffic at weekends. Get to the boathouse with the free trolley shuttle service every 15 minutes from 5th Avenue. For other bike rental

BRITTIP
May is Bike Month in the parks and over 150 bike-related events from rides, races and art shows to a film festival can be found on www.transalt.org. Keen cyclists may be interested in the Five Boro Bike Tour, a great way to 'do' New York.

information, see Chapter 4 What to See and Do Bike Tours (page 75).

BOATING

Also from the Loeb Boathouse (tel 212-517 2233, www.thecentralparkboathouse.com), you can rent a rowing boat for $10 per hour with a $30 deposit – or even a chauffeured gondola for $30 per half hour. Open 10am-dusk.

HORSE RIDING

Riding in Central Park is no longer an option now the Claremont Academy has closed, but pretty riding trails wind through The Ravine, in Prospect Park, which gives you a good excuse to head out to Brooklyn and the Outer Boroughs (page 269). Take a guided trail ride for $30 (book in advance) from Kensington Stables (tel 718-972 4588, www.kensingtonstables.com).

ICE-SKATING

The Wollman Memorial Rink, mid-Park between 62nd and 63rd Streets (tel 212-439-6900, www.wollmanskatingrink.com) is open Nov–March and rents skates for $5. It's $9.50 for adults ($12 at weekends), $4.75 and $5 for children, $4.75 and $8.25 for seniors.

The Lasker Rink, north-Park at 106th Street, is a bit rougher but less crowded at $4.50 for adults, $2.25 seniors and students and $4.75 for skate rental. Call 914-492 3857 or visit www.wollmanskating rink.com/lasker.htm for information on lessons.

ROLLER SKATING

On a hot summer's day, Central Park is filled with thousands of in-line skaters. The most popular places to skate are:

The Bandshell: for skate dancers and those who like to watch them

The Mall: between 69th and 72nd Streets, a tree-lined walkway where locals skate in summer

West Drive at 67th Street: a slalom course has been set up here for all to try

Wollman and Lasker Rinks: in summer these rinks are set up for the hot-shot in-line skater; fascinating to watch, too

If you want to join them, help is at hand from Blades, Board and Skate (tel 888-55 BLADES/888-552 5233, www.blades.com). It has 15 shops across New York, including 120 West 72nd Street between Columbus and Amsterdam Avenues, and rents skates for $20 a day. You can then join the Thursday night skaters who gather at 6.45pm May–Oct at Columbus Circle (www.empire skate.org). Practise a bit first!

◀▶ BRITTIP

The best time to go skating on the park drives circling Central Park is when they are closed to traffic, Mon–Fri 10am–3pm and 7pm–10pm and all weekend.

RUNNING

Every day, hundreds of runners encircle the Park. If you want to run here, it helps to know the distance. The outer loop of the Park is approximately 10km (6 miles). The middle loop is about 6km (4 miles) and the Reservoir loop is about 2km (1¼ miles). The Road Runners Club (tel 212-860 4455, www.nyrrc.org) can provide information on running in New York. Or, for a fun run and a chance to meet some locals join the New York branch of the Hash House Harriers (tel 212-427 4692, www.hashnyc.com), the 'drinking club with a running problem'.

SWIMMING

Cool off for free in the Lasker Pool (Mid-park from 108th to 109th Streets) - by far one of the favourite kids' activities in Central Park. It is open every day during summer 11am-3pm and 4pm-7pm. Click on activities on www.centralparknyc.org or call 212-534 7639.

TENNIS

Anyone for tennis? There are more tennis courts in Central Park than anywhere else in Manhattan. The Tennis Center can be found between West 94th Street and West 96th Street, near the West Drive (Subway 1, 6, 9, B, C to 96th Street). Courts are open April-Nov and a single play costs $7; lessons are available. Tel 212-360-0800, www.central parktenniscenter.com. For tennis courts all around the city, visit www.nycgovparks.org.

Battery Park promenade

CHAPTER 14

Taste of the Outer Boroughs

Those with limited time in New York may not be able to get as far as the outer boroughs of Brooklyn, the Bronx, Queens and Staten Island. But they do have a lot to offer in terms of museums, parks, restaurants, zoos, tours and atmosphere, so do go if you get a chance.

You may be surprised to learn that it's just a quick 10-minute taxi drive across the Brooklyn Bridge (see page 266) to Brooklyn (see opposite), a fascinating borough that houses many must-see sights, including Brooklyn Zoo, the cutting edge Brooklyn Museum, Prospect Park with its famous botanical garden and Coney Island, America's original fun park. Head north-east and you'll hit Queens, just 15 minutes from Manhattan, the largest New York borough and one of its most cosmopolitan, with attractions ranging from the American Museum of the Moving Image (to delight film buffs) to the stadium that's home to the Met baseball team and The New York Hall of Science. A trip across the East River from Harlem on Manhattan island takes you to the Bronx, once one of New York's dodgiest areas but now home to some surprisingly good tourist attractions, such as the Bronx Zoo. Of the many islands dotted around Manhattan, Staten Island, south-west of

Brooklyn and south of Lower Manhattan is worth a visit for the ferry ride alone, which passes the Statue of Liberty.

A TASTE OF BROOKLYN

Named after the Dutch city Breukelen, Brooklyn, in the very north of Long Island, was once a city in its own right, until it became part of New York City in 1898. Some still refer to the event as its annexation and the borough certainly has its own unique style and language, Brooklynese, which is most obvious in the pronunciation of words such as absoid (absurd), doity (dirty), noive (nerve) and toin (turn). One of the most populous of the city's five boroughs with about 2.5 million residents and accessed by ferries and bridges, Brooklyn houses a melting pot of nationalities that make up its colourful and well-defined neighbourhoods.

Famous Brooklynites include Woody Allen, Barbara Streisand and Mel Brooks and the John Travolta movie *Saturday Night Fever* was set in Bay Ridge, an Italian neighbourhood in the south of the borough. Its architecture has been noticed by celebrities and arty types and a whole host have moved into the neighbourhood, meaning its arts scene is getting cooler by the minute.

Brooklyn Heights brownstone houses

KIDS' STUFF IN THE OUTER BOROUGHS

These neighbourhoods are a wonderful place to spend time with children. Brooklyn in particular has a whole host of things on offer to entertain all ages. The massive Prospect Park has its own children's museum, a zoo, a boating lake and wildlife activities including the Wollman Rink, the Audubon Centre at the Boathouse, the Carousel, Prospect Park Zoo and the Lefferts Homestead Children's Museum and America's largest amusement park at Coney Island lies to the south.

Try these for size:

Astroland, Coney Island: (page 271)

Bronx Zoo: (page 273)

Brooklyn Children's Museum: (page 267)

New York Aquarium, Coney Island: (page 272)

Prospect Park: (page 268)

Queens County Farm Museum: (page 277)

The two most important 'sightseeing' areas are Brooklyn Heights and Prospect Park (Maps 9 and 10), home to the Brooklyn Botanical Gardens and the cutting edge Brooklyn Museum, but there's also fun to be had and a stunning beach at Coney Island, America's original amusement park now enjoying a rennaissance.

BROOKLYN HEIGHTS

Whether you've had lunch or dinner, a walk across the stunning Brooklyn Bridge will certainly help the digestion. It's the most famous bridge in New York and was the world's largest suspension bridge when it was completed in 1883. The views are fantastic and strolling along the wooden walkway gives an insight into why it took 16 years to build. If you've walked to Brooklyn from Manhattan via the bridge, you'll find yourself in the heart of Brooklyn Heights. Down by the water's edge is the River Café (page 149), a refined and elegant setting to soak up fantastic views of the Manhattan skyline. Night-time is best, when the twinkling lights in the skyscrapers look just like a picture postcard. Have a drink at the bar to enjoy the best views before tucking into a sumptuous supper. It is expensive and you will have to book well in advance, but it's an experience you are never likely to forget. Jackets are essential after 5pm.

The Heights themselves are home to some of the most beautiful and sought-after brownstone townhouses in New York. These were built in the early 18th century when bankers and financiers chose to escape Manhattan, yet could still be close enough to keep an eye on their money. Once again,

Brooklyn Heights is much in demand as an area of tranquillity close to the madness and mayhem of the city. If you walk along the Esplanade, you will see below you the former docks that were the setting for Marlon Brando's movie *On The Waterfront*.

BRITTIP

Brooklyn is fast becoming the hippest place to hang out in New York. Why else would Maggie Gyllenhaal, Heath Ledger and Steve Buscemi have moved into those large brownstones in Park Slope?

BROOKLYN BOTANIC GARDEN

- ✉ 1000 Washington Avenue between Eastern Parkway and Empire Boulevard
- ☎ 718-623 7200
- 🖰 www.bbg.org
- 🚇 Subway 2, 3 to Eastern Parkway; Q to Prospect Park
- ◷ Tues–Fri 8am–6pm, Sat, Sun 10am–6pm, closed Mon; Nov–mid-Mar closes 4.30pm daily
- $ $8 adults, $4 students and seniors, under 12s free

Right next door to Prospect Park and the Brooklyn Museum, the Botanic Garden has 10,000 different kinds of plants from around the world. It includes the world-famous Rose Garden, Japanese Garden, a Shakespeare Garden and the Celebrity Path, which commemorates some of Brooklyn's more famous children. It is most famous, though, for its Japanese cherry trees and huge collection of beautiful bonsai. Relax and enjoy the vibe in its Terrace Café.

BROOKLYN CHILDREN'S MUSEUM

- ✉ 145 Brooklyn Avenue at St Mark's Avenue, Crown Heights
- ☎ 718-735 4400
- ⌂ www.bchildmus.org
- 🚇 Subway 3, C to Kingston Avenue
- ⌚ July–Aug Tues–Thurs 1pm–6pm, Fri noon–6.30pm, Sat, Sun 11am–6pm, closed Mon; rest of year Wed–Fri 1pm–6pm, Sat, Sun 11am–6pm, closed Mon, Tues
- $ $5, under 1s free

A fabulous place for children, this was the first-ever museum for little ones. They can have a ball here playing with synthesisers, operating water wheels to dam a stream, dancing on the keys of a walk-on piano and playing instruments from around the world. The museum reopened above ground in 2007 following a $39 million expansion to double its size and it now has a Kids' Cafe among other exciting developments such as state-of-the-art technology, making it New York's first Green Museum. The new museum is located at the corner of St Mark's and Brooklyn Avenues, but check the website for up-to-date details, workshops, performances and events and be one of the first to visit.

BROOKLYN HISTORICAL SOCIETY

- ✉ 128 Pierrepont Street at Clinton Street
- ☎ 718-222 4111
- ⌂ www.brooklynhistory.org
- 🚇 Subway 2, 3, 4, 5 to Borough Hall, A, C, F to Jay Street/Borough Hall, M, R to Court Street
- ⌚ Wed–Sun 12–5pm, closed Mon, Tues
- $ $6 adults, $4 students and seniors, under 12s free

It's said that one in seven Americans can trace their family roots to Brooklyn and, as many American families originally came from the UK, it's well worth popping into this academic retreat to see if you can trace your family tree. Plus there are innovative exhibitions, educational programmes and a wonderful library.

BROOKLYN MUSEUM

- ✉ 200 Eastern Parkway at Washington Avenue
- ☎ 718-638 5000, TTY 718-399 8440
- ⌂ www.brooklynmuseum.org
- 🚇 Subway 2, 3 to Eastern Parkway/Brooklyn Museum
- ⌚ Sun 11am–6pm, Wed–Fri 10am–5pm, first Sat of month 11am–11pm, all other Sats 11am–6pm, closed Mon, Tues
- $ Suggested donation $8 adults, $4 students, seniors and children, under 12s free

The Spring of 2004 saw the opening of a magnificent new glass entrance pavilion, complementing the beautiful 19th-century Beaux Arts building that has housed this huge and important art museum since 1897. A new central lobby and public plaza have also been constructed, making the building the most visitor-friendly museum in NYC. With one of the best collections of Egyptian art in the world, housed on the third floor, it also has an extraordinary collection of Auguste Rodin sculptures among the million objects in its permanent collection. Well

Brooklyn Museum

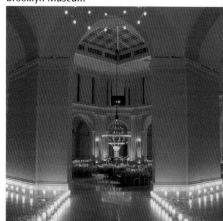

known for its African art, it was the first-ever museum to display what were once considered to be anthropological objects as fine art. The museum has a long tradition of collecting non-Western art and, since 1934, it has concentrated on fine art. The collections are divided into six departments that comprise: Egyptian, Classical and Ancient Middle Eastern Art; Painting and Sculpture; Arts of Africa, the Pacific and the Americas; Asian Art; Decorative Arts; and Prints, Drawings and Photography.

◀▶ BRITTIP

The Brooklyn Art and Garden ticket gives a 12.5 per cent saving on the cost of separate tickets if you want to visit both the Brooklyn Museum and its neighbour, the Brooklyn Botanic Garden.

The Brooklyn Museum is known for its ground-breaking art exhibitions and has a cinema theatre that screens movies and documentaries coinciding with the exhibitions. If you're heading over for the January sales and to paint the town, you could catch 'Infinite Island: Contemporary Caribbean Art', showing until 28 January 2008. In March 2007, it hosted one of the biggest arts events of the year, the opening of the Elizabeth A Sackler Centre for Feminist Art on the fourth floor. Its 8,300sq m space includes a gallery exhibiting 'The Dinner Party' by Judy Chicago, an icon of 1970s feminist art, which commemorates important women from history, and 999 others inscribed in gold on the white tile floor.

The Brooklyn Museum also organises gallery talks, films, concerts, tours and

performances for children and adults. The first Saturday of each month is known as Target First Saturdays, when a free programme of events is offered from 5pm–11pm that includes a hands-on look at art, a film, storytelling and activities for all the family and a live band to dance to. As they're popular, get there early. On the third Wednesday of every month, 5pm–9pm, is BrooklyNites, a live jazz evening, for $10. Gallery tours are free with admission Wed–Fri at 1.30pm and weekends at 2pm, 3pm and 4pm. Otherwise, you can pick up an audio tour for $3 or explore the museum with a free printed family guide.

It's useful to know that the museum has its own subway stop at Eastern Parkway, just one stop down from Brooklyn's Grand Army Plaza. This stands in a complex of 19th-century parks and gardens that includes Prospect Park, the Brooklyn Botanic Garden and the Wildlife Centre. It takes about 30 minutes to get to the museum from Midtown Manhattan.

GRAND ARMY PLAZA AND PROSPECT PARK

⊠ At the intersection of Flatbush Avenue, Eastern Parkway and Prospect Park West
☎ 718-965 8951
🖰 www.prospectpark.org
🚗 Subway 2, 3 to Grand Army Plaza; B, F, Q, S to Prospect Park
🕐 Dawn–midnight
$ Free

This urban oasis with 585 acres of meadows, waterfalls, fields and forest is one of Brooklyn's most beautiful areas. The enormous Prospect Park and Grand Army Plaza were laid out by Olmsted and Vaux after they'd completed Central Park, and many feel that these creations were even better. It contains the following:

The Arch: New York's answer to the Arc de Triomphe, the elaborately carved, 24m (80ft) arch provides a grand gateway to Prospect Park, plus a majestic overview of both the park and Manhattan. It was built as a memorial to the defenders of the Union in the Civil War, and is now the base for a series of bronze sculptures that are grouped all around the Plaza, including one of John F Kennedy.

Art in the Arch: Exhibitions are held in the spring and autumn, generally featuring artwork with a distinct Brooklyn theme. The Arch is open to the public during spring and

Brooklyn house

autumn when an exhibition is on. Weekends and holidays 1pm–5pm. Tel 718-965 8943.

Long Meadow: At nearly a mile in length, the Long Meadow stretches from the Park's northern end at Grand Army Plaza to its western end at Prospect Park Southwest. Once the home of grazing sheep and lawn tennis and croquet players, it is now frequented by strollers, kite-flyers and the Little League Baseball. At the Picnic House you'll find WCs and picnic tables, while the Metropolitan Opera and the New York Philharmonic Orchestra put on summer events here (page 258). Tel 718-965 8951.

The Long Meadow is accessible via the Grand Army Plaza and any entrance along Prospect Park West, such as 3rd Street or 9th Street. It is free to enter and is only closed 1am–5am.

The Bandshell: Close to Long Meadow, this is one of the park's main attractions for live outdoor entertainment. With its three-storey-high acoustic shell, raised stage and large circular plaza, the Bandshell features food and drinks, WCs and first-come, first-served seating in the 2,000-seat plaza or 5,000-seat lawn. In addition to musical performances, the Bandshell hosts film events on its 6.5m (21ft) high and 15m (50ft) wide movie screen. But it is best known for the Celebrate Brooklyn! Performing Arts Festival – a series of music, dance, film and spoken word performances each June to August at 7.30pm for a $3 donation, which attract nearly 250,000 people per season (page 252). For further information, tel 718-855 7882 or visit www.celebratebrooklyn.org. The nearest

subway is the F train to 15th Street/Prospect Park Station or the 2, 3 to Grand Army Plaza.

The Ravine: One of Prospect Park's most natural features, here you will find a steep narrow gorge lined with the trees and foliage of Brooklyn's only forest. Still recovering from decades of overuse that caused soil erosion, the Ravine and surrounding woodlands have been gradually restored by the Prospect Park Alliance since 1996. You can explore on your own or take one of the weekend guided nature tours.

The Ravine is open March–Nov Sat, Sun 1pm–5pm, with tours at 3pm from the Audubon Centre at the Boathouse. For information on tours, tel 718-287 3400. Best subways to take are the F to15th Street/Prospect Park or 7th Avenue or the Q to 7th Avenue.

PROSPECT PARK FOR FAMILIES

With nature trails, wildlife and activities from boating, skating and baseball to arts and crafts, there is plenty of entertainment for the family in this mini Central Park.

Audubon Center At The Boathouse

- ✉ Lincoln Road/Ocean Avenue entrance to Prospect Park
- ☎ 718-287 3400 Audubon Center; 718-965 8999 events hotline
- ⌕ www.prospectpark.org
- 🚗 Subway Q, S, B to Prospect Park
- ◷ April–Nov Thurs–Sun and school holidays noon–5pm; Dec–March weekends and school holidays noon–4pm
- $ Free admission. Electric boat tour $5 for those aged 13 and over, $3 for 3–12s, children 2 and under free

The design of this beautiful 1905 Beaux Art boathouse, with its elegant arches, decorative tiles and classical balcony, was based on a 16th-century Venetian library. Now an official Historic New York City Landmark, it is home to the state-of-the-art

Brooklyn Museum of Art

Audubon Center

Audubon Center, which is dedicated to preserving wildlife and natural education. Families can take tours along the new Lullwater Nature Trail or on the Lullwater by the electric boat *Independence* (April–Oct), as well as one of four nature trails or participate in family activities such as craftwork, music and technology sessions. Regular weekly events include Nature Babies Mon 9.30am–11am, a themed crafts, music and storytelling session for 18 months to 3 years old (tel 718-287 3400 ext 114) and free birdwatching on Saturdays noon–1.30pm for ages 9–13.

The Carousel

✉ Children's Corner, Prospect Park, at intersection of Flatbush and Ocean Avenues and Empire Blvd
☎ 718-789 2822
🖱 www.prospectpark.org
🚇 Subway Q, S, B to Prospect Park
🕐 April–Jun and Sep–Oct Thurs–Sun 12am–5pm; Jul–Labor Day (Nov) 12am–6pm
$ $1.50 per ride; 6 tickets for $8

Right next door to the zoo and museum is the magnificently carved carousel, which features 51 horses, a lion, giraffe, a deer and two dragon-pulled chariots. It is also one of the few carousels in the world that is wheelchair accessible.

Lefferts Historic House

✉ Children's Corner, Prospect Park, at intersection of Flatbush and Ocean Avenues and Empire Blvd
☎ 718-789 2822
🖱 www.prospectpark.org
🚇 Subway Q, S, B to Prospect Park
🕐 April–Dec Thurs–Sun 12am–5pm; Dec–March 12am–4pm
$ Free

Right by the main Grand Army Plaza entrance to Prospect Park stands this restored 18th-century farmhouse, once owned by original Dutch settlers in Brooklyn. Children can play with cooking tools, hunt for barnyard implements or play with toys from the era. Families can also take part in craft activities such as candle-making, sewing, butter-churning and making fire with a flint and steel. At weekends throughout the summer, stories are told under a tree, plus hoop games to play and gardening to do.

Prospect Park Zoo

✉ Prospect Park, 450 Flatbush Avenue
☎ 718-399 7339
🖱 nyzoosandaquarium.com
🚇 Subway Q, S to Prospect Park
🕐 April–Oct Mon–Fri 10am–5pm, weekends and holidays 10am–5.30pm; end Oct–end March daily 10am–4.30pm
$ $6 adults, $2.25 seniors, $2 children 3–12; under 3s free

Again close to the Grand Army Plaza entrance to Prospect Park, this is Brooklyn's only zoo. It features nearly 400 animals and more than 80 species in an environment that gives children close-up views of some of the world's most unusual ones. They include prairie dogs, wallabies, tamarin monkeys, baboons, a red panda, plus a vibrant band of birds, reptiles and amphibians. The new interactive Discovery Center is open every weekend 11am–3pm.

The Wollman Rink

As the one of the same name in Central Park, offers ice-skating in winter and pedal boats

Brooklyn Heights

on the lake in summer, and is reached through the Parkside/Ocean Avenues entrance. Ice-skating costs $5 for adults, $3 for children 14 and under and seniors plus skate rental for $5.50 and pedal boating costs $15 an hour (cash only). Hours vary by day and season; tel 718-287 6431 or visit www.prospectpark.org for details.

NEW YORK CITY TRANSIT MUSEUM

✉ Schermerhorn Street at Boerum Place
☎ 718-694 1600
⌖ www.mta.info/mta/museum
🚌 Subway M, R to Court Street; A, C, G to Hoyt-Schermerhorn Street
🕐 Tues–Fri 10am–4pm, Sat, Sun noon–5pm, closed Mon
$ $5 adults, $3 seniors and children under 12; Wed seniors free

This is a great museum for transport buffs of all ages and is located in an old subway station in Brooklyn Heights. Steel, Stone and Backbone traces the tale of the city's subway and includes old subway cars that you can get on, and you can even hang on to one of the original leather straps (nowadays replaced by metal poles and bars) that created the nickname of 'straphangers' for people who use the subway. The museum has recently undergone a major renovation and now has a new art gallery, a classroom for a children's workshop, a computer lab and a reference library. The main interactive exhibit depicts the history of buses and trolleys in the city, with a display of more than 200 trolleys and buses. There is also a film about the building of the subway, old turnstiles, maps and a gift shop.

JEWISH CHILDREN'S MUSEUM

✉ 792 Eastern Parkway at corner of Kingston Avenue, Crown Heights, Brooklyn
☎ 718-467 0600
⌖ www.jcmonline.org
🚌 Subway 3 to Kingston Avenue
🕐 Mon–Thurs 10am–4pm, Sun 10am–6pm; closed Fri, Sat (apart from select evenings)
$ £10 per person; children under 2 free

The first of its kind in the world, opened in 2004 at a cost of $31 million by Jewish Children International, its interactive multimedia exhibits entertain, educate and engage children of all backgrounds about Jewish heritage.

CONEY ISLAND

At the Southern end of Brooklyn, America's largest amusement park is undoubtedly tacky, and has definitely seen better days, but that doesn't stop children having fun, making it a great family day out.

It has around 35 rides and other attractions along a four mile stretch and the Native American Indians called it 'land without shadows' as its stunning beach was bathed in sunlight all day.

🏴 BRITTIP

Visit www.coneyisland.com for the schedule of quirky shows by the seashore such as the Coney Island Circus Sideshow and the Mermaid Parade.

Gentrification is spilling over from Brooklyn making this an up-and-coming neighbourhood, with a $1.5 billion renovation and expansion plan beginning in 2007, adding a water park, a manmade canal for boat rides, 21 rides and shopping, hotels and cinemas. In the meantime, KeySpan Park (tel 718-499 8497, http://brooklyn cyclones.com) has been bringing in the crowds to see the popular baseball league team, The Brooklyn Cyclones.

🏴 BRITTIP

Try one of Nathan's hot dogs (tel 516-338 8500, www.nathans famous.com) a Coney Island institution and still sold from its original site. Nathan holds an eating contest here every 4 July; the record is 53 hot dogs with buns in 12 minutes!

Astroland

✉ 1000 Surf Avenue between West 8th Street and Jones Walk, Coney Island
☎ 718-265 2100
⌖ www.astroland.com
🚌 Subway Q, F to West 8th Street, D, N to Stillwell Avenue
🕐 June–Sept daily noon–late evening, sessions Mon–Thurs noon–6pm, 4pm–10pm, Fri noon–6pm; winter weekends only
$ $22.99 ticket allows you on all rides (Mon–Fri only); individual rides $2.50–6

Home of The Cyclone rollercoaster, it has rides for every age and puts on fireworks every Friday evening throughout summer.

BRITTIP
The New York Aquarium is just a short stroll away from Astroland amusement park, so if the weather turns bad you can take shelter there.

New York Aquarium
- ✉ 610 Surf Avenue at West 8th Street, Coney Island
- ☎ 718-265-FISH
- 🖰 www.nyaquarium.com
- 🚇 Subway F, Q to West 8th Street, NY Aquarium
- ◷ May–Sept Mon–Fri 10am–6pm, Sat, Sun 10am–7pm; March–May and Sept–Oct Mon–Fri 10am–5pm, Sat, Sun 10am–5.30pm; Oct–April daily 10am–4.30pm
- $ $12 adults, $8 under 13s and seniors, under 2s free

BRITTIP
A stroll along the legendary Coney Island boardwalk to Brighton Beach will take you to Little Odessa, a thriving Russian community complete with traditional bathhouses, bookshops and restaurants serving borscht, vodka and caviar.

Most famous for its beluga whale family and performing lions, this excellent aquarium has another unusual exhibit showing the creatures that live in New York's famous East River. Sharks, dolphins and a re-creation of the Pacific coastline also feature.

A TASTE OF THE BRONX

Diversity definitely drives the energy of this vibrant destination in the northernmost tip of the city. Nearly 50 per cent of Bronx residents are Latino, including its most

Bronx Museum of the Arts

famous former resident Jennifer Lopez, with the highest concentration hailing from 'the islands' – Puerto Rico and the Dominican Republic – and Mexico. However, it's also a place where traditions from Italy and Ireland continue to flourish, and a growing number of Asian immigrants are now making this area their home.

The Bronx has a scary reputation, but parts of it are very safe and have attractions that make a visit here well worthwhile. The Bronx history dates back to 1609 when Henry Hudson took refuge from a storm here. It is the northernmost borough of New York and the only one on the mainland. In 1639 Jonas Bronck, a Swedish captain from the Netherlands, settled here with his wife and servants. The story goes that when people left Manhattan to visit the family, they would say they were going to the Broncks' and the name stuck.

The horrible part is the south Bronx, but even here things are improving. In the north lies the beautiful Botanical Garden that includes a huge chunk of the original forests that once covered all of New York, and the Bronx Zoo, one of the world's leading wildlife conservation parks.

BRONX MUSEUM OF THE ARTS
- ✉ 1040 Grand Concourse at 165th Street
- ☎ 718-681 6000
- 🖰 www.bxma.org
- 🚇 Subway B, D to 167th Street/Grand Concourse, 4 to 161st Street/Yankee Stadium
- ◷ Wed, Thurs, Sat, Sun noon–6pm, Fri noon–8pm, closed Mon, Tues
- $ $5 adults, $3 students and seniors, under 12s free; free Fri

Housed in an attractive glass building, the museum's collection consists of more than 700 contemporary works of art in all media by African, Asian and Latin American artists. At the end of 2006, the museum expanded into a $19 million new building that won the Art's Commission's Excellence in Design prize, giving it a major new gallery, events space and an outdoor terrace to sit and absorb the edgy vibe of this vibrant area.

BRITTIP
If you're looking to eat in the Bronx, visit the Neighbourhood section of the Bronx Museum of the Arts website www.bxma.org for some suggestions.

New York Botanical Garden

BRONX ZOO AND WILDLIFE CONSERVATION SOCIETY

✉ Bronx River Parkway at Fordham Road
☎ 718-367 1010
🖰 www.bronxzoo.org
🚗 Subway 2, 5 to East Tremont Avenue/West Farms Square
🕐 April–Oct Mon–Fri 10am–5pm, Sat, Sun 10am–5.30pm daily; rest of the year 10–4.30pm
$ $14 adults, $12 seniors, $10 children, under 3s free; suggested donation on Wed; under 17s must be accompanied by an adult; cheaper Nov–Mar; individual attractions/rides from $2–$5 each, Pay-One-Price ticket that includes admission and all rides $25 adult, $21 seniors, $19 children

The Bronx Zoo is known as New York's 'wild backyard' and respected worldwide for its tradition of conservation and ecological awareness alongside the naturalistic habitats it provides, such as the African Plains where antelope roam. It is the largest urban zoo in America and houses 4,000 animals and 560 species. The Congo Gorilla Forest is a 2.5-hectare (6-acre) rainforest, inhabited by two troops of gorillas. Other highlights include the rare snow leopard in the Himalayan Highlands and entering The World of Darkness to see nocturnal animals in action, such as a glow-in-the-dark scorpion. The latest exhibit to open is Tiger Mountain, which takes you a whisker away from the largest member of the cat family.

Disney-style rides include a guided monorail tour through Wild Asia, an aerial safari, camel rides and a zoo shuttle. There is also a children's zoo. Some of the exhibits and all of the rides, apart from the bug carousel, are open only April–Oct. For a tour by Friends of Wildlife Conservation, tel 718-220 5141.

LITTLE ITALY

Technically, this area is known as Belmont or simply Arthur Avenue, but it is tagged the Little Italy of the Bronx. Take the D train to Tremont Avenue and walk east to Arthur Avenue. Treat yourself to lunch at one of the many Italian restaurants here. The old-world Belmont District is a charming area filled with shops selling every Italian delicacy you can think of, plus the Enrico Fermi Cultural Centre in the Belmont Library (610 East 186th Street at Hughes Avenue, tel 718-933 6410, www.nypl.org/branch/local/bx/ber.cfm) and the old Belmont Italian American Theater (2385 Arthur Avenue, tel 718-364 4700), which still shows films.

🇬🇧 BRITTIP

If you're feeling peckish, pop into Mike's Deli in the Arthur Avenue Retail Market (718-295 5033, www.arthuravenue.com) for a taste of Italy.

Afterwards, walk north on Arthur, then east on Fordham Road past Fordham University to the Bronx Park.

🇬🇧 BRITTIP

If you want to discover more of Little Italy and the Irish neighbourhood of Woodlawn, contact Susan Birnbaum, who runs SusanSez NYC Walkabouts (tel 917-509 3111, www.dbsystems group.com/susansez). She leads tours around Arthur Avenue and beyond on her Bronx Walkabout.

NEW YORK BOTANICAL GARDEN

✉ Bronx River Parkway and Fordham Road
☎ 718-817 8700
🖰 www.nybg.org
🚗 Subway 2, 5 to Bronx Park East. If going direct, take subway C, D, 4 to Bedford Park and then the BX26 bus or Metro-North from Grand Central Terminal.
🕐 April–Oct Tues–Sun 10am–6pm; Nov–Mar 10am–5pm, closed Mon
$ Combo ticket $13 adults, $11 seniors/students, $5 children 2-12, under 2s free

Originally supported by magnates Cornelius Vanderbilt, Andrew Carnegie and JP Morgan, society folk still support these gardens today. Check out the Peggy Rockefeller Rose

BRITTIP

The Botanical Garden is just a road away from the Bronx Zoo – sadly that is an eight-lane highway and the entrances are a mile apart. In the absence of a pedestrian link, take a short taxi ride. Call Miles Taxi Co on 718-884 8888.

Garden, with over 2,700 bushes. This is one of the oldest and largest botanic gadens in the world, and the magnificent Victorian iron and glass conservatory near the main entrance is modelled on the one at Kew Gardens in London. It has been refurbished to perfection and is home to the gardens highlight, A World of Plants, a trip through the world's ecosystems, from dripping rainforest to dry desert. In the grounds, you can see the stunning Bronx River Gorge where the meandering waterway tumbles over a rocky outcrop formed by the retreat of the Wisconsin Ice Sheet. For thousands of years, New York was covered by a hemlock forest and a 16-hectare (40-acre) fragment remains in the gardens. Look out for the rock carving of a turtle drawn by the Weckquasgeek Indians many years ago. The 50 gardens and 100 hectares (250 acres) include The Everett Children's Adventure Garden, which is a great outdoor science experience for kids, and the Family Garden, created by children. There are also puppet shows, dance and music concerts, and other events throughout the year.

VAN CORTLANDT HOUSE MUSEUM

✉ Van Cortlandt Park, Broadway at West 246th Street
☎ 718-543 3344
🖰 www.vancortlandthouse.org
🚗 Subway 1 to 242nd Street/Van Cortlandt Park
🕐 Tues–Fri 10am–3pm, Sat, Sun 11am–4pm, closed Mon
$ $5 adults, $3 seniors/students, free on Wed, under 12s free

Once an 18th-century family-run plantation, Van Cortlandt House was turned into a historic house museum at the end of the 19th century by the National Society of Colonial Dames. Now you can walk through the family's public and private rooms, including a slave bedchamber, and see the fascinating decorative art collections from the colonial and federal periods.

WAVE HILL

✉ West 249th Street at Independence Avenue
☎ 718-549 3200
🖰 www.wavehill.org
🚗 Subway A to 207th Street or 1 to 231st Street and then the Bx7/Bx10 bus on Broadway
🕐 15 April–14 Oct Tues–Sun 9am–5.30pm; June and July until 9pm Wed; 15 Oct–14 April 9am–4.30pm
$ $4 adults, $2 seniors/students, children under 6 free; free Sat am and daily Dec–Feb

A scenic public garden and cultural centre, Wave Hill holds international events throughout the year, such as the Barefoot Dancing series when you're invited to move to the music from Kotchegna or folk music from Bulgaria. So it's worth checking the website to see what's happening when you visit. Each Saturday Jack Chu teaches Tai Chi Chuan to beginners at 10am for $10. There's a free garden and glasshouse tour every Sunday at 2.15pm and at sunset on Wednesdays throughout June and July, with entertainment and food and wine tastings from 6.30-9pm, free with admission.

BRITTIP

Sports fans can take a break and enjoy a hot dog and a drink at the Sidewalk Café on the Plaza next to Gates 4 and 6 at the Yankee Stadium.

YANKEE STADIUM

✉ River Avenue at 161st Street
☎ 718-293 4300
🖰 www.yankees.com
🚗 Subway 4, (weekdays only), D to 161st Street/Yankee Stadium
🕐 Tours daily at noon (except on game days), reservations recommended.
$ Tickets for games from $12; tours $15 adults, $8 seniors/children 14 and under

Sporting aficionados will be delighted to see the tribute to past baseball players, the field, dugout, clubhouse, locker room and press box on the one hour tour at the New York Yankees base. Babe Ruth hit the first home run in the first game played here in 1923 and other sporting greats that have played here include Joe DiMaggio, who married Marilyn Monroe, and Mickey Mantle. The record-breaking New York Yankees are the baseball team with the richest history, and going to a home game is a real New York experience (page 262).

A TASTE OF QUEENS

The largest of all the New York boroughs (Map 11) at 290sq km (112sq miles), Queens has the highest percentage of first-generation immigrants. Given the borough's suburban look, it is hard to imagine it as the densely forested area it was four centuries ago. Then it was inhabited by the Algonquin Indian tribes, who fished in its freshwater streams and creeks, hunted game and gathered shellfish from its bays. It is also difficult to picture 17th-century Queens and the borough's early Dutch and English farmers, along with Quakers fighting for religious freedom.

◀▶ BRITTIP

The Queens Council on the Arts produces an annual Cultural Guide filled with information about the borough. Order from 718-647 3377 or www.queenscouncilarts.org.

Yet there remain places where such scenes can easily be reconstructed, such as at the Jamaica Bay Wildlife Refuge (tel 718-318 4340) on open marshland, once the territory of Jameco Indians and now home to many species of birds spotted along the nature walkways, and the Queens County Farm Museum (page 277). This has the largest tract of farmland left in New York and its colonial farmhouse is thought to date back to 1772.

Today, Queens is as much about the ethnic diversity of the borough and in each of the places mentioned in this section you will find many examples of the cultures of people from Asia, the West Indies, Latin America and Greece. In fact, Queens is home to the largest Greek population outside of Greece; Astoria is the Athens of the United States, with authentic restaurants and markets on the main thoroughfare of Ditmars Boulevard. Jackson Heights is a little India, with colourful sari shops, restaurants and video stores with the latest Bollywood offerings.

In fact, so diverse is this sprawling borough that the local subway line number 7 has been jokingly renamed the International Express. It's also home to JFK and LaGuardia airports, so Queens is often the first entry point for millions of people to New York and the rest of the United States.

Top things to see in this borough include the American Museum of the Moving Image in Astoria and in Flushing, The New York Hall of Science, with 175 exhibits in a bubble-shaped space-age building, and the Queen's Museum of Art, which even has aeroplanes flying over its miniature model of New York City. A stroll through Little Asia en route to the Shea Stadium, home to the Mets baseball team, will give you a taste of the ethnic diversity of this borough. The mouthwatering smells coming from the Vietnamese, Chinese and Korean restaurants may even make you want to stop awhile.

AMERICAN MUSEUM OF THE MOVING IMAGE

✉ 35th Avenue at 36th Street, Astoria
☎ 718-784 0077
🖰 www.ammi.org
🚊 Subway G, R, V to Steinway Street
🕐 Wed and Thurs 11am–5pm, Fri 11am–8pm, Sat, Sun 11am–6.30pm
$ $10 adults, $7.50 seniors and students, $5 children (5–18), under 5s free; admission into galleries free Fri 4–8pm

If you're into the making of films, then you will want to take the 15-minute train ride out to Queens to see this museum. Set in the historic Astoria Studios, which are still used today, it is home to screening rooms, rebuilt sets, costumes, props, posters and other memorabilia.

The museum is full of interactive delights, such as the perennially popular diner set from *Seinfeld* and a life-sized dummy of Linda Blair from *The Exorcist*, complete with rotating head. Then there's the interactive Behind the Scenes exhibit, where you can see how it's all done and even make your own short film. Catch the free film screenings on Saturday and Sunday afternoons and evenings, and on Fridays at 7.30pm.

◀▶ BRITTIP

Astoria is the heart of New York's Greek community and is filled with delis and restaurants. After you've been to the American Museum of the Moving Image, head to 31st Street and Broadway for a spot of lunch.

BOWNE HOUSE

✉ 37-01 Bowne Street, Flushing
☎ 718-359 0528
🖱 www.bownehouse.org
🚇 Subway 7 to Main Street
🕐 Tues, Sat, Sun 2.30–4.30pm
$ $4 adults, $3 seniors, $2 students and children under 12

You can walk to this NYC landmark from Corona Park. Built in 1661 by John Bowne, this is the oldest house in Queens and the second oldest in New York City. It is a rare example of Dutch–English architecture, with an unusual collection of decorative arts, paintings and furniture, all of which belong to nine generations of the Bowne family. Bowne was a pivotal figure in the fight for religious freedom in the New World.

BRITTIP

For shopping, attractions, events, tours and restaurants in Queens, click on to www.discover queens.info or call 718-263 0546.

LITTLE ASIA

✉ Roosevelt Avenue and Main Street

The nearby jumble of Chinese, Korean, Thai and Vietnamese markets and restaurants offers everything from soft-shell turtles and bentwood bows to kimchi and wire baskets. At 45-57 Bowne Street is the beautiful Hindu Temple Society of North America (718-460 8484, www.nyganeshtemple.org), which is adorned with carvings of Hindu gods and is open 8am–9pm daily.

Dinner: Choopan Kabab House, 43-27 Main Street. Tel 718-539 3180. A great place to try out Afghan fare. Alternatively, you could sample Korean food at the 24 hour Kum Gang San, 138-28 Northern Boulevard between Bowne and Union Streets. Tel 718-461 0909, www.kumgangsan.net.

Nightclubs: Try Chibcha (79-05 Roosevelt Avenue, tel 718-429 9033, www.elchibcha.com, subway 7 to 82nd Street), a Colombian nightclub and restaurant. Or, if you prefer, Sunday night is Irish music night at Taylor Hall (45 Queens Boulevard, subway 7 to 46th Street). For something more exotic, there are operettas, flamenco and tango shows at the Thalia Spanish Theatre (41-17 Greenpoint Avenue, Sunnyside, tel 718-729 3880, www.thaliatheatre.org, subway 7 to 40th Street).

BRITTIP

For more information on the arts in Queens, contact the Queens Council on the Arts on 718-647 3377 or visit www.queens councilarts.org.

LITTLE INDIA

Take the International Express – subway 7 from Times Square to the 74th Street/ Broadway station and, at 74th Street between Roosevelt and 37th Avenues at Jackson Heights – to find this Indian haven. Stroll through the cumin-scented streets looking at the intricately embellished gold and silk on display. Two stops you should include are the Menka Beauty Salon (37-56, 74th Street, Jackson Heights, tel 718-424 6851) where traditional henna designs are drawn on the skin, and the Butala Emporium (37-46 74th Street, Jackson Heights, tel 718-899 5590), which sells everything from Southern Asian art and children's books in Punjabi to Ayurvedic medicine and religious items.

Lunch: Travel one stop to 82nd Street in Elmhurst for an Argentinian lunch at La Fusta (80-32 Baxter Avenue, tel 718-429 8222, www.lafustanewyork.com).

NEW YORK HALL OF SCIENCE

✉ 47-01 111th Street at 47th Avenue, Flushing Meadows/Corona Park at 48th Avenue
☎ 718-699 0005
🖱 www.nyscience.org
🚇 Subway 7 to 111th Street
🕐 Sept–March Tues–Thurs 9.30am–2pm, Fri 9.30am–5pm, Sat, Sun 10am–6pm; April–Jun Mon–Thurs 9.30am–2pm, Fri 9.30am–5pm, Sat, Sun 10am–6pm; July–August Mon–Fri 9.30am–5pm, Sat, Sun 10am–6pm
$ $11 adults, $8 seniors and children 2–17, free Sept–June Fri 2–5pm and Sun 10–11am

The bubble-shaped building features memorable daily science demonstrations and 225 interactive exhibits explaining the mysteries of digital technology, quantum theory, microbes and light and also offers slides, whirligigs, space nets and a giant teeter-totter (seesaw). Rated as the best science museum in the country, all events are free with admission.

TASTE OF THE OUTER BOROUGHS

THE NOGUCHI MUSEUM

✉ 9-01 33rd Road at Vernon Boulevard, Long Island City
☎ 718-204 7088
🖰 www.noguchi.org
🚗 Subway N, W to Broadway stop in Queens, F to Queensbridge/21st Street or 7 to 33rd Street/Vernon Boulevard (Wed–Fri), then Q103 bus or take the Sunday Shuttle from Manhattan
🕐 Wed–Fri 10am–5pm, Sat, Sun 11am–6pm, closed Mon
$ Suggested donation $10 adults, $5 seniors/students, pay what you wish first Fri of the month

If you love your ballet and Balanchine in particular, you'll enjoy seeing some of the sets created by this Japanese artist, who strove to bring art and nature into the urban environment. These were Noguchi's studios and there are now more than 300 of his works on display. A fascinating spot for art and ballet buffs.

BRITTIP

For an active tour of Queens consider Back to the Old Country – The Ethnic Apple Tour offered by Bike The Big Apple (tel 877 865-0078, www.bikethebig apple.com) a full day tour that leaves every Friday at 10.15am year round, weather permitting, and costs $75.

P.S. 1 CONTEMPORARY ART CENTER

✉ 22-25 Jackson Avenue at 46th Avenue, Long Island City
☎ 718-784 2084
🖰 www.ps1.org
🚗 Subway E, V to 23rd Street/Ely Avenue; G to 21st Street/Van Alst; 7 to 45th Road/Court House Square
🕐 Thurs–Mon noon–6pm
$ Suggested donation $5 adults, $2 seniors/students

All forms of artistic expression are found in the oldest and second largest non-profit-making arts centre, affiliated to MoMA and known for its cutting edge exchibitions. Check out paintings and videos of performance art that depict elements of American culture and life in the 20th and 21st centuries.

BRITTIP

Why not travel to Queens by Water Taxi (www.nywater taxi.com)? Cruise up the East River and get off at Hunter's Point near the P.S. 1 Contemporary Art Center.

QUEENS BOTANICAL GARDEN

✉ 43-50 Main Street, Flushing
☎ 718-886 3800
🖰 www.queensbotanical.org
🚗 Subway 7 to Main St/Flushing
🕐 April–Oct Tues–Fri 8am–6pm, Sat, Sun 8am–7pm; Nov–Mar Tues–Sun 8am–4.30pm, closed Mon
$ Free

Walk back to the north-east corner of Corona Park to see the 16 hectares (39 acres) of plants, shrubs and trees that were created for the 1939 World Fair.

QUEENS COUNTY FARM MUSEUM

✉ 73-50 Little Neck Parkway at Union Turnpike, Floral Park
☎ 718-347 3276
🖰 www.queensfarm.org
🚗 Subway E, F to Kew Gardens/Union Turnpike, then take the Q46 bus to Little Neck Parkway
🕐 Mon–Fri 9am–5pm outdoor visiting only; free tours of the farmhouse are available Sat, Sun only 10am–5pm
$ Free, $2 hayrides

This 19-hectare (47-acre) site is the only working historical farm that still exists in New York and includes the 18th-century Adriance farmhouse, barns, outbuildings, a greenhouse and livestock. Animal feed is on sale to feed the sheep and goats, making it popular with little ones, as are the tractor-drawn hayrides offered on weekends April–Oct.

P.S. 1 Contemporary Art Center

TASTE OF THE OUTER BOROUGHS

BRITTIP

Queens Theatre in the Park (tel 718 760 0064, www.queens theatre.org) at Flushing Meadows Corona Park hosts some excellent drama, dance and theatre performances, as well as music concerts and cabaret for all ages.

QUEENS MUSEUM OF ART

- ✉ New York City Building, Flushing Meadows/Corona Park
- ☎ 718-592 9700
- 🖰 www.queensmuseum.org
- 🚇 Subway 7 to Willets Point/Shea Stadium
- 🕐 5th July–3rd Sept Wed–Sun noon–6pm, Fri noon–8pm; 4th Sept–4th July Wed–Fri 10am–5pm, Sat, Sun noon–5pm, closed Mon, Tues
- $ Suggested donation $5 adults; $2.50 seniors and children; children under 5 free.

The most famous exhibit here is the miniature scale model of the entire city of New York, complete with miniature lights that turn dark every 15 minutes, and aeroplanes flying into the airports. You can rent binoculars to check out where you're staying. The museum is on the site of the 1964 World Fair, reopened recently after a $15 million renovation and which has seen new additions, including a multimedia spotlight on New York attractions. Tours of The Panorama of the City of New York are held Saturday and Sundays at 3.30pm.

SHEA STADIUM

- ✉ 123-01 Roosevelt Ave, Flushing
- ☎ 718-507 8499/Tl000
- 🖰 http://newyork.mets.mlb.com
- 🚇 Subway 7 to Willets Point/Shea Stadium
- 🕐 Ticket office Mon–Fri 9am–6pm, Sat, Sun 9am–5pm

BRITTIP

A free weekend Queens Culture Trolley (bus) (tel 718–592 9700, www.queensmuseum.org) takes you from the Queens Museum of Art noon–5pm at weekends for a journey through Flushing Meadows in Corona Park to Northern Boulevard's Restaurant Row, Corona and Louis Armstrong House and Jackson Heights

Stroll through Corona Park to the home of the Mets baseball team (see page 262). On the way you will see huge remnants of both the 1939 and the 1964 World Fairs, plus a series of weird buildings such as the New York Hall of Science. The park also has barbecue pits and boating on the lake. This is where Flushing Meadows plays host to the US Open tennis championship. As well as being a sports stadium, in the past it also hosted music concerts. Its stage has seen the likes of The Beatles, Jimi Hendrix, The Rolling Stones and Elton John.

SOCRATES SCULPTURE PARK

- ✉ 21-01 Vernon Boulevard at Broadway, Long Island City
- ☎ 718-956 1819
- 🖰 www.socratessculpturepark.org
- 🚇 Subway N or W (Mon–Fri only) to Broadway/Long Island City
- 🕐 Daily 10am–sunset
- $ Free

A great place to take children as they can climb, romp and run around these massive sculptures laid out in the park. Hard to believe it was once an abandoned riverside landfill and illegal dumpsite! It also has films outdoors in summer.

BRITTIP

If you get thirsty on your tour, pop into one of the many Irish pubs that are centred in Queens. Fun, friendly and lively, you're bound to meet locals who'll be able to give you a colourful account of life in the 'burbs. Irish Circle (101-19 Rockaway Boulevard, tel 718–474 9002), Mary McGuire's (38-04 Broadway, Astoria, tel 719–728 3434) and the newer, Woodhaven House (63-98 Woodhaven Boulevard, tel 718–894 5400) in Rego Park are highly recommended.

A TASTE OF STATEN ISLAND

With its picturesque scenery, Staten Island deserves its Indian name Monacnong, which means 'enchanted woods'. It's long been a haven for Italian-American and Irish-American populations and hasn't had a vast melting pot of cultures like the other outer boroughs. But in recent years that has slowly begun to change, with the population growing and diversifying. Hispanics now

JAZZ IN QUEENS

Queens was the home of some of the greatest jazz musicians including Louis Armstrong, Dizzy Gillespie and Count Basie. The **Queens Jazz Trail** shows you the homes and haunts of these jazz greats. It's a great tour even if you aren't a real jazz buff, as it gives an insight into the lifestyles of another era. The tour includes a visit to the home of Louis Armstrong, the Louis Armstrong archives at Queens University (fantastic views of Manhattan's skyline) and the Addisleigh Park area, home to celebrated sports stars and top jazz and pop entertainers, including Ella Fitzgerald, Lena Horne, Count Basie, Billie Holiday, Milt Hinton and Thomas 'Fats' Waller. Other famous musicians who lived in different parts of Queens include Dizzy Gillespie, Leon 'Bix' Beiderbecke, Glenn Miller and Tony Bennett. The tour includes a delicious traditional soul food lunch or dinner and a jazz concert at the newly renovated concert hall at Flushing Town Hall.

If jazz really is your thing, then avoid the tourist-trap venues on Manhattan and head out to Queens for a cheap jazz night out.

Contact **Flushing Town Hall** (137-35 Northern Boulevard, Flushing, tel 718-463 7700, www.flushingtownhall.org) for details of the Queens Jazz Trail, $35 on the first Saturday of the month 1pm–4pm. They also have details of forthcoming jazz concerts, as well as the **Cultural Collaborative Jamaica** (Jamaica Avenue and 153rd Street, Jamaica, tel 718-526 3217, www.go2ccj.org). Not only is it cheaper to get into venues in Queens, but you can also usually stay for both sets rather than being forced to leave after just one.

account for around 12 per cent of the population, while 6 per cent is Asian.

Even if you don't have much time you should try to fit in a trip on the free Staten Island Ferry, which leaves Manhattan Island from Battery Park (page 66) and offers brilliant views of Downtown and the Statue of Liberty.

◀▪▦▪ BRITTIP

Staten Island was one of the communities hardest hit by the 11 September attacks, and has constructed its own uplifting memorial, opened in 2004, that looks like outstretched wings rising from the ground or a flower about to blossom. Pay your respects as you get off the ferry. It is on the adjacent North Shore Waterfront Esplanade.

ALICE AUSTEN HOUSE

- ✉ 2 Hylan Boulevard, Staten Island between Edgewater and Bay Streets
- ☎ 718-816 4506
- ⌐ฺ www.aliceausten.org
- 🚌 Bus S51 to Hylan Boulevard from Staten Island Ferry
- ⊙ Mar–Dec Thurs–Sun noon–5pm, closed Jan–Feb
- $ Suggested donation $2 per person adult, under 16s free

A unique museum in the restored Victorian house and garden of Alice Austen, one of

America's first female documentary photographers. A great place to gain an insight into life in New York at the turn of the century.

HISTORIC RICHMOND TOWN

- ✉ 441 Clarke Ave between St Patrick's Place and Richmond Road
- ☎ 718-351 1611
- ⌐ฺ www.historicrichmondtown.org
- 🚌 S74 bus from the ferry to Richmond Road and St Patrick's Place
- ⊙ Sept–June Wed–Sun 1pm–5pm; Juy–Aug Wed–Fri 10am–5pm, Sat, Sun 1-5pm
- $ Adults $5, seniors $4, children 5-17 $3.50

A magnificent 40.5-hectare (100-acre) village that features buildings from 300 years of life on the island including the oldest schoolhouse still standing, which was built in 1695 (that's really old by American standards!). Guided tours Wed–Fri 2.30pm, Sat and Sun 2pm and 3.30pm, apart from in

Historic Richmond Town

the summer season when costumed interpreters and craftspeople demonstrate the chores, gardening, crafts and trade of daily life in this rural hamlet.

JACQUES MARCHAIS MUSEUM OF TIBETAN ART

- ✉ 338 Lighthouse Avenue
- ☎ 718-987 3500
- 🖰 www.tibetanmuseum.org
- 🚌 From Staten Island Ferry take bus S74 to Lighthouse Avenue
- ⏰ Wed–Sun 1pm–5pm
- $ Gallery $5, $3 seniors/students, $2 children 12 and under; grounds free

One of New York's best-kept secrets, which the Dalai Lama visited in 1991. It has terraced gardens and a fishpond. Inside, there are Tibetan, Nepalese and Mongolian arts from the 17th to the 19th century.

BRITTIP
Head down to the South Beach Boardwalk to catch a free concert if you're here in summer, or, if the family are in tow, to Midland Beach for sandcastle building and the Sea Turtle Fountain where kids can play under the sprinklers.

SNUG HARBOR CULTURAL CENTER

- ✉ 1000 Richmond Terrace between Tysen Street and Snug Harbour Road
- ☎ 718-448 2500
- 🖰 www.snug-harbor.org
- 🚌 Bus S40 from the Staten Island Ferry to Snug Harbor
- ⏰ Tues–Sun 10am–5pm, closed Mon
- $ $3 adults, $2 seniors/children under 12

On this plot of land once stood some rundown retirement homes for fishermen, which were going to be demolished by developers planning various money-making schemes. However, the local residents wanted it to be used for the community's benefit, and the result is a fascinating 33.5-hectare (83-acre) park containing 26 buildings modelled on historical architecture, such as Greek revival Victorian and Italian Renaissance. The various buildings are used for events throughout the year, for example the Harmony Fair in June, a celebration of music, dance, food and cultures from around the world.

The Staten Island Botanical Park (tel 718-273 8200, www.sibg.org, open dawn to dusk

daily, free) is also here with the internationally renowned Chinese Scholar's Garden, which has courtyards, pools, a Tea House and pure-flow bridge. Admission is $5 for adults, $4 students/seniors/children and guided tours are offered Wed, Sat and Sun afternoons. Also in the grounds is Staten Island Children's Museum (718-273 2060, www.statenislandkids.org), with entertaining interactive exhibitions such as crawling through an ant hill to watch butterflies emerging from the chrysalis and exploring a pirate ship and becoming a sailor. Open Tues–Sun 12pm–5pm when school is in session, 10am–5pm during school holidays, and costs $5 for the over 1s. Great Explorations takes children from the rainforest canopy to dog-sledding and building an igloo and there's a chance to be a fireman, learn dog body language, host a radio show or go to sea on an outdoors boat (weather permitting). There's daily Storytime and Feeding the Animals sessions, a range of activities for tots and weekly creative workshops including Science Thursday and crafty kids on Tuesdays, both 1.30pm–4.30pm.

BRITTIP
Download a Staten Island map, or order one by mail from www.statenislandusa.com, that gives the low-down on cultural and other attractions as well as parks and beaches.

ST MARK'S PLACE, ST GEORGE

Standing on the hill above the St George Ferry terminal, St Mark's Place is the only landmarked historical district on Staten Island. Here New York's fabulous skyline forms a dramatic backdrop to a wonderful collection of residential buildings in Queen Ann, Greek revival and Italianate styles. Visit www.preserve.org/stgeorge for a self-guided walking tour.

BRITTIP
After a day of exploration you'll be hungry, so make a reservation at one of the tasty Staten Island restaurants. Angelina's Ristorante (26 Jefferson Boulevard at Annadale Road, tel 718-227 7100, www.ange linasristorante.com) is good.

CHAPTER 15

Safety First

TRAVEL INSURANCE

The one thing you should not forget when travelling to America is insurance. Medical cover is very expensive and if you are involved in an accident you could be sued, which would be very costly indeed. If you do want to make savings in this area, don't buy it from tour operators as they are notoriously expensive. We have taken a random selection of premiums offered by tour operators specialising in North America and found that two weeks' worth of cover for one person varied in price from £42 to a staggering £90. If you're travelling for up to four weeks, the premiums go up to nearly £110 per person.

The alternative, particularly if you plan to make more than one trip in any given year, is to go for an annual worldwide policy direct from the insurers. These can start at around £60 and go up to £120, and will normally cover all trips taken throughout the year up to a maximum of 31 days per trip. These worldwide annual policies make even more sense if you're travelling as a family. For instance, cover for four people bought from your tour operator could easily cost you £160 for a two-week trip, which is little different from an annual worldwide family policy premium.

Companies offering annual worldwide insurance policies include the **AA** (0800 085 7240, www.theaa.com), **Barclays** (0800 015 4751, www.barclays.co.uk/personal), **Bradford & Bingley** (0800 11 33 33, www.bradford-bingley.co.uk/insurance), **Columbus** (0845 222 0020, www.columbus-insurance.com), **Direct Travel** (0845 605 2700, www.direct-travel.co.uk), **Norwich Union** (0800 121 007, www.norwich union.com), **Our Way** (020 8313 3900), **Post Office** (0800 169 9999, www.postoffice. co.uk), **Premier Direct** (0845 6028002, www.alliance-leicester.co.uk) and **Travel Insurance Direct** (0870 00 55 622, www.oinc.com). Many of these companies also offer straightforward holiday cover for a given period, such as two or three weeks,

which again will be cheaper than insurance offered by tour operators.

CHECK YOUR COVER

Policies vary not only in price but also in the cover they provide. In all cases, you need to ensure that the one you choose gives you the following:

➡ Medical cover of at least £2 million in America.

➡ Personal liability cover of at least £2 million in America.

➡ Cancellation and curtailment cover of around £3,000 in case you are forced to call off your holiday.

➡ Cover for lost baggage and belongings of around £1,500. Most premiums only offer cover for individual items worth up to around £250, so you will need additional cover for expensive cameras or camcorders.

➡ Cover for cash (usually around £200) and documents, including your air tickets, passport and currency.

➡ A 24-hour helpline to make it easy for you to get advice and instructions on what to do in an emergency.

THINGS TO WATCH OUT FOR

Sharp practices: In some cases your tour operator may imply that you must buy their travel insurance policy. This is never the case; you can always arrange your own. Alternatively, they may send you an invoice for your tickets that includes travel insurance unless you tick a certain box, so watch out.

Read the policy: Always ask for a copy of the policy document before you go and, if you are not happy with the cover offered,

View from the Empire State Building

Central Park in winter

cancel and demand your premium back. In some cases you will have only seven days in which to do this.

Don't double up on cover: If you have an all risks house insurance policy on your home contents, this will cover your belongings outside the home and may even cover lost money and credit cards. Check if this covers you abroad, and includes your belongings when in transit, before buying insurance for personal possessions.

MORE THINGS TO CHECK

Gold card cover: Some bank gold cards automatically provide you with travel insurance cover if you buy your air ticket with the gold card but, in fact, only the Nat West Gold MasterCard provides sufficient cover for travel in America.

Dangerous sports cover: In almost all cases, mountaineering, racing and hazardous pursuits such as bungee jumping, skydiving, horse riding, windsurfing, trekking and even cycling are not included in normal policies. There are so many opportunities to do all of these activities and more – and they are so popular as holiday extras – that you really should ensure you are covered before you go.

Make sure you qualify for full cover: If you have been treated in hospital during the six months prior to travelling or are waiting for hospital treatment, you may need medical evidence that you are fit to travel. If your doctor gives you the all clear (the report may cost £25) and the insurance company still says your condition is not eligible for the insurance you want, shop around to find the right cover.

HEALTH HINTS

Don't allow your dream trip to New York to be spoilt by not taking the right kind of precautions.

MEDICATION

If you are on regular medication, make sure you take sufficient for the duration of your trip. Always carry it in your hand baggage, in case your luggage goes astray, and make sure it is clearly labelled. If you should need more for any reason, remember that many drugs have a different name in the US, so check with your GP before you go.

IN THE SUN

Although the biggest season for New York is winter, many Brits still travel to America at the hottest time of the year, the summer, and most are unprepared for the sheer intensity of the sun. Before you even think about going out for the day, apply a high-factor sun block as it is very easy to get sunburned when you are walking around sightseeing or shopping. It is also a good idea to wear a hat or scarf to protect your head from the sun, especially at the hottest times (11am–3pm), to prevent you from getting sunstroke. If it is windy, you may be lulled into thinking that it's not so hot.

◀🇬🇧▶ BRITTIP

Always carry plenty of water, even in winter. Air conditioning and heating are incredibly dehydrating and you'll find yourself wanting to keel over very quickly without lots of liquid. It is also best to avoid drinking alcohol during the day.

SECURITY

AT YOUR HOTEL

In America, your hotel room number is your main source of security. It is often your passport to eating and collecting messages so keep the number safe and secure. When checking in, make sure none of the hotel staff mentions your room number out loud. If they do, give them back the key and ask them to give you a new room and to write down the new room number instead of announcing it (most hotels follow this practice in any case). When you need to give someone your room number – for instance when charging a dinner or any other bill to

EMERGENCIES

For the police, fire department or ambulance: Dial 911 (9-911 from a hotel room). This is a free number, even from mobiles.

If it's a medical emergency: Call the front desk of your hotel as many have arrangements with doctors for house calls. If they don't, they may tell you to go to the nearest casualty (emergency) department, but that's really not a good idea (Haven't you seen *ER*?). Instead, you have three choices: contact **New York Hotel Urgent Medical Services** on 212-737 1212, www.travelmd.com, **Dial-a-Doctor** on 212-971 9692, or walk in or make an appointment at a **DOCS Medical Center**. There are three in Manhattan: 55 East 34th Street (tel 212-252 6000), 1555 3rd Avenue (tel 212-828 2300) and 202 West 23rd Street (tel 212-352 2600).

If you need a pharmacy: There are several 24-hour pharmacies, mostly run by the Duane Reade chain. The most centrally located 24-hour pharmacy is at 224 West 57th Street at Broadway (tel 212-541 9708, www.duanereade.com), near Columbus Circle.

If you need a dentist: You can call 212-679 3966 or 212-371 0500. If you need help after hours, try the 24-hour Emergency Dental Associates on 212-972 9299, www.nydental.org.

British information services: 845 3rd Avenue, NY, NY 10022. Fax 212-745 0359. www.britain-info.org. This is the information service of the British embassy in Washington and acts as the political, press and public affairs office of the New York Consulate-General, which covers the states of New York, New Jersey, Connecticut and Pennsylvania.

your room – write it down or show them your room card rather than calling it out.

When in your hotel room, always put on the deadlocks and security chains and use the door peephole before opening the door. If someone knocks and you don't know who it is, or they don't have any identification, phone the reception desk. When you go out, make sure you lock the windows and door properly, even if you just leave your room to go to the ice machine.

CASH AND VALUABLES

Most hotels have safe deposit boxes, so use these to store important documents such as airline tickets and passports. Keep a separate record of your travellers' cheque numbers. When you go out, do not take all your cash and credit cards with you. Always leave at least one credit card in the safe as an emergency back-up and only take enough cash with you for the day.

Using a money belt is a good idea and, if your room does not come with its own safe, leave your valuables in the main hotel safe.

BRITTIP

American banknotes are all exactly the same green colour and size so familiarise yourself with the bills in the safety of your room before you go out. Keep large denominations separate from small ones.

SAFETY IN CARS

Unless you have a driver, a car in New York is not a good idea. If you do hire a car, however, be sensible. Never leave your car unlocked or leave any valuable items on the car seats or anywhere else where they can be seen. Always put maps and brochures in the glove compartment as these will be obvious signs that your car belongs to a tourist.

NEW YORK STREET SAVVY

It may surprise you to know that New York City remains the safest big city in the USA, according to the FBI. Although the city is nowhere near as dangerous as it used to be,

5th Avenue

Mounted police

it is still a large city and there are always people on the lookout for an easy opportunity. To reduce your chances of becoming a victim of street crime, follow these simple guidelines:

➡ Always be aware of what is going on around you and keep one arm free – criminals tend to target people who are preoccupied or have both arms laden down with packages or briefcases.

➡ Stick to well-populated, well-lit areas and, if possible, don't go out alone.

➡ Don't engage any suspicious people, such as street beggars, in conversation, though you can tip buskers if you wish.

➡ Visible jewellery can attract the wrong kind of attention. If you are a woman wearing rings, turn them round so that the stone or setting side is palm-in.

➡ If you're wearing a coat, put it on over the strap of your shoulder bag.

➡ Men should keep wallets in their front trouser or inside coat pockets or in a shoulder strap.

➡ Pickpockets work in teams, often involving children to create a diversion.

➡ Watch out for pickpockets and scam artists, especially in busy areas, as you would in any big city.

➡ Do not carry your wallet or valuables in a bumbag. Thieves can easily cut the belt and disappear into the crowds before you've worked out what has happened.

A useful trick is to have two wallets – one a cheap one carried in your hip pocket or

BRITTIP

It cannot be stressed enough that you should only ever walk about with as little cash as possible – and never, ever count your money in public.

bag containing about $20 in cash and some out-of-date credit cards, and another hidden somewhere on your body or in a money belt containing the bulk of your cash and credit cards. If you are approached by someone who demands money from you, your best bet is to get away as quickly as possible. Do this by throwing your fake wallet or purse in one direction, while you run, shouting for help, in the other. The chances are that the mugger will just pick up the wallet and run off rather than chase after you. If you hand over your wallet and just stand still, the mugger is more likely to demand your watch and jewellery, too. This advice is even more important for women, who could be vulnerable to personal attack or rape if they hang around.

Having given you some essential safety advice, however, it is important to remember that this is very much common sense and applies if you are travelling almost anywhere in the world, especially in a major city. New York is a busy, feisty city, but it is a great holiday destination and no doubt you'll have a brilliant time and want to come back for more!

INDEX to MAP PAGES

LEGEND
- **92** Highways/Interstate
- **3** Throughroutes
- Main Roads
- Other Roads
- Railways
- Places of Interest
- Bus/Rail Stations
- Parks
- **SOHO** Districts

MAP 8

MAP 7

MAP 6

MAP 5

MAP 4

MAP 3

MAP 2

MAP 1

MAP 11

MAP 9

MAP 10

Queens

New York

Manhattan

Brooklyn

N

Upper New York Bay

MAP 4

MAP 10

QUEENS STREET INDEX

Index